350

Career Success/ Personal Stress

How to Stay Healthy in a High-Stress Environment

Christine A. Leatz, M.S.W.

With **Mark W. Stolar, M.D.**

Medical Advisor

McGraw-Hill, Inc.

New York San Francisco Washington, D.C. Auckland Bogotá
Caracas Lisbon London Madrid Mexico City Milan
Montreal New Delhi San Juan Singapore
Sydney Tokyo Toronto

This book is printed on recycled, acid-free paper containing a minimum of 50% recycled de-inked fiber.

Library of Congress Cataloging-in-Publication Data

Leatz, Christine Ann.
    Career success/personal stress : how to stay healthy in a high
-stress environment / Christine A. Leatz.
        p.   cm.
    Includes index.
    ISBN 0-07-036966-6 :   —ISBN 0-07-036977-1 (pbk.) :
    1. Job stress.   2. Stress management.   3. Stress (Psychology)—
Health aspects.   I. Stolar, Mark W.   II. Title.
HF5548.85.L43   1992
158.7—dc20
                                                92-20848
                                                CIP

    3 4 5 6 7 8 9 0   DOC/DOC   9 8 7 6 5 4 3

ISBN 0-07-036966-6 {HC}
ISBN 0-07-036977-1 {PBK}

*The sponsoring editor for this book was James Bessent, the editing supervisor
was Fred Dahl, and the production supervisor was Pamela Pelton. It was set in
Baskerville by Inkwell Publishing Services.*

Printed and bound by R. R. Donnelley & Sons Company.

Medicine is an ever-changing science. As new research and clinical
experience broaden our knowledge, changes in treatment and drug
therapy are required. The authors and the publisher of this work have
checked with sources believed to be reliable in their efforts to provide
information that is complete and generally in accord with the standards
accepted at the time of publication. However, in view of the possibility
of human error or changes in medical sciences, neither the editors, nor
the publisher, nor any other party who has been involved in the preparation or publication of this work warrants that the information contained herein is in every respect accurate or complete and they are not
responsible for any errors or omissions or for the results obtained from
use of such information. Readers should consult with their own physicians regarding particular conditions and treatments.

Contents

Preface   ix

Prologue   1

Whom This Book Is For   1
Why Stress Management Techniques May Not Have Worked for
You Previously   2
What This Book Will Do for You   3
Our Objective for This Book   4
About Us   4
Warnings and Cautions   5

Part 1. Check Yourself Out

1. A Do-It-Yourself Stress Assessment   7

Coping Behavior Checklist   7
What the Coping Behavior Checklist Shows   9
Stress Symptom Checklist   9
What the Stress Symptom Checklist Shows   11
Life Satisfaction Checklist   12
What the Life Satisfaction Checklist Shows   15
Life Experiences and Hassles Checklist   15
What the Life Experiences and Hassles Checklist Shows   18
Work Satisfaction Checklist   18
What the Work Satisfaction Checklist Shows   21
Burn Out Checklist   21
What the Burn Out Checklist Shows   22
Company Culture Checklist   22

What the Company Culture Checklist Shows   25
Personality Type Checklist   26
What the Personality Type Checklist Shows   28

2. How Stress Works   **30**

The Physiological Side of Stress   30
Common Stress Patterns   34
Common Stress Reactions   36
Why People Perceive Stress Differently   38
How Perception Works   40

Part 2. Stress at Work

3. A Look at the New Stress-Intensive Environment   **43**

Determining Your Professional Type   43
The Continually Changing Business Environment   45
Company Cultures   46
Power, Politics, and Competition   51
Managing People in the '90s   54

4. A Compendium of Workplace Stressors   **67**

Structural Plateauing   67
Content Plateauing   70
Reductions in Force—the Receiving End   73
Promotions   90
Relocations and Transfers   98
Business Travel—Curse or Joy?   102
Information Overload and Computerization of the Workplace   110

5. Burn Out and Other Special Situations   **116**

Burn Out—When It All Gets to Be Too Much   116
The Reality of Burn Out   116
A Special Note to Those Raised in Dysfunctional Families   121
The Bottom Line   124

Part 3. Stress at Home

6. If You're Single   **125**

Stress at Home: The Myth of Having It All   125
The Single Life   126
Alone or Lonely?   126

Work Time vs. Personal Time   126
Money   128
The Chores of Daily Living   128
Relationships and Friendships   129

7. Couples   131

Work Time vs. Personal Time   131
Money   136
The Chores of Daily Living   137
The Couple's Relationships and Friendships   138

8. If You're a Parent   140

Home Life vs. Work Life   140
Work Time vs. Personal Time   142
Raising Children Today   145
Relationships and Friendships   146

9. A Special Note for Special Situations   148

The Dysfunctional Family   148
The Struggle for Intimacy   148
Seeking the Simple Life—Middle-Aged Malaise or Genuine Trend?   152

Part 4. Coping with the Effects of Stress

10. The Big Three—Diet, Exercise, Sleep   154

Coping with the Effects of Stress   154
Diet   156
Physical Fitness   168
Sleep   172

11. A Compendium of Coping Techniques   175

Behavioral Rehearsal   175
Biofeedback   176
Breathing Exercises   178
Favorite Passions: Hobbies and Leisure Activities   179
Friends, Family, and Supporters   180
A Good Cry   182
Guilty Pleasures   183
Hugs   184
Humor   184
Journals and Diaries   185

Massage   186
Meditation   188
Progressive Muscle Relaxation   189
Rewards   190
Rituals   191
Self-Talks   193
Therapy, Self-Help and Support Groups, and 12-Step Programs   198
Visualization   201
Weekends and Vacations   204
Worrying   205

Part 5. Stress-Related Problems and Disorders

12. How Stress-Related Illnesses Can Worsen   207

Stress-Related Problems and Disorders   207
It's Not "All in Your Head"   208
When You Cross the Line into Illness   209
Fatigue   213
Depression   217

13. A Compendium of Common Stress-Related Illnesses   224

Allergies and Upper Respiratory Infections   224
Chest Pain   227
Dysfunctional Eating   230
Headaches   234
Hypertension (High Blood Pressure)   239
Jaw Problems   241
Lower Gastrointestinal Tract Problems   243
Menstrual Irregularities   247
Musculoskeletal Complaints   248
Skin Problems   256
Upper Gastrointestinal Tract Problems   262

14. Special Topics in Stress-Related Illness   267

Panic Attacks   267
Hyperventilation   269
Mitral Valve Prolapse Syndrome   270
Substance Abuse   273
Stress and Sex   278
Stress and Normal Midlife Changes   284
The Effect of Stress on Chronic Diseases   286
Faux and Spurious Illnesses   287

Part 6. Adopting a Stress-Sensitive Lifestyle

15. Anger, Communication, Gentle Assertiveness, and Conflict Resolution   **290**

Anger and How It Works   290
How Communication Works   296
How Gentle Assertiveness Works   301
Win-Win Conflict Resolution: Bringing It All Together   305
Summing Up   306

16. Preparing for Changes: Values, Goals, Decision Making, and Taking Risks   **308**

Clearing Out the Garbage   309
Evaluating Your Personal and Work Values   309
Setting Personal and Work Goals   316
Evaluating Family Values and Goals   320
Dealing with Fear   326
Making Wise Decisions   328
Taking Smart Risks   332

17. Making and Living with Changes   **336**

Seeing the Effects of Change   336
What to Expect When Making Changes   336
Building a Support Network   338
When *Not* to Initiate Change   340

Good Reads   342
Index   345

Preface

While writing this book, I was working at a very demanding career, living through a reduction in force and reorganization on the job, traveling extensively to meet with vendors and my customers at FMC* Corporation's far-flung locations, and expanding and maintaining a personal and social life—an extremely stressful experience! It has been by turns exhilarating, depressing, exciting, exhausting, and fulfilling. Through it all, one person in particular helped make *Career Success/Personal Stress* a wonderful experience for me: Ivy Anderson.

This book probably wouldn't have even come to be had it not been for the encouragement and prodding of Ivy Anderson, one of my best friends and a colleague at FMC. It really was her idea, after all.

Just over a year ago, both Ivy and I were maintaining heavy-duty travel schedules at FMC. We were both exhausted—mentally and physically. One week, when I had more than a single day at my office in Chicago and had time to go through my in-box, I noticed a seminar at Northwestern Memorial Hospital on stress management for working women. Ivy was unable to attend, but I did.

The seminar was typical of the genre: hints about organization, reminders to exercise more, and encouragement to laugh more often. But in no way did the seminar address my personal frustrations and exhaustion. When you have been traveling for nearly fifteen weeks and come back to find out that a reduction in force and reorganization are brewing—and you have to help justify the existence of your department—being told to keep a joke file on your desk to look at when things get tense somehow doesn't really help.

So I hit the Chicago-area bookstores, looking for books that might give me insight in how to cope with all the stress I was experiencing. I bought lots of books, but all of them took the same approach as the stress management seminar, and they really weren't much help. Then, in one of those thunderclaps of understanding, it dawned on me that when I had been a therapist, I told my clients pretty much the same thing. I had no understanding of the pervasiveness of stress in organizations or of what my clients were really experiencing. It's very hard to write about something you've never experienced, and I realized that none of the authors of all the books I'd bought was a businessperson.

As I complained to Ivy over a take-out lunch at her desk about the worthlessness of the seminar and all the books I had purchased, she said, "Why don't you write another stress management book? *Unwinding* [my other book] was really good. You've spent nearly eight years inside big corporations, and you now know what it's like. Combine coping techniques with what is going on at work, and tell us how to cope with all the changes! All of my friends and colleagues could use a book like that!"

I thought about that suggestion for awhile, and over the course of several plane trips, drafted an outline. I decided that I needed strong medical input, because I felt it was important to cover the stress-related illnesses working people develop. Since *Unwinding: How to Turn Stress into Positive Energy* had been published, a significant amount of medical research showed that stress hormones impacted far more than just heart disease and high blood pressure. We now know that high levels of stress can help cause everything from colds and flu to gastroesophageal reflux. No other books available covered this confusing range of medical problems. I therefore felt it was necessary not only to identify them, but to help readers understand how to care for themselves, how to reduce symptoms, and, most importantly, when to seek professional medical care.

Ivy's encouragement kept me sane throughout the process of writing, and her comments and ideas were invaluable. Many of her personal experiences found their way into this book.

Mark Stolar was my personal physician at the time, and I was impressed with the comprehensive approach he took to treating my stress-related illnesses (yes, I have them too!). So I gathered up my nerve and approached him about *Career Success/Personal Stress*. To my pleasant surprise, Mark was very interested in working on this project with me. Many of his patients were suffering from stress-related illnesses, and he felt the book would be worthwhile. He was a great medical adviser, and his input was very helpful.

I owe a warm thank-you to Karen Vasudev, also one of my best friends and a colleague at FMC. Karen and I lived through a particularly stressful year-long technology implementation project at her FMC location in Santa Clara, California, and I learned much about grace under pressure from her. She served as my personal "stress-level watchdog" during the writing of this book. We talked on the phone frequently with each other, and every time she sensed my stress levels going up, she gently admonished me to "practice what you are preaching!" Karen also provided numerous insights and ideas that were incorporated into this book, for which I am grateful.

I want to thank a host of friends and supporters who provided encouragement, good cheer, and lots of examples from their own stressful lives for

Career Success/Personal Stress (in alphabetical order!): Andy Abbas; Lori Balog; Dave Banaszak; Tina Baran; Peter Braun; Matthew Bronson; Jim Bodkin; Mattie Brooks; Liz Byrum; Tom Cahill; Cindy and Bob Carolan, my sister and brother-in-law; Wanda Christopulos; Dennis Dureno; Dr. Gilchun Ergun; Jan Feder; Chef Mark Facklam; Susan Frank; Tunnie Glass; Victoria Gillespie; Millie Grohwin; Beverly Guin; Brad Johnson; Judy and Joe Kemler; Bruce Kessler; Meryl Kleiman; Dennis Kouba; Karen Krason; Don and Lily Leatz, my parents; Debra Matlock, legal advisor supreme; Leon Miller; Elaine Miologos; Kathleen Moody; Dale Morritz; Bill Mundo; Dr. Kathy Johnson Neely; John O'Brien; Sue Pawlisz; Tom Quinn; Ron Ree; Greg Reynolds; Kathy Rychel; Dr. Michael Stone; Rick Thome; Arik Vasudev; Betty Velie; Susan Weakland; Linda Weiss; Alphonzo Wesson; Karl Williams; and Claudia Wintergerst.

Special thank-you's are owed to Paul Brainerd and Bill Gates (for the software) and to Steve Jobs (for the Macintosh computer).**

Finally, one other person deserves a huge "Thanks!" because he worked to make the publishing of *Career Success/Personal Stress* possible. Jim Bessent, Acquisitions Editor from McGraw-Hill Business Books, took a chance on an outline and a few rough chapters—and for that I will be eternally grateful. His comments and ideas were excellent, and he really helped make this project a pleasant and not very stressful experience!

Thanks to all of you! You've been just great!

Christine Leatz
CHICAGO

---

*FMC Corporation is a multinational diversified company having its corporate offices in Chicago, Illinois.

**Macintosh is a registered trademark of Apple Computer, Inc.

About the Authors

Christine A. Leatz, M.S.W., has spent the last ten years as an executive for a Fortune 500 multinational corporation, experiencing firsthand the stressors facing business people today. Prior to that, she was a social worker and therapist specializing in stress management. A graduate of Michigan State University, she holds a master's degree in social work and has completed doctoral work in therapy and counseling. She is a member of the Board of Directors of the National Safe Workplace Institute and is the author of *Stress: A Family Affair* and *Unwinding: How to Turn Stress Into Positive Energy.* She has also published a number of articles on managing the introduction of technological change in the workplace.

Mark W. Stolar, M.D., served as medical advisor for *Career Success/Personal Stress.* He is attending physician at Northwestern Memorial Hopital in Chicago and teaches clinical medicine at Northwestern University's Medical School. Many of his patients are businesspeople experiencing medical problems as a result of stress on the job.

Prologue

Whom This Book Is For

Stop for a minute and think about how you are feeling, *right now*—about your life, your career, your family. Now complete this sentence: "I feel _____." If you are a typical stressed-out manager or professional, you probably put "burned out, fried, frazzled, wasted, wired, worn-out, overworked and underpaid, exhausted, worried, harried, hassled, bored, run-down," or any number of similar unpleasant adjectives, verbs, or adverbs! You may even feel that chronic stress overload has become a condition of employment for your working life.

This book is for all stressed-out working people who are struggling to achieve successful careers (not just jobs) and maintain some semblence of a personal, family, and social life. Our definition of working people includes not only those who work for large corporations, but also:

Autonomous professionals—physicians, lawyers, architects, engineers, consultants, and others who are in a solo or small practice setting

Semiautonomous professionals—people such as lawyers, physicians, architects, engineers, consultants, and others who could be out practicing on their own but have chosen to work in a larger group practice or setting

Entrepreneurs who are either starting or running their own businesses

People involved in family-owned, small, or medium-sized businesses

People in academia or service-oriented professions such as health care

Government and military managers and professionals

All of us continually try to balance the demands of our careers with our personal lives, and usually our personal lives end up getting short-changed. But that does not have to be the rule, and this book is designed to help you achieve the goal of a balanced life.

Why Stress-Management Techniques May Not Have Worked for You Previously

You may already have read a lot about stress and stress management and maybe even tried some suggested ways to relax. Most likely nothing really worked, and you find yourself asking why. There are three major reasons why stress-management techniques may not have worked well for you.

Changing Business Environment

First, the business environment has changed so dramatically over the past five years that the "threshold" of stress—the normal, day-to-day level of stress businesspeople experience—has been raised. And it has been raised to a level that in the past would have been classified a severe stress episode or crisis. In addition, the ups and downs of business have not gone away, and managers and professionals are experiencing them *on top of* that already high level of day-to-day stress.

Your Personality Style

Second, people are different; there are three common personality types who differ in their approaches to stressful situations. One type of person tends to see everything as a crisis. This person is usually hard-working, goal-oriented, compulsive, and lives a highly structured life. Some researchers have named this type of person *Type A.*

Another kind of person is a little more easygoing, slow-moving, and less outcome-oriented. These people see some situations as crises, and researchers call this kind of person *Type B.*

A third personality type views fewer situations as crises—such persons are not oblivious to what is going on around them, but they seem to be survivors and to come out of the crises somehow stronger. Such people are more concerned with the process of life and not its outcomes; they have adequate energy, feel competent, and depend on themselves to set goals for their lives. We call this type of person Type S. Type S people seem to suffer from stress reactions less frequently than either Type A or Type B, and seem to develop stress-related illnesses only after being in chronic or dangerous stress situations for a long period of time.

Type A people have been found to suffer a higher incidence of cardiovascular disease, heart attacks, and strokes than either Type B or Type S. Type Bs most often experience stress reactions when they are placed in situations in which they are expected to perform in a Type A manner. This is extremely stressful for Bs and, for them, going against type often leads to physical stress reaction symptoms.

Because these three personality types are so different, the coping technique that works well for a Type A would not be effective for a B or S. In the past you may have chosen a coping technique that didn't mesh well with your personality type. The most effective coping techniques will be those that fit almost intuitively with the way you think, and it may take some experimenting to get the mix just right.

Understanding the Causes of Your Personal Stress

Finally, you need to know about the *causes* of stress, as well as ways to cope with the effects of stress. Indeed, they are often subtle and may come from areas we do not traditionally view as stressors, such as our jobs or careers; the culture of the company or organization we work for; roles we play at home with our families and in our communities; values; goals; priorities; decision-making skills; communication abilities; and so forth—in short, all those known and unknown things that make us unique individuals. In short, stress may come from sources other than a difficult boss, burdensome workload, or economic pressures. The effects of stress—anxiety, tension, headaches, fatigue, irritability, insomnia, and so on—are fairly common. But they are only *reflections* of those individual components that cause us to experience stress in the first place.

Stress cannot be effectively managed until its causes are uncovered, dragged out into the open, and dealt with in some way. This is a tough job that requires guts—but unless you tackle it, all the relaxation techniques in the world aren't going to help you over the long haul.

What This Book Will Do for You

This book is designed to provide a comprehensive, holistic approach to helping you understand your personal causes of stress. The first part of the book helps you get to know yourself better through a series of exercises and inventories, and is geared toward providing you with information on your stress symptoms, work stressors, life experiences, coping behaviors, and personality.

It is important for you to understand how stress affects the human body, so we provide you with information on how stress works and how your body responds to a variety of common stress patterns. How you perceive stressful situations also has a tremendous impact on how stressful a situation is for you, and we explore how perception works.

Next we cover common workplace stressors—everything from managing a diverse work force, surviving (or not surviving) a reduction in force, to managing business travel and lots more. That section is followed by a discussion of stress at home and the kinds of stressors faced by singles, dual-career couples, and working parents.

Then we move on to what we call "big picture" coping techniques—a wide range of coping strategies for dealing with those stressors. But those coping techniques aren't always adequate, and you need to understand how stress impacts your body and health. Managers and professionals usually have been under a great deal of stress for a long time, and may have already begun to develop symptoms of stress-related illnesses. Solid medical information on symptoms and treatment strategies for these illnesses are covered, along with help in determining when to seek your physician's help.

Finally, we look at reassessing values and goals, decision-making skills, and communication and assertiveness capabilities—which are often at the root of stress. In this time of diminishing possibilities and rapidly changing expectations, it may very well be that the goals and expectations we have set for ourselves are no longer realistic. We may need to reexamine "what we want to be when we grow up."

Our Objective for This Book

The most stress-resistant person is someone who embodies Type S personality characteristics and behaviors. Type S folks are well-adjusted, aware of their internal needs, and sensitive to the impact stress has on their bodies and minds. They also feel that they can take active control over their lives and behaviors to ameliorate the effects of stress overload. As a result, they can be very successful in their careers *and* their personal lives.

Human beings are capable of change—and many are capable of great change—*if they are motivated.* You were at least motivated enough to pick up this book! That's a good sign!

All the information presented in this book is geared toward providing you will the knowledge and skills you need to begin to become more like a Type S person in your approach to dealing with stress. Yes, you can learn to become a Type S—people do it every day! It won't happen overnight, but it will happen—and we guarantee your body will be pleased with the results!

About Us

"Yeah, sure," we can just hear you thinking, "this sounds great, but how can I be sure this book will really work? How do I know you guys *really* know what you're writing about?"

We cannot promise to erase stress from your life completely, but we can tell you that this book has been carefully researched, is based on solid medical and mental health techniques and treatments, and has been found very useful by many managers and professionals in situations similar to yours.

In addition, we're living very stressful lives ourselves. Chris is a former therapist and medical researcher who made a career change ten years ago and moved "to the other side of the desk," as manager of information technology and systems, first for one of the top 10 financial institutions in the United States and then for a *Fortune* 100 multinational corporation. She has lived through working her way through three degrees; fellowships in community mental health and migrant worker health care; internships and assistantships in child abuse and neglect, family planning counseling, stress management, and team health care; crash hands-on courses in the business of banking and manufacturing; six major reductions in force; department and work group reorganizations too numerous to count; being one of only a handful of senior female managers in an overwhelmingly male-dominated manufacturing environment; working for demanding bosses with vastly differing management styles and personalities; "matrixed" management; coping with being in the air or on the road for up to 80 percent of her time; introducing technological changes into both a very conservative, cost-conscious corporation and one in which information about money was often more important than the money itself; overseeing technology-implementation projects domestically and overseas; consulting with senior management and company divisions in the United States, Asia, South America, and Europe; developing presentations and conferences to educate people on technology; and convincing guys on the shop floor and people in the office to try new ways of working (perhaps the hardest job of all!). Mark is a physician, researcher, and educator of physicians-in-training at a major medical school and one of the ten largest U.S. hospitals. He has lived through: medical school; internships; residency; a fellowship in endocrinology; board exams in internal medicine and endocrinology; serving as associate section chief for a large general internal medicine practice; treating a patient caseload that grows almost daily; convincing patients to change their behaviors and ways of living (a monumental task!); supervising other physicians and nurses; teaching medical students; obtaining grants for research; and writing articles and giving presentations on diabetes around the country. So we know whereof we speak!

Warnings and Cautions

This book outlines a comprehensive stress-management program, and a comprehensive *anything* takes time. This is not a crash course or a quick-fix stress-reduction program! The only way to get long-lasting results when working with a problem as complex as stress overload is to go slowly and do it thoroughly.

But any program that involves your mind and body comes equipped with a set of warnings and cautions, and this book is no exception. So take heed:

■ *If you are under a physician's care for a stress-related illness or problem, get his or her permission before you try any of the suggestions given in this book.*

■ *Don't set overwhelming expectations for yourself.* Remember, Rome wasn't built in a day, and neither was the stressful situation(s) you presently find yourself in. It stands to reason that complex problems will take time to unravel, and, while this book will help you with the unraveling process, it will not eliminate the need to examine the situation(s). So you're not doing anything wrong if you can't solve your problems overnight. (In fact, if it takes time, that's a good sign that you are doing something right!)

■ *Do a little at a time, not a lot all at once.* When you are under stress, you don't need the added stress of revamping your entire life all at once. Starting small eases the stress load, increases your confidence, and sets the stage for bigger things to follow.

■ *Not every suggestion works equally well for all people.* There is no single magic cure for stress overload. Because we are all so different and because the components of the causes of our stress are different, we may need different combinations of coping techniques to help us reduce our stress levels effectively. Experiment with the suggestions offered in this book and develop a "package" of coping techniques that works best for you.

■ *Let the people around you know that you are beginning to make significant changes in your life.* Your friends and family are used to your old patterns of behavior and may be taken by surprise when you start reacting to them differently. To prevent any additional stress, put up a sign saying, "Please excuse any inconvenience you may experience. My life is currently under reconstruction. Thank you for your cooperation!"

■ *If you feel that you are getting in over your head at any time, be good to yourself and make an appointment to see your physician or a mental health professional to talk about it.* Everyone needs someone to talk to when the going gets rough, and physicians and mental health professionals make it their business to help people through those rough times.

Fair enough? At this point, many people begin to panic! They get panicky because: (1) they are afraid that when they find out what they are really like inside, they won't like what they find; or (2) they are afraid that they will have to do something weird. Not to worry—on both counts. No one we have worked with ever found that they were terrible or awful inside, underneath it all. In fact, they all tended more to discover positive things! And nothing in this book is weird, strange, or far-out. If you feel uncomfortable about any inventory, exercise, or suggestion, skip it! Do as much, or as little, as you are comfortable doing, especially if you are under a great deal of stress already.

Okay, you'll need a pencil. Let's get going.

1
A Do-It-Yourself Stress Assessment

To combat stress effectively, it is important to know the "enemy" inside and out. In other words, we need to clarify for ourselves exactly which areas of our lives are stressful and how we react to and cope with these situations. In the last chapter of this book, we discuss how to make changes in your life designed to eliminate some of the sources of stress you are experiencing. But first you need a good handle on exactly what stress feels like and how it acts on you. The following inventories are designed to help you accomplish just that.

Please read through the directions for each inventory and then respond according to how you feel today. If you feel uncomfortable with any question or inventory, don't answer it. However, the more responses you make, the more you will learn about yourself and stress. There are no right or wrong answers. The only "right" answers are those that are true for you. So relax and enjoy the process.

Coping Behavior Checklist

The Coping Behavior Checklist, Figure 1.1, explores some coping behaviors people commonly use when they find themselves in stressful situations. Please read through the list and circle the responses that are true for you. Then add up your points and put your total score in the space provided at the end of the inventory.

COPING BEHAVIOR:

Attending plays, concerts, sports events	0 1 2 3 4 5
Balanced diet	0 1 2 3 4 5
Behavioral rehearsal or "planning your strategy"	0 1 2 3 4 5
Biofeedback	0 1 2 3 4 5
Breathing exercises	0 1 2 3 4 5
Clarifying your values	0 1 2 3 4 5
Crying	0 1 2 3 4 5
Dancing (any kind)	0 1 2 3 4 5
Deep muscle (or progressive) relaxation	0 1 2 3 4 5
Doing arts and crafts activities	0 1 2 3 4 5
Giving yourself rewards	0 1 2 3 4 5
Going out with friends	0 1 2 3 4 5
Going to a movie or renting a video	0 1 2 3 4 5
Having sex	0 1 2 3 4 5
Hobby or hobbies	0 1 2 3 4 5
Hugs (getting and giving)	0 1 2 3 4 5
Imagery training	0 1 2 3 4 5
Listening to music	0 1 2 3 4 5
Massage	0 1 2 3 4 5
Meditation or "centering"	0 1 2 3 4 5
Organizing your living/working space	0 1 2 3 4 5
Organizing/planning for reports, presentations, etc.	0 1 2 3 4 5
Physical exercise (any kind)	0 1 2 3 4 5
Playing with your children	0 1 2 3 4 5
Playing with/caring for a pet	0 1 2 3 4 5
Playing a sport	0 1 2 3 4 5
Practicing saying no	0 1 2 3 4 5
Reading things unrelated to your job	0 1 2 3 4 5
Reordering priorities	0 1 2 3 4 5
Scheduling/budgeting your time	0 1 2 3 4 5
Seeking professional help	0 1 2 3 4 5
Shouting	0 1 2 3 4 5
Sleeping	0 1 2 3 4 5
Taking a vacation	0 1 2 3 4 5
Taking a walk	0 1 2 3 4 5
Taking breaks	0 1 2 3 4 5
Taking courses to improve job skills	0 1 2 3 4 5
Taking courses to learn new leisure activities	0 1 2 3 4 5
Taking naps	0 1 2 3 4 5
Talking to family members, spouse, or significant other	0 1 2 3 4 5
Talking to friends	0 1 2 3 4 5
Tending indoor/outdoor plants	0 1 2 3 4 5
Thinking about your goals	0 1 2 3 4 5
Thought-stopping exercises	0 1 2 3 4 5
Using community services	0 1 2 3 4 5
Warm baths (or bubble baths)	0 1 2 3 4 5
Watching a sunrise or sunset	0 1 2 3 4 5
Watching television	0 1 2 3 4 5
Window shopping or buying things	0 1 2 3 4 5
Yoga or stretching exercises	0 1 2 3 4 5
Other:	0 1 2 3 4 5
Other:	0 1 2 3 4 5
Other:	0 1 2 3 4 5
Other:	0 1 2 3 4 5
Other:	0 1 2 3 4 5
Other:	0 1 2 3 4 5
Other:	0 1 2 3 4 5
Other:	0 1 2 3 4 5
Other:	0 1 2 3 4 5
Other:	0 1 2 3 4 5

Figure 1.1. Coping Behavior Checklist

Key to Responses:

0 Never used

1 Tried once

2 Used more than once in lifetime, but not monthly

3 Use 1–3 times per month

4 Use 1–2 times per week

5 Use 3 or more times per week

What the Coping Behavior Checklist Shows

The higher you score on the Coping Behavior Checklist, the greater chance you have for successfully coping with stress and preventing stress overload.

Score Between 0 and 100:

Most people have tried several of these coping behaviors at one time or another, maybe without even knowing they were coping behaviors. A score of between 0 and 100 is fairly typical.

Score Between 100 and 150:

If you scored between 100 and 150, you show a higher-than-average awareness of coping techniques; however, you might want to consider experimenting with some of the listed coping techniques that you haven't tried before.

Score Between 150 and 200:

If you scored between 150 and 200, you most likely use a variety of coping techniques to get you through tough times, but you might not be aware that using coping techniques regularly has a preventive effect as well. Regular use of coping techniques can enhance recuperation times between crises and help your body function more effectively during crises.

Score Over 200:

If you scored over 200, you are using a variety of coping techniques regularly to enhance your effectiveness in coping with stress. As your life changes, your need for different coping techniques change as well. You might want to experiment with some new coping techniques from the list to increase your "bag of tricks" for future stressful situations.

Stress Symptom Checklist

The Stress Symptom Checklist, Figure 1.2, explores some common reactions people experience when faced with stressful situations. Please read through the list and circle the responses that are most true for you. Then add up your points and put your total score in the space provided at the end of the inventory.

Key to Responses:

0   Never experienced

1   Experienced once

2   Experienced more than once in lifetime, but not monthly

3   Experience 1–3 times per month

4   Experience 1–2 times per week

5   Experience 3 or more times per week

STRESS SYMPTOMS:

"Lump" in throat	0 1 2 3 4 5
"Scratchy" or sore throat	0 1 2 3 4 5
"Stuffy" sinuses	0 1 2 3 4 5
Abdominal pain	0 1 2 3 4 5
Absentmindedness	0 1 2 3 4 5
Accident proneness	0 1 2 3 4 5
Acne	0 1 2 3 4 5
Anxiety (feeling "uptight" or "nervous")	0 1 2 3 4 5
Back pain - lower	0 1 2 3 4 5
Back pain - upper	0 1 2 3 4 5
Biting fingernails/lips	0 1 2 3 4 5
Blushing	0 1 2 3 4 5
Chest pain	0 1 2 3 4 5
Cold hands or feet	0 1 2 3 4 5
Cold sores	0 1 2 3 4 5
Constipation	0 1 2 3 4 5
Crying	0 1 2 3 4 5
Diarrhea	0 1 2 3 4 5
Dry mouth	0 1 2 3 4 5
Eczema	0 1 2 3 4 5
Excessive perspiration	0 1 2 3 4 5
Excess "gas," burping, or belching	0 1 2 3 4 5
Fatigue	0 1 2 3 4 5
Feeling "blue" or depressed	0 1 2 3 4 5
Frequent urination	0 1 2 3 4 5
Hair loss	0 1 2 3 4 5
Headache	0 1 2 3 4 5
Hives	0 1 2 3 4 5
Inability to concentrate on a task	0 1 2 3 4 5
Inability to respond sexually	0 1 2 3 4 5
Increased alcohol use	0 1 2 3 4 5
Increased desire to eat	0 1 2 3 4 5
Increased drug use	0 1 2 3 4 5
Increased time spent sleeping	0 1 2 3 4 5
Indigestion (upset stomach)	0 1 2 3 4 5
Insomnia (trouble falling asleep)	0 1 2 3 4 5
Itching skin (dermatitis)	0 1 2 3 4 5
Loss of appetite	0 1 2 3 4 5
Menstrual irregularity	0 1 2 3 4 5
Mental confusion	0 1 2 3 4 5
Migraine headache	0 1 2 3 4 5
Nightmares	0 1 2 3 4 5

Figure 1.2. Stress Symptom Checklist

Figure 1.2. (*Continued*)

Pounding heart	0 1 2 3 4 5
Recurrent dreams	0 1 2 3 4 5
Sexual problems or loss of interest in sex	0 1 2 3 4 5
Sore or tense muscles in arms or legs	0 1 2 3 4 5
Sore or tense neck muscles	0 1 2 3 4 5
Sore or tense shoulders	0 1 2 3 4 5
Stomach pain	0 1 2 3 4 5
Suicide - attempting	0 1 2 3 4 5
Suicide - considering	0 1 2 3 4 5
Sweaty palms	0 1 2 3 4 5
Teeth grinding	0 1 2 3 4 5
Tendency to startle easily	0 1 2 3 4 5
Tics	0 1 2 3 4 5
Trembling/shaking	0 1 2 3 4 5
Troubled breathing	0 1 2 3 4 5
Waking up early and being unable to go back to sleep	0 1 2 3 4 5
Waking up often at night	0 1 2 3 4 5
Other:	0 1 2 3 4 5
Other:	0 1 2 3 4 5
Other:	0 1 2 3 4 5
Other:	0 1 2 3 4 5

What the Stress Symptom Checklist Shows

The higher you score on the Stress Symptom Checklist, the greater is the likelihood that you are a victim of stress overload.

Score 0 to 100:

Almost all people have experienced several of these stress-related symptoms at some time during their lives, so scores between 0 and 100 are normal.

Score 100 to 150:

If you scored between 100 and 150, your body is telling you that you are in a high-stress situation, whether you are aware of it or not.

Score 150 to 225:

If you scored between 150 and 225, you are most likely in a chronic stress situation, and the suggestions provided in this book will be very helpful for you.

Score Over 225:

If you scored over 225 points, your chronic stress is very severe. It might be a good idea for you to make an appointment for a checkup with your physician, who can help take care of your physical problems while you work on increasing your coping techniques by reading this book.

Life Satisfaction Checklist

The Life Satisfaction Checklist, Figure 1.3, helps you explore which areas in your life are currently stressful for you. Please answer the following sections according to how you feel today.

Employment

Examples: My job is the pits.
            I worry a lot about getting laid off.
Your thoughts: _____
Overall are you
                _____ satisfied?
                _____ dissatisfied?

Education

Examples: I'm thinking about going back to school.
            My education isn't enough to get ahead on the job.
            I need some new job skills.
Your thoughts: _____
Overall are you
                _____ satisfied?
                _____ dissatisfied?

Friends

Examples: I have lots of good friends.
            My best friend recently moved away or was transferred.
            I'd like to meet some new people.
Your thoughts: _____
Overall are you
                _____ satisfied?
                _____ dissatisfied?

Family

Examples: I enjoy visiting my family.
            My parents are pressuring me to get married and settle down.
            My kids and spouse drive me crazy sometimes.
Your thoughts: _____
Overall are you
                _____ satisfied?
                _____ dissatisfied?

Personal Life

Examples: My boy/girlfriend and I broke up recently.
            My spouse and I have been quarreling a lot.
            My lover and I have been getting along well.

Figure 1.3. Life Satisfaction Checklist

Your thoughts: _____
Overall are you

_____ satisfied?

_____ dissatisfied?

Sex

Examples: It's hard for me to ask my lover for what I want.
I really enjoy having sex with my lover.
Sometimes I just don't feel like making love.
What's a sex life?

Your thoughts: _____
Overall are you

_____ satisfied?

_____ dissatisfied?

Energy

Examples: I'm tired much of the time.
I can always get geared up for fun things.
I'm really tired by Friday and look forward to the weekends.

Your thoughts: _____
Overall are you

_____ satisfied?

_____ dissatisfied?

Health

Examples: Basically, I can't complain.
I get lots of headaches.
I'm worried about my health.

Your thoughts: _____
Overall are you

_____ satisfied?

_____ dissatisfied?

Personal Appearance

Examples: Some days I can't even stand to look in the mirror.
I'm definitely a "10."
I think I need some help in sharpening up how I look.

Your thoughts: _____
Overall are you

_____ satisfied?

_____ dissatisfied?

Personal Influence

Examples: I feel like a slave at work.
I have a lot of credibility at work.
I look forward to going to work.
I get along well with my colleagues.
My department is being reorganized, *again*.

Figure 1.3. (*Continued*)

Your thoughts: _____

Overall are you

_____ satisfied?

_____ dissatisfied?

Mood

Examples: I find my moods go up and down a great deal.

I worry about many things.

Some days I just feel blah.

I'm up most of the time.

Your thoughts: _____

Overall are you

_____ satisfied?

_____ dissatisfied?

Habits

Examples: I really should quit smoking.

I'm thinking about jogging again.

Basically I'm doing okay.

Your thoughts: _____

Overall are you

_____ satisfied?

_____ dissatisfied?

Living Environment

Examples: I'm getting tired of hearing the neighbor's music through the walls of my apartment.

I think I've finally got my house just the way I want it.

I really like my condominium.

Your thoughts: _____

Overall are you

_____ satisfied?

_____ dissatisfied?

Leisure-Time Activities

Examples: I spend most of my free time watching TV.

I've been thinking about learning how to do cabinetry, so I can redo my kitchen.

I have lots of fun doing crossword puzzles.

I enjoy coaching my kid's Little League team.

Your thoughts: _____

Overall are you

_____ satisfied?

_____ dissatisfied?

Community Involvement

Examples: I'm very active in programs with my church.

I vote, but that's about it.

Sometimes I think I spend too much time on all my volunteer activities.

Your thoughts: _____

Overall are you

_____ satisfied?

_____ dissatisfied?

What the Life Satisfaction Checklist Shows

This checklist is geared toward helping you focus on various parts of your life and then think through whether you are satisfied with them as they are or whether you'd like parts of your life to change. The greater the number of areas in your life that you are happy with, the lower is your potential for stress overload. If you are dissatisfied with any parts of your life, try to think why you might be dissatisfied. What obstacles are keeping you from having your life as you would like it to be? Can you think of ways around those obstacles? Think, too, about whether your expectations for changing your life are realistic. Too often we think that if we lost 50 pounds, won the lottery, or got a different job, people would think we were witty and intelligent, and our lives would suddenly be fantastic. In reality, that never happens. If you keep pushing for unrealistic goals, you only add needlessly to your stress levels. Are any of your expectations unrealistic?

Life Experiences and Hassles Checklist

Experts have found that there is a very strong correlation between the number of stressful episodes people experience during their lives and the state of their relative health or illness. Looking at recent experiences in our past often gives us a clue about vague feelings of stress that we may have, as well as helps us clarify values, goals, and priorities.

The Life Experiences and Hassles Checklist, Figure 1.4, is an adaptation of two surveys—a Life Experiences Inventory developed by John Schneider, a professor in the Department of Psychiatry, College of Human Medicine at Michigan State University; and an Everyday Problems Scale developed by Nancy Burks and Barclay Martin. Dr. Schneider took the best aspects of a variety of life-experiences measures and developed a way for people to rate for themselves the impact the event had for them. Ms. Burks and Dr. Martin believed, as we do, that ongoing, everyday problems can also add up, increasing our "stress quotient."

Look over the events in this checklist and decide whether you have experienced any of them in the past year. Also include any events that did not happen within the past year but that still affected you during that time, such as a divorce or the death of a family member. Then rate the impact the experience had on your life.

When you have finished, total the negative numbers and then the positive numbers you circled. Write both numbers in the spaces provided at the end of the checklist.

Key to Responses:

- −3 Very negative
- −2 Moderately negative
- −1 Somewhat negative
-   0 No impact
- +1 Somewhat positive
- +2 Moderately positive
- +3 Very positive

LIFE EXPERIENCES & DAILY HASSLES:

Marriage	-3	-2	-1	0	+1	+2	+3
Divorce	-3	-2	-1	0	+1	+2	+3
Separation	-3	-2	-1	0	+1	+2	+3
Reconciliation	-3	-2	-1	0	+1	+2	+3
Marital difficulties, without separation	-3	-2	-1	0	+1	+2	+3
Remarriage	-3	-2	-1	0	+1	+2	+3
Single parenting	-3	-2	-1	0	+1	+2	+3
Disabled child	-3	-2	-1	0	+1	+2	+3
Difficulty finding the romantic relationship you want	-3	-2	-1	0	+1	+2	+3
Engagement	-3	-2	-1	0	+1	+2	+3
Breakup with significant other	-3	-2	-1	0	+1	+2	+3
Reconciliation with significant other	-3	-2	-1	0	+1	+2	+3
Problems getting along with significant other	-3	-2	-1	0	+1	+2	+3
Death of spouse or partner	-3	-2	-1	0	+1	+2	+3
Death of close friend	-3	-2	-1	0	+1	+2	+3
Death of close family member	-3	-2	-1	0	+1	+2	+3
Carrying on long-distance romantic relationship	-3	-2	-1	0	+1	+2	+3
Parents or family members having marital difficulties	-3	-2	-1	0	+1	+2	+3
Spouse or partner starts work or school	-3	-2	-1	0	+1	+2	+3
Spouse or partner stops work or school	-3	-2	-1	0	+1	+2	+3
Trouble with in-laws or parents	-3	-2	-1	0	+1	+2	+3
Trouble getting along with close family member	-3	-2	-1	0	+1	+2	+3
Concern over possible pregnancy of self or partner	-3	-2	-1	0	+1	+2	+3
Birth of child or adoption	-3	-2	-1	0	+1	+2	+3
Miscarriage, abortion, or pregnancy	-3	-2	-1	0	+1	+2	+3
Infertility	-3	-2	-1	0	+1	+2	+3
Sexual difficulties	-3	-2	-1	0	+1	+2	+3
Child starts school or college	-3	-2	-1	0	+1	+2	+3
Child leaves home	-3	-2	-1	0	+1	+2	+3

Figure 1.4. Life Experiences and Hassles Checklist

Figure 1.4. (*Continued*)

Child returns home	-3	-2	-1	0	+1	+2	+3
Serious illness of family member (emotional or physical)	-3	-2	-1	0	+1	+2	+3
Less serious illness of family member (emotional or physical)	-3	-2	-1	0	+1	+2	+3
Loss of old friendship(s)	-3	-2	-1	0	+1	+2	+3
Formation of new friendship(s)	-3	-2	-1	0	+1	+2	+3
Illness/injury of close friend	-3	-2	-1	0	+1	+2	+3
Disagreement or misunderstanding with close friend	-3	-2	-1	0	+1	+2	+3
Dissatisfaction with housing	-3	-2	-1	0	+1	+2	+3
Having problems with neighbors	-3	-2	-1	0	+1	+2	+3
Taking on a mortgage over $100,000	-3	-2	-1	0	+1	+2	+3
Taking on a mortgage under $100,000	-3	-2	-1	0	+1	+2	+3
Taking on a loan of over $10,000	-3	-2	-1	0	+1	+2	+3
Taking on a loan of under $10,000	-3	-2	-1	0	+1	+2	+3
Bankruptcy	-3	-2	-1	0	+1	+2	+3
Loss of job	-3	-2	-1	0	+1	+2	+3
Start of new job	-3	-2	-1	0	+1	+2	+3
Beginning of new school experience, for example, college or graduate school	-3	-2	-1	0	+1	+2	+3
New responsibilities on the job	-3	-2	-1	0	+1	+2	+3
Business readjustment	-3	-2	-1	0	+1	+2	+3
Salary increase	-3	-2	-1	0	+1	+2	+3
Salary decrease	-3	-2	-1	0	+1	+2	+3
Promotion	-3	-2	-1	0	+1	+2	+3
Career change	-3	-2	-1	0	+1	+2	+3
Outstanding personal achievement	-3	-2	-1	0	+1	+2	+3
Start of major project at work or school	-3	-2	-1	0	+1	+2	+3
Completion of major project at work or school	-3	-2	-1	0	+1	+2	+3
Conflict on job/at school	-3	-2	-1	0	+1	+2	+3
Trouble with employer or instructor	-3	-2	-1	0	+1	+2	+3
Work required by job was boring or unpleasant	-3	-2	-1	0	+1	+2	+3
Had to work too long or too hard on the job	-3	-2	-1	0	+1	+2	+3
Unemployment	-3	-2	-1	0	+1	+2	+3
On strike	-3	-2	-1	0	+1	+2	+3
Own retirement or graduation	-3	-2	-1	0	+1	+2	+3
Spouse's or partner's retirement or graduation	-3	-2	-1	0	+1	+2	+3
Jail term	-3	-2	-1	0	+1	+2	+3
Christmas	-3	-2	-1	0	+1	+2	+3
Own birthday	-3	-2	-1	0	+1	+2	+3
Anniversary of significant event	-3	-2	-1	0	+1	+2	+3
Moving	-3	-2	-1	0	+1	+2	+3
Change in residence	-3	-2	-1	0	+1	+2	+3
Change in number of arguments with partner or spouse	-3	-2	-1	0	+1	+2	+3
Change in social activities	-3	-2	-1	0	+1	+2	+3
Change in eating habits	-3	-2	-1	0	+1	+2	+3
Change in sleeping habits	-3	-2	-1	0	+1	+2	+3
Change in exercise patterns	-3	-2	-1	0	+1	+2	+3
Change in opportunities to relax	-3	-2	-1	0	+1	+2	+3
Major personal illness/injury	-3	-2	-1	0	+1	+2	+3
Chronic personal illness	-3	-2	-1	0	+1	+2	+3
Menopause or midlife crisis	-3	-2	-1	0	+1	+2	+3
Change in smoking habit	-3	-2	-1	0	+1	+2	+3
Change in alcohol/drug use	-3	-2	-1	0	+1	+2	+3
Loneliness	-3	-2	-1	0	+1	+2	+3
Major personal weight gain or loss	-3	-2	-1	0	+1	+2	+3
Vacation	-3	-2	-1	0	+1	+2	+3

Figure 1.4 (*Continued*)

Crime victimization	-3	-2	-1	0	+1	+2	+3
Commuting	-3	-2	-1	0	+1	+2	+3
Other:	-3	-2	-1	0	+1	+2	+3
Other:	-3	-2	-1	0	+1	+2	+3
Other:	-3	-2	-1	0	+1	+2	+3

What the Life Experiences and Hassles Checklist Shows

Research has shown that both positive and negative life experiences can produce stress reactions and symptoms. Most people, however, experience more severe stress reactions and symptoms from negative life experiences. Ideally, you would want to have a larger positive total than negative total. If your negative total was larger than your positive total, pay careful attention to coping techniques listed in this book. If you are experiencing stress symptoms, consider checking them out with your physician.

Now disregard the positive and negative signs on your totals and add the two numbers together, giving you one large number. The higher this number is, the greater your chance for experiencing stress overload and resultant physical and mental symptoms. We've found that most people can tolerate a score between 0 and 50 points fairly well; hence, this range is considered normal. If you scored between 50 and 100 points, you may be beginning to experience stress overload and its accompanying symptoms. The techniques and ideas in this book could help you prevent the stressful situations from becoming chronic. If you scored over 100 points, you are probably in a chronic stress situation. You, especially, will benefit from the techniques and exercises in this book. Plan to work with your physician to maintain your level of physical health, too.

Work Satisfaction Checklist

The following checklist will help you explore which areas at work are currently stressful for you. Please answer the following sections according to how you feel today.

Job Responsibilities and Functions

Examples: I have many responsibilities but very little authority.
             I enjoy the functions I do on my job.
             The tasks I am required to do are challenging and continually changing.
Your thoughts: _____
Overall are you
        _____ satisfied?   _____ dissatisfied?

Office Politics

Examples: Where I work, office politics are serious and can be deadly.
I feel I know the terrain when it comes to office politics and know what I have to do to be "safe."
I *hate* office politics!

Your thoughts: _____

Overall are you

_____ satisfied? _____ dissatisfied?

Relationship with Your Boss

Examples: I get along fairly well with my boss and have established credibility.
My boss is definitely moody, and I have to know what "hot buttons" not to push.
I just got a new boss, and I haven't figured her/him out yet.

Your thoughts: _____

Overall are you

_____ satisfied? _____ dissatisfied?

Relationships with Co-workers

Examples: It's us against the world.
Sometimes I think my co-workers act like little kids.
We tolerate each other and help each other out when we can.

Your thoughts: _____

Overall are you

_____ satisfied? _____ dissatisfied?

Relationships with Subordinates

Examples: I have to manage many people, and keeping up with all they are doing is a real challenge.
The people who report to me are great; I wish I had more authority to provide larger salary increases and bonuses to reward them.
My subordinates come from different cultures than I do, and sometimes I have difficulty understanding them.

Your thoughts: _____

Overall are you

_____ satisfied? _____ dissatisfied?

Office Morale

Examples: My company is doing really well, and everyone is very excited about it.
We just went through a major reorganization, and now no one knows what is going on.
I'd have to say morale is at an all-time low.

Your thoughts: _____

Overall are you

_____ satisfied? _____ dissatisfied?

Red Tape and Bureaucracy

Examples: My company has made a conscious effort to push decision-making down to lower levels in the organization.
I get so tired of dealing with all the red tape and rules that sometimes I want to scream!
Most of the time bureaucratic baloney is kept to a minimum.

Your thoughts: _____

Overall are you

_____ satisfied?   _____ dissatisfied?

Salary, Bonuses, Benefits

Examples: My salary is pretty much in line with my peers in other similar-sized companies.
I think I am underpaid for all the responsibilities I have and the quality of work I do.
My company has eliminated bonuses at my grade level and lengthened the time
between salary reviews.
The cost we have to pay for health insurance and prescriptions just went up.

Your thoughts: _____

Overall are you

_____ satisfied?   _____ dissatisfied?

Professional Growth and Development, Training

Examples: My company does formal professional development planning.
I can get reimbursed for at least part of my tuition if I go back to school to get
another degree.
Our budget for attending conferences in our industry was slashed this year.
I need more training on how to use a computer on my job, but I'm told there is no
money for training.

Your thoughts: _____

Overall are you

_____ satisfied?   _____ dissatisfied?

Opportunities for Advancement

Examples: I have already bumped my head against the "glass ceiling."
I think I have a great deal of potential for advancement here.
We can't get promotions around here, but we are encouraged to make lateral moves.
Only "fast-trackers" get promoted where I work.

Your thoughts: _____

Overall are you

_____ satisfied?   _____ dissatisfied?

Control Over Your Own Work Pace

Examples: I get to set my own priorities and decide what needs to be completed when.
There is so much work to be done that I have to work fast all the time.
The demands of the situation determine the pace at which I have to work.

Your thoughts: _____

Overall are you

_____ satisfied?   _____ dissatisfied?

What the Work Satisfaction Checklist Shows

This checklist is geared to help you focus on all the various parts of your work
life and then to think through whether you are satisfied with them as they
are or whether you'd like parts of your work life to change. The greater the
number of areas in your work life that you are happy with, the lower your

potential for stress overload. If you are dissatisfied with any parts of your job, try to think why you might be dissatisfied. What obstacles are keeping you from having your job be "perfect"? Can you think of ways around those obstacles? Think, too, about whether your expectations for your job are realistic. Given the way business has changed in the last decade, many of the ideas we have about our jobs may no longer be achievable or even realistic. If we keep expecting the impossible or unattainable, we only add needlessly to our stress levels. Are any of your expectations unrealistic?

Burn Out Checklist

When you have been in a stressful job for a long period of time, you run the risk of burning out, or developing feelings of detachment, apathy, cynicism, or rigidity on the job. Not everyone in stressful jobs burns out, nor do people who develop burn out do so in the same way or in the same time frame. But examining your feelings about your job can provide you with some valuable information on your potential stress level (Figure 1.6).

Key to Responses:

1   Strongly disagree
2   Disagree
3   No feeling one way or the other
4   Agree
5   Strongly agree

BURNOUT POSSIBILITIES:

I find myself becoming bored by the things I do on my job.	1 2 3 4 5
I sometimes feel "scattered" at work.	1 2 3 4 5
I sometimes feel "trapped" in my job - and I don't feel I can change jobs or leave my present job.	1 2 3 4 5
I feel overworked and underpaid.	1 2 3 4 5
My skill level at my job is not as good as it once was.	1 2 3 4 5
My boss doesn't always listen to, and value, my input and opinions.	1 2 3 4 5
I don't control my own time and work pace at work.	1 2 3 4 5
I don't see the impact or effect of my work.	1 2 3 4 5
I don't hear when I do well, I just hear when I do badly.	1 2 3 4 5
I don't have enough time to do all the things I am *required to do* on my job.	1 2 3 4 5
I don't have enough time to do the things I *want* to do on my job.	1 2 3 4 5
My work is not challenging or stimulating.	1 2 3 4 5
The workload for my job comes is not well distributed - it's either feast or famine.	1 2 3 4 5
Staff meetings are a pain in the neck.	1 2 3 4 5

Figure 1.6. Stressful Situation Checklist

Figure 1.6. *(Continued)*

Politics at work prevent me from discussing job concerns with my colleagues.	1 2 3 4 5
My colleagues are not supportive - they all have their own fires to put out and problems to worry about.	1 2 3 4 5
I'm going nowhere, I'm stuck in my job and don't see a career path.	1 2 3 4 5
I don't have much energy to try and change things in my company.	1 2 3 4 5
I do significantly more in my job than I want to.	1 2 3 4 5
Some days I'm just wiped out by the end of the day.	1 2 3 4 5
I get a greater sense of accomplishment from the things I do outside of work than I do from my job.	1 2 3 4 5
We seem to reorganize departments at my company every time I turn around.	1 2 3 4 5
My work is extremely difficult and overly demanding.	1 2 3 4 5

What the Burn Out Checklist Shows

The higher your score on the Burn out Checklist, the higher the likelihood that you have begun to burn out on your job.

Score Between 0 and 40:

Most people feel frustrated, overwhelmed, and unappreciated on the job once in awhile, so a score between 1 and 40 is fairly typical.

Score Between 41 and 80:

If you scored between 41 and 80, you are beginning to show some of the signs of burn out. You might want to see if you can reduce some of your current work commitments, talk with your boss about getting more control over your work, or begin to develop a network of colleagues at work to provide mutual support.

Score Over 81:

If you scored over 81, chances are good that you are in the process of actively burning out. Burn out is hazardous to both your emotional and physical well-being. People who are burned out very often suffer from stress-related illnesses. This book may help you cope with some of the stresses of your job, but it might be a good idea for you to make an appointment for a checkup with your physician.

Company Culture Checklist

Every company or organization has a culture—a distinct personality that permeates the way everything is done in the company. No one overtly teaches it to you when you join a company, understanding the culture is something you learn through the unwritten codes of behavior; stories of organization heroes; and hints on how to navigate the maze of bureaucracy that are passed on during coffee breaks, while standing at the copier or fax machine, or after hours when colleagues stop for a drink after work.

Understanding your organization's corporate culture is very important—if you know what makes a company tick, you can use it to your advantage to succeed in your career. It is equally important to understand what kind of corporate culture you personally feel most comfortable in, because a misfit between employee and company is a very common cause of stress on the job.

This checklist is an adaptation of one developed by Warren Strugatch, and it looks at a variety of ways in which an organization's culture can manifest itself.

Please work through this checklist *twice*—first checking off the answer that best matches your company, and then checking off the answer that best matches the kind of organization you would be happiest working in. After each pass through the checklist, total up the number of As, Bs, Cs, and Ds you checked, and put the number in the space provided at the end of the checklist.

---

1. The accepted style of dress at your company is:
   A. Formal. There is a dress code (either an actual written code or one that everybody follows), and everybody dresses pretty much the same. Executives look like executives, and junior staffers look like junior staffers.
   B. Whatever "middle America" is wearing at the moment, with no extremes in dress.
   C. Individualistic. Either everyone wants to stand out from the pack and style is very important, or no one cares how you dress.
   D. Basically conservative, but there is a little more flexibility. Men can work in shirt sleeves and women wear mostly dresses.

2. Offices at your organization:
   A. Get bigger and fancier the higher up the ladder you go.
   B. Are decorated in the style of the moment and get flashier the more successful you are.
   C. Are low rent, but there are lots of cubicles and conference rooms for people to get together to talk and hatch ideas. Cubicles are full of personal mementos and "stuff"—the more outrageous the better.
   D. All look pretty much the same. Everything is standard issue, from the in boxes to the art on the walls.

3. Employees move through your organization:
   A. Vertically—up the proverbial career ladder.
   B. At a speed dependent on their sales volume.
   C. Who moves? Most people move out to start their own businesses.
   D. Very slowly. People can stay for years in a position while multiple bosses are promoted to higher positions.

Figure 1.7. Company Culture Checklist

Figure 1.7. (*Continued*)

4. Your company most values:
   A. Hierarchy—playing by the rules and working through proper channels.
   B. Conformity and fitting in—we're all team players here.
   C. People who produce, no matter what the cost. Short-term results are what count.
   D. The process, not the final result.

5. The most successful and revered employees at your company are:
   A. Specialists who spent a long time at the company learning their area of specialization.
   B. Those who made the difficult sale.
   C. The stars and the comers who are aggressive, whether right, wrong, or indifferent.
   D. Those who do their job neatly and competently and follow the rules, whether the rules make sense or not.

6. The interview process you went through before you were offered your job was:
   A. Very intense. It seemed as if you had interviews with nearly everyone in the company.
   B. Very fast. Everybody asked direct questions and seemed to make up their minds very quickly.
   C. Very fast. They expected you to tell them why you thought you were good, and good for the organization.
   D. Very lengthy. In fact, the interview process lasted as much as a month or more.

7. My company considers its retirement and pension plans:
   A. More important as you go higher up the career ladder and stay with the company longer.
   B. Important, but not the be all and end all.
   C. What pension plan? Their attitude is: "If you are the kind of person who wants a pension, you're not the kind of person we want working here."
   D. A vital part of the total compensation package.

8. The preferred way to handle a crisis in your company is to:
   A. Call a meeting of people in the company who have lived through that kind of crisis before, and learn from their experience.
   B. Call an emergency staff meeting and get everyone to help develop a strategy.
   C. Work out your own plan to handle the crisis; then document it in a memo to your boss.
   D. Turn it over to someone who has been trained to handle that specific kind of crisis.

9. Most decisions and ideas in your company are generated:
   A. In conference rooms during scheduled meetings.
   B. On the golf course and in task force groups.
   C. By someone working alone.
   D. Very slowly and are implemented over a long period of time after much debate and discussion.

Scores for your company:	Scores for your ideal company:
_____ As	_____ As
_____ Bs	_____ Bs
_____ Cs	_____ Cs
_____ Ds	_____ Ds

What the Company Culture Checklist Shows

No company or organization is a pure type, but most organizations tend to fall into one of the following four categories:

Mostly As:

The *Bet-the-Company Organization* praises hierarchy and specialization and believes in long-term commitment—both to the employee and the company. In this organization decisions often risk the future of the entire company and take years to prove out. Examples of this type of organization include most large capital-goods companies, oil companies, investment banks, architectural firms, computer-design companies, and mining companies.

Mostly Bs:

The *Work Hard/Play Hard Organization* values activity and persistence more than anything else because volume of sales is the goal. Management likes to think of the company as one big, happy family. Good examples of this type of organization include mass-consumer products companies, retail stores, real estate agencies, computer companies, any door-to-door sales organization, and small manufacturers.

Mostly Cs:

The *Tough-Guy Organization* values people who hit a home run the very first week on the job. The environment is usually very high-pressure, and short-term results are what count. Tough-Guy Organizations are typified by organizations involved in construction, cosmetics, management consulting, venture capital, advertising, the entertainment industry, and surgery.

Mostly Ds:

The *Bureaucratic Organization* seems always to be bound up in red tape or memos. There are right and wrong ways to do *everything*. The Bureaucratic Organization is typified by government agencies, the health-care industry, banks, insurance companies, financial service organizations, utilities, and heavily regulated industries.

If your present company and your ideal company match, lucky you! Bet-the-Company and Bureaucratic Organizations share some similar characteristics, so if your present organization is the Bet-the-Company type, but you prefer a Bureaucratic company (or vice versa), chances are good that your company's culture suits you well enough that it won't be a major source of stress on the job. The biggest potential for serious stress occurs if your present company is a Bet-the-Company or Bureaucratic organization, but you prefer a Tough-Guy or Work Hard/Play Hard company (or vice versa). Corporate culture clashes could be a major source of work stress for you, and it may be time to rethink your job strategy. This book can provide you with coping techniques to help you deal with the stress, but working through the values and goals section of this book will be very important for you to help clarify what is important for you in your work environment.

Personality Type Checklist

People seem to be of three common personality types, that differ in their approach to stressful situations. These types are referred to as A, B, and S for convenience' sake. This checklist will help you determine which personality type you are and give you some insight into how other personality types function in stressful situations.

Read through the following situations and then decide which of the available reactions would most resemble yours. After you have finished the checklist, add up the total number of As, Bs, and Ss you checked and write them in the spaces provided at the end of the checklist.

---

1. It's 4:45 p.m. on Friday, and you need cash for the upcoming weekend. You most likely would:
   A. Throw papers into your briefcase, break all traffic records to get across town to your bank, and curse loudly as the bank manager locked the door at 5 p.m.
   B. Clear off your desk and head for the bank, figuring that if you didn't make it in time, you'd borrow some cash from a family member or cash a check at the grocery store.
   S. Finish work and take a leisurely trip to the bus stop, the train, or your car. You did your banking at lunch at an ATM.

2. You're sitting in a staff meeting and not much is going on. You most likely would be:
   A. Thinking about all the work piled up on your desk, wondering if you were getting any important calls, fuming because you really had better things to do, chewing on your fingernails, and hunting for antacid tablets.
   B. Daydreaming about something else—a trip to Hawaii, sex, playing for the Chicago Bulls or Bears—anything other than what you were *supposed* to be doing.
   S. Writing a memo that you wanted to get out today.

Figure 1.8. Personality Type Checklist

Figure 1.8. (Continued)

3. A friend is talking about life in New York City. You find yourself:
   A. Interrupting him to talk about the hot restaurants you read about in the *New York Times* on Sunday.
   B. Wondering why on earth anyone would want even to visit such a huge, busy, crime-ridden city.
   S. Listening carefully and filing away bits of information for your next business trip to New York.

4. You've been asked to address a national conference in your area of interest or specialization at work. As you are giving your speech, you:
   A. Use lots of gestures, change your tone of voice, and find yourself speeding up at the ends of sentences. You also notice some puzzled looks on the faces of some of the people in the audience.
   B. Find yourself slowing down and really enjoying the experience. You also notice a couple of people have fallen asleep.
   S. Keep the pace of your speech upbeat, throw in some jokes and side lines, and even use some slides to illustrate your points. Afterward, several members of the audience ask you to speak at their company.

5. When you turned on the radio this morning, you learned that, because of the ice storm last night, most businesses in the area are closed, including your company. You most likely would:
   A. Put on your boots, warm up the car, and head into work anyway, thinking that it would be an excellent time to catch up on all that paperwork sitting on your desk and in your briefcase.
   B. Turn off the radio, unplug the coffee pot, and go back to bed.
   S. Fix yourself a fancy breakfast, spend time reading the newspaper, and do something around the house you've been wanting to do, but haven't had time to start.

6. You're having lunch with your best friend, who asks if you notice anything different about him. You most likely would:
   A. Be taken aback. You can't see anything different and don't know what to say. You mumble something about not being too observant these days, and your friend chuckles knowingly.
   B. Compliment your friend on a 10-pound weight loss. You knew right away that he must have really lost some weight! You tell your friend he looks fantastic and decide to skip dessert.
   S. Comment on the fact that your friend looks positively glowing and healthy, asking his secret for looking so great when everyone else is falling apart. You know your friend looks different, but you're not exactly sure why. You hope it's because he's been taking better care of himself.

7. You have been thinking about getting better organized at home and at work, and making better use of your time. You hope this will:
   A. Help you do more in less time, so that you can fit more things into your day.
   B. Give you a few tips on how to look organized, even if you really aren't—that way maybe everyone will get off your back about being disorganized.

Figure 1.8 (Continued)

    S. Give you some ideas on shortcuts so that you can spend more time doing things you *want* to do, instead of things you're *supposed* to do.

8. A genie in a magic bottle says she'll grant you three wishes. You wish for:
    A. Presidency of the company, membership in the country club, and one hundred more wishes.
    B. Long, happy lives for you and your family, a chance to be a better person, and maybe a new car—if it wouldn't be too much trouble.
    S. Besides world peace or a cure for cancer, you really can't think of anything you want so much that you couldn't live without it.

9. When you play sports, you:
    A. Become very competitive. Your killer instinct functions at top form and you want to win!
    B. Like to be sociable and have a good time. You like it best when no one keeps score and you head for the club house or snack bar afterward for a cool drink.
    S. Actually, the thing you hate about sports is the competition part. It takes all the fun out of it. You are into achieving your personal best. You know you will never be champion material, but somehow you really don't care.

10. It's Saturday morning, and you are standing in the checkout line at the neighborhood grocery store. Most likely you would be:
    A. Trying to figure out if any other line would be shorter, thinking about all the other things you want to get done before noon, and mentally concentrating on throwing daggers at the woman ahead of you, who just decided to try and cash a check without three pieces of ID.
    B. Scanning *People* magazine and maybe even *National Enquirer*, if you felt wicked enough. You might also be watching the other people and wondering how that woman in the next line could possibly feed all her children without going broke.
    S. Sorting through your coupons, checking to see if you got everything on your shopping list, and contemplating the fact that you can learn a lot about people by what they have in their grocery carts. You try to picture what kind of life the man ahead of you in line must have with caviar and diapers in his cart.

                           TOTAL As _____
                           TOTAL Bs _____
                           TOTAL Ss _____

What the Personality Type Checklist Shows

Each of the situations mentioned in the checklist represents a situation that the three stress-personality types would handle very differently. The letter for which you had the highest total indicates the personality type you most resemble. Few people are pure types (that is, have all their answers for one personality type); most people are a mix of all three types. However, you probably resemble the personality type for which you had the highest total.

If You Had More A Answers:

Type A people are usually hard-working, striving, competitive people. They try to do a lot in very little time and often feel rushed because they don't plan for the unexpected in their overcrowded schedules. Research has shown that Type A people have a much higher risk of cardiovascular disease, heart attacks, and strokes than either Type B or Type S. If you resemble Type A, study the techniques and exercises presented in this book carefully—they might save your life!

If You Had More B Answers:

Type B people are typically more laid-back than Type As. They don't feel compelled to prove how great they are and are content to enjoy life as it comes. If you resemble a Type B, you might want to study the ideas presented in this book to help you cope with Type As! Type Bs most frequently experience stress symptoms when Type As expect them to behave like As. Be good to yourself if you're in that kind of situation. The exercises and techniques presented in this book have a preventive effect, too, and can help you prepare for a world full of As.

If You Had More S Answers:

Type S people are somewhat rare, mainly because it takes a high level of maturity and self-acceptance to be a Type S. Type S people are more concerned about the *process* of tasks and events than their *outcomes*, and measure their successes and failures differently than either Type B or Type A. Of all the personality types, Type Ss usually exhibit fewer stress symptoms and problems, mainly because their psychological mind set toward life is accepting and philosophical. They know they will fail sometimes, so they don't worry about it. They usually develop stress-related illnesses only after being in chronic stress situations for an extended period of time. On the outside, Type Ss may look like Type As. Type Ss are very active, have lots of energy, and accomplish many things. They work hard, but they also like to play and relax.

We'd like everyone to become a Type S, mainly because Type S usually enjoy their work so much that it becomes play. These people truly enjoy what they are doing, and sometimes even feel guilty about being paid for having so much fun! We've found that a B can easily become a S—and many seem to do so naturally as they get older—but it can be difficult for an A to become a S. Type As can effect behavior changes, however, and—who knows—with all the drive Type As have, they just might make it to S if they really want to!

2
How Stress Works

In order to combat stress effectively, you need to know the "enemy" inside and out. If you know how stress affects your mind and body, you will be able to determine how to short-circuit the process—which is what this chapter is all about.

The Physiological Side of Stress

The grandfather of human stress research is Hans Selye, who first documented some of the physiological aspects of stress in the 1930s. What he found out then still holds true today.

Acute Stress

Selye discovered that there are two kinds of stress. The first kind, which he called acute stress, occurs when there is an immediate threat to a person's life or physical well-being, and the person has to respond instantaneously. A good example is going into a skid on an icy road while driving your car. You have to be able to react fast, and if you've ever been in a similar situation, you probably noticed that your hands shook, your heart raced, and maybe your knees felt a little weak afterward. That reaction happened as a result of adrenaline (epinephrine) and norepinephrine, two messenger chemicals produced by your body to decrease your reaction time and sharpen your senses, preparing for the "fight." Adrenaline and norepinephrine produce a "rush," leaving you feeling a little drained when the crisis is over.

Chronic Stress

A second kind of stress is one Selye called chronic stress—the kind most managers and professionals in business today are experiencing. Chronic stress occurs when a crisis situation is prolonged without any rest or recuperation time for your body. It can also occur when one crisis follows another crisis too quickly, giving your body insufficient time to recuperate from the previous crisis.

Chronic stress situations trigger the production of different hormones in our bodies. The cortex of the adrenal glands, two small organs that rest atop the kidneys, produces hormones called glucocorticoids (steroids) in an effort to help your body respond to a stress situation. Glucocorticoids have the potential to be harmful. While adrenaline and norepinephrine are easily and rapidly metabolized by your body, steroids are too large structurally and too long-acting to be eliminated the same way. Unless they are biochemically altered in some way, steroids remain in your system, where they are capable of raising your blood pressure, changing your mood and stamina, increasing the likelihood of cardiovascular disease by facilitating the adhesion of fats to the walls of arteries and veins, and causing a whole host of other problems. Steroids are also capable of actual physical tissue damage. Chronic stress increases the amounts of acid secreted by your stomach, which is why you may get heartburn and stomach pain when you are under stress.

Physiological Reactions and General Adaptation Syndrome

What triggers acute and chronic stress reactions? Researchers have found that, given the right conditions, a person may perceive any situation as stressful. Selye found that *both* chronic and acute stresses produce a definite series of reactions in the human body, which he called the general adaptation syndrome (GAS). This syndrome works as follows.

The Alarm Phase.   The first phase is the *alarm phase*. It occurs when your brain and body perceive in the environment some sort of threat to you or a situation that requires your immediate attention. Adrenaline is rapidly secreted and rushed throughout your body to prepare you for action.

The Resistance Phase.   The second phase is the *resistance phase*. This occurs when your body readies a particular organ or muscle group to cope with and resolve the stressful situation. Most of the time your body chooses the organ group most suited to handling the crisis situation: your leg muscles if you need to run, for example; your arm muscles if you need to strike out at something; and so on. If it is not safe for you to do anything about the situation, such as when you have a quarrel with a coworker or with your spouse, your body may shift the coping responsibility to your heart or stomach.

The second phase is crucial for coping with the effects of the stressful situation and preventing tissue damage. If you are able to act in some way to resolve the situation so that no threat to your well-being remains, GAS ends here. You have either fought or fled the stressful situation. But—and this is a big but—if you are not able to affect the situation to alleviate the crisis, your body responds to it as a chronic stress situation, and both adrenaline and steroids begin to be secreted in large amounts.

The Exhaustion Phase. If the stressful situation has not been resolved by the time you have come to the end of your "organ chain"—or your rope, so to speak—your body will reach what Selye calls the *exhaustion phase*. This phase results in severe illness or death. You've used up all of your reserves and resources, and your body can no longer handle the stressful situation.

It usually takes a long time to reach the exhaustion phase. But if for some reason your body picks your weakest organ or muscle group to handle the stress first, you may reach your *personal exhaustion point* much faster than someone else.

Coping Determinants

During the first part of the resistance phase, your body shifted the coping responsibility to an organ or muscle group in your body. An organ group can last only for a given amount of time before it becomes exhausted and can no longer cope with the stress situation effectively. How long and how well any particular organ or muscle group will cope depends on the following:

Your Heredity. Heredity affects your ability to cope with stress because, to some extent, your family genes play a role in the overall wellness of a particular organ or muscle group. Some families have a predisposition to heart disease, others to stomach problems, and so on.

Your Overall Level of Health. The healthier you are to begin with, the longer it will take the stress to have an impact strong enough to exhaust the particular organ or muscle group.

Your Environment. Environment can contribute significantly to how well you are able to stand up to stress. It can either add to the damage going on or increase your overall level of wellness. For example, consider the following situation: A manager's family has a predisposition to stomach ulcers, and lately she has been having problems with heartburn and upset stomach. This morning she had to attend a staff meeting that took longer than she had anticipated. It is 2 p.m. and she is late for a meeting with a major customer. She must grab a quick lunch on the run, and the closest spot for that is a taco stand. She chooses a couple of spicy burritos and washes them down with strong coffee. She gets stuck in traffic on her way to the customer's office. When she does get there, she learns that the customer is dissatisfied with the quality of the product he is purchasing from the manager's company, and has begun to look for other suppliers. Once back at her office, the manager notices that she has a terrible stomach ache and starts looking around for her antacid tablets. Chances are good that the manager's stomach isn't going to last long at this rate!

The Severity of the Stressful Situation. The more severe the stressful situation, the higher your hormone output will be. With lower levels of stress, your steroid secretion is lower, which gives your body a chance to metabolize the steroids, effectively removing them from your bloodstream.

Your Energy Level. You, like everyone, have an optimal amount of physical and mental energy you can command at any one time. This optimal level of energy is determined by your overall level of health, daily nutrition, upbringing, and personality. When more than one worry or crisis is occurring at the same time, your mental and physical energy has to be diverted to handle all of the crisis situations. This means that you have less energy available to handle each individual crisis. The less energy you can supply to an organ or muscle group, the faster it will fatigue, and the less able it is to respond to stress.

Eventually your body's "first-choice" organ group will become exhausted and ultimately damaged. If the stressful situation is still present, your body will switch the coping responsibility to another organ or muscle group. That's why some people get a skin rash after they get asthma or develop low back pain after they get an ulcer. If the stressful situation is still not resolved, eventually the second organ or muscle group will become exhausted, and your body will shift the coping responsibility to a third organ group, and on and on.

There are ways to short-circuit GAS:

1. Act to resolve the stressful situation during the alarm phase, thus inhibiting steroid secretion.

2. Get some form of physical exercise while you are in the resistance phase. Researchers have found that physical activity and the hormones your body produces during such activity can counteract the effects of the steroids.

3. Allow adequate resting time for your body between stressful situations. Your body is capable of repairing initial tissue damage if given enough recuperation time. Recuperation time can be shortened if you practice some sort of stress-reducing or relaxation technique during resting times.

Later chapters in this book will help you determine which techniques could be most useful for you.

Common Stress Patterns

The Optimal Stress Pattern

What kind of stress patterns do people commonly have? Ideally, your stress pattern should look like the one shown in Figure 2.1, entitled *Optimal Stress Pattern*. This stress pattern allows adequate rest and recuperation time between crises. How much time you need for rest and recuperation depends on the severity of tissue damage and your overall level of health. Thus everyone has a different optimal resting time.

Figure 2.1. Optimal stress pattern

The Typical Stress Pattern

Most people have stress patterns similar to the one shown in Figure 2.2, the *Typical Stress Pattern*. Here, resting time between crises is less than adequate. However, you can enhance your body's recuperative powers by practicing coping and relaxation techniques and including wellness behaviors in your daily life. If you take care of yourself, it is possible to survive even a severe stressful situation with minimal damage to your body.

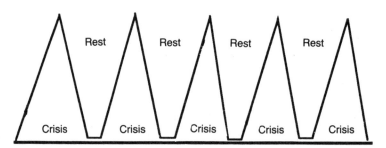

Figure 2.2. Typical stress pattern

The Chronic Stress Pattern

The third stress pattern, Figure 2.3, is called a *Chronic Stress Pattern* and is considered harmful. This drawing represents a chronically stressful situation that begins and doesn't let up. This situation is one that many managers and professionals find themselves in today. Levels of hormone production are high and can cause actual tissue damage. However, your body can learn to adapt to high levels of stress hormones and function adequately in such situations as long as is needed to preserve your survival. Problems occur *after* the stressful situation has ended. Very often people who have survived such stress patterns develop delayed stress reactions, ranging from mental problems to heart disease and death. Many people who fought in the Vietnam War developed delayed stress reactions several years *after* they had returned to their families in the United States—reactions that caused nightmares, personality changes, violent behavior, and chronic physical problems.

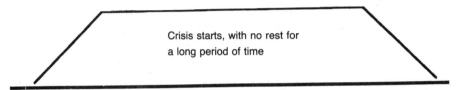

Figure 2.3. Chronic stress pattern

The Hazardous Stress Pattern

The fourth stress pattern, depicted in Figure 2.4, called *Hazardous Stress Pattern*, is the one researchers previously consider to be the most dangerous. This pattern is made up of a series of crises coming rapidly one right after the other, with very little resting time between each crisis. The tiny resting period is enough to allow the body to begin reestablishing a new equilibrium, but then suddenly it has to gear up to cope with a new crisis all over again. This type of yo-yo syndrome is *extremely* hard on the body, and people experiencing this type of stress pattern reach the exhaustion phase faster than with other stress patterns.

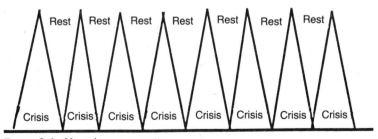

Figure 2.4. Hazardous stress pattern

New—The Dangerous Stress Pattern

A fifth stress pattern has recently emerged, one that we call the *Dangerous Stress Pattern*, shown in Figure 2.5. In this pattern, which combines aspects of *both* the chronic stress pattern and the hazardous stress pattern, stress levels do not dip low enough for the body to recuperate and repair damage. Essentially, given the demands of business today, our "resting levels" of stress have been ratcheted upward, toward what would once have been considered severe chronic stress levels. On top of that, we have the peaks and valleys of stress caused by the ups and downs of our company's business— plus the stresses of our personal lives. Businesspeople who are lucky enough to have good health, lots of energy, and no weak organs can appear to tolerate this environment well—for a period of time. But over time, the body begins to use up its reserves, damage caused by excessive hormone production is not repaired, and stress-related problems and illnesses develop. At first those problems are rather minor—frequent colds that seem to take a long time to go away, frequent sore throats or sinus infections, upset stomachs and heartburn, even hypertension. The symptoms are a nuisance, but don't seem too serious.

But after three, four, or six years, people in the dangerous stress pattern start showing symptoms of significant stress-related illnesses, such as peptic ulcers, reflux esophagitis, ulcerative colitis, heart disease, and others. By this time, damage has been done to the body, and repairs take a long time.

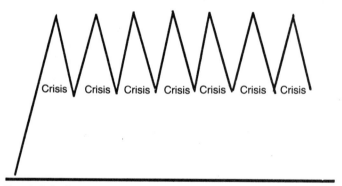

Figure 2.5. Dangerous stress pattern

Common Stress Reactions

When people find themselves in stressful situations, how do they respond? The most effective reaction is to find some way to deal with the situation actively and resolve the crisis it has caused. But sometimes we cannot do that. This is particularly true in business because many of the stressful situations we encounter are truly beyond our control—brought on by business conditions, industry events, corporate decisions on policies, etc. We have to make the best we can of the situation, preferably while keeping staff morale up and company profits high!

Typically, people react in one of seven ways when they encounter a stressful situation:

1. *Most people's first response is tolerance.* They just put up with the situation and go on as best they can. Businesspeople refer to this phase as "getting with the program," "keeping a stiff upper lip," and "being a good team player."

2. *After a while, though, tolerating the situation isn't enough. Most people try diversion next*—doing anything to take their minds off the situation for a while and get a much-needed mental or physical break. Common diversions are: commiserating with colleagues; picking on subordinates; signing up for *any* conference *anywhere* that is out of town and where the weather is decent; taking long lunches (preferably on an expense account); playing sports; fighting with a spouse or significant other; eating; making love; kicking the dog; and so forth. Diversion doesn't involve working directly on the problem to resolve it, but doing something to expend the energy and feelings of frustration produced by the stressful situation.

3. *If the stressful situation still hasn't been resolved, some people begin to practice withdrawal* by removing themselves physically or mentally from the stressful situation. Common withdrawal techniques range from procrastination, oversleeping, "forgetting" a staff meeting has been scheduled, holing up in the office with the door closed and phone forwarded, or getting drunk after work—to more serious withdrawal responses, such as suicide, drug abuse, or deep depression.

4. *If withdrawal doesn't work, many people practice denial.* In effect, they deny to themselves, and often to others around them, that there is a stressful situation at all. They try to fool themselves by pretending that things are just as they were before the stressful situation began—and start living in sort of a fantasyland. They may tune out valuable information from the office grapevine, ignore rumors that have credibility, and fail to plan appropriately for upcoming crises. Denial usually makes the stressful situation worse and adds to the toll already taken on the body.

5. *Another response some people choose in extremely stressful situations is "going crazy."* Sometimes going crazy is a very sane thing to do—a last-ditch attempt at self-survival in an overwhelming situation. Long-term "craziness" is not especially beneficial to most people, but it can provide a breathing space and make an intolerable situation bearable for a little while. It might also keep a person alive.

6. *If toleration, diversion, withdrawal, and denial haven't worked, people often respond by developing some sort of illness.* The steroids produced as a result of the chronic stress situation have done actual tissue damage, making

the person ill. Physicians often call these illnesses psychosomatic, and we usually think that means that our aches and pains are all in our head. Not so! The steroids our bodies are producing damage tissue and wear down our reserves of energy, making us more susceptible to a wide range of illnesses.

7. *If all the previously mentioned responses haven't worked to alleviate the stressful situation, death can result.* It is the end result of GAS and biochemical damage. In the recent past, the Japanese work ethic bred businesspeople who literally worked themselves to death. In fact, they have even coined a new term for death by overwork—*karoshi*. It was not uncommon for managers and professionals to put in a full 8- to 12-hour day six days a week on the job, and then spend another 4 or 5 hours after the formal workday with their colleagues and supervisors, having a drink to talk over problems or gathering in quality circles to talk about how they could do the job better. Workaholism was raised almost to an art form, with businesspeople striving to complete one assignment rapidly, and take on another—for the good of the company and the country. Such drive made Japan an international economic powerhouse, but it took a tremendous toll on businesspeople. In one, not uncommon case, a son recalls life with his businessman father in an interview in *Fortune* magazine:

> "He worked like mad, often until midnight. He had to go out with his colleagues after work. That taxed his nerves, wore out his health. His heart failed."

Most people are lucky enough never to reach this final stress point, and the purpose of this book is to make sure you never do either.

None of these common responses to stress—toleration, diversion, withdrawal, denial, going crazy, illness, or death—is an effective way to cope with stress over the long term. The only really effective way to deal with stressful situations is to resolve them. But it is important to respect these other common reactions for what they are—valiant attempts to survive in overwhelming situations. They are not bad or wrong. They just are.

Why People Perceive Stress Differently

What makes one person respond with withdrawal while another person responds by actively confronting a stressful situation? The answer to that question lies in how people perceive stressful events. Our perceptions are based on our values, resources, track record, feelings of control, and personality style.

Your Values

Your values play a big part in your perception of a situation as stressful because they determine the meaning the situation has for you. It stands to reason that you will be more upset and stressed if something goes wrong in a situation you care a great deal about than you would be if the situation were not important to you.

For example, a technical professional in research and development at a mid-sized corporation had always felt that his job was the most important part of his life. He was very good at what he did, loved doing research, and had progressed regularly up the career ladder in his division. He was well regarded by his peers, and in his industry. When his company was acquired by a much larger company, the larger company decided that the profession-al's company would no longer be responsible for research and develop-ment—all of that would be done by the larger company. The professional was "RIFed" (reduction in force)—along with all the other research and development staff members. But because his work, and all the positive feelings and benefits he received from it, was the most important thing in his life, he was devastated. He was embarrassed to tell others he had been let go, even though it was not his fault. He didn't even want to apply for unemploy-ment compensation. Being unemployed felt to him as though he had done something wrong, and his self-esteem dwindled.

This professional put a high value on being viewed as a competent re-searcher, and when his life situation changed, and he was no longer a researcher, a severe stress situation resulted.

Your Resources

The amounts and kinds of resources you have available to use in coping with a crisis can determine how stressful the crisis will be for you. People usually think *resources* refers to money, education, job skills, or savings. But re-sources are much more than that. Resources are anything that help you cope more effectively with a crisis situation. Resources can include family, friends, physical health, availability of information, knowledge of relaxation techni-ques, communication skills, organizational ability—in short, your bag of tricks. If you can increase the number and kind of resources in your bag of tricks, you can greatly increase your ability to cope with stressful situations effectively.

Your Track Record

Your track record is built on your past experiences with stressful situations. If you have handled crisis situations to your satisfaction in the past, chances are you feel good about yourself. If you feel good about yourself and your abilities, you're more likely to believe that there is something you can do about a crisis, and you will at least begin to find some ways to cope. But if your past experiences with handling crisis situations have been negative, you might give up in a new crisis situation without even trying. In addition, if you have handled stressful situations effectively in the past, you probably learned a wide variety of problem-solving skills you may not even be aware you know.

Your Feeling of Control

If you believe you can control the *outcome* of a situation in any way, you will feel less threatened by that situation and may be able to tolerate higher levels of stress. It's the situations you feel you have no control over that are stressful and frustrating.

We often have more control in situations than we think we have. Even if we cannot control the outcome of a situation (such as a transfer to another division or a reduction in force), we may be able to have some sort of impact on the process leading to the outcome (arranging for your company to help your spouse find a job in the new city, or getting a larger termination package or longer outplacement time in the case of the RIF). If that fails, we are *always* capable of changing our perceptions of the situation itself (for example, "I'm not losing a job, I'm getting a chance to determine whether I want to change careers at this point in my life").

How Perception Works

People perceive situations as stressful based on their values, resources, track records, feelings of control, and personality styles. You can *change* your perception of a stressful situation by changing any one, or any combination of, these five components of perception.

Since our modern lifestyles are often collections of habits, clarifying our values for ourselves is very important. It's important to find out, not only what our values are, but also whether these values are currently useful for enhancing our lifestyles. Values we may have acquired as children (such as roles for adults to play on the job, and even what is considered a "good" job) may no longer be useful, given the massive changes the business world has gone through in the recent past. Holding on to values that aren't helping us get on with our lives is stress-producing. But it is possible to sort through our values, toss out those that are no longer useful, and keep those that are life-enhancing. Later chapters in this book will help you do just that.

Developing your bag of tricks by increasing the resources at your command for coping with stress is probably the easiest component to work on. That's what a major segment of this book is about! Every new skill and technique you learn will add to your ability to cope—even if you don't use it until several years from now. It's an immensely reassuring feeling to be sitting on a bulging bag of tricks!

Improving and building on your track record is a little harder to do, but it can be done. Each new situation you handle to your satisfaction, no matter how small, increases your positive track record—and the effect is cumulative. It's also helpful to focus clearly on your successes rather than keep all your attention on your failures. If you're like most people, you know every single one of your failures in great detail, but when asked to talk about what you do well, you're at a loss for words. Give yourself a pat on the back when you do well. You're not bragging or blowing your own horn—you're being realistic!

You can reclaim control of your own life and the situations you find yourself in. Try repeating the following thoughts until you've internalized them:

> I am in charge of myself, my feelings, and my actions. No one has control over me unless I give him or her that control.

And whatever you've given away, you can take back.

Of all the components of perception, your personality style is probably the most difficult to change. Even if you can't change it you can get to know it better and build in allowances for it when you are in crisis situations.

Let's look at a simple example and see how the perception and coping processes work.

Not too long ago a manager at a large foreign bank lost her job when corporate staff positions were cut back due to a recession and repercussions from a series of bad loans.

Assume for a minute that she needed 100 points overall for her "perception quotient" in order to cope effectively with this crisis situation.

Values: She rated herself -60 points because she had very strong feelings about having a job, being able to eat, and keeping a roof over her head. She also had recently purchased a condo, and valued highly being able to make her mortgage payments. (Strong values are rated negatively, not because its bad to have them, but because you get upset when these values are upset in some way.)

Resources: She rated herself $+70$ points because she had a variety of salable job skills, knew how to write a good resume and give a good interview, had kept up contacts with head-hunters, knew where to look for new jobs, had a wide circle of supportive friends, and had a family she could count on to back her up. She was also familiar with a variety of stress-management techniques.

Track Record: She rated her track record $+50$ points. She had experienced similar situations in the past and had handled them effectively. She had been able to find new jobs before and adjust to them successfully.

Feeling of Control: She rated her feelings of control at -20 points because the loss of the job wasn't her fault and because nothing she could do would erase the recession and bad loans.

Personality Style: She was a Type S so she scored $+30$ points. Type Bs would score $+20$ points; and Type A people, $+10$ points.

After adding up her scores, she came up with 70 points overall, still well below the 100 needed to cope effectively with the situation. What should she do?

She decided she didn't want to change her values in this area, couldn't change her track record, and didn't want to change her personality style. But she *could* increase her resources and feelings of control.

So she increased her resources by +10 points, bringing her new resources total to +80 points. She did that by making full use of outplacement services her company offered as part of the severance package, networking with friends still employed at other corporations, and investing her 401K plan funds wisely.

But, most importantly, she added +*20* points to her feelings of control by seriously thinking through what she wanted to do with the rest of her working life. She figured that maybe she didn't want to spend the rest of her life in a corporate setting. She decided that if she didn't find a new job within three months, she would apply to a nationally known culinary institute to become a chef—something she had always wanted to do, but never had the opportunity even to consider.

The total of her new "perception quotient" turned out to be 100 points—the amount necessary to cope effectively with the stressful situation, and she was able to weather the storm and keep a roof over her head! As a result the crisis was uncomfortable and stressful, but it was not devastating. Most importantly, it did not turn into a chronic stress situation—and she is very happy being a chef!

This whole process was not that difficult to accomplish. You are fully capable of doing the same thing. The rest of this book will show you how!

3
A Look at the New Stress-Intensive Environment

Determining Your Professional Type

When we look at the world of work, we see three types of managerial and professional workers—determined by the kind of environments in which they work:

The corporate professional

The semiautonomous professional

The autonomous professional

Each of these types experience stress on the job—but the causes and types of stress are qualitatively different, due to the pressures and demands of their different environments.

Given these differences, the various potential work stressors discussed in this chapter will impact these three types of professionals differently, and certain situations may be more stressful for one type of professional than the others.

In order to get the most out of this chapter, it is important to determine your professional type:

Corporate Professional A corporate professional is the type of person that comes to mind for most people when they think of a "businessperson"—someone who works for a company or organization (which may be large or small) where progression through the ranks is fairly clear; supervisor-subordinate relationships are defined and managed; and professionals have little if any control over their environment, work flow, or work speed.

They may have staff members to whom they can delegate work, but in most corporations today, staff size is shrinking—and many specialized corporate professionals, such as engineers, scientists, lawyers, and technical specialists, have no one on whom they can off-load tasks. If they do have staff to manage, they rarely have final say over promotions, rewards, salary increases, or even firings or layoffs—they have the responsibility of managing people with little of the authority necessary to do so effectively.

Many corporate professionals used to work fairly independently, but, with today's trend toward matrixed management, more and more are having to work on projects in teams or work groups. Many corporate professionals find such groups very stressful: first because their backgrounds did not prepare them for such teamwork and, second because the success of these groups is determined by whether a specific objective is met, and most corporate professionals have little control over those with whom they work in teams.

In the worst case, they may feel like cogs in a machine and see no real impact on the business as a result of their hard work. The major sources of a corporate professionals' stress are lack of control over their work lives; office politics and competition; and rarely seeing a finished product from their labors, which makes proof of their accomplishments hard to document.

Semiautonomous Professional. Semiautonomous professionals are those who, given the nature of their professions, could be in private practice or out on their own, but, for whatever reason have chosen to work in a group or team setting. Examples can include lawyers, architects, or consultants in a firm; physicians, dentists, or specialists in a group practice or health maintenance organization (HMO); advertising or graphic arts professionals in a small agency; or engineers, scientists, or technical specialists in a consultancy.

The majority of semiautonomous professionals have no direct reporting relationship to a supervisor or manager; also, they may be partners in the group, but they usually have no one to whom they can delegate work or stress. They *can* see the results of their efforts—in an expanding client base, increased profitability, completed projects, or new products, but there is often the added pressure of bringing in more business to keep the group afloat. Compensation or rewards are often ill-defined, and may not be directly tied to individual effort.

In short, for them, the buck stops here. Given the nature of their professions, they often *expect* to be in control of their working environment and work flow, but most of the time decisions of that nature are made by "the group," and the results may or may not be most appropriate for the group's individual members.

In the worst case, semiautonomous professionals can feel like hired guns—with all of the responsibility, but little of the authority to make decisions on how the business is run and managed. The major sources of their stress from the job are having no control over their working environments, and dealing with the expectation that they will be able to handle continually expanding work loads. In addition, their professions can often be considered service or helping professions, which means that they have to cope with other people's problems all of the time—and that can be extremely stressful.

Autonomous Professional. Autonomous professionals are individuals in private practice by themselves or entrepreneurs who are starting up or running a small company. This category can include lawyers, physicians, dentists, consultants, architects, graphic artists, writers, and others who run their own businesses with no other partners, as well as people responsible for start-ups or family-owned companies.

They may or may not have staff, depending on the size and profitability of the business, but, if they do, they can off-load work to those staff members. They also have the responsibility and authority both to hire and fire these personnel. In many cases, they do *everything* relating to the business—from negotiating contracts to emptying out the wastebaskets and cleaning the bathrooms.

These professionals *do* see the results of their work in increased profits, new products, or an expanding customer base. The downside, and their major stressor, is that they have near-total responsibility for the success or failure of the business—and that heavy burden can be extremely stressful. In addition, most autonomous professionals eat, sleep, and breathe their developing business—24 hours a day—because it is *their* business. The business often becomes an extension of themselves and their personalities—and its success or failure directly impacts how they feel about themselves.

The Continually Changing Business Environment

Business has changed irrevocably over the past decade—and it has changed for all types of professional workers. Virtually no industry has entered the nineties unscathed by this massive break with the past. Technology, reduced head count, and increased competition all play a role in what amounts to a complete reworking of the "business of business."

The level of stress prevailing in business today has been raised to an extreme that would previously have been considered chronic stress. And, unless the underlying assumptions regarding how business is done are examined and questioned, that stress level *never* goes away. On top of that, all professionals are trying to cope with the additional stresses of crises that crop up on the job and at home. A new, stressful order is the rule today.

If you think back to the previous chapter and what was termed the *Dangerous Stress Pattern* (shown again in Figure 3.1), you can begin to understand why we are so concerned about professionals today. This new, stressful order can be damaging to the human body, but it has become a fact of life that we, as professionals, will have to learn to manage. And we believe it can be managed to ameliorate at least some of its harmful effects. Doing so requires us first to examine exactly where potential stressors occur at work and at home, which is what the rest of this chapter, and the following chapters, will help you do.

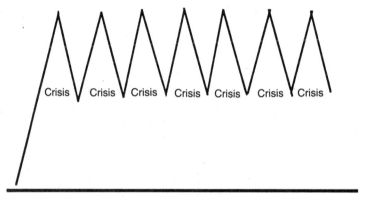

Figure 3.1. Dangerous stress pattern

Company Cultures

Every business, organization, or company is made up of people—and exists only in the hearts and minds of those people. To coalesce those individual hearts and minds into an entity that gets work done and products or services out the door, every organization has to develop an essential "way things are done around here," and to convey that essence to its employees. That is what a company's culture is—the personality of a company, its (usually) unwritten rules, values, and guidelines for how business is done.

The Importance of Company Cultures

Company cultures are critically important, because they impact literally *everything* in an organization—from promotions and how decisions are made, to where employees live and how they dress. It is a stressor that can operate just outside the range of awareness, causing a kind of stress that is particularly frustrating because it is so hard to identify.

If you learn more about the different types of company cultures, you can reduce many of your stressors at work. You can do this either by making a conscious effort to fit in and readjust your personal style and expectations—if that is what you choose to do—or by finding an organization that is more compatible with your personal style and values. But first you have to understand the various types of cultures that exist.

Identifying Your Organization's Culture

In their book *Corporate Cultures: The Rites and Rituals of Corporate Life,* Terrence Deal and Allen Kennedy identify four primary types of company culture. If you haven't already done so, take a few minutes to fill out the Company Culture Checklist in Chap. 2 of this book—it will help you determine your organization's culture, and, more importantly, the kind of culture in which you would be most comfortable. Then read through the rest of this section to get more background information on those cultures.

The Tough-Guy Organization.   In *Tough-Guy Organizations,* high risks are taken on a regular basis, and there is quick feedback on the results of those decisions. Financial stakes are high, and in most cases, employees know within a year whether or not their decisions were on target. In some cases, such as the entertainment industry, fortunes can be made or lost literally overnight. The environment is usually very high-pressure, the hours grueling, and the players highly individualistic—but the rewards can be great. Because of these demands, employees tend to burn out before they reach middle age.

Tough-Guy Organizations are typified by companies involved in construction, cosmetics, management consulting, venture capital, advertising, the entertainment industry, and surgery. Police and fire departments are classic examples of this type of organization, because life and death decisions are made on a daily basis.

People who do well in this environment have to be tough—they need to be comfortable making quick decisions and able to accept that they may call the shots incorrectly—and find that out very quickly. Internal competition is usually brutal. Only gamblers need apply here!

People also do well in Tough-Guy Organizations if they are good at what they do, know it, and are temperamental. This is the only environment that tolerates "star" behavior—because these organizations could not survive without their stars. Women and minorities can do very well here, because a star is a star, after all.

The Word Hard/Play Hard Organization. The *Work Hard/Play Hard Organization* is benign and hyperactive—think of sales organizations where everyone is relatively relaxed (except at the end of the quarter when they have to make sure they meet their quotas) and generally has a good time. But, for the most part, risks are small and feedback is quick—either the sale is made or not. Besides, the system has lots of checks and balances to keep things from getting out of hand.

Good examples of Work Hard/Play Hard Organizations include mass-consumer products companies, retail stores, real estate agencies, personal computer and office equipment companies, and any door-to-door sales organization. In many cases, manufacturers would also fit the bill: They have to keep at the job on a daily basis, and everybody knows right away when something isn't working properly on the line.

To work successfully in Work Hard/Play Hard Organizations, people have to value their customers and strive to fulfill the needs of those customers. For the most part, there are few individual stars (and few individualists, for that matter), but lots of star *teams*, because teams, not individual people, produce the volume. People who succeed here tend to be, friendly, like to go along with the crowd, are outgoing, sociable, truly enjoy people, and have a gift for gab.

The Bet-the-Company Organization. In the *Bet-the-Company Organization*, risk is continual, but the feedback is a long time in coming. Financial risks are very high, and employees often literally risk the future of the entire company when they make decisions. Working for such a firm is a very-high-stakes game; only those with guts and stamina, who can tolerate minimum feedback, need apply.

Given this environment, the importance of making the "right" decisions means that decisions are made very deliberately, when all the data are in, and after much analysis and discussion—and they flow from the top down. Think months and years ahead instead of hours, days, or weeks. Investments are made for the future, but only when everyone has bought into a shared vision for the future.

Examples of this type of organization include most large, capital-goods manufacturers; oil and chemical companies; investment banks; architectural firms; the aerospace industry; computer-design companies; mining and smelting companies; and the military.

You have to like business meetings to work in this environment—because meetings drive Bet-the-Company organizations. You have to be patient as well, because nothing—including movement up the corporate ladder—happens quickly. It helps if you are conservative and analytical; respect authority, hierarchy, and technical competence; and are comfortable sharing your hard-won knowledge. Mentoring plays a big role in these companies, and people become highly dependent on each other—so no one screams, fights, or treats anyone badly. Miss Manners would love Bet-the-Company Organizations!

The Bureaucratic Organization.   The *Bureaucratic Organization* is based on situations that involve low risk and minimal feedback. Financial stakes are relatively low, in contrast to Bet-the-Company and Tough-Guy Organizations, and no one decision will make or break any employee. But pressure comes from the fact that most workers have no idea whether they are doing a good job until someone blames them for something. In this kind of situation, the first thought of most employees is likely to be "How can I cover my butt on this decision?" In such a climate, the process—*how* something is done—becomes more important than the final outcome—*what* is done.

Organizations that exemplify the Bureaucratic culture include academia and higher education; most health-care providers and hospitals; pharmaceutical and chemical companies; government agencies; banks; insurance companies; financial service organizations; utilities; and most heavily regulated industries.

The employees valued in this type of environment play by the rules; are orderly, punctual, and detail-oriented; and carry out procedures whether they make sense or not. They don't question authority (at least openly), and understand that playing politics well can mean survival. Long meetings that focus on how a decision should be made, as well as titles and formalities, are commonplace. In many instances, the Bureaucratic Organization's tightly structured hierarchies come to resemble turn of the century class systems—and employees have to understand and respect those hierarchies.

The Bottom Line on Company Cultures

Because company culture is so pervasive in the workplace, a clash between your preferred culture and your organization's existing culture can be a powerful stressor. Companies rarely, if ever, change their cultures, so changes have to be made by you. In such a situation, you have three options:

- *Alter your style to accommodate your organization's culture.* We recommend this option *only* if you do not have to compromise any of your most important values or priorities, if you plan on doing so only for a relatively short period of time, or if you feel it is not in your best interests to begin looking for another employer. Changing yourself is hard work, although it can be done.

  If you choose this option, study carefully your company's existing culture, understand what is expected of you, and then devise a strategy for rolling out the new you. Poorly implementing a new you or creating one that is incongruent with the prevailing culture is far more detrimental to your career than sticking with your old style.

- Understand also that you may pay a personal price for this transformation: Submerging your true personality and style for an extended length of time is exceedingly stressful, and people who do so often develop health problems. In addition, we have found that most people revert to type over the long haul because it is difficult to keep personality buried forever.

■ *Find another department or work group in your company that more closely matches your preferred style.* When it comes to company culture no company is purely one type. True, some prevailing values always exist across a company, but different work groups and departments may display those values somewhat differently. For example, let's assume that your preferred company culture is Work Hard/Play Hard. Even in Tough-Guy or Bet-the Company Organizations, the sales and marketing departments tend to be more Work Hard/Play Hard–ish than the information systems or business development departments. So do some investigative work.

■ *Find another employer that more closely matches your preferred cultural style.* If all else fails and you find your stress levels increasing, it just might be time to look for a new job in a more compatible company. As you interview for new positions, check out the company's culture just as you would its benefits package. Deal and Kennedy suggest the following techniques:

Study the company's physical setting. Bricks and mortar tell you a great deal about culture—whether the buildings' style is modern or traditional, the plants clean or grimy, the offices adequately equipped or filled with castoffs, and so on.

Watch how you are greeted when you go to an interview. Reception areas and receptionists can speak volumes about a company's culture. Is the reception area formal or informal, relaxed or busy, elegant or plain? What is the receptionist's attitude like? Do you have to endure a lot of signing in and assignment of visitor badges?

Read what the company says about its culture. Annual reports, quarterly statements, posters and plaques, and advertising materials often reveal more than we would expect. The only caution here is that management may say it believes in certain things, but pay only lip service to them.

Interview the people who interview you. Ask about the history of the company, why the company is a success, who its heroes are, what kind of people work there, who gets ahead, and so on. People, being human, love to talk about where, and with whom, they work. Besides, you'll come across favorably as someone seriously interested in learning more about the company!

Watch how employees spend their time. Always remember, what people do is determined by what they value—what is important to them. Comparisons between what people say and what they do can give you insight into a company's real culture.

The bottom line is that you will be more successful in maintaining lower stress levels if your preferred company culture matches that of the organization in which you work. And, in the long run, isn't that as important as salary and benefits?

Power, Politics, and Competition

Office politics have long been a dirty little secret of working life; given today's shaky economic environment, its role is neither little nor secret. In an era of downsizing and layoffs, being smart at office politics is an important part of being able to survive and reduce your stress levels. Corporate and semiautonomous professionals live with it on a daily basis, but an autonomous professional may or may not deal much with politics. Indeed, one of the reasons professionals leave corporations and group practices and become autonomous is to escape politics.

Some Definitions

Before you can master something, you have to understand what it really is. So first, let's review some definitions. *Power* is simply the capacity to accomplish things through others. The things that are accomplished with power can be either good or bad, but power in and of itself is neutral—it just helps you get things done. When used positively, power can help you motivate others, encourage cooperation, shine the spotlight on good work, and help yourself—and others—excel at what they do.

Politics are the techniques used to gain power. Some of these techniques are overwhelmingly negative—such as sabotage, backbiting, credit mongering, and others—but political techniques also include friendliness, the ability to get along with people, cooperation, willingness to assist others, and so on. Another way to look at it is to consider politics the unwritten rules of how to make sure you are considered a key player in your organization and widely liked and respected. The people who play the office politics game poorly are the ones who give it a bad name. The ones who play the game well get promoted.

Competition is what happens when many people want the same few resources. No matter whom you work for, you compete (as well as cooperate) with colleagues every day because there are limited rewards to go around—be they promotions, perks, raises, enhanced titles, trips to conferences or meetings, budget dollars, your boss's time and attention, access to staff and secretarial time, being recognized at meetings, or convincing others of your position in a disagreement.

Sometimes competition comes from directions you would least expect. Secretaries, staff members, or colleagues may want to see a boss or best friend succeed—either because they like that person (having been the object of successful office politics) or because they believe their stature will be raised in the organization if their boss or friend gets promoted. Subtle sabotage, delays in granting your requests or completing tasks for you, gossip, and innuendo can result. This kind of competition can be extremely frustrating because it usually doesn't *look* like direct competition. You may not be able, at first glance, to determine what the person gains by competing with you.

Discrimination and sexual harassment boil down to competition in its crudest form. Some people feel the shortage of rewards so intensely and feel so insecure about their own abilities to obtain them on their personal merits, that they become threatened by people who are different from them. Harassment and discrimination then become ways to exclude important segments of the work force from potential access to rewards, and to preserve a larger portion of those finite rewards for themselves.

To net it all out: *Because there aren't enough rewards to go around to satisfy everyone's needs, people will compete for the few that exist. Power determines who gets or distributes rewards, and politics influences who has the power.* Although while there are no politics in the animal kingdom, the fittest survive. And in the business world, the most fit are the most political!

Why Power and Politics Are Important

In the best of all possible worlds, how far and how fast we move through our organizations, and how smoothly we are able to reach our goals, would depend solely on how well we fulfill the requirements outlined in our job definitions. But in the real world, people's perceptions of how well we fulfill those job requirements are filtered through lenses colored by—and potentially molded by—politics.

Take performance appraisals, for example. They are supposedly designed to assess objectively an employee's motivation, productivity, problem-solving skills, and knowledge. In the real world, however, performance appraisals more often represent bosses' subjective assessments of an employee's ability to help them meet the objectives and goals that have been established for them. And, although appraisals are intended to be an objective measure of how an employee performs against a stated objective; many managers measure their staffs by perceptions that have little to do with performance evaluated against an objective—and such perceptions are shaped by office politics.

Visibility to management in an organization is important when it comes to surviving layoffs—if the powers that be like you and remember that you did something very useful or great for the department, chances are you will not get axed. But how will they know you are out there if other people don't talk about your successes? And what makes people talk about your successes in a positive way? They must like and respect you—and that happens because of politics.

A common misconception is that the higher you are promoted, the more power you will have. True, with promotion you receive formal authority that you can use to get people to do things they really don't want to do. But the amount of power you have doesn't necessarily correlate with your formal authority. You acquire power and influence, even without significant amounts of authority, if people perceive you as someone who can help them reach mutually beneficial goals. People's perceptions of you are determined by your willingness to cooperate, your friendliness, and so on—again, all techniques of politics.

The bottom line is that, in today's world of matrixed management, a big chunk of managers' and professionals' jobs involves convincing people over whom they have no direct control to support their ideas and projects.

How to Play the Game: Win-Win Politics

Because politics is so important to your business survival, you can not opt out of the game: Changes in the business environment make it too risky to count just on doing a good job to see you through. Not playing the game at all can be more stressful than playing it well.

"But I don't want to be a shark," we can hear you saying. "I'm a nice person—I don't want to be mean and sneaky and manipulative. I want to be able to do good things for my organization and the people in it." (Women tend to feel this way more often than men, who are socialized to appreciate power, politics, and competition in our culture and through organized sports.) You don't have to be mean. But if you do want to do good things, you still have to play politics. Consider playing "win-win politics."

Win-win politics is like a win-win approach to negotiating: Everyone gets at least some of what they want, and nobody really loses. Win-win politics involves bringing out the best in people and facilitating mutually beneficial goals and objectives. In the best case, everybody wins.

Now that may sound great—but how do you do it? The specifics may sound trite, but the basics include: saying hello in the morning and goodbye at night; sharing the spotlight; giving credit where credit is due; thanking people for a job well done (publicly if at all possible); sharing information gladly, sometimes without even being asked first; finding out what people really want and then doing your best to help them get it; cooperating with others; encouraging people when they need a lift; taking time to chat and get to know people as human beings; keeping up on your field and keeping your skills current; being diplomatic and gently assertive (see Chap. 15 for information on gentle assertiveness); completing assignments or tasks on time or when promised; keeping promises that you make; meeting your budget objectives; being a good listener; remembering the little people as well as the big shots; sending thank you notes and flowers; remembering birthdays and special occasions; not throwing your weight around unless it is absolutely necessary; making sure people feel that they are all part of the team; and so on. Generally, being good at office politics means being a nice, thoughtful person!

But Do Win-Win Politics Really Work?

Believe it or not, it does! In fact, "win-win" politics works far more effectively than negative politics—and is mentally healthier for you. If you think for a minute, you can probably name several people at work who play negative politics. Do you like them? Do other people respect them? Do they have real power, or just authority? Would you fire them if you got a chance to do so?

Negative manipulators expend personal energy, knowing that people don't like or respect them, and have to be continually on their toes to make sure someone doesn't stab them in the back. Imagine the energy it must take to remember to whom which lie was told. Such an office style is very stressful. Win-win politics gamespeople have far lower stress levels, because they can look at themselves in the mirror and be comfortable with the reflection there, and they receive positive "strokes" from coworkers. Think about people who use the win-win approach at your office. Are they liked and respected? Do people feel manipulated by them? What are their chances of getting cut in a reduction in force? Would you like to work for them?

Managing People in the '90s

Managing people has never been more difficult or more stressful for both the manager and the managed. All professionals are feeling the squeeze. Downsizing has pruned staffs and greatly reduced the number of promotions that can be offered to promising employees. The sluggishness of the economy allows raises barely to keep pace with inflation. Industry downturns have reduced profits, and most companies have had to reduce or restrict benefits to employees. But work has not gone away—in fact it is increasing. And managers and supervisors find themselves the most visible emissaries of the company to its employees—who may no longer trust or respect management.

The effects of stress on both sides are evident in infighting, reduced productivity, resistance to change, and increased health-care costs for stress-related illnesses. The good people who remain in our organizations are more important to their organizations' success and longevity than ever. Given this situation, what can be done to motivate people while reducing stress for all involved?

Developing a New Management Mind Set

1. *Win-win politics can help tremendously.* Treating people fairly, with respect and humanity, goes a long way in reestablishing trust and lays the groundwork for positive communication.

2. *A manager's focus should be on motivating, not controlling.* The vast majority of employees want to do a good job, and will do so if given half a chance. Motivation is the key: encouragement to perform at the highest level possible. Today wise managers view themselves as coaches and teachers who provide people with the feedback they need to continuously improve their performance and productivity. To be most effective, feedback and encouragement must be structured differently depending on the type of employee.

3. *Managers need to lead, not just oversee.* Leadership goes far beyond that. Leadership requires that people be able to grasp the big picture, synthesize information to create a customized vision for performance and quality for their work groups or departments, and then explain and live that vision for employees in a way that is meaningful to them. Very few managers and professionals do this well. We have been trained to be good "project managers"—people who can identify all the tasks necessary to complete a project, put them in the proper order, and then execute the plan to complete the project on time and within budget.

Leaders inspire loyalty and serve as role models. This is not easy, and the skills take much practice to perfect. But in today's working world, where people's company loyalty has eroded, the way to keep good performers is to help them develop loyalty to their work group and their peers.

4. *Managers and supervisors need to begin "thinking outside the box" to foster innovation and creativity.* The old, traditional ways of working and managing people need to be reevaluated in light of the rapidly changing business environment. Most of the assumptions under which firms have operated are no longer appropriate in the new environment. Organizations may not be most effective as hierarchies; it may be more appropriate to reward performance rather than seniority; and intimidation and confrontation may no longer be the best ways to manage. A healthy skepticism, disregard for rules, and respect for risk taking are required for businesses to succeed and grow.

5. *It needs to be understood and respected that the work force is changing dramatically.* No longer is it made up primarily of white males. Women, minorities, and people from other cultures will continue to make up greater percentages of our staffs, whether we like it or not. Successful managers will be those who come to grips with this dynamic situation, begin to learn how to relate to a diverse work force, and find individualized approaches to motivating and encouraging workers to achieve their personal best.

This is a tall order. These "new age" skills and capabilities are not something most managers and professionals learned at college or grad school. Hands-on learning in the real world—which may often be unforgiving of mistakes—is needed. Changing the way we work and the way we think about our work is always stressful.

This may all sound rather depressing and demoralizing, but really it is not. In front of us is tremendous opportunity to reengineer the way we do business and the way we relate to our employees.

Understanding Employees Today

Some of the greatest stress producers in the work place today include communication problems and inappropriate expectations. Most of us assume that everyone thinks like we do, wants to receive information the way we do, and has the same sets of expectations and desires we do. Nothing could be further from the truth.

Not only are people from different cultures and sexes working together in work groups, but in many cases people from different age groups are working together. This situation sets the stage for potential conflict unless we understand where people are coming from and how best to communicate with them. Furthermore, what people from different groups are looking to get from their careers is often quite different, and we need to gauge our expectations accordingly.

Experts believe that the following thumbnail sketches of different groups of employees may be helpful in developing strategies for effective communication and motivation. Although these sketches are not all-inclusive, they can give you clues for getting started on your own explorations geared toward reducing everyone's stress. Later chapters focus on effective communication and negotiation skills.

Age Differences.   Experts offer these insights on intergenerational differences among staff members:

- *"Baby busters"—people born from 1961 to 1979.* These workers are the first group to grow up with computers, VCRs, and video games—and in dual-career families. They learned independence early in life, so they prefer to work on their own, and regard autonomy highly. They are not particularly loyal to an organization, but tend to stay put when they are involved in a project that is interesting and challenging—for them, job satisfaction is very important. Busters tend not to be intimidated by authority figures, and are comfortable with women in leadership roles. Most of all, they like to have choices—choices for what they do in their spare time, choices in what they eat, and choices in how they go about completing tasks at work. They are naturals for projects involving quality management and customer satisfaction. They have a clear picture of the kind of life they want. And in that life, work definitely plays a secondary role to a rewarding personal and family life.

- *Baby boomers—people born between 1943 and 1960.* These folks are comfortable with computer technology, and anxious to use it to give themselves greater productivity and more time to do more things. The 1960s left an indelible mark on them; they still want to make this world a better place, and now they are focusing on the work place. Struggling to balance home and career, they are causing organizations to rethink flextime, job sharing, and child and elder care. Boomers are also approaching midlife and taking a hard look at where they thought they wanted to go and whether or not they will get there. This reevaluation of their lives often results in their personal and family lives taking on a renewed importance. They are not afraid to take risks, and vastly prefer participatory management and teamwork. Nor are boomers afraid of getting emotionally involved with coworkers and projects—they *become* the projects they are working on. Money will always be a motivator for them (remember the 1980s), but now it is because their families are growing and they are planning college educations for their children. But make no mistake about it, even though they work hard, they are not loyal to organizations—they view working as a means to personal growth and meaningful experiences.

- *Fifty Plus-ers—people born between 1925 and 1942.* These workers are mostly male, and have worked their way steadily up the career ladder, doing whatever the organization asked of them. They like formal hierarchies and have trouble adapting to all the changes happening in the workplace. They are very loyal and do their jobs well because they believe it is good for the company. These people watched their parents battle their way through the depression and have never forgotten that. For them, jobs aren't careers, and they aren't necessarily meant to be enjoyable—they are something you do to earn a living and support a family. Status and security are very important to them.

As you can see, these three different age groups look at life, and work, very differently. There is bound to be conflict when they are brought together in work groups, because their perspectives are so different. Managers and professionals can make joint projects less stressful by making sure all team members feel valued for their individual skills and perspectives. They all have an insatiable need to know what is going on and how they are doing, so regular updates on projects and your organization's goals are vital to forming a cohesive work group. Put your own biases aside when dealing with people outside your own age group—it is easy to feel resentful when a "computer baby" demands a raise, or a "radio baby" gives you a lecture on what it was like when he was your age. Keeping things in perspective will help you achieve your goals and lower your stress levels.

Cultural Differences. The Hudson Institute raised everyone's awareness that traditional organizational management was going to have to change when they predicted that by the year 2000, only 15 percent of the new entrants to the labor force would be white male, with nearly 61 percent female and 29 percent minorities and immigrants. What a change from the work force most organizations are used to!

If organizations are going to attract the best and brightest workers from this diverse group, they are going to have to change the way they hire, treat, promote, and reward people. Doing so will be stressful for those currently in charge, but if it is not accomplished, organizations will ultimately fail—which is even more stressful!

As managers and professionals, how can we begin to prepare, not only ourselves, but our staffs and our management for these stressful changes? Experts tell us that understanding how we have been shaped by our own culture is the most important first step—exploring our own assumptions, biases, expectations, stereotypes, and behaviors. Most of the time, we don't even think of these things: They operate almost transparently in our lives, but they color everything that we think, say, and do.

Iris Randall, a management consultant specializing in diverse work forces, has categorized typical behavior styles. Although an individual may exhibit one of these behavior styles or a mix them, the following categories are useful starting points for understanding them.

- *Type D or Dominant Behavior Style.* These managers and professionals make decisions rapidly and are most interested in results—the bottom line. They are analytical and are more comfortable with data than with people. Most often, people from a Euro-American background exhibit this style, particularly white males.

- *Type I or Influencing Behavior Style.* Managers and professionals using this style are very verbal and are excellent at influencing and persuading others. They like people and are great cheerleaders for organizations' goals and objectives. Hispanics, African-Americans, and women frequently use this behavior style.

- *Type C or Cautious Behavior Style.* Taught not to shoot from the hip or be confrontational, managers and professionals who use this style are cautious. They like to think before they speak and make sure that they have all the facts and figures before making a decision. This style is seen most frequently among Asian professionals.

- *Type S or Steady Behavior Style.* For the most part, managers and professionals exhibiting this style are good team players, have no trouble recognizing and supporting the person in charge, and will hang in there to do what needs to get done. Native Americans often exhibit this behavior style.

While these behavior styles are all very different, it is important to recognize two things. First, they complement each other. Second, each has capabilities and strengths that are vital to the success of an organization that is undergoing rapid change. Even though it may be stressful to manage, or work, in such a diverse group, the rewards for working together can be very great—both for the organization, and the people involved.

The best way to encourage higher productivity in people with different behavior styles is to understand what motivates them and to communicate by "speaking their language." This requires development of a high degree of flexibility on the part of the manager and professional, as well as an appreciation for the differences in people. So check out your attitudes and start learning about the people with whom you work!

Understanding the Price People Pay for Success

What is the price of success in business today? If asked that question, most white male professionals would say the cost includes: hard work in college and graduate school; long hours at work; lots of travel; missing family activities; putting up with grief from bosses or subordinates; maybe compromising some values or goals along the way; and having to work with, and for, people you don't personally like. Although all that is stressful, for white males the path to success is usually clearly defined, and their capabilities and ways of thinking are valued. In addition, the rewards of success are things that white males can identify with and enjoy.

But the price is often much higher for women and minorities—precisely because most organizational structures are designed to reward behavior and work styles commonly exhibited by white males.

What is it like to make a journey into white male corporate America? Dr. Theophilus Green, a Chicago psychotherapist who works with African-American high achievers, says it's like "walking into a buzz saw." Many of his clients still say that the easiest way to succeed is to make themselves over into people similar to those who manage them. That means wearing the same clothes, playing the same sports, talking the same way, moving into similar neighborhoods, taking on the same values and goals, and treating people the same way they see people being treated. All of this is on top of doing a great job, being innovative and creative, and growing professionally and personally.

Women face much the same situation. For some women, although the color of their skin is the same as that of their white male counterparts, their innate behavior and work styles are often fundamentally different—and are not ones valued by most organizations. To succeed, they must make themselves over in much the same way as their minority counterparts.

But even more importantly, minority and female workers have to give up a significant part of themselves, of their very souls, to succeed in today's workplace. Their values, feelings, priorities, and cultural mores are ultimately discounted by the organization's establishment—which is reflected over time in feeling, as one woman executive said, "I'm not *me* anymore, and even worse, I'm not sure I like the person that I've had to become." A staff member who reaches this point is well on the path to burn out.

So what does this mean for managers today, and why should they be concerned about it? The obvious reason is that the best and brightest women and minority professionals are the ones who want to be successful, and they are at the highest risk for burn out, that is, for reduced productivity and high health-care costs due to stress-related illnesses. But the skills, behaviors, values, feelings, and priorities these people bring to organizations could very well be the salvation of the corporation in the long run. With business changing so dramatically, we need all the new ideas, approaches, and working styles we can get—there is no guarantee that the way we have been doing business in the past will serve us well in the future.

Overseeing Downsizing and Layoffs

Downsizing and layoffs are incredibly stressful for everyone involved: for managers who must make decisions about who will go and who will stay; for people who are laid off; and for the people who remain behind. No one escapes unscathed. Managing a layoff is a gut-wrenching experience, particularly if you care about the people reporting to you.

The stress experienced during this time can range from great, to very great, to off the chart—depending on how management has decided to handle the situation. In many cases managers need to keep the situation a secret from their staffs—that means having to disguise your normal feelings and reactions and behave in an entirely different manner. As the downsizing progresses, not only do you have to deal with your feelings about laying off your staff members, but with your own fears about your job security and that of your friends, and with your concerns about how staff members will take the news. All of this takes a phenomenal amount of energy, and leaves you feeling exhausted and drained.

It is not uncommon for managers in this situation to experience a wide range of stress-related problems. Insomnia, nightmares, upset stomach, heartburn, depression, headaches, fatigue, overeating, lack of appetite, increased smoking or drinking, backaches, and flare-ups of chronic medical conditions are common problems for managers during downsizing.

How can you, as a manager who will have to lay off staff members, cope with all this stress? People who have been in this uncomfortable situation offer the following suggestions:

✔ *Increase your use of coping techniques.* Later chapters outline a wide variety of coping techniques that will help to ameliorate the effects of stress on your body. Start using several regularly, and increase their use as you move farther along in the downsizing process.

✔ *Maintain or begin an exercise program.* Exercise is a great stress reducer, especially when you are angry or frustrated. In addition, if you are experiencing fatigue, depression, or insomnia, regular exercise can help counteract those problems.

✔ *Develop a support system outside work.* You will need people who can listen to you vent, provide encouragement and support, and be there for you when you are really upset or depressed. Depending on colleagues at work for these purposes is probably too risky, because downsizing plans usually have to be kept strictly confidential. Friends and family members can fill the bill, and it is important that you give yourself permission to lean on them when the going gets rough.

🖊 *Work on compartmentalizing your work life and keep it separate from your personal life.* Now more than ever you need to leave your worries at work at the end of the day. A more complete discussion of compartmentalizing is included in the section on burnout in this chapter, and later chapters contain some ideas for a successful transition between home and the office.

🖊 *Whenever possible, be honest with your staff members and keep them informed as to what is going on.* They are going to pick up a sense that something is brewing anyway, and it is best all around if management doesn't try to lie or hide the fact that downsizing is being considered. Most people would much rather know the truth—even if it is negative—than be left to imagine what could happen, because we all can imagine something much worse than reality. Openness will help reduce your staff members' stress levels, and keep yours at a manageable level.

🖊 *Confront rumors directly, and deal with them immediately.* The office grapevine will be working at warp speed, and it is vital that you derail rumors that you know are false. Encourage your staff members to talk to you about rumors and be as honest as you can in responding to them. Ignoring them is the worse thing you can do. They won't go away, they will only get worse, and reduce worker productivity and morale as they fester.

🖊 *During a layoff, treat your staff members with dignity and respect—and let them know they will be missed.* This may seem like a small point, but you would be surprised how many managers let their feelings get in the way of being a class act when it comes to dispensing pink slips. It *is* hard to see people you've worked with and coached be terminated, but there is no excuse for not being present and available for them when they are actually laid off. Let your people know how much care and thought went into the decision-making process. Be able to look at yourself in the mirror after a layoff is all over and say that you did your best, in the best way you knew how.

🖊 *After you have dispensed the layoff notices, get out of the office and go home to your friends and family.* You will feel sad, depressed, exhausted, frustrated, tense—in general, like you've been hit by a truck. You won't be any good to anyone, so go home and take care of yourself. Play with your kids, talk it over with your partner, force yourself to eat something, and go to bed. Be good to yourself so that you can have the strength to help the survivors cope with the aftermath.

🖊 *Be scrupulously honest with your staff members who survived the reduction in force, and help them understand what the downsized work place will be like and what their roles in it will be.* Readjusting to life after a layoff will be difficult both for you as a manager and for the survivors. A later section of this chapter describes the phases survivors go through as they adjust to the changes, and it is important that you understand what these stages are. Gauge your expectations for performance accordingly. Doing so will reduce your stress, and help them manage theirs.

Managing Terminations

Another great challenge of managing is handling terminations for employees who are not functioning at their jobs in an acceptable manner. These are not fun either; no manager enjoys firing people. Unpleasant as firings are, all managers are ultimately faced with this—at least once during their careers. Although not as nerve-wracking as layoffs and downsizing perhaps, terminating employees is very stressful for a number of reasons.

First, in a certain sense, having to terminate an employee for performance reasons involves admitting that you were unable to motivate or coach that employee to achieve an adequate level of performance. Many managers look at this as a personal failure—which is stressful. Given the actual situation, you as a manager may or may not bear some responsibility, but it is important that you clarify for yourself its extent. Having to deal with guilt in this situation dramatically compounds the stress produced.

Second, most companies have very strict protocols and procedures that must be followed during the requisite probationary period—all of which are necessary to prove no liability should the employee decide to sue. Great care must be taken to inform the employee adequately of his or her status, exactly how performance is lacking, and what can be done to improve the situation. Documentation must be maintained as to what transpired during meetings with the affected employee, how the employee's performance did or did not change, and how that performance was measured. Just maintaining the paperwork can add stress on top of an already large work load.

Third, you will have to deal with an unhappy and potentially destructive employee in your work group during the probationary period. It will take extra effort on your part to make sure those feelings do not damage the work group's morale or productivity. You may need to reassure work group members that they are not at fault.

Finally, prepare yourself mentally for the possibility that the employee may decide to take the company to court over the dismissal. If you are lucky, this won't happen, but there's no guarantee, particularly in today's litigious society. Make sure you have your documentation in order, that you handle each encounter with the employee in a professional, aboveboard manner, and that you leave nothing to chance.

How can you cope with the stress you will experience managing your employee's termination process? All of the tips mentioned in the previous section on managing downsizing will be useful to you. In addition, it is vital that you build a strong relationship with the human resources department, and rely on them for advice and guidance throughout the process. This is *not* a time to try to handle things on your own, particularly if you might end up in court. Also, keep your boss well-informed, and ask for help in determining what strategies to use. This is not so much "covering your butt" or "sharing the blame" as making use of all the experience and knowledge you can to handle the situation effectively.

Managing Upward

Almost everyone has a boss. Corporate professionals definitely do. Semi-autonomous professionals often have bosses, or they may have a group of other partners to whom they are responsible. Autonomous professionals often report to someone, even if that someone is an investor or venture capitalist. So bosses are a fact of life, something we have to deal with throughout our careers.

There are good bosses, average bosses, and bad bosses. Unfortunately, the good ones are few and far between, but if you are lucky, a good boss may change your life and serve as a role model. Everyone seems destined to work for at least one or two bad bosses during their working life. Average bosses outnumber either of those—the ones that don't harm you, but they don't help you, either.

Bosses can either create or remove stress for you. The good ones reduce stress for you by shielding you from the vagaries of senior management, helping you reach your goals, and coaching you in ways that increase your capabilities. Bad bosses can make your time in the office a living hell, damage your self-esteem, and multiply the stress you experience at work.

If you find a good boss, enjoy your luck, do whatever you can to please, and stick with him or her as long as you can. If you have an average boss, do what you can to foster improvement, or stick with the situation until you can find something else.

But if you have a bad boss, be careful. The impact of the stress such a person can create for you is insidious and dangerous. The longer you stay in the situation, the greater is the chance of developing stress-related problems. After you work for a difficult boss for a period of time, the stress you experience begins to feel normal. After a while, you may not be consciously aware of it—that is, until you start developing health problems. But once you get out of the situation and go to work for even an average boss, you will be amazed at how much stress you were really experiencing.

Identifying Difficult Bosses. One of the best ways to reduce the stress you experience due to your boss is to take a hard look at a potential boss's management style before you accept a new position. Difficult bosses always give out warning signals—such as harried staff members who roll their eyes every time the boss speaks; the casual comment that a "good" manager is identified by the amount of pain inflicted on employees; or the fact that everyone in the work group comes in early, stays late, and gives up weekends to meet the boss's demands.

There are several kinds of difficult bosses:

- *The Slave Driver.* These managers believe that people are lazy and unmotivated. They treat staff members as slaves because they think that is the only way to get people to accomplish the tasks at hand. Their demands are never-ending, everything is always high-priority and has to be done right now, and they push their people to the limits of their endurance. The best way to deal with them is to negotiate: You'll meet this request, but you expect to get something back in return.

■ *The Tyrant.* Tyrants love to intimidate staff members. The vast majority of such bosses are insecure and afraid that their lack of talent or skill will be found out. They scream, throw tantrums, and generally control through fear. The best way to cope with a tyrant is to keep your performance cranked up to the excellent level in an effort to reduce the number of tantrums. And if a battle ensues, resist the impulse to fight back. If you don't react, you take away the thrill and sense of power.

■ *The Credit Monger.* These bosses steal the credit for a good idea, successful project, or an increase in sales. The best way to cope with this kind of boss is always to back up your ideas and successes on paper, and send a copy to your boss's boss. Never present an idea until you have thought it through completely.

■ *The Chameleon.* These bosses are wishy-washy, and blow wherever the prevailing corporate winds go. They are afraid of making a decision for fear of making the wrong one. It is very stressful to work in an environment where the rules are constantly changing, so the best way to cope is to get clarification on all decisions, and then follow up with a memo outlining what you and your boss have agreed to do. You may even want to go so far as getting your boss to initial the memo. Keep this kind of boss informed regularly of your progress on the project, so you'll know early on about potential changes to the terms of your agreement. Getting this kind of feedback from you also helps the chameleon feel more secure and facilitates more effective interactions with higher levels of management.

■ *The Best Friend.* This situation seems ideal—the boss as friend. Such bosses typically are uncomfortable with authority, and usually want everyone to like them. Unfortunately, they find it very difficult to give criticism, even if it is needed. They also find it hard to push their staff members to be as productive as they should be—and people who work for them often don't feel that they have the opportunity to take on challenges and grow. If you are a self-starter and have definite career goals, working for a "best friend" can be tremendously frustrating. The best way to cope is to start asking directly for what you want.

■ *The General Incompetent.* You'd be surprised at how many of these are around in large organizations. They are living examples of the "Peter Principle"—promotion to their highest level of incompetence. They make bad decisions, they can't teach their staff members anything new, get mired in trivia, and end up wasting organizations' time and money. The best way to cope with them is to try to educate them in a nonthreatening way in the areas in which they are weak. Capitalize on their strengths. Above all else, find a way to get information reliably to and from them—whether by written reports, regular meetings, email messages, or whatever.

■ *The Jekyll-and-Hyde.* These bosses are tremendously moody: their treatment of subordinates varies according to the mood of the day. The major stressor here is uncertainty—the best way to cope is to try and determine a pattern to the moodiness. If you can figure out the highs and lows, you can avoid your boss when the lows hit. In the meantime, document your plans, ideas, and decisions so that you have backup if you need it during a mood swing. Maintaining excellence in your performance may enable you to escape the worst brunt of a black mood.

- *The Egomaniac.* These bosses are impatient, judgmental, vague, full of themselves, and usually not very smart. Often they are secretly insecure and threatened by competent staff members. Egomaniacs rarely listen to what people tell them, and they always think they know everything there is to know about anything. Often it is extremely difficult to figure out exactly what it will take to get a good performance appraisal from an egomaniac. This is stressful, especially for people who are really good at what they do, because performance appraisals tend to favor "brown nosers" over those doing excellent work. The best way to cope with a boss like this is to discover the boss's hot buttons, and play those buttons the best you can. Always be as specific and concrete as possible when you discuss issues, ideas, or projects, so that the egomaniac will know exactly what you want. Get other staff members' support for your ideas. Finally, try selectively ignoring some of your boss's more stupid demands. Such bosses are often "idea people" who spew out ideas without thinking them through. They ask you to follow up, and then promptly forget about it. So stash some of those requests for a day or two and see if you really do need to follow up on them.

No doubt you can come up with even more kinds of crazy, bad bosses. The point is that when you do have a difficult boss, you have three options open to you. You can quit. You can try to ignore your boss and get on as best you can. Or you can try to manage your boss effectively and get at least some of your needs met while keeping your stress levels tolerable.

Quit only if you have another job to go to right away. Ignoring the situation may make you terribly stressed-out, and perhaps ill. The most effective approach is to figure out what makes your boss tick and to use that knowledge to get your job done in the best way you can.

Managing Your Manager. All bosses—whether good, bad, or indifferent—need to be managed so that you can accomplish your career goals and objectives and get good performance appraisals. Win-win politics works just as effectively with your boss as with peers and subordinates. To be successful, help your boss reach his or her goals and objectives. If you can develop your boss as a mentor or supporter, you can dramatically reduce your stress levels at work.

Try these tactics with every boss—even the good ones:

- *Find out how and when your boss likes to receive information, and then make sure you supply regular updates on your progress.* Most managers will tell you how they like to get information; if not, you can experiment and see what method elicits the best response. Some bosses prefer memos, weekly status reports, email messages, regular project reports. Timing is also important: Nearly everyone is more receptive to information and ideas at certain times. Once you figure out what works, use it *regularly.* The more information you can give your boss, the easier it will be for him or her to look good to the bosses higher up.

✔ *Do an excellent job.* This should be obvious, but some people ignore it. It doesn't matter how well you manage your boss if your performance is lacking. Doing a good job can help you avoid some of the worst aspects of your boss's personality.

✔ *Find out what your boss really values, and then make sure that what you do supports those values.* Your boss is measured against certain goals and objectives. If you know what they are (and most managers will tell you if you ask), you can build in support for those objectives in the projects you undertake.

✔ *Never make your boss look bad.* Again, this should go without saying, but some folks just don't seem to grasp it. Never gossip or gripe about your boss to other employees.

✔ *Always own up to your mistakes.* Again, this should be obvious. Let your boss know as soon as things go wrong; don't wait until you have a total disaster on your hands. You may be able to salvage the situation with your boss's help—and save both of you from embarrassment.

✔ *Ask for what you want and need.* Your boss can't read your mind, and if you aren't clear about what you want, chances are you won't get it.

✔ *Ask for your boss's opinion, consultation, or assistance once in awhile,* even if you don't really need it. Like everyone else, bosses like to feel needed. And you might be surprised to find out that your boss has some great ideas after all!

✔ *Once in awhile, go out of your way to help your boss out.* Most bosses recognize when extra effort has been expended on their behalf and they are appreciative.

Managing your boss simply means learning to work effectively with him or her—just what you would like your subordinates to do for you. Think of it as doing unto others what you would like to have done unto you! The boss-subordinate relationship does not have to be an adversarial one, it can become one of mutual respect and support. And that's the best way to assure that your stress levels stay low!

4

A Compendium of Workplace Stressors

If you feel dead-ended in your job, it may be because you've reached a plateau. You can feel "stuck" in your job for two major reasons:

1. If your organization has nowhere to promote you, you can reach a *structural plateau.*
2. If you know everything there is to know about your job, you can be at a *content plateau.*

Neither is a great place to be: People who remain at a plateau for a long time experience considerable stress because their progress is blocked. While they may not be actively *un*happy, they are just not happy—not motivated or creative or innovative at work. Frustration can spill over into their personal lives, spreading stress to friends and family.

Structural Plateauing

All people reach a structural plateau at some point in their working lives— including CEOs. Very few people reach their structural plateau at the executive level; estimates put that number at less than 1 percent. The rest top out at less lofty levels. At present, it appears that baby boomers in business are reaching their final promotion far earlier than their parents did.

The 1950s through the 1970s were years of unprecedented growth. It was relatively easy to climb the career ladder if you were a good performer. Most of our parents got their last promotions between the ages of 45 and 50, when they rose to the highest level in their organizations for which their abilities were suited.

But baby boomers are starting see their last promotion arrive when they are between 35 and 40 years of age—well before their capabilities would normally justify a structural plateau. Why? Many of the changes impacting business today are responsible: downsizing, competition, implementation of technology. All these factors have served to reduce significantly the number of middle management and executive positions available. In addition, a far greater number of people are between the ages of 25 and 40 than when our parents were that age—and these people comprise one of the most highly educated, competent, skilled work forces ever, all competing for a rapidly shrinking pool of high-level positions. This situation is not going to go away. The "big squeeze" will likely become an even bigger squeeze—because, even if the economy improves, business seems intent on remaining lean and mean during future boom times.

For those managers and professionals geared to strive for the top, do their best, and compete with their cohorts, this new reality of early structural plateaus can come as a real shock. They are used to being promoted every three to four years, gaining increased responsibility, and reaching for a personal vision of success—a vision formed as baby boomers watched their parents climb the career ladder. The vast majority have dedicated themselves to their jobs, firmly believing in the theology of work. They are used to thinking of people who have reached their plateaus as dead wood—living examples of the "Peter Principle."

Thinking of yourself in those terms can be extremely stressful when you haven't even turned 40, but haven't been promoted in six years. Realizing that you may never achieve your personal vision of success—be it to run the company, have a corner office, make executive vice president, or get promoted out of middle management—is very depressing. Most people begin to think that something is wrong with them—they haven't worked hard (or long) enough, they don't have the right credentials, or they failed a test at some point

True, some people reach a plateau in an organization because they lack capability. But the real reason most managers and professionals are hitting a wall so early in their working lives is simply demographics. It's not their fault, it has nothing to do with their capabilities or worth as a person, and it has nothing to do with how well they do their jobs. But it still feels rotten.

Special Structural Plateaus: The Glass Ceiling and Discrimination

Women and minorities feel the effects of a structural plateau far more keenly than do their white male counterparts. The U.S. Department of Labor states that women hold only 6.6 percent of executive positions, and minorities hold an even smaller percentage—only 2.6 percent. That's because, in many organizations, they very frequently reach a plateau far earlier than either the big squeeze or their talents would justify. They see equivalently educated, skilled, and talented white men promoted above them or given opportunities to acquire new skills that would make them more promotable. The so-called glass ceiling prevents women and minorities from reaching the highest levels.

The glass ceiling is a mind set deeply embedded in management today that persistently encourages hiring, grooming, mentoring, promoting, and working only with people who are like themselves—meaning white and male, because those are the people who largely populate management today. It is rarely given voice—rather it is a complex web of subtle attitudes and prejudices. In its less malignant form, it takes the shape of relying on word-of-mouth and employee referrals to fill management and executive positions. At its worst, women and minorities are not given the crucial early training that would make a promotion a possibility. In all cases, talented people are passed over and organizations are deprived of those capabilities and skills.

Although all public organizations have to adhere to governmental equal employment opportunity guidelines, there is great leeway in how those standards are implemented and enforced. The height of the glass ceiling varies from business to business, industry to industry, and sometimes even within a company. It tends to be lower for minorities than for women, and even lower for gays. It is always a problem in companies whose top officers have not committed themselves to fostering the talents of a diverse work force.

Because this web is so subtle, it is hard to prove that it exists or that a specific person has been plateaued because of it. The person who is held at a plateau by the glass ceiling experiences additional stress because the questions never go away. Is it because I don't have the right skills? Why don't I have the right skills? Is it because management is afraid I might get pregnant and take off work? Is it because of the color of my skin? Is it because of my preference for a life partner?" Asking yourself why all the time can make you crazy.

Most people who hit the glass ceiling regroup, work harder, work longer, and try to break through it a second time. They may even try a third or fourth time. But eventually they give up. It is important to understand, however, that not only the affected employee suffers. The organization suffers as well by not taking advantage of the unique capabilities these talented people bring to the workplace.

Will the glass ceiling ever go away? That is hard to tell. Right now there is little incentive for organizations to do away with it, or even raise it, for women and minorities. Structural plateaus inflicted by the glass ceiling will probably be around for a long time to come, and managers and professionals will need to learn to cope with the problem as an unfortunate, but omnipresent, fact of corporate life.

Common Reactions to Structural Plateaus

Most people, when confronted with a structural plateau, think about changing jobs: Maybe changing venues will help; maybe another organization can offer greater opportunities for promotion. Others think about changing careers: If they have topped out in a large corporation, maybe they would have a better chance owning their own businesses and being their own bosses.

Sometimes this works—particularly if the new job or new career is different and rewarding enough that scaling the heights of the career ladder there becomes irrelevant. But most of the time people move to similar jobs at another organization, and eventually reach another plateau. Demographics catch up with them once more.

Some people feel defeated, and mentally "check out" of their jobs. They plan just to do what they have to do to get by until they retire. But most achievers aren't happy with this attitude, and depression, passivity, anger, and boredom settle in. People in this situation aren't actively unhappy, but they know they aren't happy either. Although they may be unaware of the stress this situation produces, it acts on them just the same.

Others decide to go all out one last time. They put in the hours, make the sacrifices, do what has to be done—all in an effort to get that one last promotion. They become prime candidates for burn out, especially if that last promotion turns out to be the job they already have.

Content Plateauing

Some people who reach a structural plateau decide simply to focus on doing their job really well. As they spend more years in their position without promotion, they may eventually come to feel that they know everything there is to know about their jobs and the way they currently perform tasks. The longer they are in a position, the greater the chance they will plateau in terms of their job's content.

Although all people reach a structural plateau at some point in their working careers, most people don't have to reach a content plateau. Rarely do people ever know absolutely everything about their professions. The content plateau is preventable, and, if it has occurred, is remediable.

At first glance, you might not think that a content plateau could cause as much stress as a structural plateau. But it does because of the mind-numbing repetitiveness of the job. This stress has nothing to do with how much work you do—you can feel harassed by your job, but if you are still learning things and solving new problems, you have not reached a content plateau. The human mind needs challenge; it needs constant exercise or it gets flabby—just as your body does when you don't follow your exercise program. The *process* of learning and mastering a task is usually more fulfilling than what we ultimately learn. When we miss out on that experience, we get frustrated and bored. Very often that frustration is just outside the fringes of our awareness, so it is hard to pinpoint and define—which can make it incredibly stressful.

True, some people don't like challenge. They are very uncomfortable taking risks—which is what learning new things is all about. But such people are in the minority. Most people operate from a stable base and are comfortable taking moderate risks. These folks are most prone to depression, boredom, and frustration when they reach a content plateau.

Others are what plateauing expert Judith Bardwick calls risk creators—people who know that a change involves risk, but the risk holds no fear for them. When they get bored they *create* change for themselves, because they feel most alive when they are out there trying new things, living new experiences, and putting themselves on the line. According to Bardwick these people don't wait until other people offer them opportunities, "they wrest them." They also experience very little stress at plateaus, because they do something to keep themselves from staying there very long.

Dealing with Boredom and the "Blahs"

To reduce their stress levels when they reach a plateau, people need to become more like Bardwick's "risk creators." We need to make changes in our jobs and our lives. *Only we can do that for ourselves—no one else can get us unstuck when we reach a plateau.* We have to decide that we are not satisfied being where we are and that the stress is uncomfortable enough to justify the risk, and make up our minds to change. The following ideas might help:

- ✔ *Reevaluate your values, goals, and priorities.* Given that life in business has changed, we have to face the fact that many of the visions of success we once had must change. Otherwise we will continually frustrate ourselves and dramatically raise our stress levels for no good reason. Later chapters of this book provide you with a variety of tools to help you through this process.

- ✔ *Change your perspective when it comes to your work flow.* Most jobs have periods when things are slow, and we can get very bored during those times. Track those slow times, and plan projects to take advantage of them. Such projects can be as mundane as planning to build a customer database and entering all your customers' names or as extensive as exploring a new technology to see whether it can be used by your organization. You can even offer to help colleagues out if they are swamped—you'll not only learn something new, but help to foster better working relationships as well.

- ✔ *Evaluate what you can change within the limits of the job procedures you are required to follow.* If your job has a number of repetitive tasks, ask yourself what aspects of those tasks you could do differently. Maybe you could find out more about your customers or clients when preparing a bid or computer program or taking a medical history. You could challenge yourself to see how efficient you can become at performing the task—how quickly you can pull together the data for the report and how many new sources for data you can identify and learn to use. Whatever challenge you choose will give you something new to learn, and that is the key.

✔ *Act as mentor to someone younger or less skilled.* When you have years of real-life experience doing what you do best, you have the potential to be the best kind of teacher. Sharing your knowledge and helping someone else grow is very rewarding and fulfilling, and you enhance your credibility, visibility, and self-esteem in the bargain.

✔ *If your industry is in a downturn, learn about topics that will be valuable when it revives.* Almost every industry has some area that will be up and coming. Spend some time learning more about it—even become something of an expert on the topic. You could find yourself in the enviable position of having the skills your company needs when the business situation changes, or you may create a new niche for yourself.

✔ *Improve your profile.* Join organization or industry committees, task forces, or working groups that you ordinarily wouldn't have time for. Make speeches or write articles and increase your visibility while you are stretching your managerial or professional skills in a slightly different arena. Or simply take a look at your department and see what tasks you could assume or assist with that would help the department achieve its goals while you learn some new skills. The visibility won't hurt, and the confidence you gain by doing this can significantly reduce your stress levels.

✔ *Build (or rebuild) your professional network.* Maintaining networks takes time and energy, both of which we usually have very little of when our jobs are very busy. A plateau may offer you the opportunity to have the time to nurture those relationships and expand your field of contacts. Join professional organizations, attend conferences and briefings, ask people to lunch. Not only will this help you in your current position by exposing you to different ways of thinking about major issues in your industry and providing you with sources of information and counsel, but it could prove invaluable should you decide to leave.

✔ *Give something back to your community.* Join a community group, volunteer for a charitable organization, help out at your children's school, participate in a political organization, do work for your church. Many such organizations could benefit greatly from your managerial and professional skills; and, not only will you be faced with challenges and learn new things as you stretch your skills in a completely different venue, the sense of accomplishment you will receive is extremely rewarding and life-enhancing.

✔ *If you have spent most of your time focused on work, use the space given you by your plateau to enhance and expand your personal life.* Spend time with your partner, your kids, your friends, your family. Take a vacation. Take a class that looks interesting. Start a hobby or pick up an old one again. Learn a new sport or spend more time perfecting your skills at one you already know. Read the books you always wanted to read. Vegetate, and let yourself dream new dreams and fashion new visions of success for yourself. Decide what you really want to be when you grow up. All these things take time, and none of them can be accomplished adequately when we are busy. It is only when we give ourselves space, and permission not to "work at" them, that they evolve and bloom. Enhancing your personal life is one of the best stress reducers around.

. ✔ *If you know that you won't be happy at a plateau on the job for the rest of your working life, carefully assess your alternatives and options.* Talk to career counselors; explore options in other organizations, industries, or careers; determine what new skills you will need and get the training you require; and assess financial requirements. Then build a master plan—and start implementing it.

Reductions in Force—the Receiving End

Every time you open a newspaper or turn on television news today there seems to be another story about a company planning massive layoffs or reductions in force. The managers and professionals most frequently impacted by RIFs are corporate professionals, although some semiautonomous professionals—particularly those in law and health care—have also been affected.

What causes such massive layoffs?

1. Many corporations foresee an upswing in the economy that will impact their businesses favorably and want to get ready to take advantage of the improved economy. By reducing costs they expect to improve their profit margins when customers are ready to buy their products once again. A time-honored way to reduce costs is to reduce head count.

2. Management believes, rightly or wrongly, that stockholders are clamoring for better returns on their investment dollars. Again, one way to increase that return is to reduce costs by cutting head count.

3. Some companies have truly been able to reduce the need for middle management staff through more effective use of technology, redesign of territories, or restructuring of job functions.

Today, you work for yourself, your real family comes first, and no big organization is going to take care of you anymore. It is time to begin managing your (own) career.

Can It Happen to You?

Layoffs are likely to be with us for some time, and today no job is safe. Yes, you read that sentence correctly. Business has changed so drastically that no matter how long you may have worked at a corporation, no matter how good a job you do, or how effectively you have managed your budget and staff, no one's job is completely safe.

How can you tell if a RIF is brewing? These signs should clue you in:

- Plans are made to consolidate operations, warehouses, or branch offices or to close remote offices, data centers, or warehouses altogether.

- A hiring freeze is implemented and jobs that become vacant through attrition are not filled, or open requisitions for positions are closed without being filled.

- Sales are decreasing, or target revenues for the month, quarter, or year are not being met.

- Budget projections become extremely pessimistic.

- Management prolongs the length of time between salary reviews (for example, from every 12 months to every 18 months).

- Managers appear worried and spend a great deal of time in closed-door meetings.

- You are asked to justify the existence of your department, work group, or your own job.

- You are asked to list your successes or customers to whom you provided value over the past year.

- You are asked to prepare various work plan scenarios based on the assumption that your budget were reduced by a certain amount or your staff were reduced.

True, all of these "signs" taken individually may *not* mean that management is considering head count reductions, but if more than two or three of these signs are present, it's time to start developing "plan B."

Developing Your Plan B

Everyone (or at least *most* working people) have a "plan A"—that is, a plan to continue working at their present jobs, do those jobs well, and progress up the career ladder. Very few people have a "plan B"—what they will do if plan A gets derailed. *Everyone* should have a plan B, given today's business environment. Such a plan can greatly reduce the stress or fears of a layoff because it gives you a feeling of control over your own career.

When should you develop your stress-reducing plan B? As soon as possible, or as soon as you learn that a layoff may be brewing. First, reassess your values, goals, and priorities in relation to your career. Later chapters include exercises to help you do just that. Once you know what you really want to do with your career, you can fill in the details of plan B. Based on our personal experience and information from *Business Week's* Bruce Nussbaum, we find that the following areas are crucial components of a solid plan B:

- ✔ *Increase your skills.* Managers and professionals today need a wide variety of skills that can be sold to an ever-changing market. Enhanced skills can give you the flexibility to change companies or even industries. Develop any capability or talent that more than one company could find useful.

🖊 *Consider moonlighting.* You can develop new skills by moonlighting, in addition to gaining experience being on your own, building up cash reserves, making valuable contacts, getting experience selling yourself directly to customers, and increasing your self-confidence. Help a start-up company, do consulting, write a book, teach, sit on boards of smaller companies—anything to expand your horizons. Establish a Keogh-type plan or a Simplified Employee Pension (SEP) plan for saving some of your self-employment earnings for retirement. Should you get RIFed or decide to go out on your own you will have your financial arrangements already set up.

🖊 *Expand your credentials.* More and better credentials are always a plus. Get another degree (your present employer may even help defray the cost); take a midcareer development program; sign up for conferences and seminars in your field; give presentations at industry conferences; author papers and articles if doing so is appropriate for your job; learn a foreign language (very important in today's global markets); head up a task force or work group; go for a computer class—anything that interests you and fits in with your goals and priorities.

🖊 *Choose assignments with visibility.* Whenever possible, select (or volunteer for) projects at work that will be successful and provide you with a measure of visibility. Those projects include any hot new product or service that will get sold to customers. And customer contact is a definite plus. Hands-on management is an important skill today; so if you are in a staff job, look for line responsibilities. If you are in a line position, look for projects that provide planning or development experience.

🖊 *Stay flexible.* Being flexible today means survival. Think of your skills or profession, instead of defining yourself by your industry. You may need to jump to a totally different industry later in your career. Join professional organizations that cut across industries—you not only learn more about other industries and the options they may hold for you, but you can build networks of contacts that can prove valuable later on.

🖊 *Network, network, network.* Today everyone needs a *permanent* network of contacts, so start building it now. Nurture those networks—develop business friendships; call people regularly and share industry gossip; take people to lunch; provide information and job leads freely when asked; watch trade papers for information on promotions and people's movements to other companies; pass on information when you come across something you think a contact might find valuable—in short do all those things you probably now skip because you are too busy. Check out the new permanent job-networking groups that many professionals have started or Exec-U-Net, a nationwide networking organization for managers and professionals. Revitalize any contacts from graduate school or previous employers: they maay prove valuable if you get laid off.

🖊 *Rewrite your resume or vita.* All professionals should keep an up-to-date resume or vita in their top desk drawers. But in today's business climate, that resume should focus on skills, experience, and credentials that foster your employability. Forget "career objectives" and focus less on titles. Consider consulting a professional resume writer. Sometimes it is very hard to "think outside the box" of how we have always written our resume or vita, or we feel uncomfortable "selling" ourselves.

✔ *Make friends with head-hunters.* Head-hunters can be a valuable source of job leads, advice, and contacts, but most people use them only after they have been laid off. It takes time to develop a relationship with a head-hunter and to find one whom you will work well with, so start now. Broaden your scope to include head-hunters in your profession, not just your industry. Make appointments to visit a number of head-hunters, and interview them as you would interview a prospective physician. When you find a mutually satisfactory relationship, nurture it—start listening to job leads as the head-hunter comes across them. It is always easier to find a new job when you are already employed than it is when you are out of work!

✔ *Reassess your health benefits, pension, and stock plan.* Look at these benefits with the possibility of being laid off in mind. Would it be beneficial to get some extra life or disability insurance now? What about setting up an Individual Retirement Account (IRA) or some other retirement fund in addition to your company's pension plan? Should you diversify your stock holdings? A financial planner can help you assess your options, and many offer an initial consultation for free. Remember, the more prepared you can be for the worst, the easier it will be to ride out the difficult times.

✔ *Listen to rumors, scuttlebutt, and office gossip.* True, only about 60 percent of what you hear is accurate, but office grapevine usually has a good deal of accurate information about the general direction of events. It can be a valuable early warning system and give you additional information on which to base your decisions. Do what you can to provide *accurate* information as well—nobody likes someone who only takes and never gives information, but keep a tight rein on your mouth. Don't start a panic, don't betray true confidences, and don't pass on something you know is not true.

✔ *Keep a copy of important work-related personal records offsite.* Keep at home copies of all performance appraisals, letters of commendation, nonconfidential samples of your work, thank you letters from customers or contacts, and anything else you think could be useful to you in a job search. Include a copy of your employee handbook that covers descriptions of your company's policies and procedures. Add to that copies of phone numbers of contacts from your Rolodex. Start collecting the home telephone numbers of colleagues at work as well—if you all get laid off, you'll want to stay in touch. While this sounds rather extreme, most people are in such a state of shock when they are told to clean out their desks that they don't think clearly about what they should take with them when they leave. Being prepared leaves you covered in case you are *not* allowed to clean out your desk yourself.

✔ *If possible, get on the health-care plan provided by your spouse's employer*—even if it costs you a little more each month, consider this alternative as soon as you hear rumors of layoffs. The security of knowing that you will be covered no matter what is very important. Given the high cost of health care today, you can't run the risk of being without adequate coverage.

✔ *Establish a "worst-case bare-bones budget.* Think through your monthly expenses and determine the amount of money you would need to get by. Write it down.

The budget you come up with is likely to be more accurate than the one you will struggle to develop if you actually face a layoff.

✔ *Think through what you would require in a severance package.* Later sections of this chapter discuss in detail the ins and outs of severance packages. It is important to have a good sense of your requirements, even as part of a plan B. If you make your assessments now, they are likely to be more accurate than they would be when you are in the situation of actually being let go.

Plan B should include a hard look at your personal day-to-day financial picture. Living beyond one's means is a great stress producer, and makes no sense with the potential for a layoff hanging over your head. The standard rule of thumb is that, as a cushion against job loss, you should have three months' living expenses in savings that are liquid and easily accessible. But the more you earn, the longer a job hunt will take. Experts now figure you should count on spending approximately six weeks for each $10,000 of salary you are looking for in your new job.

So reassess spending habits: cut back on credit card debt; set up a budget and stick to it; reevaluate your housing situation; and look for creative ways to save a few bucks here and there. Anything you can do to reduce your overhead, build up your liquid assets, and plan for the future can pay big dividends and at the same time reduce your stress levels—even if you don't get laid off or decide to strike off on your own from your present company.

What to Expect if You Are Laid Off

Layoffs, furloughs, RIFs—no matter how you say it, the ultimate result is that someone loses a job. For many people, it is the most stressful experience they will have during their lifetimes. Even if you followed all of our advice and have a solid plan B in place, getting laid off will *still* be stressful. The coping techniques listed in later chapters can help ameliorate some of the physical impact of this kind of stress, so make good use of them. But you also need to know how to deal with the immediate feelings and fears layoffs create.

First of all, being laid off *is* different from being fired. It may feel the same, but the cause is different. When you are fired, it is because your performance was lacking. For layoffs, performance is rarely cited as the reason: Usually the reasons are economic—your department or job is being eliminated or reorganized to reduce costs. And remember, no matter how rejected you feel, your employer's reason for your departure is the official reason—even if your boss may have implied that your performance was shaky. Don't be ashamed to tell head-hunters or potential employers that you were laid off—everyone understands that today and no one will be surprised.

Typically, the feelings that follow a pink slip or termination notice are similar to those for any major loss.

The first stage is *denial:* For a fleeting period of time you believe this has all been some gigantic mistake, you believe that your employer will hire you back as soon as things turn around, or you just feel numb.

Next comes *self-blame:* "If I hand't screwed up that last presentation..." or "If I were really good at my job, they would have laid someone else off."

Then comes *anger:* You get angry at your boss, coworkers who survived the cuts, **your boss's boss, senior** management, your partner, your kids, the government for **messing up the economy—in** short, you get mad at everyone for everything.

Depression comes next: You don't want to get out of bed in the morning and nothing seems worth the effort.

Finally you get to *acceptance:* You come to terms with being let go, and decide to get on with your life and look for another job.

The length of time a person stays in any one of these stages is idiosyncratic. It is affected by a wide range of conditions, including, how the termination was handled by your employer; reactions of family and friends; your personal financial situation; how important your job was to you in terms of defining your self-worth; how well you handle vulnerability; how important having control over your life is to you; your flexibility; how well you handle stress and the specific coping techniques you use on a regular basis; and so on.

There is a tendency to avoid going through these stages of loss for one's job—but, remember, you have to work through each stage to be able to move successfully on to the next one. You can't skip stages, so even if you feel you are going crazy, realize you are adjusting to a loss, and it is *normal* not to feel like your usual self.

It is important to get control over as much of your life as you can after you have been laid off—and as soon as possible.

Negotiating a Severance Package

One of the first things you can get control over is your severance package. True, severance deals are usually offered to you at the worst possible time: Most people are in shock and their minds turn off temporarily. But experts feel that you need to take an active role in negotiating a generous severance package and a graceful exit. Don't take your employer's offer as the last word; there are ways to get more if you persist and can play the game well.

The first step is determining what will most likely be in your severance package. Most companies today offer two weeks pay for each year of employment, although this can vary somewhat by industry and job level. Health-care insurance, which you would pay for at the rate your company currently pays for it, is typically made available in companies with more than

20 employees for a period of at least six months. You can probably expect to get reimbursed for unused vacation time and sick leave, plus receive any bonuses, profit sharing, stock options, tuition reimbursement, or retirement monies due you. Beyond that, you should consider anything else provisional, depending on your organization's specific personnel policies and how well you play the negotiating game.

So how can you play the game more effectively? The following tips may help:

✔ *Buy some time.* Most employers will inform you of your termination, offer a severance package, and ask you to leave the premises on the same day. But you don't lose leverage or bargaining power if you keep your cool and simply say "I'll need some time to think this over." If you are pressured, reiterate that you will think it over and get back to them in a day or two regarding the severance package.

✔ *Consult a lawyer specializing in employment issues if you suspect discrimination or a termination that does not follow standard company policy.* Most companies have standard severance packages and termination policies outlined in employee handbooks. Look them up in yours ahead of time, so you know what to expect. The vast majority of employers typically offer one to two weeks of severance pay for every year on the job—but your employer may be different. In cases of discrimination or an unusual termination, a lawyer can help you determine the potential value of your severance package.

✔ *When you go back to talk about your severance package, go prepared.* Bring with you a written statement outlining specific accomplishments, difficult assignments, or projects and relocations taken at the company's request. It doesn't hurt to attach favorable recommendations or commendations from customers.

✔ *Keep the attitude of working out a "reasonable" package.* Hold your temper, keep your words diplomatic, and maintain the attitude that you are two adults solving a practical problem—how you will get the resources you need to find another job. It does not hurt to mention that it will be difficult to find another job in your field during a recession (if it is true), or that you have extenuating family circumstances (such as being the sole support for a child or parent).

✔ *If more money isn't an option, ask for additional services.* Outplacement services can be invaluable in helping you land another job. Ask your employer about the possibility of the company picking up the tab for such services or allowing you to choose your own outplacement service. A good outplacement service provides counseling, an office with access to phones and computers, secretarial services, and support groups of others looking for work.

Ask about access to your employer's Employee Assistance Program (EAP) or counseling services while you are unemployed. Although you may not feel the need for it right now, a time may come when you could benefit from counseling or participation in a support group when the stress just gets too great to handle on your own. EAPs often provide such services, not just for the person who has been laid off, but for partners and family members as well. Such counseling and support can go a long way in helping you cope more effectively with the stress of being out of work.

If you are offered these services as part of a severance package, and you feel you won't need them or can get such help elsewhere at a better price, ask to get the cash equivalent of them included as part of your severance. The cost for outplacement and counseling services varies, but in many cities it can run nearly $100 per hour. Determine the number of hours of service your employer is willing to provide, and determine the cash equivalent from there.

✔ *Negotiate health-care insurance coverage costs.* Most employers have to offer you coverage under their health-care plan for six months: What is negotiable is the price you will have to pay to be covered by your company's plan while you are unemployed. If your company offers access to a health maintenance organization and it costs less than standard health insurance coverage, see if you can opt for the HMO and get a cash equivalent of the difference as part of your severance.

✔ *Ask about continuation of severance pay or outplacement assistance if it expires before you find another job.* Sometimes companies will authorize such an extension, especially if you can prove that you have been looking hard for another position.

✔ *Get a letter of reference from your boss.* Even if you have to write it yourself and ask him or her to sign it, it's worth it.

Surviving a Layoff

So you have survived the initial pink-slip meeting with your boss and have gotten some time to negotiate your severance package. You feel incredibly stressed out or just completely numb. What should you do before you walk out of the office that day or for the last time?

First, take what is legally yours: your Rolodex; samples of your work that are not confidential; copies of performance appraisals, salary reviews, and letters of commendation—all of which can be useful in either presenting your case for a better severance package or finding another job. It is not legal to take home: work in progress; company confidential information; company telephone books; computer software; or office supplies. Second, try to secure a letter of reference from your boss, and ask other executives you have worked with for letters, too.

Finally, thank everyone who has helped you before you leave. Yes, we know you will be feeling numb, angry, or just plain rotten, but exiting with class is very important. *Never* burn your bridges. Don't let your upset show. Phone in your thanks, or stop by on your way out. And don't forget the little people who have helped you—you never know when your paths will cross again.

Once you've left the office, what then? Now comes the hard part: getting your life back together again. Give yourself a few days to let it all sink in, feel the stress, and begin to cope with it. Three broad areas of your life will need attention: your finances, job hunting, and your personal life.

Your Finances

Probably the first thing people worry about when they get laid off is money: making sure there is enough of it and wondering how long what they have will last. Jane Bryant Quinn, financial expert, has some solid suggestions that may help reduce your financial stress:

- *Apply immediately for unemployment compensation.* This seems obvious, but many people put off applying until they have used up most of their reserves. You are entitled to unemployment compensation—your employer paid into the program—so take advantage of it. It may take several weeks for payments to start, so the sooner you apply, the sooner you will see cash coming in.

- *Set up a bare-bones budget.* List essential expenses, such as rent or mortgage, utilities, insurance, car loan, food, gasoline, job-hunting costs. Pay these bills; put all other bills in a box marked "later." Then add up your income, including your partner's pay, unemployment compensation, interest on savings, and any other income. Determine the gap, if any, between your income and your essential expenses.

- *Get rid of most optional expenses, but save one you can use as a special treat to yourself.* These can include health club, hair stylist, manicures, entertainment, cleaning service, purchases of new clothes or other major expenses (unless absolutely necessary), vacations, and so on. Obvious frills must go; don't dip into your savings or use credit cards to prop up your lifestyle.

  Setting aside money for one special frill that really makes you feel good is important. It could be cable TV if you are a sports freak or dinner out once a month. Anything that makes you feel good is a powerful stress reducer.

- *Assess your cash reserves.* These include severance, bank accounts, any liquid investments such as stocks and mutual funds. This reserve should be used to fill in the gaps in your layoff budget each month.

- *Don't pay what you can't afford to pay.* Make no payments on postponable bills, including credit card or department store bills, and student, car, or personal loans, and so on. For each of these bills, write to the head of the credit department and explain your situation. Send monthly good faith payments to prove that you will pay some now, with more when you get another job. This won't work forever, but most creditors will be reasonable for up to six months—especially if you refrain from using the credit or department store cards or taking on any more expenses from them. Don't worry about your credit rating—it's repairable.

- *Decide what to do about your retirement savings.* If you had contributed to a tax-deferred 401(k) retirement savings plan offered by your employer, you may be offered a lump-sum payout of those funds, or the option of keeping the money in your previous employer's 401(k) plan. Quinn advises taking the money out of your old 401(k) plan—if you don't, the money might be tied up until you are 65, and you may not be able to retrieve it later if you need it to live on.

  However, you shouldn't plan on spending those funds immediately. If you do so, you run the risk of: (1) paying income taxes on it, (2) paying a 10 percent penalty if you are under age 59½, and (3) losing the tax shelter that lets those earnings compound tax-deferred. Your best bet is to roll the money into an Individual Retirement Account (IRA) vested in a money-market mutual fund or a bank money-market deposit account. It is best to use a separate IRA for these funds, rather than one you already may have, because if you segregate the funds, you may be able to roll them back into a 401(k) program at the next company you join.

Dip into these 401(k) funds only if your other savings run dry. You will pay taxes and penalties on the money withdrawn, but you can stop the withdrawals at any time and protect what IRA money you have left.

- *Consider getting inexpensive term life insurance.* Consider this if you have a family and relied on your previous employer to cover most of your life insurance. You can't afford to go without life insurance if you have a family. You can skip it if you are single.

- *Call utilities or social agencies to see if you qualify for special utility bill payments.* Many cities and counties have special programs for the poor or unemployed. It doesn't hurt to check it out.

Although being laid off is very scary, if you have developed a solid plan B and adhere to the suggestions listed in the foregoing, a family might make it for 9 to 12 months—long enough for you to find another job and begin again.

Job Hunting

After a couple of days for recuperating, get started on finding your next position. We cannot emphasize enough that finding a new job requires dedication, effort, and persistence in today's market. No job will come to you, you have to find it. The rule of thumb today is that you should plan on spending approximately six weeks for each $10,000 of salary you are seeking. The following ideas can help you begin that search and reduce some of the stress associated with it:

- *Contact your favorite head-hunter.* If you have developed a solid plan B, you should have developed relationships with head-hunters already. Let them know what has happened, and tell them to start looking for you. Bring over a copy of your revised resume and talk seriously about your alternatives.

  If you haven't established a relationship with a head-hunter, start now. Call colleagues and friends for referrals, or pick up a phone book and start calling. Set up appointments and meet prospective head-hunters. Find two or three you like and start working with them.

- *Go to the outplacement service provided by your employer.* If you are offered this service, take advantage of it. It sounds obvious, but many people never take full advantage of the outplacement services offered to them. Even though it may be stressful to see other laid off colleagues there, you need to support each other, and you need the support and services an outplacement firm can provide.

- *Call on your network of contacts and friends when you are ready to start searching seriously for a new job.* Sometimes it is best to work first with head-hunters and outplacement firms, because, if you call your contacts immediately on losing your job, you may send out a message of fear: at that point you *are* afraid. If you wait a week or so, you will feel more in control and will be able to convey that message to your contacts. But, remember, experts say that more than 70 percent of managerial and professional jobs come from networking, so your contacts are invaluable to you.

- *Don't limit your job search.* Consider moving to another state, if that is where the jobs are. Now is not the time to limit yourself to a particular industry, either. Be flexible, because the more broadly you cast your net, the greater the number of alternatives you make available to yourself.

- *Keep a log of all job hunting expenses.* Such expenses may be tax deductible, but you will need adequate documentation for accounting purposes. Keep any and all receipts in one place, such as a special folder or notebook.

- *Keep a log of all job-hunting activities.* Get a big notebook, and every day write down whom you called, the gist of your conversation, and when your contact promised to get back to you. You may need this information as proof for continued qualification for unemployment compensation, and you want to keep straight what you said to whom. If your contacts don't call back, follow up.

  Also, track letters and inquiries you send out, noting the date you sent the letter, the date you received a reply, and the results of your inquiry.

- *Keep expectations for each job interview low.* Great highs and terrible lows will make you feel like you are on an emotional rollercoaster. Riding it out and dealing with the stress will be easier if you keep your expectations for each interview low. That way you won't be devastated when an interview doesn't turn into a job offer. Realize that many of them *won't* result in an offer—but that fact is no comment on your capabilities or qualifications. Employers today are getting incredibly picky because they have a larger pool of very qualified applicants from which to choose. They feel they can wait for exactly the right person to fill their slot, even if their expectations are unreasonable. Even though this may sound completely crazy, *don't take it personally.* Your prospective employer certainly isn't!

- *Consider all aspects of a new job offer.* The biggest mistake people make is accepting the first job offer that comes their way. A new job is more than just a paycheck, it is the people you will work with and report to—so take time to assess that aspect as well.

Job hunting is not easy; it is stressful, exhausting, and sometimes depressing. But don't let it get you down. The more you open yourself to new options, the larger the number of alternatives you will ultimately have to choose from for your next position. The people who are most successful are those who keep at it and follow through.

Your Personal Life

It may sound strange to be talking about your personal life when you have
lost your job, but during this stressful time the quality of your personal life
becomes crucial to determining how well you will survive a layoff. Now,
more than ever, you need the support and encouragement of your family
and friends. But they may not know exactly how to provide you with the
support you need—they may be afraid of saying the wrong thing, asking the
wrong question, or offering assistance that may be unwanted. So help them
help you by asking for what you need. There is nothing wrong with asking
for support, in fact, it is the first step on the road to getting your life back in
order.

Beyond letting your friends and family help you, there are things you can
do to help yourself and control your stress levels. Our own experience has
shown us that the following ideas can help:

✔ *Maintain a daily routine.* Get up when you would usually get up to go to work, set
aside specific times of the day to make calls and write letters, go to your outplacement office on a regular schedule, set aside time for being with friends and
family, and make time every day to do something you enjoy. Don't force yourself
to job hunt 24 hours a day—you'll just burn yourself out and make yourself
harried and frustrated. Instead, plan to get in 4 to 6 solid hours of job hunting
work every day. It's persistence that pays off, not the total amount of hours spent.

✔ *Stay busy.* Don't vegetate. Continue or start volunteering for a favorite charity.
Doing so will remind you that you still are a competent, capable human being, and
will bring you in touch with people who look at things from completely different
perspectives. Spend time doing hobbies or leisure activities you enjoy, or take a
class to learn something new. Read the books you never had time to read, pick up
the projects you had set aside when you got busy at work, or play with your kids.
Try out several new stress-coping techniques to see which ones work best for you
now. If you are home during the day, cook dinner for your partner or family, or
take on more chores around the house. The key here is to keep yourself active and
occupied so you don't dwell on your situation and make yourself depressed.

✔ *Maintain or start an exercise program.* Exercise is one of the best stress reducers
around. You've got the time now. In addition, when you see your body change as
it gets into better shape, you begin to feel that you have control over at least some
part of your life. The compliments you will receive will definitely be a boost!

✔ *Call friends and business acquaintances, and don't hide your jobless status.* Talk to
people you haven't talked to in awhile, and make arrangements to visit friends
you haven't seen in ages. Accept all invitations and give a few of your own. Be
frank about your situation. Simply tell business acquaintances you left your
employer and are looking for alternatives or working on independent projects.
Either way, you can foster relationships and continue to network.

✔ *Seek counseling if things get to be too much to handle on your own.* If you feel you're getting bogged down and not being able to get a grip, do yourself a favor and get professional help. Talk with your physician, ask about a referral to a therapist. Don't suffer in silence. If you experience appetite loss, excessive drinking or eating, sleeping too much or too little, or withdrawal, see your physician or therapist—you may be developing a real depression. Relationships have been known to buckle from the strain, and your partner may be as stressed out as you are due to concern over your welfare. People do bounce back, especially if they get the help they need.

✔ *Don't become obsessed about what cannot be changed.* Most people's initial reaction to losing their job is to rehash the past, to sort through all the "clues" they missed, to berate themselves for trusting the wrong people, and so on. Doing so is a tremendous energy drain. Chances are you wouldn't have done anything differently anyway. Instead, write these issues down as they occur to you. Then replace each one with a positive statement about what you learned or what you will do next time.

✔ *Spend time doing whatever makes you feel better.* Remember, no time is wasted doing something that raises your spirits, gives you courage, reduces your stress, or makes you happy. You are a worthwhile, deserving person—prove it to yourself!

Unfortunately, there are no easy, pat answers to how to make unemployment less stressful. Individuals have to go through the experience in their own way, at their own pace, in their own time. But, remember, it is not the end of the world, and we can honestly say that each person we have known or counseled ended up going on to a job or position that was more fulfilling or made them happier than the one from which they were laid off. As corny as it may sound, it really is true that sometimes these things happen for the best.

What to Expect If You Are a Survivor

Suppose you're one of the "lucky" ones. You survived a layoff. Everyone tells you that's great; you should be relieved and happy. Then why do you feel so depressed, scared, worried, and stressed-out? Why do you have this sick, sinking feeling? What's wrong with you?

Actually, nothing. The emotions and stresses you are experiencing are perfectly normal. Although hardly anyone talks about it, layoffs are almost equally hard on those who remain as on those who are let go. Believe it or not, the experience is very hard on managers and supervisors who had to tell people that they were being terminated.

Survivors go through all the stages of adjusting to a loss: denial, self-blame, anger, depression, and finally acceptance. As a survivor, you have to adjust to the absence of colleagues who will no longer be working with you and the loss of the relationships you had with them; a job that typically is changed significantly by the layoffs; loss of trust in management, your boss, and your employer; and, maybe most importantly, the evaporation of your sense of personal security about your job and financial future.

You experience a number of worries, starting on the day the layoff is announced. You worry about your friends and colleagues who were laid off and how this will impact their lives. You wonder what work will be like without them, and whether it will be as enjoyable. If your best friends or buddies were RIFed, you wonder who you will turn to when work gets crazy and you need to gripe or vent about it. You want to support your friends, but you don't know how to do that in a way that would make them feel better— and chances are you feel guilty about keeping your job.

You think that it could just as easily have been you getting the pink slip, and you fear you might be the next to go. You wonder whether you could get a good job, whether the changing technology has made your skills obsolete, and whether you should try to get more training somehow.

You worry about the reorganized department or company and, if you end up with a new boss, whether your working relationship will be a good one and whether you will be able to perform adequately. You wonder how all the work that the people who were laid off used to do will get done, and by whom. You just don't see how you can possibly get it all done on top of the mountain of your own work you already have to do.

It is not at all uncommon to feel paralyzed by all these conflicting worries and stresses. The best thing is just to let the feelings and worries wash over you—feel and acknowledge them. Go home and be with friends and family, and let them support you and listen while you talk out your worries and fears. Your stress levels will be very high, so practice additional coping techniques to help counteract the impact on your body.

When you go back to work, don't expect to get any work done right away. The layoff will be the major topic of conversation for a good two weeks or more. All the survivors will feel guilty and frightened. Expect the office grapevine to be working overtime, and filled with stories about how people were told about their terminations, what kind of severance packages were offered, how people reacted, how management acted, and so on.

Then anger will set in. It is not at all uncommon to feel great anger toward management or your boss during this time, particularly if you feel the people who were terminated got a bad deal. Everyone at work will seem cranky, cross, and snappish, with everyone about everything. Anger can last several weeks to several months, particularly if management did not handle the terminations well.

Once anger fades, depression takes its place, especially if you are expected to shoulder the burden of additional work that previously had been handled by the people who were terminated. You will likely hate your job, loathe coming in to work now that everything is so different, and lack the energy to build a new work support group if your friends were RIFed. Very little will cheer you up—even things that used to work, whether it was reading the *Wall Street Journal* first thing in the morning, learning a new computer program, flowers on your desk, that great coffee from the little place around the corner, or lunch at your favorite watering hole. You feel as if a big gray cloud descended on the office, and everyone is in the depths of despair. Expect a great deal of talk about how good things used to be, how much people miss the people who were laid off, and how crazy you were not to like your job the way it used to be.

Eventually, people will come to accept the situation as it is now, and get on with mastering their restructured jobs and taking care of business. How long this whole process will take is hard to say—there is no way to cut it short, as survivors have to go through each stage in order to come to grips with the new situation. Much depends on how management handles the adjustment phase—whether they let survivors know they care and whether they show that they did agonize over the terminations. In the best case, the process will probably take about 3 months, from denial to acceptance. But we have seen companies where, at 6 or 7 months and counting, employees are still in the anger phase.

Unfortunately, many employers expect the survivors to carry on as if nothing had happened. They may even tell you that you are lucky to have a job in today's economic environment. But this attitude is completely unrealistic. Something very big did happen—your employer broke the "psychological contract," the one that said that if you did a good job, you would continue to be employed. And basic issues of trust and credibility have been brought up and need to be dealt with.

Surviving as a Survivor

How can you cope as a survivor? First, realize that you won't feel like your typical self for awhile, and that what you're feeling is normal.

Adjusting to a Larger Work Load. Get ready for a greater work load. When people get laid off, the work they used to do rarely disappears; it just gets put on the shoulders of those who remain. Many survivors are doing the work that used to be done by three or more people. It is very common to feel overwhelmed, overloaded, overworked, and overcommitted—and if you are used to feeling confident and capable, these feelings can be very frightening. You may begin to wonder whether you are losing your touch or are able to handle work at all any more—and, more importantly, if you say no to the additional work, will you be the next to go.

Sometimes these feelings go away once you have mastered the new tasks you have been given, reprioritized your projects, and delegated some of the work to other staff members. Expect that the first three to six months may require burning the midnight oil or coming in earlier than usual just to get your head above water.

The key to being a successful survivor is to keep telling yourself that you cannot do it all—no one can; you certainly cannot do it all perfectly, and that is OK! You have to set limits for yourself: on the amount of time you spend on particular tasks and projects, on the length of time you spend each day at work, on the number of lunch hours and weekends you give up, and on the number of new projects you undertake. Those limits will feel unfamiliar, and probably uncomfortable, because you may not be able to do things as thoroughly as you would like. But remember, it doesn't have to be perfect, it just has to be good enough.

The ability to grasp quickly the essence of a situation, to assess the tasks involved in completing a project, and to prioritize and reprioritize your work load become absolutely crucial to survival. Now is the time to force yourself to master these skills if you haven't already. If you aren't so good in these areas, ask your boss for assistance, talk to colleagues, and talk with your customers to learn what they think is important for you to do. You may be surprised at the results!

If after three or four months, you still feel overwhelmed and overworked, it's time for a frank discussion with your boss. Many companies today consciously load more and more work on survivors until those survivors nearly reach the breaking point—then they back off. Why they do this is a mystery. Maybe they can't judge well the amount of work people can do, maybe they want to make a point about something. What is certain is that the effect of such overloading can be disastrous, both to morale and to physical health.

It is *your* responsibility to be assertive and let your boss know when the added work gets to be too much. Approach the boss in a problem-solving frame of mind—you're both adults and you are here to solve a problem. Ask for clarification of responsibilities and priorities, help in assessing what is worth doing excellently and what can be done "well enough"—perhaps a restructuring of projects and help in deciding who could provide assistance with important tasks. Keep your wording diplomatic and negotiate to get the results you want—and need—to remain a productive employee.

Making Use of Coping Techniques.   You will need to practice as many stress coping techniques as you can. Try some new ones that appeal to you from later chapters of this book. Watch your diet, make sure you get adequate exercise and rest, and spend more time with friends and family. If you start to develop physical symptoms of a stress-related illness, make an appointment with your physician. If you feel yourself getting stuck or immobilized by the events you've been through, either talk to your physician about getting a referral to a therapist or support group, or check in with your employer's Employee Assistance Program. Some EAPs have begun support groups for layoff survivors, where you can talk out your fears and feelings and get support from others going through the same experience.

Developing Your Personal Plan B.   All these good things will help you bring your stress levels into the tolerable range and get you ready for the work that needs to follow—establishing a plan B for yourself. You owe it to yourself and your family to follow the steps outlined earlier in this chapter to work up an alternative plan for your career. Eventually the anxiety about your own job will fade away, and the biggest mistake people make is to get complacent, thinking they are safe now and forever.

No one is completely safe from a layoff today, and the sooner you develop a plan and begin to implement it, the sooner you can dramatically reduce your stress levels for the long term. Remember that you have the freedom to leave your employer when you feel the time is right for you to move on—and plan B can help you determine when that time is.

How Employers Can Help Survivors

If the reorganized company is to avoid stagnation, employers have to pay attention to the survivors, as well as to those who were laid off. Because employees need to trust their leaders, they need to know they are being told the truth, and, although no one can say today that there will be more layoffs, at least there will be no surprises.

Costs are involved if survivors aren't supported during the transition. The question facing management is, are they acceptable costs?

Increased stress results in more frequent occurrence of stress-related illnesses—which raises employers' health-care costs.

Downsized staffs are likely to be demoralized and less productive.

Information doesn't flow well when people are confused and concerned.

There is always the chance that the best people, even if they have not been laid off, will leave—out of frustration, anger, or fear—or they will decide that there is no longer any point to putting in 60-hour weeks or working excessive overtime, and will quit doing so.

Management must recognize that the adjustment will be difficult, and make sure that survivors have the tools and capabilities they need to make the transition. That may involve extra training to handle new responsibilities, rewriting job descriptions, clarifying company policies, discussing management's vision for the newly restructured company, and providing a clear picture of where survivors are on the career path through the organization.

Some companies have regularly scheduled work group or department meetings to discuss the aftermath of layoffs, but this works only if management is truly willing to listen to what employees have to say. Very few employers provide support groups or workshops for survivors to help them gain their sense of mastery, control, and confidence.

Minimally, management should communicate honestly why and how the terminations occurred, deal immediately with rumors, and not pull any surprises. There is much to be gained by these efforts.

Promotions

Promotions is a word corporate and semiautonomous professionals hear less frequently in today's business climate, given downsizing and the shrinking of middle management. Many, many baby boomers are reaching the age where they could begin to be promoted into senior levels of middle management, so many of us are caught in a squeeze, with fewer high-level positions being competed for by more people. Lateral moves are common, as are ceremonial title changes—while salaries increase at the "standard rate," which means barely keeping up with inflation.

But promotions are possible. They just are rare, and are no longer something you can assume will automatically happen to you every few years. You have to work harder, and longer, to get them. But maybe that's for the best, because they certainly are sweeter when you have made a significant personal investment to achieve them!

Managing a Promotion

Dealing with a promotion involves two challenges, both of which can significantly raise your stress levels. First, you must cope with feelings of being in over your head and fear of failure—both of which are common in all new jobs. Second, you have to learn to manage the increased or new authority that comes with your new position.

Adjusting to Your New Position

Everyone gets a little nervous on accepting a promotion, but if you are confident of your capabilities, just plunge in and do it. This kind of stress is the good kind. We call this period the honeymoon phase; it usually lasts a few weeks to a couple of months. People are excited about their new position, look forward to coming into work, and learn many new things.

But after a bit reality starts to sink in, particularly in "stretch" promotions that force you to grow. Then the first wave of negative stress hits. Your staff may start asking you questions for which you don't know the answers; new peers may appear to have their own secret agendas, and management may seem to speak in code and be very hard to read. You come from a position where you had mastered all the requirements and could perform easily. Finding out that the same knowledge base isn't adequate is scary and nerve-racking. You may begin secretly to doubt your ability to handle the new job, and wonder if you are in over your head.

Don't worry. All these feelings are perfectly normal, and even proper. A certain amount of ignorance is a good sign. A certain amount of stress is to be expected. If you have already mastered every skill that is needed to perform a new job adequately, the new job probably isn't worth taking.

The higher up you go on the career ladder, the less important specific technical knowledge becomes. The ability to see the big picture is far more critical—in fact, that is what most management is paid for. To achieve that, you need to know who has the answers you need, how to assimilate and synthesize information, how to delegate responsibilities (so you have time to look at the big picture instead of putting out brush fires all the time), and how to coach your staff to produce their best work.

In addition, relationships, allies, and support systems are extremely important as powerful stress reducers. Spend more time building and nurturing relationships, not only with peers and your staff, but with people both above and below you because most work is accomplished through other people.

The more of a "stretch" position this promotion is for you, the more you will need to rely on your staff to provide you with accurate, timely information and good work. Win-win politics can definitely help, as can appropriate handling of authority. Fairness, firmness, and respect go a long way in winning over a new staff.

Those below you can make or break you in your new position, particularly if you need their cooperation to achieve goals and if you do not have direct authority over them. Innuendo or sabotage are not unheard of, particularly if lower ranking people have a vested interest in the success of one of your peers. Once again, win-win politics can pay big dividends.

Getting the support of your peers and those above you requires power of persuasion—you may need their assistance but cannot command it. Win-win politics can help you develop, not only supporters, but allies, who are invaluable as you progress up the ranks—because so much of what is accomplished is achieved through a Byzantine network of favors and good words. Allies can provide you with valuable feedback on your performance, how business is run, and the intricacies of life in higher levels of management—where there are definitely rules and codes of behavior, but none of them are ever written down.

Failure is a possible fact of life in promotions—particularly "stretch" positions—but not because people are incompetent or lacking in talent. Most people would not have been promoted in the first place had this been the case. People can fail because they are poor delegators, handle authority inappropriately, misread crucial business decisions, fail to resolve conflicts, and so on.

But more people fail because they didn't listen to feedback than for any other reason. Your peers, superiors, staff, and those below you will let you know, both directly and indirectly, how you are doing. That feedback is very, very valuable. *The key is not to get defensive, but to listen to that feedback and use it to improve and enhance your performance.* Truly successful people succeed and have less stress beacause they are able to discern what is *not* stated, and can read signs along the way. Remember that the vast majority of people want to see you succeed!

Handling Authority Comfortably

Promotions usually mean additional authority. And for baby boomers, authority carries mixed messages. When we were in our teens and twenties, authority was closely linked to tyranny and repression—it was something we rebelled against. Remember "Power corrupts and absolute power corrupts absolutely"? We actively wanted to rid the world of authority and say no to it. Some of us were intimidated by authority and feared it.

Have things ever changed! Governmental politics aside, most of us now realize that authority is sometimes necessary to accomplish goals and objectives, and that business has a difficult time running without it. But old habits die hard. Dealing with authority, and handling our own, is stressful for us. How can we become more comfortable with authority so we can use it wisely?

A fundamental rethinking of what authority means is required. As we said earlier, power means the ability to achieve shared goals and objectives through others. As a corollary, *authority is the ability to* enforce *shared goals and objectives.* And because of that, it needs to be handled carefully, fairly, and appropriately.

The way to do that is to use win-win politics principles when exercising your authority. The win-win scenario enables you to achieve power while being respected and well liked. Authority does not give you license or free reign to trample on others—with authority comes tremendous responsibility to use the power that comes with it respectfully and fairly.

If you want to be comfortable in your authority, be clear and consistent about rules, use a personal approach to encourage your people to do their best work, and be scrupulously fair. Don't betray your knowledge or experience or give in so that your people might love you for the moment. It is more important that they respect you than personally like you.

Handling authority does get easier—both with time in the position and with age. As with any other skill, mastery takes time. Somehow the things that bothered us or seemed earth-shakingly important when we were younger no longer seem important as more priorities compete for our attention—

in both our work and personal lives. You realize you can compromise more in some areas without giving up your authority. And if you are able to build a self concept that doesn't need validation from above or below, so much the better. The French call this "being comfortable in your own skin"—and that is key for reducing your stress levels!

Handling the Transition

Making the transition into a new position is always stressful, whether you come from the outside or were promoted internally. Both situations have their pros and cons. If you come from the outside, you don't have to deal with the potential problem of managing your office buddies. But you don't have the inside track—you don't know who is good at what, who works hard, and who sloughs off. If you are promoted from within, you know the lay of the land, but managing close associates can be very difficult.

Leaving Your Old Job

How you exit your old job is crucial, and may significantly affect subsequent stress levels. If you don't manage the transition, and both your old and new boss, you could end up working two demanding jobs at the same time. Therefore, you need to develop a transition plan with *both* bosses. This transition plan should cover:

- *A complete written listing of all current projects for which you have responsibility.* Many professionals write up brief case reports of their projects, explaining exactly what has transpired up to this point, what needs to be done next, what is already underway, who major contacts are, and which staff members are responsible for which parts of the project (if appropriate). This should be reviewed and signed off by your old manager. Such a document will be a godsend for the person promoted to take your place.

- *An agreement on how and when you will leave your old job.* This is so obvious that most people overlook it, especially if they are moving on to a new position within their own company. But if you, your old manager, and your new manager don't formally agree on an ending date for your old job, you may find yourself in the untenable position of having to continue to carry your old work load while you are trying to master your new one. People who have found themselves in this unfortunate situation tell us they wouldn't wish it on their worst enemy—stress levels skyrocket because you feel pushed and pulled by the two managers competing for your time and energy.

  An agreement on how you will be involved in the search for the person to take your place. Again, this agreement should involve not only you and your old boss, but your new boss as well, especially if the search process continues after your official starting date on your new job.

✔ *An agreement on how, or even if, you will provide "telephone support" for the person taking your place.* This agreement covers whether or not you will be allowed to act as a helpful advisor to the person taking your place, exactly what you will or will not do, and how long you will offer such assistance. These details also need to be hammered out between you, your old boss, and your new boss, to make sure everybody agrees how your time will be used.

✔ *An agreement on how your salary will be covered if you end up continuing to do part of your old job while you also start doing your new job.* This can get very, very sticky, and we strongly discourage agreeing to a dual-job situation, unless there is absolutely no way you can get around it. Your old manager and your new manager will need to determine both the length of time and the percentage of time you will spend on each job, with your input. Then the two of them have to decide whose budget pays for what. But all of this should be determined prior to your transition, so that you don't have to deal with frustration or resentment on the part of your new boss.

This all sounds like a great deal of work, and, truthfully, it is. But working through these details ahead of time can go a very long way in reducing stress levels for everyone involved as you move into your new position.

Managing Your Old Peers

Perhaps one of the most stressful spots to find yourself in managerially is being promoted to lead your current work group or department. In this special case, you end up managing people who had been friends, confidants, and peers—your work support group, which greatly helped you reduce your personal stress levels on the job. Now you don't have that support group to help you cope. From the point of view of your coworkers, you are suddenly the one who determines their salary increases, writes their performance appraisals, and in short, decides their futures. And you know all the rotten things they said about senior management! The transition can be a difficult time for all of you.

The relationship between you and your office buddies changes inexorably once your promotion takes effect. You can no longer be office friends in the way in which you had been. Given your increased authority, it is important to establish a professional distance immediately—you can no longer be one of the group, even if you really enjoyed that. Trying to maintain camaraderie only serves to increase stress all around.

The best way to handle the situation is to discuss it with your new staff, either in a group meeting or individually. The former members of your group need to be reassured that they are important to you and that you value their special talents.

Can you continue to socialize with your former coworkers once you supervise them? The answer to that is yes, but probably not in the way you used to do. One successful executive told us her rules of thumb were never to socialize individually with people whom she managed (as a way of preventing any feelings of favoritism), and never to do anything with a former coworker that she wouldn't do with her best client or customer (so commiserating about love lives over a few beers is definitely out!). The key here is to maintain some semblance of a professional distance, because blurring boundaries after work or on the weekends only makes things more confusing during the work week.

You may run into resistance from coworkers who had competed for your new position. They may not take you seriously, or they may harbor resentment and anger if they had competed with you. If either situation happens, it is critical that you nip it in the bud immediately, or you risk having the resulting frustration undermine your efforts.

If your new staffers don't take you seriously, you may have tried to be overly nice and accommodating because you wanted to show you still thought of them as buddies and you wanted them to like you. That approach almost always fails. As we said before, it is more important that your staff members respect you than like you.

To get respect, act as though you believe you deserve it. As one successful elementary school teacher told us in describing how she handled her class during the first few weeks of a new school year, "In the very beginning, it's best to start off very strict, but polite—while you very clearly outline expectations for new roles. You can always lighten up later on, once new norms of behavior have been established. But if you start out being overly accommodating, you can never get back the authority and respect you gave away." What holds true for children in school also holds for staff members (and there are those who would say that sometimes they also act like schoolchildren!).

It is not uncommon for former coworkers who had competed for your new position to feel angry and frustrated, and to take this out on you. Taking it personally is a sure-fire way to make yourself stressed out. In this instance, confront the situation directly, in private, with the individual(s) involved. Allow them to vent their frustrations and anger. Commiserate with the very true assessment that "We don't always know exactly why decisions get made the way they do around here, but the fact of the matter is that a decision has been made. So let's strive to work together to achieve the goals that have been given to us for this department." But leave no doubts as to who is the boss.

If either situation continues for more than a couple of weeks, it's time for another private discussion with the staff member. Only this time be firmer, and make it clear that the anger or frustration is affecting the rest of the work group or department, and that is not acceptable.

If problems persist, do yourself a favor. Don't try to deal with it on your own. Talk to your boss. Ask your boss to help you develop an action plan to cope with the situation. Giving your manager a progress report, not only provides valuable information, but sets the groundwork for reducing your stress levels by enlisting your boss's support early on—in case the situation should escalate.

And escalate it might. Be aware that transfer or termination of the problem employee may ultimately be necessary. But if you do everything you can to make the situation work from the beginning, you will be able to tell yourself in all honesty that it is not your fault—which goes a long way in helping you adapt to the stress of such a situation.

The Imposter Phenomenon

All people worry, when they accept a promotion, whether they have what it takes to be successful at the new job. For some people, this fear does not go away once they begin to master the new position and evidence of their success is visible. Suffering from the "imposter phenomenon," these people are unable to trust their own competence. Instead they believe their success is unrelated to their own abilities.

People who believe they are imposters exhibit these private fears and stresses in one of several ways:

- *Workaholic imposters.* These sufferers believe that because they really aren't competent, the only way to succeed is to work two, three, or four times as hard as everyone else. This common myth is believed by many women and minority professionals, who have always had to be at least twice as good as their white male colleagues in order to be taken seriously or promoted. The thinking goes like this: "If I were really capable, I wouldn't have to work so hard to be successful." The fact that hard work plus talent are required for success doesn't even occur to them.

- *Lucky imposters.* These folks always attribute their success to luck. A project was completed early because it was unexpectedly easy to do, an important piece of information was chanced on, or a customer was ready to close the deal anyway— any reason will do except the one fact that says the sufferer did a really good job. These beliefs leave the lucky imposters with no sense of control over their working lives: Success depends entirely on fate.

- *Charming imposters.* Charmers use the power of their own personality and charisma to succeed—or at least to draw attention away from what they believe are their serious shortcomings. They cajole, flatter, bolster egos—anything that will keep others from seeing the real them. When they are successful on the job, they discount it. Their feeling is that people were swayed by their personalities and cannot accurately judge the quality of their work.

You may have seen aspects of yourself in these descriptions—experts say that as much as one third of the work force struggles with these delusions. Living this kind of double life is very stressful. Most people try to eradicate these feelings by going after more and bigger successes and positions, in the hope that, by doing something really terrific, they themselves will come to believe that they are competent. But that rarely happens—nothing ever turns out to be quite terrific enough—so imposters find themselves on a never-ending treadmill.

If you identify with any of the imposter behavior patterns, you can do several things to develop a more realistic picture of your capabilities:

- *Talk to successful friends you trust about your feelings of being an imposter.* You may be surprised to find that some days all of us feel we are winging it and would classify ourselves professional fakers!

- *Examine compliments you have received, and what you do to deflect them, then try doing the opposite.* Let the compliments sink in and see what it feels like to enjoy them.

- *Take a hard look at your track record.* Does your past really warrant such fear when you tackle new projects? Weren't you able to handle similar situations in the past?

- *Accept that you don't have to be perfect.* To some extent we all carry around unrealistic expectations for ourselves and our performance. Do you really expect everyone else to do things perfectly all of the time? No. No one expects you really to be perfect—except you.

If you feel that you are an imposter, do yourself a favor. Discuss your feelings with your physician, clergyperson, or Employee Assistance Program (EAP) personnel. They can refer you to counseling or a support group to help you break this cycle. It really does take professional help to eliminate this potent stressor from your life.

Turning Down Promotions

Not every promotion is worth taking. That may sound like heresy, but it's true. Given the current high levels of stress present in working life, it is appropriate to examine situations carefully to make sure the benefits outweigh the costs. Very few people today automatically accept a promotion, no matter what it is or what conditions come with it.

Sometimes it is easier to determine which promotions are *not* worth taking than to define those that are. A promotion may *not* be worthwhile if: You have already mastered all the skills needed to manage the new position successfully; you will be required to act against deeply held values, goals, or priorities; there seems to be little payback, either careerwise or monetarily, for the responsibilities you would assume; several other people have turned the position down; work duties would seriously cut into valued personal or family time or throw off the balance between your work and personal life; or your gut just tells you not to do it.

Later chapters in this book help you explore your values, goals, and priorities, and discuss successful risk taking. Making a change is scary, and you owe it to yourself and your family to go into a promotion with your eyes open. In most companies, not accepting a promotion is no longer enough to throw you off the career track. It may slow you down a bit, but it won't derail you. And that may be a small price to pay if you are already under a great deal of stress.

Relocations and Transfers

A fact of life for many corporate professionals today is being offered a transfer to a new company location as part of a promotion or lateral career move. Transfers may also become necessary due to layoffs or reorganizations. Semiautonomous professionals may be affected if they decide to join a small group elsewhere, and even autonomous professionals may at some point decide to relocate their practice or small company to another city.

By far the greatest impact is felt by corporate professionals, for whom moves every two to three years may be common. The stresses faced by people or families being relocated include: loss of support networks and valued people or things; taking on greater role burdens (one partner taking on the hassle of handling the move while the other partner goes on ahead to start the new job); the possible loss of the other partner's job or the impact on that partner's career that results from stepping off the fast track; financial hardship if one partner cannot quickly find a new position at a comparable salary; and interruption of personal growth and development (a partner may end up leaving a fulfilling career, children may have to leave behind membership in a sports team, or a teenager may give up some autonomy when forced to leave a part-time job).

The Human Side of Relocation

For the person being offered the relocation, the move is toward something, but for the family or partner, it may be a move away from things they already know—friends, family, fun activities.

Every relocation is disruptive.   Transferees have to find a new place to live, a new place of worship, schools, clubs, sports facilities, physicians, dentists, hair stylists, grocery stores, malls, friends, babysitters, and so on. Local mores and traditions have to be learned, along with how to get around in the new location. A partner may have to start looking for a new job in an unfamiliar market where former contacts and networks are of no help. All of this comes on top of mastering a new job and learning about all the new people at work!

Dual-career couples can face special stressors, especially when one partner is being asked to give up a fulfilling position or cannot quickly find a comparable position in the new location. Power conflicts and feelings of competition can be ignited, and it is tough to determine whose career is more important and whose career can go into neutral for a while. Negotiation is crucial for successful resolution of these issues.

Impact of Relocation on Children

We tend to think about the impact of relocation on adults, but moving can be even more stressful for children. As long as parents are happy with a relocation and help them deal with the inevitable disruptions at home, very young children handle transfers well. But school-age children, who may worry about coming into a new school in the middle of the year when friendship groups have already been formed, have a much more difficult time. Textbooks may be different, and the child may be ahead of or behind where the new class is in those textbooks. Even what clothing is considered in style may be different. Certain neighborhoods may be more or less receptive to outsiders in terms of forming friendships away from school. Moves are always much more disruptive for teenagers, for whom stable social relationships are so important.

Most families can handle these disruptions adequately, particularly if moves are infrequent, and there are no other major stresses on the family. However, research has shown that frequent transfers can trigger a group of stress reactions called the mobility syndrome, which can include depression, deterioration of health, strong dependency on one's partner or family for emotional satisfaction, little community involvement, lack of desire to build new friendships, feelings of social anonymity, a significant rate of alcoholism, marital discord, acting out behavior on the part of children and teenagers, and a high divorce rate. While coping techniques can help in some cases, a couple or family may find it necessary to get professional help.

Research is starting to emerge indicating that adults who as children moved very frequently due to parental job transfers may find it difficult to form lasting friendships and intimate relationships later on in life. For some of these adults, forming close relationships is scary because for them, ending relationships has always been painful—so they may choose to avoid close relationships altogether. Others never learned the skills necessary to foster the development of close personal relationships because, as children, they never lived in one place long enough to have time to develop such relationships.

Some of the ways you can help your children cope with a move are very simple:

✔ *Enlist children's help in determining what features are desired in their new home.* It's a small thing, but letting kids voice their opinions about what features they would like in the new family home helps them feel they are a part of the process, and fosters their buy-in on the move.

✔ *Take your children with you when you go house hunting.* Yes, that may be a hassle, but seeing a variety of new houses, getting comfortable with the new city, and, most importantly, being with their parents during this confusing time—are very reassuring for children. Participation in the choice of a new home greatly lowers their stress levels because, if left to their own devices, their imaginings are likely to be far worse things than the reality of their new environment.

✔ *Work with your relocation people to identify places in the new city that would be important or special to your children, and then make sure you visit them on house-hunting trips.* The idea here is to show your children, literally, that many of the same things they like about where they currently live are also present in their new town. Depending on your children's interests, this may mean visits to nearby fast food restaurants, shopping malls, playgrounds, zoos, libraries, skating rinks, public parks, video rental shops, and so on.

✔ *Take your children to visit their new school for a day before you move.* All schools will gladly arrange for your children to visit their new school and spend a day in the class they will be joining after the move. This simple tactic can go very far in easing your children's worries about what their classmates will be like, how hard the teachers will be, whether the textbooks will be familiar, and so on.

You might consider taking pictures of the new school and classmates for your child to take home if there will be a gap of several weeks from the date of the visit to starting at the new school. The pictures will help your child to keep fresh mental images of the new school, and make the move something to look forward to.

If your children attend religious education classes, you might consider doing a similar visit to your new place of worship.

✔ *After a house is selected, take pictures of it to bring home to your children.* Take pictures of the outside, where the children will play, their bedrooms, and important rooms where the family will spend much of its time. This way, the house will feel more familiar when the children actually move in, and they can picture where their things will go in their new living space.

If you are building a new home, take pictures of it at varying stages of construction, and start a scrapbook. This helps children, even small children, grow gradually more comfortable with their new environment.

✔ *Make the new environment special by letting your children decide how their new rooms will be decorated.* This can range from simply letting them pick out the color of the paint on the walls of their bedrooms to letting them select new curtains, furniture, or sheets and blankets. The idea here is to make the new place different and the move something exciting—not scary.

✔ *Before you move, help your children make a scrapbook of their old environment.* This means taking pictures of their friends, teachers, school, playground, bedrooms, and old house, as well as any other places that are special for your children. Such a scrapbook will help your children preserve memories of their old town and old friends. Add addresses and telephone numbers of special friends, so your children can keep in touch with them.

✔ *Let your children help prepare for the actual move.* Let them pack their own belongings, and even help you with packing other items. Doing so helps them feel important, and a part of the preparations. Ask your children to pack special suitcases of their favorite things to take with them when they make the trip— things not to be sent with the movers. That way, favorite toys are available on the trip itself, and immediately in the new house. Also, if the movers get delayed, your children won't be separated from special comfort items, like stuffed animals or books.

✔ *Once at the new home, let your children help with unpacking and turning the strange house into a home.* Again, the idea is to let the children feel they are active participants in the process. Let them unpack and put away their own belongings, even if they do so in a messy way! You might want to consider taking before and after pictures of the new home—what the rooms looked like empty, and what they looked like after your family's belongings were in place. This helps children see that there is a real impact on the new house.

Clarifying Pros and Cons

How are other professionals today deciding whether or not to accept a transfer? For the first time, many managers are assessing not only the career, financial, and housing implications of a move, but whether or not it will improve the quality of life for them and their families. This is a major shift for businesspeople, because the conventional wisdom has always been if you turned down a transfer, you would be removed from the fast track.

This attitude comes at a time when relocations are becoming a much more important mechanism for broadening an employee's capabilities and knowledge about the company. As fewer and fewer upward promotions become available, lateral moves are being used much more frequently as ways to keep star performers interested in and involved with a corporation. The changing business environment also requires that managers and professionals have experience working with different businesses, functions, and locations—even globally—to have a better understanding of the company's business and customers once they take on senior positions.

In this kind of a situation, long-range planning for career moves becomes crucial, and employees need a better understanding of how long a commitment is required for transfers. For such moves, many professionals would prefer structured, centralized career planning that would include an evaluation of their partners' aspirations and alternatives. Few companies provide this kind of planning, and far fewer communicate effectively what the repercussions are if a transfer is turned down.

So how do you decide whether to take a transfer or let it pass? Perhaps the most important thing is for you and your partner to reassess your values and goals, and those you hold for your family. Rethinking priorities is very useful, as well. Chapter 16 "Preparing for Changes" can provide concrete information on how to do this. Then take a hard look at the new position in terms of career enhancement, contents of the relocation package, finances, housing costs in the new city, etc., and determine whether it matches your goals and priorities.

Ask if your employer will make relocation assistance for your partner part of the relocation package. Many companies don't broadcast the fact that they provide such services but, when pushed, will provide assistance at least in locating executive search and employment consultants. Some go further than that by picking up the costs for such consulting; others use their own contacts to help a partner find a new position. Either way, it doesn't hurt to ask.

Also ask whether your company provides access to, or covers the expense of, relocation experts. Several types of experts are available who can help reduce the stress of moving for you. One group of people can arrange hotel or temporary housing, airline reservations, babysitters, car rentals, movers, and so on—all those things that can make house hunting and the actual move itself easier. Most large corporations even provide this service in-house. Other experts can help you set up house inspections; gather financing and mortgage information; put you in touch with the right appraiser, realtor, and broker; gather information on where you can pursue your favorite activities in the new city; provide lists of physicians and dentists; and so forth. This whole area is booming now, and many such experts are available to help you lessen the disruptions of relocation. Take advantage of them!

If your assessment is positive, great! Then just consider using the additional coping techniques provided later in this book to help you reduce the impact of relocation stresses on you and your family. If your assessment is negative, then it is time to think about turning down the relocation. Doing so always carries risk and Chap. 16 can help you determine your level of comfort with taking risks. But you may be surprised: In today's world, turning down transfers may not be as detrimental to a career as it has been in the past.

Business Travel—Curse or Joy?

Business travel seems so glamorous on television and in the movies, doesn't it? The reality is that it gets very old very quickly—usually within a couple of months if you travel frequently on business. For most of us, the scenario goes something like this: Work at the office until the last possible moment; frantically flag down a taxi; careen through traffic to the airport; find out that your flight has been delayed or, worse yet, cancelled; grab an airport hot dog and coffee; shuffle on board the plane and stuff as much as possible into the overhead compartment; chew a couple of antacid tablets to counteract the hot dog and coffee; try to do paperwork or read while a baby several rows ahead of you has a screaming fit; stagger off the plane and hunt down the car rental desk; get lost on the way to the hotel; check in and find out: (a) there is no 24-hour room service; (b) housekeeping is closed and you can't get an iron and ironing board; or (c) the company travel agent forgot to request a nonsmoking room for you; sleep fitfully, if at all; meet people for a "power breakfast"; spend the day (or days) giving your presentation and trying to convince people to do something they really don't want to do and to spend money they really don't want to spend; race to the airport at the last minute through terrible traffic; run through the airport and make your flight just as the doors are closing; get stuck in the middle seat; swallow a couple of aspirin to relieve a pounding headache; work on your expense and call reports while the guy sitting next to you wants to tell you his life story; wait in line for a cab; arrive home very late to 17 messages on the answering machine and the urgent need to do laundry so you will have something clean to wear to work the next day. Yes, business travel isn't pretty, and only the strong, and prepared, survive!

Preparing for Business Travel

Yes, you read that title right. Preparing properly for business travel can significantly reduce opportunities for stress. It goes without saying that, if at all possible, complete preparation of speeches, presentations, or reports before the last minute. *Double check all flight and hotel reservations*—this seems obvious, but many people forget to check. Finding out that a flight has been delayed or cancelled or that a hotel room wasn't guaranteed for late arrival and was given to someone else can be incredibly stressful. Give yourself plenty of time to get to the airport. Beyond that, fellow business travelers have come up with a wide variety of helpful tips that may be useful for you:

✔ *Set up and maintain a travel profile with your travel agent.* Such a profile contains, not only information on your frequent flyer and credit card numbers and airline preferences, but also such things as preferred seat assignments, hotel room preferences, requests for special meals on the plane, rental car specifics, your preferences for health club facilities at your hotel, and any other pertinent information that can help make your trip more pleasant. This way you don't have to remember to tell the travel agent all these details every time. Travel profiles can be updated at any time.

✔ *Find out your hotel telephone and fax numbers.* Keep these with your travel documents and distribute them to staff members who may need to reach you. Nearly every hotel has a fax machine today, and most will not only receive your fax for you, but deliver it to your hotel room—a big stress reducer if a crisis flares up and you need to look at hard copies of documents.

If your company has standard fax cover sheets that are used as the first page of fax documents, you should add several blank ones to your briefcase.

✔ *Make arrangements for your in box or electronic mail messages to be delivered to you on the road if you are going on a trip over two days in length.* Have your staff or secretary express mail important items from your in box or electronic mail queue to your hotel every couple of days. That way you can keep crises to a minimum, and keep from feeling overwhelmed when you walk back into your office for the first time on the day you return.

If you are going to be out an entire week or more, consider having your in box packed up and delivered to your home before you return. That way you can peruse the contents at your leisure, rather than feel you have to drag yourself into the office over the weekend. If you don't have a computer at home that can dial in to your email system, have someone print off your email messages and add that to the package being delivered to your home. Once again, this will help keep you from feeling overwhelmed when you return to the office.

✔ *Take a sturdy notebook in your briefcase.* Use this notebook to record notes to yourself, follow-ups you will need to do on your return based on your responses to voice or electronic mail messages or faxes you received on the road, or promises you made on your trip. Little scraps of paper invariably get lost. Keeping all your notes together in one place makes it much easier to follow through.

✔ *Take along an empty express mail envelope and label.* That way, if you collect a lot of papers or materials while you are on the road, you can ship them back to your office.

✔ *Put a just-for-fun magazine, book, or tape for your Walkman in your briefcase.* Having one of these available can make airline delays more bearable and long flights more pleasant.

If you plan to be gone longer than a couple of days, add to your suitcase some things you really enjoy for doing in your hotel room in the evening or if you can't sleep. These could be lightweight hobby materials, notepaper or cards to write letters, catalogues from which to shop, home- (as opposed to work-) related magazines or books, or anything else you enjoy doing.

Consider bringing along home "administrivia"—bills that have to be paid, applications or forms that need to be reviewed, birthday or Christmas cards that need to be addressed, recipes that you want to copy onto cards, and so on. The key here is to keep up on home tasks so you don't feel you are behind schedule when you finally do get home.

✔ *Put your traveler's first aid kit in your suitcase before you put in anything else.* In a plastic bag assemble:

- *Your physician's daytime and emergency telephone numbers*

- *A list of all the medications you are currently taking, plus a list of all the medications to which you are allergic*

- *Pain medication*—either acetaminophen or ibuprofen

- *Decongestant*—either nasal spray or tablets to help you fly safely if you develop a head cold. If you fly with a bad cold, the changes in air pressure may force bacteria or viruses up into your ears or sinuses, setting the stage for infection. Check with your physician to determine whether you can use over-the-counter medications or need to have something special prescribed.

- *Diarrhea medication*—Imodium AD is available over the counter now, and will quickly relieve diarrhea

- *A selection of bandages*—you never know when you might need them

- *Oral thermometer*—if you do get sick, you need to know if you are running a fever. Hotel gift shops never seem to stock these.

- *Antacid tablets*

- *Small tube of petroleum jelly*—it has a million uses

- *An extra pair of glasses or disposable contact lenses* if you wear them

- *Copies of prescriptions for any medications you may be taking*

✔ *Keep a complete set of your favorite toiletries or personal grooming aids packed and ready to go.* Put them in a waterproof plastic bag or carrier, and don't snitch from this stash when you run out at home! If you do snitch, replenish the supply immediately! This way, if your luggage gets waylaid on your return flight, you won't have to stop on your way home from the airport at an all-night drug or discount store to purchase shampoo, mousse, makeup, razors, shaving cream, toothpaste, toothbrush, and so on. This is not only stressful, it can be expensive!

✔ *Toss your workout gear in your suitcase.* If you carry it with you, you are more likely actually to make use of any health club facilities associated with your hotel.

✔ *Pack something to remind you of home.* This could be a picture of your family or significant other, a travel pillow if you can never sleep with the ones hotels give you, or something that has meaning to you. It may sound a little dumb, but it makes coming back to an impersonal, empty, alien hotel room a little more pleasant.

✔ *Take along an adequate supply of disposable contact lenses or any prescription medications you may be taking. If you wear glasses, take an extra pair along.* If you are going overseas, pack *twice* the amount of medications you will need, and pack each batch in different places, in case one piece of luggage gets lost or delayed.

   If you are going overseas, also pack over-the-counter medications you use that you may not be able to get overseas. It is also helpful to take prescriptions for any medication you are taking regularly, just in case.

✔ *Bring along healthy snacks so you don't raid the honor bar in your room or feel tempted to make a foray to the hotel gift shop for junk food.* This works best if you are checking your luggage through to your destination. Few people want to be weighed down with food when they are carrying on all their luggage. Pack your favorite healthy munchies: rice cakes, fresh fruit, bagels, whatever—or stop at a grocery store on your way to the hotel. You'll save money, and your body will thank you.

✔ *Wear comfortable clothes on flights over two hours.* If at all possible, wear comfortable clothes, not standard business suits, so you can walk around, move, and stretch easily. You can even change in the bathroom at the airport if you leave directly from the office. If you're concerned about the extra weight of a change of clothes, consider that comfortable clothing can make a huge difference on long flights.

✔ *Verify pet sitting, house sitting, mail pickup, or plant care arrangements.* Just as you would double check your travel arrangements, double check any arrangements you made for taking care of things at home. It can be tremendously stressful to envision hungry pets or dying plants when you are several thousand miles away!

✔ *Make sure your answering machine is turned on and working properly.* If you don't have a machine, purchase one that lets you access your messages remotely. Failing that, if you have call forwarding on your home phone and voice mail at work, forward your home phone to your voice mailbox. That way, you can pick up messages from family and friends while you are on the road, and you won't feel that you are out of touch. You also won't feel overwhelmed when you get home and find 15 or 20 messages on your home answering machine.

✔ *Prepare for your return.* For many, the most stressful part of a business trip is the return—particularly for singles. So many things are vying for our attention when we are crabby, tired, and hungry—laundry, mail, messages, hungry pets, and so on. Plan ahead—straighten up so that things don't look like a cyclone hit the place when you first walk in the door. Have a frozen meal in the freezer to heat up to eat if the airplane food was awful and make sure you have something for breakfast. Set aside a complete (from the skin out) clean outfit to wear to work the day after you return, so you don't have to do laundry at midnight. Do anything you can think of to make it easier to get your act together for the upcoming day at work.

If you travel a great deal, and you are single or your partner travels, too, consider hiring a cleaning service. Make arrangements to have the cleaning people spiff up your living space on the day of your return.

If you live in a high-rise building with a doorkeeper or have a friendly neighbor, you may even be able to have your dry cleaning delivered, groceries brought in, and mail delivered to your door.

Surviving Business Travel

After preparing for business travel, comes *surviving* it.

✔ *Don't eat standard airline food.* Standard airline fare is usually tasteless, low in fiber, and high in fat and calories. All major airlines today offer a variety of special meals that can be requested at least 24 hours in advance. These special meals cover dietary restrictions including vegetarian, low-fat, low-calorie, bland, low-sodium, and so on. Your travel agent should be able to give you information on the specific types of special meals your airline offers.

If you are really organized, you might want to carry on a meal with you. Or pack something at home to bring along.

✔ *Reduce your caffeine and alcohol intake on the plane, or eliminate it completely.* Both are dehydrating and the air on the plane is already very dry, so plain water or fruit juices are much better for your body. This is particularly true for long flights, when caffeine and alcohol can compound jet lag.

✔ *When in restaurants, stick to your diet resolutions.* Don't eat what, under normal conditions, you wouldn't even look at. This is particularly true for foreign travel. Business trips are *not* the right time to experiment with new or unusual foods, except under very controlled conditions such as if a colleague recommends the restaurant, the restaurant is clean, and you try only a *little bit*.

Remember, as long as you are paying for it, you have the right to request that food be prepared to your liking. So if a waiter gives you a difficult time about a special order, simply say "If the chef wishes to treat me to dinner tonight, I'd be happy to have the meal prepared the way he or she prefers. However, since I am paying for my dinner, I'd like it prepared this way...." It does work!

Your healthiest option is to stick to high-carbohydrate, low-fat, high-fiber foods while on the road. But most restaurant food is low in fiber and high in fats. The easiest way to cope with this is to follow your **ABC**s:

Ask for sauces and dressing on the side.

Baked, broiled, boiled, or grilled meats and seafood are wise choices.

Create your own meal from appetizers.

Divide dessert with one of your dinner companions.

Extra food can go home in a bag; you don't have to clean your plate.

Fill up with fiber from grains, fruits, and vegetables.

Glass of wine is a healthy substitute for multiple mixed drinks.

✔ *Watch out for food poisoning.* If you travel or eat out a great deal, there is really no way to avoid completely the risk of food poisoning. Most food poisoning results in diarrhea, nausea, stomach cramps, and vomiting, but it can sometimes lead to a variety of long-term health problems, and, rarely, even death.

How can you avoid food poisoning? Although you can't completely, you can reduce your risk by passing up foods that have been handled a great deal such as hamburgers (the meat has to be ground up, which requires additional handling) and tuna or chicken salad; avoiding rare beef, fish, poultry, and pork; steering clear of raw shellfish; avoiding raw eggs (which are a prime source of salmonella bacteria) used in Caesar salad dressing, uncooked hollandaise or bearnaise sauces, or homemade mayonnaise and switching to firmly cooked eggs, whether they are scrambled, poached, boiled, fried, or done over easy. Pass on buffets, too—food that sits around and is kept neither hot nor cold enough is a prime breeding ground for bacteria.

Symptoms of food poisoning can appear between 1 and 24 hours after you eat the contaminated food—usually they appear within 6 hours. The symptoms can include cramps, vomiting, pain above the navel, and diarrhea. Sometimes the symptoms appear very suddenly.

Contact your physician if you have been vomiting for more than three hours or if you show signs of dehydration—lethargy, weakness, or light-headedness. If you are far away from your physician, contact the hotel's front desk or concierge, and ask for help to find a physician. Most hotels have arrangements with local physicians for situations like this.

If your diarrhea or vomiting becomes uncontrollable, you develop a fever over 100 degrees or shaking chills, or if abdominal pain worsens or persists beyond 24 hours, it would be wise to go to an emergency room. You may need to be admitted to the hospital and be given intravenous fluids or antibiotics.

✔ *If you do get sick on the road, adjust your travel schedule accordingly.* Most of us plan our travel itineraries assuming we will be healthy the entire trip: We cram as much as we can into as little time as possible. If you do pick up a bug, a bad cold, or something else, it may not be wise to continue with your aggressive schedule. Phone your physician for an opinion on how to alter your travel plans. Then follow those recommendations! You don't need to be a road warrior or hero—you are worth far more to your company healthy than ill!

✔ *Beware of traveler's shoulder and elbow.* You wouldn't think of carrying your 9-year-old son or daughter over your shoulder as you ran past 27 gates through the Dallas–Fort Worth airport, because you know your shoulder and elbow couldn't stand the strain. So why do you think nothing of doing the same thing with a suit bag and briefcase that weigh the same as your child? Perhaps the most common complaint of business travelers is strained muscles in the shoulder, neck, elbow, or back—all from carrying too much luggage that is too heavy for too far a distance.

So learn to pack light; check your luggage; invest in a sturdy luggage cart—the fold-up kind you can either carry on the plane or check through to your destination; or hire a sky cap (admittedly a rare sight in airports today). If you buy a luggage cart, spend the money to get a good one—sturdy and large enough to handle the weight you typically carry with you. After you've bought it, use it! Don't think that only oldsters drag carts through the airport: Have you ever seen a flight attendant without one of those little carts? Maybe they know something you don't.

If you do pull a muscle, give it a rest. Switch to the other arm, or check your baggage. If the pain persists, try cold compresses or heat, whichever feels best to you. Aspirin, ibuprofen, or acetaminophen can help relieve pain. Make an appointment to see your physician if the pain persists for more than a couple of days; the pain is severe or gets worse over time; you feel tingling in the affected limb; or the discomfort significantly limits your range of motion, prevents you from sleeping comfortably, or keeps you from doing your daily activities. Medication, physical therapy, or other treatments may be required to get you back to normal.

✔ *If at all possible, stick to some variant of your exercise regimen.* Probably the last thing you feel like doing when you finally drag yourself back to the hotel is working out. But exercise is a powerful stress reducer and can help you fall asleep later on. So if you exercise regularly, continue to do so on the road. If nothing else, take a long walk (even in a mall) or do some exercises in your hotel room at least once a day, to stretch your legs, take a break, and maintain some level of fitness.

✔ *Get enough sleep.* This is easier said than done sometimes. Most hotel beds are either too hard or too soft; the room temperature is too cold or too hot and you can't regulate it easily; it is too noisy or too quiet; or the air is too dry and you get a scratchy throat that keeps you up. On top of that, if you've changed time zones, your biological clock may be off.

How to cope? If the bed is really too soft, pull the bedspread and blankets off the bed and sleep on the floor. If it is too cold, call down to housekeeping and ask for more blankets, or block the air vents with towels. If the air is dry, block the vents with *wet* towels. If it's too noisy or too quiet, turn on the room ventilation system fan to provide some "white noise" to block out outside noise and create some sound inside. Some people swear by leaving the TV on all night at low volume (just make sure you don't leave the TV set to a pay-for-view movie channel!).

Some business travelers recommend keeping to your normal sleeping and wake up times if you are only one or two time zones away from home. Others recommend staying out, working in your hotel room, or reading a boring book until you are ready to fall asleep. Try both and see what works for you.

✔ *Keep up with friends and family.* Would you normally be talking with friends and family if you were at home during the time you are on a business trip? If so, call them from the road. Don't let your relationships with friends and family slide because you are traveling. Although we may think of calling our immediate families when we travel, we rarely chat with friends. Being cut off from friends and social life is stressful. With telephone calling cards, you can bill your long-distance calls to your home phone if you don't want them to show up on your hotel bill. This is a powerful way to make yourself feel better about traveling and to make other people feel good, too.

✔ *Take some time to enjoy where you are and see a bit of the surrounding area.* Too often business travel becomes all work and no play, as we try to cram in a maximum of business and visits with as many people as possible. But it makes a huge difference to your state of mind if you take time to stick your nose outside the office and see what's there. Local people love to show off their home town.

Dealing with Jet Lag

Jet lag is a term most business travelers are intimately familiar with, yet few understand that it is a true medical condition. Everyone has an internal clock that dictates when we are hungry, tired, and wide awake. When we cross several time zones, our day, as measured by a clock, becomes longer or shorter, and our bodies aren't able to adjust immediately to that change. The result is fatigue, poor memory, reduced physical and mental activity, and the inability to sleep. Those who have experienced its effects say that when jet lag is really bad, "your brain goes out to lunch," and you can find yourself not remembering what you said in business meetings!

Jet lag tends to be worse when flying east (which shortens our day) than when flying west (which lengthens it). It is more likely to affect people over thirty who normally follow an established daily routine. Many business travelers have found that it can take up to half a day for their bodies to adjust for each time zone crossed.

What is the best way to cope with jet lag? Research has shown that the "feast and famine" diets for several days prior to a long flight don't work as well as was once thought. If you are going east, you might try going to bed earlier than usual for a few days before you leave, and if you are going west, try staying up later. Taking evening flights often helps, particularly if you can sleep on the plane; as does avoiding alcohol and heavy meals. If it is a relatively short flight, you might try timing your arrival so that you arrive in the early evening and can go to bed early. For a long flight, which gets you at your destination midday, forego a nap once you get to your hotel. Try to stay awake and go to bed slightly earlier on local time. Getting regular exercise once you arrive can also help readjust your body rhythms. Smart travelers allow a full day to recuperate before starting business meetings if they are going to Europe from the United States.

Then again, "terminal jet lag" can be a good excuse for minor lapses in performance, or for just about anything you need a socially acceptable excuse. So we leave it up to you to determine whether fighting jet lag has positive, or negative, benefits!

Information Overload and Computerization of the Workplace

The Information Tidal Wave

If you feel that you are literally drowning in a sea of information, you are not alone. All types of professionals are caught in an "information squeeze"— the volume of information we need to absorb to do our jobs is growing exponentially, just as our careers and family commitments are taking more and more of our time. We have more to read than ever before, and less time in which to read it. That in itself can be stressful, but the rapidly changing business environment, which requires continued monitoring, has made it even worse.

Now we feel guilty about that rapidly growing stack of journals, newsletters, newspapers, and magazines on the floor in our living rooms and on the bookshelves in our offices. You could say we suffer from "information anxiety"—the gap Richard Wurman describes in his book *Information Anxiety* as the "widening difference between what you think you *should* understand and what you *can* understand."

And paper information is not the only problem. Almost all of us have had computer information forced on us, along with faxes, voice and electronic mail, cellular phones (so we can't even escape the phone in our cars or on airplanes), answering machines, VCRs, audio and videotapes, and cable television. Every way we turn, some form of information is pulling at us. We also feel we have to have an opinion on all of it. Wasn't the computer age supposed to make things easier for us?

The problem is that computers haven't developed to the point where they can really help us, because what we need is not information, but knowledge. We need a sifting and synthesizing of all that data to find patterns—to make sense of it. And that is still a long way off.

Coping with Information Overload

There are some tactics you can use to help you cope with this sea of information. Some people like yourself who deal with it on a daily basis provided the following tips:

✔ *Give yourself permission not to know everything about everything.* Most of us feel that we have to know absolutely every current thing going on in our fields. We feel that if we don't, something will come up of which we were unaware, and we'll look stupid. That rarely is the case. No one can know everything! Instead of straining for omniscience, practice asking for clarification when you are unfamiliar with something that comes up in work-related conversation. Not only will you get the information you need without having to dig for it, chances are the other person will feel flattered that you asked.

✔ *Determine exactly what information you need to do your job adequately.* Don't say "everything"! Since we have so much to skim through, we have to work with a purpose. And that purpose should be to find information that is relevant to what we need to know to do our jobs. Much time is wasted reading irrelevant information—so don't get caught in this time trap.

✔ *Practice "rip and read."* As soon as you can after you get a new journal, newspaper, or other publication, quickly scan the table of contents. Then flip to the articles that are of interest to you, and rip them out of the publication. Staple the pages together, put them into a file folder marked "reading," and *toss the rest of the publication into the wastebasket.* You accomplished three things: First the scan of the table of contents gave you a quick mental picture of what was important in the publication, and you absorbed more information from that scan than you might think. Second, you have determined what is relevant to you from that publication, and set it aside to be read. Third, you have eliminated a visual stressor from your workplace—the growing stack of publications.

Be honest: If you let the publications stack up, how likely are you to go back and even open them for the first time? You are more likely to take the folder of ripped-out articles with you on your commute or on plane trips than a stack of publications. The folder is less daunting, it weighs far less, and you choose the articles.

✔ *Always take your reading file with you on business trips.* Sitting in the airport, on planes, or in a hotel room just demands that you have something to read. And if you have your reading file along, you can get something useful accomplished while you kill time. The same concept applies if you commute by train or bus. Reading can help you unwind after a long, stressful day at work!

✔ *Let others do the scanning for you.* Another option is to put a route list of colleagues and staff members (with your name last) on relevant publications, with a note asking them to highlight information or articles they think are important. By the time the publication gets to you, you can skim what everyone else highlighted, learn what is relevant, and be done with it very quickly.

If you do have a staff, assign important work-related books to be read, and have them prepare a short report. The reports can be distributed or discussed at staff meetings, which serves the purpose of keeping everyone up to date on the latest in their field—not just you.

✔ *Try audio information sources if reading is just too time consuming.* Common sense dictates that you shouldn't read in some places, such as driving a car on the commute home, during your early morning run, or when you are doing physical tasks around the house. Today, a wide variety of collections of important business information are available on audio tape. Some even come out weekly or monthly. Some people find they retain the information better when they listen to it.

To find these audio collections, check out professional societies, professional journals, or audio tape stores. Yes, there are audio tape stores where you can rent tapes by the day or week—just as you would a tape for your VCR. Most major bookstores carry cassettes of major business books. You can ask your company librarian to research them for you—and share the tapes with your colleagues.

The same concept holds true for videotapes. If you like to turn into a couch potato when you go home, but can't find anything worth watching on TV, you might want to explore educational videotapes. Not only are digests of important industry news available, but you can watch presentations by major business consultants or interviews with industry executives, or even learn a new computer skill.

✔ *Set up a customized search profile on major on-line databases used in your field.* More and more on-line data sources are allowing users to establish customized search criteria that are stored on a computer and then run daily against new information added to the database. If any new, appropriate information is detected, it is either sent to you via fax, or electronic or express mail, or downloaded directly to your computer—without your ever having to lift a finger to retrieve that information. Unfortunately, the price tag is high. You are paying for convenience but, in some circumstances, it may be worth it.

✔ *Ask to have your name removed from distribution lists for interoffice reports and mailing lists for publications that do not apply directly to your job or field.* This sounds like a small thing, but it really helps. For some reason, many people feel they have to at least look at every piece of paper or publication that crosses their desk—even materials that are not totally relevant to their job. You'll save yourself time, guilt, and stress if you simply prevent irrelevant publications from hitting your in box!

You can winnow your inflow even more if you work at it. For the next couple of months, keep track of which publications really provide you with the information you need to do your job—not just one or two articles, but several—all of which are relevant to what you need to know to stay abreast of changes in your field. The number usually is less than 5 or 10. Then look for duplication of information in those publications—which you will probably find. After you've done that, select the 3 to 5 publications that give you the most bang for your buck, and *read those religiously.* Trash the rest! You'll still be well informed, but a lot less stressed out!

So if you are creative, there are ways you can reduce your "information anxiety" and make keeping up with your field far less stressful. A very nice side benefit is that research has shown that you retain more information when you are not stressed out while you read it!

Creeping Computerization

As mentioned earlier, computers were supposed to help us, to save us work by doing work for us. Many professionals from all fields would argue this point, for it seems that computerization has *increased* the work we have to do—what with word processing, spreadsheets, electronic mail, presentation preparation, and so on. And it has allowed management to reduce support staff head count. Now, if you want copying done, you have to do it yourself.

We seriously doubt that these trends are going to be reversed. So we're going to have to find innovative ways to cope with this situation, ways that will help us get our work done without spending lots of time doing it. The following tactics may be useful:

↙ *If you use a computer application, take a class to learn how to use it effectively and efficiently.* Too many people think that they can learn an application simply by playing around with the software. This is partially true—you may be able to learn the basic concepts behind the software and happen upon ways to perform certain of its functions. But continuing to use that certain way to get something done without thinking much about it—even if it takes seven steps to perform that function—is probably not the optimal approach. Chances are good that there is a way to do that function with only one or two keystrokes, but you won't discover it unless you take a class.

If you don't have time to go to class or are uncomfortable in that environment, try some of the widely available computer-based training materials. These include audio tapes with tutorials, videotapes that show you what to do, and even special training disks that you use in conjunction with a workbook. All can be used at your convenience, and in the privacy of your office or at home.

Understand that all software has a learning curve, meaning that it takes a given amount of time to get the hang of it, and to be able to use it well enough to see improvements in your productivity. This learning curve varies for every application and for every person—some people take to computers faster than others. So don't expect to become an expert right away. But anyone can learn how to use a computer effectively—it just takes commitment and effort.

However you do it, get the training you need to be effective and efficient. You pursued advanced education in your field because you couldn't pick up enough information on your own, didn't you? Why do you think using a computer should be any different?

✔ *Turn on the prioritization features of your electronic and/or voice mail system(s).* Most systems today have a feature that lets you determine which incoming messages are urgent or from certain important people—or at least let you scan the names of the senders of the messages. Think of it as "Robo-mailman" inside the computer. Few things are more stressful than being faced with 11 voice mail messages (at least three minutes each in length), only to find that the most important one is the next to last message. The same holds true for electronic mail messages, which at least *seem* to take longer to get through because you have to read them and you can't put them on the speaker phone and do something else while you listen. If you don't know how to initialize prioritization features on your systems, ask someone who does know!

✔ *Set aside a fixed period of time each day to go through your voice and electronic mail messages, faxes, and in box; and let people know not to interrupt you during that time.* Our tendency is to attend to each message as it hits our computer screen or lights up the little red blinking light on our phones, and address each fax or piece of mail as it crosses our desks. But that interrupts our work flow and thought processes. As we track down information and try to resolve the problems brought to us with these missives, other tasks get set aside and nothing gets completely finished. For most of us, this state of affairs is very stressful.

If we go through these messages at a fixed time, we can determine which are important and prioritize, delegate, and act on them—helping us gain more control over our work day and our time. Getting control means reducing stress levels.

You may need to experiment a bit to find which times work best for you. Some people go through their electronic and voice mail messages first thing in the morning and then again late in the afternoon. Others just do it once a day—when they first arrive. Ask yourself if you really need to check those messages more frequently than that. Some managers and professionals go through their regular in box just once a day or handle faxes as soon as they come in. Whatever works best for you, stick to the routine. This technique helps only if you practice it regularly.

✔ *Make it a habit to forward your phone for a block of time each day while you attend to urgent business and decision making.* Again, the goal is to reduce interruptions so that you can have a concentrated block of time to get priority tasks out of the way. You will be amazed at what you can accomplish when you remove distractions and focus on getting the job done.

✔ *Make full use of the information technology at your disposal.* Most people are only partial consumers of the technology that is available to them—usually because they never take the time really to understand what the technology can do for them. Instead of just leaving your name and number, send detailed voice mail messages; send an email message instead of a paper memo; try conference calls between several locations instead of holding a meeting; experiment with videoconferencing instead of traveling—in short, make creative use of technology to help reduce the number of situations that can cause you stress.

✔ *If at all possible, don't overdo office technology at home.* The point here is to maintain a separation between work and home to help you compartmentalize your life and reduce your stress levels. Although it may be helpful to have a computer at home to catch up on work once in awhile, to work on an emergency presentation, or for your children to do their homework on, draw the line there. Unless absolutely necessary, skip the fax machine, leased telephone line to the overseas offices, and 35 mm slide maker. All these items will do is provide a constant reminder of the problems at work or make you feel guilty that you aren't using them. Either way, they bode ill for reducing your stress.

These are just a few ways you can personally customize your use of technology to help you function more effectively. We strongly support the use of anything that will help you reduce your stress levels, but although it can be tremendously powerful and help us totally change the way we conduct business, technology can also become a major stressor. By experimenting and learning, you will be able to determine what is the appropriate use of technology for you. Don't be afraid of it, but don't become a slave to it, either!

5
Burn Out and Other Special Situations

Burn Out—When It All Gets to Be Too Much

As you can see, working life today can be extremely stressful. What happens when motivated, idealistic, committed, bright people choose a career because it promised a lifetime of satisfaction, would give their lives meaning, and maybe, would make the world a little better place—only to find several years later that stress seems to be unrelenting, they really won't be able to achieve the high career goals they set for themselves, and they probably won't make a major impact on their company? These top performers are prime candidates for burn out.

The Reality of Burn Out

Burn out is physical, emotional, and mental exhaustion caused by long-term involvement in situations that are emotionally demanding and very stressful, combined with high personal expectations for one's performance. It happens when work loses its meaning, and the ratio of stress to rewards leans heavily towards stress. People who are most prone to burn out are those who need and want to feel that they are doing something useful and important at work—in short, the best and brightest.

Some theorists contend that *all* jobs have three stages—which they call the "learn-do-teach" cycle of work. In the first stage, you learn your job—the skills, specific tasks, and politics of a specific job function. This period is typically very stressful, but workers handle the stress well because they are challenged and excited by the new job and because they are rewarded by seeing results coming from their growing mastery of the position. The length of time a person stays at this stage is determined by the complexity of the job, the existing knowledge a person already has, and the available learning and support sources.

After the basics have been mastered, a worker moves into the do phase— you "just do it" every day, every week, and feel a sense of satisfaction and mastery in getting the job done well. If the rewards are adequate, and stress and frustration are kept to tolerable levels, employees can stay in this part of the cycle for a very long period of time.

Eventually, however, you learn all that you can about your job and its intricacies, and you reach a point where you feel you can do it with your eyes closed. At that point, it becomes important for you, as an expert, to pass on your knowledge and skills to others—to teach—so that you can move on to something else, learn something new, and repeat the learn-do-teach cycle with all of its excitement and rewards.

If you are prevented from moving on to learning new things (which is very common in some organizations that don't want to promote valuable team players out of the position they have mastered), or if stress, pressure, and frustration continue at high levels, the symptoms of burn out can begin to creep into your working life.

Symptoms of Burn Out

Sometimes the symptoms of burn out can be missed and attributed to other situational stresses or life changes. But close examination reveals that there are three sides to burn out:

- *Physical exhaustion.* This aspect is characterized by fatigue, nausea, muscle tension, changes in eating and sleeping habits, and generally a low energy level. Probably the first symptom most sufferers notice is a general malaise, an ennui with no apparent cause. Sometimes people say, "I don't know, I just get so tired by lunch or early afternoon."

- *Emotional exhaustion.* This is expressed as feeling frustrated, hopeless, trapped, helpless, depressed, sad, apathetic about work. People say they feel that their "soul is dying" or report frequently feeling irritated or angry for no specific reason. The scariest part is when they just don't care anymore about parts of their job that were really important to them earlier in the cycle.

- *Mental exhaustion.* Sufferers are dissatisfied with themselves, their jobs, and life in general, while feeling inadequate, incompetent, or inferior—even though they are not any of those things. Over time, mental exhaustion causes people to see customers, patients, clients, or colleagues as sources of irritation and problems rather than as challenges or opportunities. They also tend to believe that there is something wrong with themselves because the work that once gave them such pleasure has gone stale and flat. Then they add self-blame to the mental exhaustion mix.

Although many of these symptoms occur in other stress-related problems, such as depression and alienation, there are significant differences. Clinical depression tends to affect all aspects of a person's life, whereas people suffering from burn out can function very well in the nonwork aspects of their lives. Alienation is common in people who never expected anything from their jobs but a paycheck, while burn out candidates are highly motivated, committed workers. The time component is indicative: Burn out occurs over a long period of time, in contrast to other responses to severe situational stress that happen rapidly when a particular stressor occurs in a person's life.

Reactions to Burn Out

People typically respond to burn out in a number of ways—all of which impact their job performance:

- *Change jobs.* This is the first thing most people consider during the early stages of burn out. They look around inside their present organization to see if there is something else they could do that would get them away from the demands of their current job. If nothing appears appropriate, they may look for a similar position with a different organization, thinking that a change is all that is needed. Sometimes this works, and both the company and the employee benefit. But for many people, burn out comes back.

- *Move up to a management position.* A burn out victim who had been in the front lines of customer, client, or patient contact, may think that moving to the administrative arena would relieve some of the pressure and stress. Occasionally this works, because some people *are* better suited to administration than to the front lines, and they can be valuable contributors to the organization from a different position. Others find that their burned out attitudes are transmitted to the people they now manage.

- *Endure it.* People who value stability and emotional security often decide just to stay where they are, hang in there, and wait it out until retirement. These are the employees most organizations consider dead wood, and today are often prime candidates for layoffs. If they are able to function adequately in their positions, the drain on the company may not be too great. If, however, they block change and improvement, the cost to the organization can be very great.

- *Change professions.* Some burn out sufferers decide that maybe they made a mistake when they originally chose their professions, and they make a career switch. They go off into business on their own or to a completely new field.

Sometimes this works, but very often they have feelings of failure and guilt, and regret having wasted their time—especially if they invested many years in school and training. The loss of trained professionals is a high cost for companies to pay. After making a change, some people go on to do well in their new career, others find that the depression and feelings of self-doubt follow them to their new job.

- *Move ahead.* This response is the most productive of all, as it uses burn out as a launching pad for personal growth by reassessing priorities, tapping unused skills and potential, and cultivating new strengths and abilities.

Causes and Cures

It is important to understand two things about burn out. First of all, the root cause *does not* lie within the person suffering from it. The biggest cause is a dysfunctional work environment—a work environment that permits unrelenting levels of stress, frustration, and pressure for long periods of time, yet offers few rewards to people for putting up with all of that. Second, if we subscribe to the learn-do-teach cycle theory, there is the potential that burn out can occur several times during our working lives—as we master each new job function we are given.

This means that if we want to conquer burn out, there are two fronts for attack. The first is to take a hard look at the work environment itself. Chronic work overload, dead-end jobs, excessive red tape and paperwork, poor communication and feedback, lack of rewards, and absence of a support system are all major contributors to burn out. They are also components that can be changed, if management is willing to do so.

True, a cost is associated with making a change. Redesigning jobs to give people a sense of their importance to the organization and opportunities for growth takes time and effort. Making sure employees aren't overcrowded means providing more office space, good lighting, comfortable furniture, and appropriate technology—which is a capital expense. Assuring that workers aren't assigned an overload of customers, clients, or patients may mean hiring more workers. Increasing work breaks and vacation time costs money. Assuring that management provides adequate feedback, encouragement, and compliments takes effort, but it is probably the most important means of avoiding employee burn out. Rebuilding the organization's reward and promotion structure is often a major undertaking. And reassessing policies, rules, and regulations to reduce red tape, paperwork, and bureaucratic bungling takes commitment, time, and effort—all of which come with a cost.

The key is understanding that there is a high cost to be paid for fostering conditions that promote burn out—contrary to what many managers believe today. That cost comes from absenteeism, lowered performance and morale, increased turnover, and, ultimately, decline in employees' physical health—which is reflected in rising health-care costs for stress-related ill-nesses.

Second, because we all will go through the learn-do-teach cycle several times during our working lives, there are some things we can do for ourselves that may help, at least to some degree, to counteract an unhealthy work environment. Not only will these coping strategies help us in our work life, but they can help us in our personal and family life as well:

✔ *Understanding your personal work and stress reaction styles.* If we work to understand our reactions more completely, we can learn to identify behavior patterns that are no longer working effectively for us. Once we have identified them, we can go about changing those patterns. Chapter 1 of this book provides you with questionnaires and surveys that help you learn more about yourself. The rest of this book can help you begin to change unproductive behavior patterns.

✔ *Reassessing your values, goals, and priorities.* Unrealistic goals for our careers and performance virtually guarantee that we will become frustrated and disillu-sioned. Most of us set vague career goals for ourselves early in our lives, and we never stop to see if they are still appropriate, given how both we and the business world today have changed. We may be operating under goals that no longer make sense for us, or priorities that are no longer important. Later chapters will provide you with tools to take a good look at what you want, where you are going, and how to get there.

✔ *Compartmentalizing your life.* By compartmentalizing, we mean *segmenting* the different parts of your life: work, home, community, and so on. Focus as much as possible on each compartment when you are in it—and then don't think about it when you move on to another compartment. For example, you would immerse yourself totally in your job when you were at work, but leave it behind, along with its paperwork, frustration, and worries, when you headed for home.

This skill is definitely an acquired one. But compartmentalizing is an important skill to master, because people who let work and nonwork stresses overlap tend to have higher rates of burn out. Later chapters of this book will provide you with information on a variety of decompression and coping techniques that can help you begin to reduce your areas of stress overlap and start determining appropri-ate compartments for your life.

✔ *Building a social support system.* Everybody needs friends, and this is particularly true for people in high-pressure positions. We need many kinds of friends and colleagues. We need people who: will lend a willing ear and a soft shoulder just to listen to us vent, without judging our words, thoughts, or actions; are knowledge-able in our field, have our best interests at heart, and can give us honest praise and criticism when we need it; will back us no matter what, think we are terrific, and serve as our own private cheering sections; share our interests, values, views, and priorities, and provide us with a reality check when things get crazy; and like to do the same hobbies, pursuits, and fun stuff we like to do.

It is highly unlikely that any 1 (or even 5 or 10) person(s) can fulfill all these different kinds of needs. We need to continue to develop and nurture friendships and relationships throughout our lives.

So if you think you are experiencing burn out, take heart. It does not have to be devastating, and we have found that it can actually be growth-promoting. You can survive and come out happier, healthier, and stronger. Burn out is simply an opportunity for change, and it is up to you and your employers to take advantage of that opportunity when it presents itself.

A Special Note to Those Raised in Dysfunctional Families

Whether we are aware of it or not, all of us attempt to duplicate our family of origin in the workplace. Our coworkers become our siblings, and our managers and supervisors become our parents. Just as we did at home as children, we squabble with our coworkers and seek approval from our bosses. For most of us, this doesn't cause any major problems (except for the occasional stress flare-up when we get into a disagreement with a coworker).

But recently it has become clear that people raised in dysfunctional families—where alcohol or drug abuse, emotional or physical abuse, neglect, incest, or severe workaholism were present—carry vestiges of the problems caused by their family of origin with them well into adulthood. These issues commonly come to the surface in intimate relationships and on the job. These are also places where other kinds of stress are found as well, and unresolved family issues can dramatically compound those stressors.

The Struggle for Success in the Workplace

Overall, these folks make wonderful employees. The vast majority are superachievers who are superresponsible. They are hard workers, dedicated, loyal, competent, resourceful, and adept at figuring out other people's needs—all qualities they had to develop at home in order to survive. Most of the problems they experience are internal—the stresses they feel are based on their perception of themselves as not good enough, not capable enough, or not worthy of the successes they achieve. Children learn to believe in themselves when their parents provide a stable, loving, caring, respectful environment for the child. But people from dysfunctional families may not have had that, so they haven't learned how to feel good about themselves.

As a result, they try to overcompensate for their perceived failings by taking on more projects, working longer hours, helping colleagues out of jams, doing everything perfectly, and overcommitting themselves. This sets the stage for severe stress overload, which can easily lead to an early burn out.

Common Myths

People raised in dysfunctional families often carry around with them a host of myths about working and work relationships. Not every person believes every one of these myths completely, but most can see themselves in at least three or four. In her book, *The Self-Sabotage Syndrome: Adult Children in the Workplace,* Janet Woititz outlines these common myths:

■ *"If I don't get along with my boss, it is all my fault."* People from dysfunctional families believe that if a relationship does not go right, there is something wrong with them. They will do everything they can think of to help make the working relationship work. If it does not, they take it as a sign of personal failure. But sometimes something is wrong with the boss, or the work situation is simply wrong for the person.

■ *"If I am not productive, I am worthless."* As a child, many people from dysfunctional families had to take care of themselves and sometimes their siblings. So they are used to working hard all of the time. Working hard was also a way many people proved to their families that they were worthwhile. After awhile, working hard became an automatic response, and many people from dysfunctional families carry that over to the workplace. They are the people who put in the extra hours, take on the extra projects, are always there when you need them—in short, excellent workers. But this sort of workaholism can lead to burn out because they are continually trying to prove to themselves and those around them that they are worthwhile.

■ *"If I am not suited for the job I'm supposed to be suited for, there is something wrong with me."* Almost all of us at one time or another have had someone tell us that we would make an ideal physician, teacher, manager, scientist, or even cab driver. We may try one of these jobs, only to find that it just doesn't fit us. But people from dysfunctional families don't trust their gut reactions—for a long time they have believed that other people knew what was right for them far better than they themselves did, so they stick with careers or promotions for which they really are not suited.

■ *"I am afraid they will find out that I am not capable of doing the job, and I am not worthy of having it."* This is an exaggeration of the imposter phenomenon, discussed earlier. These folks feel that if they don't continue to prove themselves, people will find out that they really don't know what they're doing. This happens because they got double messages from their parents as they were growing up. Whenever they did a great job or brought home a good report card, there was always a "but" attached to it—as in "That's great, but you didn't do...." or "A B+ is good, but why didn't you get an A?" After you hear this for awhile, especially from your parents, you start to believe that you aren't capable and that you can't do anything really well.

This mind set is terribly destructive, especially in a work environment where the person is treated with respect and valued—and is successful. People from dysfunctional families desperately want recognition, but they don't trust its accuracy— which creates an excruciating approach-avoidance conflict. They are terribly afraid that if their employers and coworkers *really* knew them, they would see what awful people they really are—even though there is not a shred of truth to back that up. This feeling is very hard to shake. It is also a potent stress inducer.

■ *"I should be able to do whatever is asked of me. If I say no, I will be replaced."* People from dysfunctional families spent most of their lives dealing with unreasonable demands from family members. So the unreasonable becomes normal. They also believe that they could easily be replaced, which they heard often enough growing up. So no matter how outrageous the demands at work, they believe that they do not have the right to say no, to say that what they are working on currently has a higher priority.

■ *"Anything that goes wrong is my fault. Anything that goes right is the result of fate, luck, or chance."* These people have been told this all the time they were growing up, and by now the feeling is an automatic response to a situation where something goes wrong. In the workplace, if someone is unhappy, the person from a dysfunctional family will think that it was something they did. If the report isn't quite right, even though they weren't responsible for the section that was wrong, they will worry about it. But if something goes well—if, for example, they land the big account—they discredit the success by believing they were just lucky.

■ *"I shouldn't have to ask my boss for what I need."* This doesn't mean that they think their boss should be a psychic or clairvoyant; rather they believe that they would be imposing to ask for what they need. And when they asked for something in the past at home, they rarely got it; or, if they did, even bigger problems came up. So they don't ask—they make do, they take care of it themselves—just like they have always done.

Much of the time, this may not be a problem. But suppose a situation developed where they really did need a boss's help on a project. People from dysfunctional families find it very difficult, if not impossible, to ask for assistance. Unfortunately, if they don't get the help they need, a work project may suffer, which reinforces all the negative feelings they have about their capabilities.

■ *"I should be able to fix it."* It doesn't matter what *it* is—these people spent their whole lives attempting to fix everything that was wrong in their families. It is what they know how to do best. In the workplace this is a wonderful skill, but many coworkers (and bosses) take advantage of it, take credit for the success, and take the person from the dysfunctional family for granted. In some ways, this is approval-seeking behavior, but it can backfire when the person ends up overcommitted, overworked, and overstressed.

■ *"Change is threatening. I should try to keep things the way they always were."* People from dysfunctional families always have to know where they stand, where the exits are, what their options are. They like to have all their bases covered, so they can plan a reaction to any eventuality. This behavior pattern served them well growing up because they were continually faced with not knowing what was going to happen next. But, as a result, they crave stability. Sudden change, such as a reorganization, move to a new facility, or switch in projects, can be completely unnerving for them, because they haven't had time to work through the possibilities. So they may overreact to changes or try to prevent them—even though they know they are necessary for the business.

Dealing with the Myths

Unfortunately, these myths about the workplace and working relationships don't go away by themselves. They go away only if they are brought into the open and dealt with by the person raised in a dysfunctional family. The amount of stress these myths can cause impacts not only performance on the job, but physical health.

So if you (or someone you supervise) comes from a dysfunctional family and you think that the previously mentioned myths may be impacting your performance at work or causing undue stress, do yourself a favor. Talk with your physician or clergyperson about it. Get a referral to a therapist who specializes in this sort of problem, a support group, or a therapy group. More and more support groups are being formed, and there are a number of books available on the subject. But get yourself the help you need, because you deserve a rewarding, fulfilling, low-stress work life.

The Bottom Line

The bottom line is that working life has gotten more stressful over the past five years, and we do not expect this pattern to change. If anything, work will continue to become even more stressful. In order to cope successfully with these higher levels of stress, we must not only understand the causes, but also expand our use of coping techniques to ameliorate the damage to our bodies these stressors can cause, and then do everything we can to balance our work life with a fulfilling personal life. The rest of this book will help you achieve this personal bottom line.

6
If You're Single

Stress at Home:
The Myth of Having It All

Everyone experiences stress at home. Yes, *everyone*, whether they are single, part of a couple, or parents. That is because everything in life is a trade-off: Every time you say yes to one thing, by default you say no to something else. The great myth today is that you can have it all, but that notion is just that—a myth.

In reality, everyone has only 24 hours a day. If you try to fit everything in that you want to do or feel you *should* do—work, quality time with your partner and family, exercise, friends, hobbies, spirituality, self-improvement, stress-coping activities, and so on—you run the risk either of feeling inadequate because you aren't able to do it all, or of totally exhausting yourself. Both lead to stress overload. You need to determine what is *really* important to you, set priorities, and weed out the rest. Subsequent chapters help you do just that.

The other myth is that the grass is greener on the other side of the fence. Singles think couples have it made, couples envy singles, and working parents often wish they were anyone else! We're here to tell you that each group has its own special joys, and its own special hassles. Although singles can experience significant amounts of stress at home, dual-career couples experience most of the same stressors and additional challenges since two people's needs and desires have to be accommodated in the relationship. Parents are faced with most of those same potential stressors, *plus* additional issues and concerns in raising and providing for their children.

In Chaps. 6–9 we explore the nature of stress as experienced in the home by single people, couples, and parents.

The Single Life

Recent estimates indicate nearly 10 percent of all Americans—approximately 23 million—live alone, either by choice or by circumstance. That number is huge, and it gets larger every year. More and more people are staying single longer than ever before, and even more people find themselves living alone due to divorce or death of a partner.

Given the prevailing cultural bias toward coupledom, many single adults are exposed to additional stress because of their marital status. Those singles view living alone to be less desirable and frustrating—and they hope it is only a temporary condition. That is not to say that there are no benefits from being single. Greater independence, freedom, and more time for oneself and one's interests are a real luxury. Many singles don't focus on these benefits, though. They just look at the negatives, causing increased stress for themselves.

Alone or Lonely?

Our society links being alone with being lonely, which is terribly unfortunate. Alone simply means apart from anything or anyone else, whereas lonely means unhappy at being alone; longing for friends, etc. It is definitely possible to be alone without being lonely.

In her book *Positive Solitude: A Practical Program for Mastering Loneliness and Achieving Self-Fulfillment*, Rae Andre reminds us that loneliness isn't a true emotion. She believes the word is a convenient way to mask deeper issues, such as fatigue, insecurity, frustration, stress, anger, boredom, and disillusionment. The key is that these issues are tangible and correctable, using many of the coping techniques outlined later in this book.

Work Time vs. Personal Time

Building a career, especially in the early stages, takes a tremendous amount of time, effort, and energy. However, it is particularly easy for singles to get trapped or become overcommitted by their work loads. This occurs for several reasons:

1. In many companies, managers and supervisors tend to give to singles assignments requiring extra hours or travel, simply because they assume there are no family responsibilities that could cause conflicts. This can be boon or a bane, depending on the person's situation. If the projects are interesting, rewarding, and career-enhancing, the extra hours might not be stressors. If the projects are drudgery, keep the person away from friends and family, or hamper development of new relationships, this common practice may unwittingly become a major cause of stress.

2. Many singles also take on additional work when their social and personal lives are not going as well as they would like. It's a logical, human reaction: If you're not going out frequently with friends or dating, you have hours that need to be filled. Work can consume all that time and more. Unfortunately, working long hours eventually reduces their personal lives even more; to fill the void, they make even more work commitments until all the person is doing is working. This pattern can go on for a very long time, particularly if the work is enjoyable and they get "strokes" and rewards for being diligent and dedicated. The problem arises when someone interesting *does* come along or an exciting opportunity for fun presents itself, and they can't take advantage of it because of previously made work commitments. If a crisis arises—an illness or a situation where they need to rely on someone for assistance—they may find that there are no friends or support network left.

3. Singles also tend to do the same sorts of things on the weekends that they do during the week, and this can greatly add to stress overload. When they get swamped at work, they either bring it home or go into the office on the weekend. If they don't go into the office, they may tend to develop projects or tasks at home that they treat like work projects!

You can use some of the following strategies to prevent yourself from falling into these traps:

1. *First learn to "just say no" to some commitments, assignments, or projects—at work and at home.* You don't have to accept or do *everything* that comes your way, just because it is offered. Nor do you have to take on new or additional tasks and projects at home, just because all your friends or neighbors are doing similar things.

2. *Make sure your weekends are different from your work weeks.* Read through the "Weekends and Vacations" section of Chap. 11. Do at least two relaxing activities each weekend. To be really relaxing, they should be completely different from what you do at work. Get away for awhile. Give yourself a change of scenery—where you can't see your work. Whatever you do, don't let chores take up a full day. Set a time limit and do the most urgent jobs first. When you reach the time limit, quit!

3. *Also important is setting aside time to "transition" into your life at home.* This means establishing a routine for decompressing from work either on the way home or immediately upon arrival home. Check out the section "Making the Transition between Work and Home" in the "Couples" chapter for ideas on how to set up your routine.

4. *Next, be kind to yourself.* Again check out the coping techniques compendium chapter to get ideas on hobbies, friends and supporters, "guilty" pleasures, etc.—activities that can fill up your time while providing you with an opportunity to recharge your batteries and expand your network of

friends. Think of yourself as a cup holding a liquid that corresponds to all the ways you give to other people. By the time the weekend rolls around, chances are that your giving levels are very low, and need to be replenished. Hobbies, friends, exercise, grand passions, and activities that you do *just for you* provide the self-nurturance you need to get your cup filled up again for another week.

5. *Force yourself to "stay in the market" and actively pursue a social life.* It takes effort and energy and you run the risk of rejection, but human beings need other human beings, and friends and lovers don't just magically appear.

Money

"What problems can singles possibly have with money?" you can just hear couples and parents asking. Singles do view money as a stressor, and that stress usually comes from not having enough. Costs are so out of hand today that it seems that two incomes are required to maintain even a middle-class lifestyle. With only one income, it is hard to keep up with friends and neighbors, and for many singles, this can be very stressful. Sometimes this fuels the drive for the next promotion or transfer at work—with all the pressures that entails. Other times it leads to overextending oneself with credit cards or loans—or spending everything on needs today, and not setting aside enough for the future and retirement.

The only real way to deal with money is to get a firm grip on your values, goals and priorities. Once you have a true picture of where you want to be financially, you can begin to determine how to use the funds you have available to you to move toward that lifestyle. Too many singles don't take the time to do this, thinking that it matters only if you have a spouse or family. But how can you know whether you have arrived if you don't know where you are going? Get expert help if you need it, but do develop a long-term plan. Working toward that plan actually *reduces* stress in the long run.

The Chores of Daily Living

Just because you're single doesn't mean you don't have to get groceries, pick up the dry cleaning, maintain the yard, take the car in for repairs, do the laundry, take your pet to the vet, and clean your living space. It just means you don't have another person to help you do these chores! Given the time crunch all of us operate under, nearly everyone, including singles, often wishes for someone to take on the role of housekeeper.

If you don't have such a person, why not hire someone for those chores you hate to do? Many singles say the best thing they ever did was get a maid service or cleaning lady to maintain their living space. There is nothing quite like the feeling of coming home late from a hectic, stressed-out day to a sparkling clean space. True, cost is involved, but it may not be as much as you think. Even in large cities, $30 buys you a couple of hours of cleaning time—a small price to pay to remove a major stressor from your life. And you may be able to get by with a biweekly cleaning.

Other singles have found unique solutions to the time and chore crunch. Some swear by hiring high school students to do yardwork. Others rely on grocery stores that take orders over the phone or via fax and then deliver the goods. Still others have found that by using the free personal shoppers provided by most major department stores, they have been able to reduce the amount of stress experienced when looking for clothing, gifts, and other home purchases. Some entrepreneurs will even stay at your home and wait for the plumber for you!

Relationships and Friendships

Singles say that it has become very difficult to find a mate today. Why is that? What has changed? First, our expectations have changed—often dramatically. Popular culture leads us to believe that our partners should be "true soul mates" who make each other feel complete. Being very attractive, well-off financially, socially acceptable, politically correct, fun and funny, sexy and sensual, totally devoted to meeting our needs, and having an interesting career never hurt either. After all, that's the way it works out in the movies and on television!

Second, by being more rigid in our standards, dating has become a "data dump," an exchange of resumes, as singles strive for enough information to see if the potential mate meets his or her requirements. This creates an atmosphere where the "interviewee" feels resentful at being treated like a work project.

Our culture has instilled in singles a fear of settling. Now no one knows *exactly* what settling means, but it sounds pretty negative, and most people take the term to mean accepting someone less worthy than they are or someone who doesn't meet all of their exacting criteria. After being told for years to "be all that we can be," why would we accept someone less than ourselves? That's because our culture has come to view our partner as a measure of our value, a statement of "who we are." This is the "mate as an accessory" school of thought.

The dating scene today is pervaded by an air of desperation. Society is so geared toward coupledom and families there there is tremendous pressure to get coupled—*fast.* We expect to be able to find the perfect partner just as we would find the perfect job—and on about the same timetable, too. Such desperation doesn't allow time for people to fall in love naturally, after first becoming friends. The more desperate people become, the more foolish their choices are likely to be.

Finally, culture has instilled in us from preschool on that if something comes too easily, it can't possibly be worth too much. In other words, if it doesn't take much effort or work to make a relationship click, it must be somehow inferior. But sometimes the best relationships do come easily, and we no longer trust our gut instincts about them.

The result is a dating environment so stressful that many singles have simply dropped out. Those who still play the game do so defensively and with trepidation. Can you remove the stress from the dating game? Not entirely, because meeting new people, facing rejection, expending effort, and taking risks are stressful by nature. But you can reduce your stress, or keep it a more positive, rewarding kind, if you keep the following in mind:

✔ *Don't take it personally.* Relationships may not work out for a variety of reasons— timing, nonnegotiables (things you won't compromise on), background, upbringing, and so on—all of which have equally to do with both people involved. Don't assume just because one relationship didn't result in marriage that you are doing something horribly wrong or that you are defective.

✔ *Lighten up!* True, looking for a partner is serious. But too many singles approach it with the same level of intensity and drive that they would making a major deal at work. Love tends not to develop in that kind of a situation—it needs space to grow at its own pace, in its own way. So relax a little! Try to have some fun!

✔ *Remember that meeting people is a numbers game, so keep in circulation.* The more people you meet, the greater your chances of finding the Mr. or Ms. Right. There is more than just one, and that's true for everyone. So keep going out, meeting people, and expanding your social sphere. If the old ways of meeting people don't seem to be turning up potential partners, try new ones: Check out singles support groups, political and volunteer organizations, groups geared toward your hobbies and interests, and adult education classes—things you enjoy doing. Your chances of finding someone compatible are much greater when you are participating in an activity you enjoy, because you already have something in common with the other people there.

✔ *Reassess your evaluation criteria and nonnegotiables.* Many singles have a list of criteria for partners that goes on for pages. It would be hard to find anyone to meet them! Revisit your "list" periodically to see whether all the criteria are still important to you and to determine whether they still fit with where you are going in your life. Are criteria on the list because they truly are important to you, or because you think they *should* be there? Rank them in terms of their importance, and focus only on the most essential. You may find that you have a much wider pool of eligible potential mates this way.

A balanced life, one composed of work, friends, family, and activities that make you feel good, is the best preventive medicine for stress overload. Singles deserve, and can achieve, that kind of balanced life just as well as couples and parents. All it takes is a conscious decision to make it a priority!

7
Couples

In 1969, Rapoport and Rapoport developed the term *dual-career* to mean a marriage in which both partners are committed to active pursuit of their own demanding and continually evolving managerial/professional careers, as well as to the development of their relationship and/or family life. We apply the term to any couple in which both partners are pursuing their own careers—married or not, gay or straight.

Since that time, mountains of articles have been written about such couples. The bottom line for all the articles is that loving and working concurrently is no easy task. More importantly, it can be especially difficult because there are no traditional or conventional role models to follow as guidelines. Today's dual-career couples are making it up as they go along.

Although being part of a dual-career couple has a downside, there are benefits. Some are economic: Two managerial/professional incomes allow couples to live very comfortably. A partner is also relieved of the responsibility of being the sole breadwinner. Other benefits are social: Today many senior-level managers and professionals find it advantageous socially to have a partner who has an interesting, successful career. It validates their worth in the sense that they must be pretty interesting and important, too, to attract (and keep) such a partner. Again, this is the "mate as an accessory" school of thought.

Work Time vs. Personal Time

Managing Two Careers

Dual-career couples feel many of the same work-related pressures as singles, but there is a significant difference. The other person's needs, desires, and wishes—and career—have to be taken into account. That consideration is involved for nearly every work-related decision: from whether one partner stays late at the office to whether a promotion or transfer is accepted.

Many people assume that their mate's views about work match their own. This is rarely true, but most of us never take the time to check it out for certain. Guilt, resentment, frustration, and anger can erupt over seemingly inconsequential events, such as whether the couple go to one of the partner's annual company picnic. Sometimes it boils down to "who's job is more important, anyway?"—particularly when a partner has to put in long hours at work or do heavy traveling, while the other partner needs accommodation due to job pressures.

It is very important for couples to understand clearly the values, goals, and priorities each other have regarding their careers. And sometimes we move along in our careers without really thinking about whether the objectives we have set for ourselves are still realistic, given changing business conditions and our personal growth and development as people. Several of the values and goals clarification exercises later in this book can help you in this. Negotiation and compromise are key—but first you have to know your priorities.

Career Changes

If you are like most people, you know at least one friend who has recently made a major career switch. Some people make the change voluntarily: They decide finally to take a shot at doing something they truly want to do with their lives. But the majority have it forced on them, often as the result of corporate downsizing or layoffs due to tough times in their industry or profession.

Although many would argue that making a switch is worse if you have been laid off, even in the best of cases, changing careers is tremendously stressful. Most people today define themselves by what they do, and when that job is no longer there, they can feel a tremendous sense of personal loss. Changing careers is scary—it requires learning new ways of working and different skills; facing the potential for failure and rejection; investing personal savings and capital; frequently spending more time away from home because you are starting your career over from ground zero; and putting yourself on the line in ways you haven't done for quite awhile. It can also bring tremendous feelings of guilt (for making your partner go through this experience), frustration, and a great need for support and nurturing from your partner.

The other partner goes through many changes as well. Economic expectations change, and he or she may worry about being the primary breadwinner until the new career begins to pay off. There is often frustration and anger over the situation and the stress it causes. And there is always guilt—for almost everything—from guilt over feeling frustrated and angry to guilt over sometimes wishing the partner would not have made the career switch.

Supporting and nurturing a partner through this experience is demanding and draining; and if the partner is going through difficult times at work as well, his or her "giving" levels end up at all-time lows. People who have gone through it say the following situations are very stressful: Money, what should be eliminated from the budget, and how remaining funds will be spent; watching what and how you bring up issues or even talk about your own job with your partner; having always to be there to listen; not asking about how things are going with the career switch too often or in the wrong way; and being constantly aware of the partner's mood and adjusting accordingly.

There is no way to get through this period of transition painlessly. It is critical for the partners to talk honestly about what they are feeling, how they are experiencing the change, and what their expectations are of themselves and each other. Later chapters focus on anger, communication, gentle assertiveness, and conflict resolution—good guidelines for facilitating this process.

To adequately support the partner making the change it is also important for the supporting partner to do several self-nurturing things. Self-nurturing activities can range from spending time with hobbies and friends, to getting outside help from a therapist or support group. The coping techniques chapter can give you some ideas. Remember, you can't give to others unless you first give to yourself. And since you are so important to your partner's well-being during this phase of your life together, it's too big a risk not to take adequate care of yourself.

Making the Transition between Work and Home

Five days a week you and your partner do it—come home from work. What do you usually do when you walk in the door? If you start talking about everything that went wrong at work during the day, you are like most dual-career couples. While this may feel natural, it prolongs your work day and causes you to bring work pressures home with you—not good for your stress levels! And you may find that you continue to worry about work while you are home, so you find yourself not refreshed the next day.

If one partner is experiencing stress at work while the other is not, the stress from work can poison the home atmosphere—which neither of you need. How does this happen?

Some men feel they need to solve their partner's work problems, just as they solve problems at work, and often start giving advice when their partners bring up work issues. Many times advice is not wanted or needed, the partner simply wants to sound off or vent feelings. Advice-giving can lead to misunderstandings, and stress for the man, because he may feel pressured to solve a situation that is beyond his control. One way to handle this is to be clear with your partner up front as to whether you want advice or just someone to listen.

Sometimes the stressed-out partner is drained by the end of the day and too tired to talk, share feelings, help around the house, or make love. Dealing with the situation at work has completely depleted giving ability.

Alternatively, partners who communicate or interact with others and solve problems all day long may simply be unable, or unwilling, to do so at home. It is almost as if people can only talk so much in a day, and, if that "talk quota" gets used up at work, may have a real need for being noncommunicative at home in order to "recharge" for another day of communicating at work. In either case, the preferred mode of operation at this point is to turn into a couch potato or simply collapse into bed.

But intimacy requires constant nurturing through communication and sharing, and if this scenario goes on too long, either the nonstressed partner can become stressed out by the lack of attention, or the fragile structure of intimacy can be seriously damaged. Either way, the prognosis is not good for the relationship, and the damaged relationship can become a powerful new stressor.

In the second scenario, the stressed-out partner comes home desperately needing support, nurturing, and unconditional love and acceptance. This is a tall order for the other partner to fulfill—even under the best of circumstances. Most loving partners will try to meet the needs of the suffering partner, and keep on meeting them as long as the need exists. The danger is that the needy partner can become fixed in this behavior. The other partner may continue to give—only to find that no amount is enough.

If this stressful situation goes on for an extended period, the nonstressed partner's "giving levels" become depleted, and frustration and anger can creep into the relationship. This does not bode well for either partner or for the relationship. The stressed-out partner has become a "carrier" of stress, causing the other partner new problems.

Couples should try to avoid either of these scenarios. They put undue stress on an intimate relationship—a relationship that is more important than just about anything. If you see yourself in either scenario, you need to decompress: Establish a daily transition time immediately after you leave work.

That means setting up a routine to follow for the first 20 to 30 minutes after work. It doesn't matter what you do—you could read the newspaper or your favorite mystery paperback on the commuter train on the way home; listen to favorite music on your car radio; or simply meditate quietly. The point is to choose something that relaxes you. Do it regularly—*no matter what*. The routine will give your body a cue, "Relax," and your body will soon learn to do just that for you. But you have to practice using the routine every day to achieve this level of bodily training.

Developing a routine for the first hour or half hour immediately after you arrive home is also important—again to program your body to relax even further. Some people change out of their business clothes into old jeans and a T-shirt or a comfortable robe. Others exercise, do a chore that involves physical labor, take a shower, or work on a hobby until dinner. The key is that this activity should be low-key and quiet—and *should not* involve talking about work.

The whole point of these routines is to help your body learn to relax and leave the pressures of work behind. You may also find that you will get a second wind in the evening, rather than feel that all you can cope with is collapsing in front of the TV. You and your partner will enjoy each other more, and will be able to give each other the support and nurturing you need.

Managing Time

A major stressor for dual-career couples is time management. Time can become a stressor in two ways:

1. Sometimes one partner is "in charge" of time and scheduling, and inadvertently overcommits the other partner or "steals time" that partner needs for other things. The partner in charge may do this unconsciously—because of wanting to spend more time together or the feeling that the other person is working too much. The social calendar becomes a weapon—which is not good for the relationship if "creative scheduling" is used to vent anger or frustration with one's partner.

2. Most couples simply do not have sufficient time for themselves or to spend with their mates, as they juggle career, family, community, religious, and social demands.

Again, unfortunately, there is no easy solution to the problem. You need to realize that you cannot do everything that comes your way, no matter how tempting. Then you have to make a conscious commitment to taking back the control over your time that you previously had given up to others.

The way to do that is to decide what is most important to you, individually and as a couple, and clarify as a couple priorities relating to time and the amount spent on the different parts of your lives. Once both partners have clarified what they want to do, what they have to do, and what they feel they should do, they can negotiate with each other to determine what is really important to do. It is very important to talk about feelings and values around this issue, and work towards a win-win situation. We guarantee an interesting discussion!

The solution becomes careful planning, organizing, and scheduling of time by both partners—for work, community and social life, and for home— religiously. It involves being as considerate of your partner in this regard as you would a colleague at work: When something comes up to change your schedule at work and that will affect others, you let your colleagues know as soon as possible, don't you? Treat your partner with the same respect. But be prepared for the unexpected: Flexibility is the key here, as in all aspects of a successful partnership.

Some couples set aside some time at the beginning of the week (or even daily) to go over their calendars and schedules, and bring each other up to date on work, social, and personal commitments. This way, everyone knows what is going on, and there are no surprises. Other couples go as far as planning intimate time together—sort of like regularly scheduled dates. Don't laugh; This works and is visible proof to partners that they have a high priority to each other. The practice also has an unexpected bonus: When you are under a great deal of stress, these regularly scheduled "breathers" can be a godsend.

It may sound weird, but you might consider planning for sex. We know that everyone says that the "best" sex is spontaneous, but that's a myth. Think about it: When was the last time you did something spontaneously as a couple? Most dual-career couples can't remember. In fact, if most of us were honest, we'd admit that we're so busy we don't have time to do *anything* spontaneously. Many couples in this situation have found that if they don't make sex dates, they don't make love—all that's leftover is the dregs of their days, and then they're too tired. But if you plan time with your partner this way, you can actually *enhance* the experience—especially if you set aside more than half an hour! Think about a session of heavy necking on the couch, a mutual massage, taking a shower or bath together, sharing a bottle of wine or champagne, trying out some new positions. . . .

Money

Some couples say that in relationships, everything boils down to money. While that is sad, it is an accurate representation of the importance of money in our culture. As the song says, "money changes everything"—and not only because it seems there isn't enough of it!

Invariably, couples hold very different ideas about the importance of money: how it should be spent or saved; how it should be managed and who should do it; and whether making more money means more power in the relationship in terms of decision making, accommodation, and compromising. Most of us never stop to reevaluate these beliefs once they are formed during our childhoods. We may not even be able to articulate what our "rules" are. It is also sad, but true, that most couples spend very little time discussing these issues and understanding their differences. Money, and our feelings about it, are still treated as "dirty little secrets" in our society.

As a result, most couples have their fiercest battles and most heated discussions over money-related issues. And they become even more heated when income is threatened or drastically reduced—through unemployment, career change, or illness. Concerns that previously could be comfortably overlooked can take on lives of their own in these situations. Many people also have real fears about the potential of financial insolvency, and can overreact when income or savings drop below acceptable levels.

Couples can greatly reduce the amount of stress generated by misinformation, frustration, and even anger surrounding money matters by clarifying their values, goals, and priorities for money—for the individual and for the couple. The exercises on values later in this book can help, especially those exercises identified for families. Be forewarned that money is an emotionally laden subject for many people, and both partners will have to agree to significant compromising and negotiation to resolve these issues.

The Chores of Daily Living

Couples have the same problems with household chores that singles do, except that there is one more person to contribute to the mess and clutter. True, there is another person available (usually!) to help clean up, but it also means that there is a different interpretation of what "clean up" means! The household often is the most important "territory" for each partner; for that reason minor issues may become major, and unnecessary, disagreements.

Everyone has internal standards concerning what constitutes acceptable cleanliness and unacceptable messiness—we're usually fanatics in one area (for example, the kitchen) and could care less in other areas (such as dust bunnies under the bed or the speed with which laundry is ironed and put away). There is probably not a couple on earth whose cleanliness and messiness standards match exactly.

Differing standards mean that most couples continually drive each other crazy. Accommodation is usually the rule, but in times of stress, people often feel they need to control at least some portion of their lives, and the shared living space becomes the focal point for that control.

Interestingly, it is human nature to assume that your partner approaches household chores with the same mind set as yours, and if some part of the living space is not kept up to your standards, to assume that the partner is doing it deliberately to bug you or get back at you for something you said or did. When was the last time you felt this way? True, sometimes people do retreat to these types of passive-aggressive behaviors when they are angry, but that's the exception rather than the rule. Now think about what you are really asking your mate to do—*read your mind*. Can you read minds? What makes you think your partner can?

Frequently the woman gets stuck with doing most of, or at least overseeing the completion of, household tasks. This is like adding another half-time job to the one she already has. This arrangement breeds stress, exhaustion, and frustration. A rearrangement of our culture's traditional division of labor is needed here: He or she who makes the mess should have an equal hand in cleaning it up! After all, a household is a community effort, and everyone needs to share the responsibility for it.

Rather than fight, many couples hire a cleaning or maid service to clean up. The weekly fee is a small price to achieve domestic tranquility. Other couples decide to divide up the chores—going with each partner's fanaticism. That means whoever is pickiest about the cleanliness of a certain part of the living space handles the maintenance of that part.

Few couples sit down and talk about how to handle household chores and even fewer clarify cleanliness/messiness standards and what will absolutely drive them crazy. But to do so is a useful exercise. Working together through your cleanliness expectations, including who should do what, in what manner and when, is a valuable opportunity to communicate with your partner and significantly reduce a major stress producer. How you handle the clean up is only limited by your imagination and creativity.

The Couple's Relationships and Friendships

While couples may no longer be dating, the relationships and friendships arena is still not devoid of stress. Successful relationships require work on the part of both mates; they don't just magically happen. Most of us underestimate the amount of work it takes, and this can be a significant stressor.

Power Conflicts.   If asked, most working couples would say that they are peers and equals in their relationship. They strive to take both partners' needs into account when making decisions and make heavy use of compromise and negotiation to solve problems. Unfortunately, our cultural upbringing does not support this sort of egalitarian approach, and husbands and wives are often surprised to find themselves muttering the equivalent of "well, Dad (or Mom) never had to put up with this!"

Dual-career couples report that power conflicts often crop up when, and usually boil down to, deciding which partner has or will have preferential influence over a given decision. Here our culture often speaks through us. Historically, males, for the most part, due to their roles as breadwinners, had the deciding vote. But when the woman has a successful career, then what? Chances are pretty good that she will be uncomfortable having him make all the decisions—particularly if she is used to making them at work.

Many couples try negotiating a mutually acceptable compromise for most decisions. Others divide them, and give one partner overall authority to make decisions in certain areas. This works well if: one partner has a particular skill in a particular decision area; or one mate really doesn't care at all about a particular area. Sometimes couples are lucky, and the decision areas each wants to take on don't overlap (or at least overlap only minimally).

In any situation, we encourage win-win techniques. It takes a fair amount of skill in communication, decision making, and risk taking to reach win-win resolutions. Later chapters focus on these skills, and can be very helpful in brushing up on these techniques.

Competition

Though most couples are loathe to admit it, competition also comes into play in dual career relationships. Partners often compete with each other for a very scarce resource in their relationship—nurturing. Everyone needs to be appreciated, given recognition and positive "strokes," and provided with support and "mothering" from time to time. (See the earlier section on career changes.) When we are under a lot of stress, nurturance can become very important, as it is a powerful stress reducer.

Competition surfaces when nurturing is limited, which occurs when both spouses are tired and drained from work and home demands and look to each other for support, help, and emotional nourishment. Their "giving levels" are low, and they haven't the ability to support each other adequately. Both partners end up feeling bad—one for not getting the needed nurturing, the other for "failing" the needy partner.

Admitting that competition exists is an important first step. Competing is a normal human reaction when a needed resource is in short supply. There is no reason to feel guilty. It is neither good nor bad, it just *is*. But only when you acknowledge its existence can you confront and deal with it.

Most couples try to deal with competition by embracing equity. Equity means each partner believes and anticipates that, over the course of their life together, opportunities, benefits, and constraints will be fairly distributed. In other words, I may give to my partner today (or this week or this month), and when I need to receive, he or she will be there for me. This can be hard to implement because it requires maturity on the part of both partners—an ability to delay gratification and a promise not to keep score.

Separate Activities and Friendships

Both partners need to work at maintaining their self-identities, and self-esteem as well, doing things just for themselves that they enjoy. These activities will help keep "giving levels" high, so nurturing does not become a scarce commodity. Couples still need to maintain and make friendships. In some ways, friendships become even more complex and potentially stressful, as the couple has to deal with the third entity of their own relationship as a couple. Most of us underestimate the amount of work it takes to maintain these friendships, and that can become a powerful stressor.

8

If You're a Parent

Working parents experience most of the same work-versus-personal-life stressors singles do, as well as *all* of the ones that frustrate dual-career couples. In addition to all those concerns, they have responsibility for children, who have pressing needs that must be attended to around the clock every day. Raising children today is a stressful proposition. Single parents feel the stresses even more keenly.

Home Life vs. Work Life

It is very difficult not to think about your family at work during a crisis at home or when there are unfinished tasks that need doing. It is also very difficult not to think about work at home, particularly if there is a crisis or projects have been left undone. Most parents are caught betwixt and between, and feel guilty if they think about home life at work or work life at home. For many people, this conflict is a potent stressor. Rest assured every parent experiences this; it is perfectly normal. Unfortunately, there is no cure for this parental affliction. The best you can hope for is moderation and balance, so neither part of your life has excessive negative impact on the other. But sometimes you can unknowingly poison your home life as a result of life on the job.

If you have had a rough day (or week or month) at work, it is difficult to turn off your frustration, anger, or depression when you return home. Many parents find that carrying work stress home can negatively impact their children. This can happen in several ways:

1. In the ever popular kick-the-cat syndrome, working parents growl at their partners, who in turn snap at the children, who then fight with each other or take their frustration out on the family pet. In this scenario, everyone felt fine before the working parents got home, and then everyone

quickly got upset. If this continues for extended periods, children can learn to avoid their parents, and working parents can be surprised to find that their families function much more happily and effectively when they aren't around.

2. Another scenario involves stressed-out parents who return home, try to act normally, but without dealing appropriately with their stress overload. Children are very perceptive, however, and they invariably pick up on their parents' moods, feelings, and anxiety. If this occurs regularly, children may begin to think that they are causing the problems. Children often begin to try to "do everything right" so that the parent will be less upset or angry. It is tremendously stressful for children when no matter what they do, the parent remains upset.

3. Parents who are very stressed out may also come home and be simply unable to give anything, or even talk to, their partners or children. They have only enough energy left to eat dinner and collapse in front of the television. Over time, children's needs are often ignored. They learn that adults can't be trusted to meet their needs, and they withdraw from their parents. This produces stress for both child and parent.

4. Conversely, stressed-out parents may feel a strong need to get something accomplished at home, particularly if overwork has led to chores piling up around the house or if they don't feel that things are getting done at work. These "projects" become another source of stress for parents and, in an effort to get them completed, parents may brush off a child's attempts to get attention or pleas to play. Sometimes strict adherence to a work plan blinds us to the needs of our partners and children—which is causing them increased stress.

In all these situations, stressed-out working parents act as carriers for stress that they bring home from work. They then "infect" their partners and children with that stress, resulting in increased stress levels all around.

Sometimes the stress from work is not what causes family problems, but the kind of person we have to be at work and the way we behave there. We all have a "business mind set"—a Polly or Peter Professional persona—that we developed as a way to cope with and be successful on the job. This person is the one who meets goals, sets agendas, gives orders, establishes priorities, and communicates using big words and complex ideas. But the same skills that bring success at work can cause havoc at home and keep us from developing close relationships with family members. You can't run your family life like the office.

How does this work, and where does the stress come from? Little children don't understand big words or complex ideas, and it is very hard to switch from being a business professional to being a mommy or daddy able to talk on a child's level. Giving orders at work can become a habit that is carried over to home—but in most cases, you can't order your partner or children around the way you can your staff—at least not without repercussions! Children don't often adhere to a schedule—and may need a little tender loving care and attention at a time that is not convenient for the parent— which may mean not giving time or attention to something (or someone) else. Children may also have a different agenda for spending time with a parent, and different notions of what is fun. Parents who must appear confident and in control at work may find it difficult to avoid making snap decisions at home. However, making decisions for the family without consulting them can often mean jumping to conclusions, and can cause great frustration and anger on the part of family members. Finally, many working parents have high expectations for organization and order at work. If they are unable to scale back those expectations at home, the usual clutter associated with children can cause enormous frustration.

The bottom line is that work behaviors *usually* are not appropriate at home. Working parents need to understand this and examine whether their "professional personae" are having a negative impact on their home lives. Taking time to decompress and make a transition between work and home can help alleviate this problem. The "Making the Transition between Work and Home" section of the "Couples" chapter can provide many ideas on how to develop such a decompression routine. Also, try some of the coping techniques outlined later in this book, which can even involve other family members, and provide an opportunity to become closer.

Work Time vs. Personal Time

Parents need to balance the time they spend on themselves, their partners, their child(ren), and the family as a whole, with the time spent on their careers. This is not easy! Nothing ever seems to go according to plan, things they want to do won't get done (or will get done later), and everyone and everything seem to want some of their time. Children, especially small ones, are very demanding, and they have a way of making their needs known— very loudly!

It is a fact of family life that parents will have less time for their own activities and personal pursuits (and perhaps careers) because they have children. Parents have to come to terms with this and accept it. Many parents do not anticipate the impact children will have on their time, and feel the children are infringing on their personal "rights." Understand that the demands on your time will change during your children's growing years, based on their ages, the type and variety of after-school activities they are involved in, and how much involvement is required of you. Things get better over time, because the most demanding years are birth through age 11 or 12.

If you can survive that, you can definitely survive your children's adolescence! Flexibility is the key to making things work in today's families.

The Superwoman Myth

Some would argue, loudly in fact, that the whole issue of personal versus work time is a "woman's" problem, because, except in rare instances, the woman is the one who coordinates child care; oversees household chores; stays home with infants until they are old enough to go into day care; takes time off when the children are ill, or tracks down someone to care for them; and is often told "just do your job and manage like everyone else."

So it is most unfortunate when women blame themselves if this whole crazy, fragile network breaks down—as it is guaranteed to do every time there is the smallest hitch, or childhood illness. This is an incredibly potent stress producer. Your own perceptions of how you should be and what you should do can cause more anguish than anything anyone else can do to you.

How did today's moms get the notion that they are failures if they can't make everything work—even when logically, realistically, and analytically it is not their fault and there is no way they can do it alone? It is partly because most women in their thirties and forties were raised to be ambitious—to want to do more than their mothers did with their lives. But the vast majority were raised by mothers who stayed home and took care of their families—the idealized version of motherhood working women aspire to today and want for their children. Women were raised with the expectation that they would be able to manage career and family if they organized their time well and kept their lives compartmentalized—as men are brought up to do. But no one ever prepared women for the ongoing, push-pull of the underlying struggle, which occurs every time reality departs from the ideal. No wonder today's working mothers feel such pressure.

Working Fathers as Heros—Sometimes

Today more and more fathers are realizing that it is both very important and very rewarding to be involved more fully in their children's lives. Some are even turning down promotions and relocations; but in these instances, the man *chooses* to do so. Fathers get peer support and approval for doing so; women who do the same thing tend just to get more guilt.

But sharing the burden of child care, which more men are beginning to do, is something else. There can be financial drawbacks, to be sure, but many men also fear damage to their careers. Part of this problem is that corporate cultures haven't adjusted, even when companies have begun to implement leave policies for fathers. Although unspoken, the theme is that men who want to share parenting can't be serious about their work. In essence, they face the same discrimination working mothers face.

Possible Panaceas?

The media has recently made much of corporations that are beginning to be more innovative and flexible when it comes to retaining valued employees faced with family pressures. The operative word here is *valued*, and the vast majority of workers affected by this new flexibility are senior managers and professionals who possess skills or knowledge that employers believe are critical to the company's success. But the options are worth exploring:

- *Flexible work schedules.* This option has been interpreted differently by different corporations. In some, flextime may mean a choice of starting work between 7 and 9 a.m. and leaving between 4 and 6 p.m. In others, it means work weeks can be scheduled in four 10-hour days, instead of five eight-hour days. For still others, it may mean a break during the day to take a child to day care after preschool, with work resuming until the normal 8 hours are completed.

- *Part-time work.* This option has always been considered a panacea, especially for women who could afford not to work full-time. It does allow skilled people to keep up with their fields, making it a potentially valuable option to corporations as well. Sometimes it works out to be a viable option; sometimes it becomes a hassle—especially if workers feel their careers become sidetracked.

- *Job sharing.* When a position can't be cut up into chunks and handled by part-time personnel, some corporations consider allowing two people to share a position. Prospective sharers need to consider carefully how the sharing will work, how long it will last, what happens if one leaves the company, how problems will be handled, and so on. This option works only if both sharers are highly motivated, can work well together, and are detail-oriented. In many cases, the corporation comes out ahead: Job sharers are so eager to please that they end up working extra hours, and the employer gets the productivity equivalent of three people.

- *Job splitting.* This option works somewhat like job sharing, but differs: The working partners reach a consensus on their overall strategy, and split up, not hours, but responsibilities, and sometimes even subordinates. Typically the partners keep each other up to date on projects so that, in a crisis, they can fill in for each other. This approach works best if both workers work three days a week, with a day's overlap for extended information sharing.

- *Home-based work or telecommuting.* A few corporations have begun to experiment with home-based work or telecommuting. This works best with professionals who do not need to be at the office to do their work, such as programmers, writers, systems analysts, engineers, architects, and, in some cases, lawyers. Computers, modems, fax machines, voice mail, answering machines, and call waiting have made it possible for these professionals to keep in touch with work while keeping an eye on their children. Whereas some people really like this option; others find home provides too many distractions to work effectively.

- *Freelancing and starting your own business.* This option has always been around, and has often been used by professional women with skills that are in high demand, such as writers, programmers, consultants, graphic artists, and others. It can be risky financially, and, if successful, as demanding as a full-time position. It's not for everyone, but can work well for many professionals.

What Working Parents Really Need

In all honesty, what you can do for yourself to reduce the stress of career and family is minimal: The significant action has to come from government and corporations. The bottom line is that *all* working parents—both moms and dads—need parental leave, flexible work schedules, the ability to take advantage of the other job options listed, on-site or quality day care provided by trained child-care workers, child-care deductions, and an understanding on the part of big business that personal and family problems are a part of doing business. Only working parents can convince their communities, governments, and employers of the importance of this bottom line—so speak up!

Raising Children Today

Ask parents to list their top five pet peeves and we guarantee that somewhere on the list will be: people who give unsolicited advice on how to raise children. So, the objective here is not to tell you how to raise your kids, but that dealing with how to raise children and prepare them for the rapidly changing world is very difficult, very time-consuming, and very stressful.

A major stressor for many parents today is determining the "right way" to bring up their children. Both parents typically come from different backgrounds, with different experiences, and can have very different ideas on what the right way should be. Grandparents, other relatives, close friends, and "experts" also have their views of the "right way." Sorting through and dealing with those differing views can be confusing and difficult.

Would it surprise you to know that most parents would honestly say that they don't know the right way to raise their children? It's true—you are not alone. *Everyone* is winging it to some degree. It's not even certain there is a single "right way"—it depends on the parent, the child, the family, and the community. Parents have to come up with their own way. Clearly, flexibility is vital, as is agreement between parents about goals for their family and core values that they want to pass on to their children. Beyond that, little is certain because our society is changing so rapidly. The behaviors and habits we learned as children may not serve our children well when they are adults.

So how do you cope with this tremendous source of stress? First, listen politely to people who offer their opinions about child raising, assess what they say, and then "take the best and leave the rest." Just because someone gives you advice (or criticism) doesn't mean you have to take it to heart.

Second, help your children understand what their current limits are, and expect them to adhere to those limits. Teach your children that the limits will change as they themselves change and grow, and as situations change. This lesson is a valuable one for children to learn in a world that is constantly changing—limits are definite, but do not always have to be permanent and can be changed through consensus.

Finally, a family is a small community, and everyone has to be involved if that community is to be successful—including children. This is a timeless lesson for children to learn. Participation may involve doing age-appropriate chores, being respectful of other people and their property, participating in family decision making, doing well at school, or whatever both parents agree is important. Active participation helps children feel that they are truly part of the family, and it provides many wonderful opportunities for parents and children to become closer.

Relationships and Friendships

The typical working parent is running from early morning until late at night. In order to meet all the demands on you, you first cut back on time for yourself and on your grand passions and guilty pleasures. Then you cut back on seeing friends and other family members. If you still feel the time crunch, you cut back on spending quality time with your mate—thinking that you are both too tired to do anything together anyway. This pattern is truly dangerous to your mental and physical health.

Your Relationship with Your Partner

Working parents are expected to satisfy peoples' demands on them at work, provide support to their spouses, and be on 24-hour call for nurturing their children. That is a tall order, one that is impossible to fill without continually replenishing their "giving levels."

The only way to do that is to set aside time to do something just for yourself and to commit to spending even a short amount of face-to-face time with your partner—*every day*. Yes, we did say "every day." Although that sounds impossible, it's not, *if you make yourself and your partner a priority in your life*. It doesn't matter what you do that's just for yourself—it can be anything from reading a novel for half an hour to soaking in the bath—but it's crucial that you do *something*. What you and your partner do together can be as simple as holding hands on the couch while you watch the evening news or snuggling in bed before falling asleep, but healthy relationships require that time be spent on them, every day. You and your mate deserve that sort of special, private time!

Friends: Yours, Mine, and Ours

Each parent needs to maintain a circle of personal friends. Finding the time to nurture such friendships is difficult. Sometimes our friends and our partner are not particularly compatible. But the support and encouragement that such friends can offer are powerful "destressers." Having friends who like you because you are you, not because you are part of a couple or a family or some other group, is especially beneficial. These relationships come about as close to unconditional acceptance as you can get, and everyone needs regular doses of this to cope with stress adequately.

Partners may need to reach an understanding about how much time is spent with personal friends—again flexibility is valuable. There may be times when it is appropriate for your partner to meet or socialize with your friends, and we believe that partners should make every effort to do so, if only to show respect to the other partner. If you are lucky, "your" friends can become "our" friends.

Parents also need to have a group of "our" friends—friends they see as a couple and whom they both enjoy and feel close to. Such friends help us reaffirm our "coupleness " and our identity as parents. As such they can be an invaluable source of support for both parents, as their relationship and family grow and change over time. Again, such friends can be powerful destressers.

Too often parents get so wrapped up in their children that they lose touch with their friends, only to wake up when their children leave for college to find that they have no one with whom to enjoy their new-found leisure time. Good friends are hard to find, and the positive stress-reducing benefits they can offer make them definitely worth working at keeping throughout one's lifetime. So take a few minutes and go call a friend!

9
A Special Note for Special Situations

The Dysfunctional Family

Although everyone struggles to some degree to develop healthy intimate relationships, people who were raised in a family with a background of some dysfunction, such as alcoholism, emotional or physical abuse, drug abuse, incest, or severe workaholism, often struggle more than most. People raised in dysfunctional families carry with them well into adulthood the vestiges of problems caused by their family of origin. These issues commonly surface in intimate relationships and on the job—both places in which the normal human behavior is to try to recreate a family setting. In addition, unresolved family issues can dramatically compound the stresses ordinarily associated with work and intimate relationships.

The Struggle for Intimacy

Most people from dysfunctional families are giving, caring, sensitive people. They are good at perceiving people's needs—even anticipating them. They take relationships, and people they care about, very seriously. These are all wonderful characteristics! So why do they often have difficulty achieving intimacy?

The reason is simple. Children learn intimacy by watching how their parents manage it. Frequently, dysfunctional families are not successful at being intimate, so people who grow up in them may not know what is normal when it comes to intimate relationships or how to go about developing one. To love someone else, you have to be able to love yourself. Children learn self-love when their parents provide them with a stable, loving, caring, respectful environment. But people from dysfunctional families may not have had that kind of environment, so they haven't learned how to love themselves.

Common Myths

Children of dysfunctional families often carry with them a host of myths about intimate relationships. Such excess baggage may cause stress for both partners in the relationship and can impact both desire and performance. Not everyone from a dysfunctional family believes every one of these myths completely, but most can see themselves in at least three or four. In her book, *Struggle for Intimacy*, Janet Woititz outlines those common myths:

- *If I am involved with you, I will lose me.* Many people do not develop a clear sense of self as children—the messages they got from their parents about themselves may have been too confusing. So they feel insecure and afraid that someone else's opinions will affect them too deeply.

- *If you really knew me, you wouldn't care about me.* This myth is a big one for people from dysfunctional families. As children, many were continually told that they weren't good enough or they were the cause of the family's problems, or, conversely, they were ignored. To cope, they put on a good front, tried to be all things to all people, and gave and gave and gave—especially to people they cared deeply about. But because they may not want their partners to know who they *really* are, they may try to keep a distance between themselves and their partners. And distance is an intimacy killer.

- *If you find out that I'm not perfect, you will abandon me.* People from dysfunctional families can be their own severest critics. They're often ruled, even in adulthood, by "if onlys" and "buts." They sometimes believe that if they do everything perfectly, and make everything perfect for everyone else, the people they love won't leave them. This comes from childhood, when the people whom they loved and most needed love from (their parents) continually did abandon them—at least while the parents were drinking or working long hours. These peoples' fear is that the person they love will not be there for them tomorrow.

- *We are as one.* Many people raised in dysfunctional families did not experience the bonding found in normal homes as children, especially if their mother was dysfunctional somehow. Bonding requires that needs be met in a consistent way, which may not have happened in their families. Sometimes when they invest in an intimate relationship (if they ever invest at all), they invest quickly, heavily, and on a very deep emotional level. In doing so, they risk smothering their partner and may worry excessively if they think their partner doesn't feel the same way, or they may expect unrealistic things of the intimate relationship.

- *Being vulnerable always has negative results.* The only way to achieve intimacy is to allow yourself to be vulnerable with your partner. But when people from dysfunctional families were growing up, being vulnerable brought pain. As a way to cope, some decided that *they* were responsible for their own happiness and that people could make them unhappy only if they let them. Survival entailed building a wall around their feelings and trying not to let down their guard. Those feelings may stay with them, making it difficult to be emotionally accessible to their partners.

- *We will never argue or criticize each other.* This is a great myth, isn't it? While people know intellectually that every relationship involves conflict and anger, some people had so much conflict as children that they desperately want their intimate relationships to be conflict-free. Some people raised in dysfunctional families found that expressing anger in their families only made things worse. Even as adults, some bury their anger, rationalize conflicts, and ultimately become depressed. They are terrified that if they lose their temper, bad things will happen. Having someone else's anger directed toward them can also be frightening; they immediately reflect back to how they felt as children.

- *Anything that goes wrong is my fault. I am a terrible person.* The reason some people believe this myth is simple—they heard it all the time as they were growing up. And when you hear something often enough, especially from your parents, you start to believe it—whether it's true or not.

- *In order to be lovable, I must be happy all the time.* If you ask people from dysfunctional families to describe their childhoods, the most common answer is, "I never had a childhood." And many never did—they had to take care of adult responsibilities because their parent(s), when they were drinking or taking drugs or weren't able to handle those responsibilities. They worried about their families and siblings and kept waiting for another "bomb" to drop. In some families, it is even worse. There are strict rules about not letting people outside the family know about the family's problems, and parents demand that children put on a good front at all times—smart, perky, and happy, and mask any crying on the inside. Many never got to be normal kids and learn how to have fun. So, since they may carry a tinge of sadness with them all the time and might not know how to have fun, they're convinced they can't *really* be lovable.

- *We will trust each other totally, automatically, and all at once.* We learn to trust as children by having our needs met consistently by our parents. Most people from dysfunctional families had some of their needs met, but those needs were met inconsistently. So, to them, trusting someone likely involves being hurt. They may find it hard to trust others, particularly their partners—even though they desperately want to. Their "magical" thinking is that, when they are in an intimate relationship, trust will happen immediately. But we all know that trust is built slowly, over time.

- *We will do everything together; we will be as one.* Some people have trouble with boundaries between themselves and others. As children, boundaries were confusing—it was sometimes hard to tell who *really* was the mother or the father or the child in a dysfunctional family. Intimacy involves establishing new boundaries between yourself and your partner, boundaries that help you become closer. But boundary definition can be stressful for people from dysfunctional families.

- *You will instinctively anticipate my every need, desire, and wish.* When they were growing up, some people learned it was easier not to have expectations: At least then you wouldn't be disappointed. They cut their losses as a way to cope; but they also cut their gains. Their magical thinking tells them that the person they love will be a mind reader able to tell what they *really* want without their having to voice it—because expressing their needs and expectations can be too stressful. They may also not know what a reasonable expectation is, because for their entire life they've been dealing with someone else's *unreasonable* expectations.

- *If I am not in complete control at all times, there will be anarchy.* The biggest lesson many people from dysfunctional families learned as kids was "If I am not in control, everything will fall apart." Often this has more to do with controlling the environment than controlling people: They learned early on that controlling people was impossible. They may feel a need to know all their options, have all their bases covered, and understand all the escape routes and scenarios. They can be frightened of depending on someone, because when they tried that before, they were hurt. These folks may feel they have to do everything themselves. But successful intimate relationships involve give and take and shared responsibility.

- *If we really love each other, we will stay together forever.* People from dysfunctional families are often very loyal, and offer loyalty in all relationships. Sometimes they are loyal far longer than is good for them, when evidence proves they have no reason to be loyal any more—because they want to avoid the pain of loss. In an intimate relationship, loyalty is best based on a mutual decision about the limits of the relationship. And we all know that, especially these days, partners do not always stay together.

- *My partner will never take me for granted, and will always be supportive and noncritical.* People from dysfunctional families need to have their feelings validated, because their feelings were discounted by their parents during childhood. So they worry about whether or not their feelings are legitimate. When their partners criticize them, or behave in a way they perceive as nonsupportive, they can be devastated.

Dealing with the Myths

Unfortunately, myths don't go away by themselves. They go away only if they are brought into the open and dealt with—by both the person raised in a dysfunctional family and his or her partner.

So if you or your significant other comes from a dysfunctional family and you think that the previously mentioned myths may be affecting the quality of your relationship or causing you stress, do yourself a favor. Talk about it with your physician or clergyperson—someone who can refer you to a therapist specializing in this sort of problem, a support group, or a therapy group. More and more support groups are being formed, and a number of books are available on the subject (see the suggested reading list at the end of this book). But however you do it, get yourself the help you need. You deserve a rewarding, enriching intimate relationship.

Seeking the Simple Life—Middle-Aged Malaise or Genuine Trend?

Pick up nearly any magazine today, and you're bound to see an article about the "new pioneers"—people who have given up high-stress, high-profile careers to pursue simpler lives. Most of the time these people are senior executives who leave large corporations to run smaller companies, or Wall Street types who pack it in to start a business of their own in the country. Many of us fantasize (sometimes daily!) about doing the same thing— chucking the rat race to become our own boss.

But then reality intrudes on this lovely fantasy. Most working people cannot afford to quit their jobs and bravely try on an entirely different lifestyle. They have responsibilities and obligations, and today most of those require two incomes to fulfill adequately. They can't make a sudden shift in careers, but the *desire* for change is pervasive as more and more people say they are dissatisfied with their jobs and the toll their careers extract from their lives.

What is Happening Here?

In some cases what people are reacting to is the American work ethic gone slightly haywire in the 1980s. For the media, and for many people, work has become a substitute for religion—not only was it going to give a paycheck, but it would enhance self-esteem, broaden horizons, and provide a reason for living.

At least that is what many consultants and corporations' human resources departments want us to believe. The problem is that during the past decade most companies became even more numbers-, goal-, and investment-oriented than ever before, creating an environment completely counter to the kind that would help us discover our best selves. So our expectations did not match reality, and we are struggling with the resulting letdown and disillusionment.

In addition, it's a matter of demographics. By becoming parents and reaching middle age, the baby boomers are entering two of life's major passages simultaneously. And when baby boomers get the sniffles, society gets pneumonia—simply because there are so many of them.

What happens when you hit middle age (aside from seeing far too many wrinkles and gray hairs)? Most people realize for the first time that their energy is limited and their days are finite. Time passes more quickly, or at least it feels that way. You find out that the true cost (in time and energy) of maintaining a job, marriage, children, and home is very high. That fact, combined with diminished energy, means boomers are choosing to focus on their children and families, while slacking off a bit from work.

Realistic Downshifting

Suppose you are a boomer: You want to focus more of your finite energy on your family, but you and your partner can't afford to quit your jobs and try something new. Besides, most of the time you value your career and enjoy what you do for a living. So how can you downshift or become a "domo" (downwardly mobile professional)?

You might start with the words of Thoreau, "Simplify, simplify." Examine your life carefully; then take the best and leave the rest. Reassess what is most important to you, and make a conscious decision to make those aspects of your life a priority. Later chapters can help you clarify your goals, values, and priorities—which is a good place to start.

Start thinking about work in a new way. In *Small is Beautiful*, the counterculture bible of the 1970s written by E.F. Schumacher, work has three functions: "To give people a chance to utilize and develop their faculties; to enable them to overcome their ego-centeredness by joining others in a common task; and to bring forth the goods and services needed for a becoming existence." Schumacher also states that, "Work and leisure are complementary parts of the same process. They cannot be separated without destroying the joy of work and the bliss of leisure." Think about it. We need work and we need leisure—but we need them to balance each other. Maybe what has happened is simply that we have lost sight of that powerful truth.

The Bottom Line

The bottom line is that whatever you choose to do with your personal life, there is a price to pay—just as there is in your working life. All the more reason to understand your values, goals, and priorities.

10

The Big Three—Diet, Exercise, Sleep

Coping with the Effects of Stress

In Chaps. 6–9, we talked about all the things that can cause us stress on the job and at home. What about things that can help us cope with these stressors? This section covers a wide variety of techniques and tricks that are helpful in coping with the effects of stress. Effects of stress are the emotions, feelings, and physical symptoms mentioned earlier in this book that are signs of stress overload. *The coping techniques offered here can help you control your symptoms while you work on solving the problems causing stress in the first place.* As such, they are a means to an end, not an end in themselves. They can provide you with breathing room so that you can start afresh.

These coping techniques will not reduce stress for you. The remaining chapters of this book will provide concrete ways for you to do that. But in order to tackle those areas, you've got to have energy. These coping techniques will help you free up some of your energy.

We believe that everyone feeling the effects of stress overload will benefit from following a healthier, well-balanced diet and increasing their level of physical fitness. Because diet and exercise are so important, they are the first two coping techniques we cover. These two proven stress busters can help you combat the impact of stress hormones by making it easier for your body to repair the damage caused by those steroids.

But not all the other coping techniques will work equally well for all people. It's up to you to experiment with a selection of the techniques offered here to come up with the coping package that works best for you. As your life situation changes and the sources of your stress change, you may need to alter your personal coping package to meet these new demands. We have included a wide range of coping techniques for you to choose from including:

A good cry

Affirmations

Behavioral rehearsal

Biofeedback

Breathing exercises

Friends, family, and supporters

Guilty pleasures

Hobbies and leisure activities

Hugs

Humor

Journals and diaries

Massage

Meditation

Progressive muscle relaxation

Rituals

Rewards

"Self-talks"

Therapy

Visualization

Weekends and vacations

Worrying

Think of Chaps. 10 and 11 as a giant bag of tricks you can pull out and try on for size when you are feeling the effects of stress overload.

A few words of warning first, however:

- *Check with your physician before you make any drastic changes in your lifestyle through exercise or diet.* Don't try to do everything at once. Go slowly! Progress won't be made overnight, but it will come.

- *If you have any physical problem or injury, check with your physician before you do any relaxation or fitness-oriented exercise.* The operate rule is: First do no harm! You don't need to add to your stress level by injuring your back or knee.

- *It's better to practice a few coping techniques consistently than a lot of coping techniques sporadically.* Our bodies respond best to habit, so make your coping techniques an integral part of your daily life. They have a preventive as well as a restorative value.

- *If you find yourself getting in over your head emotionally, talk to friends, family, or coworkers.* You might want to consider talking with your physician or a mental health professional.

- *Let the important people in your life know you are trying new ways to cope with your symptoms and feelings.* They're more likely to be supportive and tolerant if they know what is going on.

- *Do not discontinue any medication or treatment regimen prescribed by your physician without checking with him or her first!* These coping techniques will help you feel better, but do not stop *anything* your physician may have told you to do unless you get his or her approval first.

Now that that much is clear, you can get ready to unwind!

Diet

Most people watch their diets to lose weight, manage their nutrition, or prevent health problems. Although maintaining your weight at a healthy level and making sure you are getting adequate nutrition are good ideas, prevention of health problems is key, and something we frequently ignore. When you are under stress, it is important to take a good look at your diet because what you are eating, or not eating, can affect your overall level of health. The following guidelines are useful whether you are trying to prevent health problems, maintain proper nutrition, or lose weight.

Processed foods contain high levels of salt and, when additional salt is added to food during cooking or at the table, an average American gets 12 grams of salt each day. High levels of salt over the long term significantly increase blood pressure and, when combined with increases in blood pressure caused by stress hormones, can cause serious side effects such as permanent hypertension and, ultimately kidney damage. Salt also causes water retention.

Cholesterol, common in the typical American diet, has been linked to premature cardiovascular disease, a problem all too commonly seen in workers with high levels of stress. The refined sugars and saturated fat present in our daily diet increase triglyceride levels in the blood, raising the risk of cardiovascular disease. They provide quick energy, but fast drops in blood sugar levels cause fatigue, not to mention extra pounds.

B vitamins, which have been found to play a role in maintaining good health under stress, are not present in significant amounts in highly processed foods and foods made exclusively from white flour.

If you think your diet is sound, take a second look. Most of us could benefit from cutting back on salt, sugar, saturated fats, cholesterol, and refined foods. That's also easy to do (if you are not on a special diet recommended by your physician) if you are willing to try the following suggestions:

✔ *Eat more fresh, raw fruits and vegetables.* They have more vitamins, minerals, natural sugars and carbohydrates, and fiber than processed fruits and vegetables. *Try to get at least four servings each day.*

✔ *Eat more complex carbohydrates.* About 60 to 65 percent of your daily calories should be foods that are high in complex carbohydrates—vegetables, fruit, cereals, pasta, noodles, rice, whole-grain products and breads, peas, and beans. Your body metabolizes these foods slowly, and they provide energy for the long haul. They have lots of fiber, make you feel full, and usually are very low in fat. *Try to get at least four servings each day.*

✔ *Steam or microwave fresh vegetables instead of using canned or frozen vegetables.* Canned vegetables lose most of their nutritive value during processing, and frozen vegetables often have salt added to them. If you use frozen vegetables, check the label, and purchase those vegetables that have no sodium added. Invest in a food steamer (usually under 10 dollars in most variety and discount stores) and learn to appreciate the goodness of tender-crisp vegetables. If you own a microwave, you are in for a pleasant surprise. Microwaving either fresh or frozen vegetables is fast, keeps in nutrients, and maintains the fresh colors of the vegetables.

✔ *Switch to soft margarine in tubs instead of butter or margarine in sticks, and cut back on how much you use.* Soft margarine has less saturated fat than butter or hard margarine, and after a while the difference in taste will not be noticeable. We also tend to use too much margarine. Stop and think before you reach for the margarine—do I really need to put it on this food item? Most of the time, our food tastes just fine *without* it.

✔ *Whenever possible use polyunsaturated oils in cooking to replace shortening or lard.* Corn, safflower, vegetable, sunflower, olive, peanut, canola, and sesame oils are high in polyunsaturates and do not increase your chances of cardiovascular disease as do shortening and lard. Because these oils are high in calories, try to cut back on their use as well, using nonstick cookware and one of the new cooking sprays.

✔ *Eat fewer egg yolks per week to limit your cholesterol intake.* Experts say that healthy people with no cardiovascular disease can tolerate up to three egg yolks a week. Most people can do just fine without that many. We recommend that you experiment with the egg-substitute products, such as Eggbeaters or Scramblers. These are made mostly from egg whites, which contain no cholesterol. These egg-substitute products also work very well to replace regular eggs in most recipes. They are also great in the microwave because you can make an omelet or scrambled egg with no additional fat to coat your frying pan.

✔ *Cut back on luncheon meats, beef, pork, and organ meats while increasing your use of poultry and fish.* With rising food prices, you may be doing that already! Poultry and fish are usually less expensive than other meats, and are also lower in saturated fats and cholesterol. Deli-style meats are tasty but deadly, they have a very high salt and fat content.

✔ *Switch to peanut butter that is low in cholesterol and does not contain hydrogenated fats.* That kind of peanut butter is an excellent inexpensive source of protein.

✔ *Stop adding salt to food at the table and in cooking.* You may want to phase out salt gradually, giving your taste buds a chance to adjust to lower levels of salt, or switch to a salt substitute. You can get all the sodium (the major component of salt) you need from vegetables, fruits, and protein sources. There is no need to add any extra salt to your diet. Eliminating salt in most recipes doesn't significantly affect the resulting product.

✔ *Cut back on the amount of refined sugars used both in preparing and in serving foods, and reduce your intake of packaged or prepared foods.* An occasional candy bar won't do you in, unless you have a medical condition that forbids it. Most recipes turn out just fine with little appreciable difference in taste if you use only half as much sugar as suggested. Nondessert recipes can usually have the sugar eliminated entirely without noticeable effects. You can reduce the amount of sugar you add to coffee, tea, cereals, fruits, and so forth, and gradually cut back on your daily intake of candy bars and other goodies. Prepared or packaged food also contains high amounts of sugar, as well as being very expensive. By cutting back on these items, you'll be helping your checkbook as well as your body!

✔ *Increase your fiber intake.* The typical American diet provides approximately 12 grams of dietary fiber a day—experts believe we should have at least 30. Increased dietary fiber may help reduce risks of various bowel cancers and can reduce constipation or diarrhea—common side effects of stress overload.

Raw fruits and vegetables are good sources of fiber, as are foods made from whole-grain cereals and flours. Another alternative to try is psyllium hydrophilic mucilloid, a completely natural fiber source, found in products such as Metamucil or Hydrocil. *Go slowly in increasing your intake of fiber, especially if your present diet is lacking in it.* It takes your body awhile to get used to handling large amounts of fiber, and you may notice bloating and excess gas at first. If this happens, reduce your intake by half for four or five days, and gradually work up to your desired level. It is also wise to spread your consumption of fiber out over the course of a day to avoid a sudden overload of your digestive system.

Table 10.1 gives you an idea of the fiber content of a variety of food items.

✔ *Eat breakfast.* It's the most important meal of the day. Skipping meals often leads to rebound fatigue, headaches, and poor performance. Calories are also burned most efficiently early in the day. And we don't mean "grab a doughnut and a cup of coffee on the run!" Every body needs refueling after 8 to 12 hours without food. Ideally, breakfast should combine members of the complex carbohydrate, protein, fat (just a little, please!), fruit, and milk groups. But that doesn't mean it has to be cold cereal or fried eggs. You can try: leftovers from dinner the night before; a breakfast shake made from nonfat milk, yogurt, and fruit; hot cereal with nonfat milk and fruit; a bowl of soup and a sandwich on whole-grain bread; a breakfast salad made from low-fat cottage cheese, fruits, and lettuce; or even (radical thought!) your "main meal"—what you would eat for dinner.

We recommend the breakfast cereals listed in Table 10.1 because they contain no fat and are high in fiber.

✔ *Cut back on whole milk products to reduce your fat intake.* Skim milk, nonfat milk, evaporated low-fat milk, low-fat yogurt, low-fat cottage cheese, and reduced-fat cheese products are all better for you than their higher fat counterparts. You will also rapidly become used to minor differences in taste.

Table 10.1. Fiber Content of Common Foods

Food	Serving size	Grams of fiber
Bran muffin	1 small	2.5
Whole-wheat bread	1 slice	1.4
Macaroni	1 cup	1.6
Spaghetti	1 cup	1.1
Spaghetti (whole wheat)	1 cup	3.9
Fruits		
Apple (with skin on)	1 medium	3.5
Banana	1 medium	2.4
Grapefruit	1/2 large	3.1
Orange	1 medium	0.8
Blueberries	1/2 cup	2.6
Prunes	3 medium	3.0
Vegetables		
Kidney beans (cooked)	1/2 cup	7.3
Navy beans (cooked)	1/2 cup	6.0
Lima beans (cooked)	1/2 cup	4.5
Beans, green (cooked)	1/2 cup	1.6
Broccoli (cooked)	1/2 cup	2.2
Peas (cooked)	1/2 cup	3.6
Potato (baked with skin)	1 medium	2.5
Spinach (cooked)	1/2 cup	2.1
Celery	1 stalk	1.1
Lettuce	1 cup (sliced)	0.9
Mushroom	1/2 cup	0.9
Spinach (raw)	1 cup	1.2
Sprouts, bean (raw)	1/2 cup	1.5

✔ *Decrease your caffeine, theophylline, and theobromine intake.* Caffeine is primarily found in coffee, theophylline in tea, and theobromine in chocolate. All act as stimulants. You don't need to eliminate them entirely, provided your physician does not recommend restricting your intake, but it will be better for you at least to cut back. Decaffeinated coffees, teas, and colas are widely available. Herbal teas are good, too, providing you do not have allergies to the herbs in them.

If you drink coffee, as millions of people do, it is important to know that some coffees have more caffeine than others. There are two kinds of coffee

Table 10.2. Recommended Breakfast Cereals

Breakfast cereal	Fiber (grams per ounce)	Calories (per ounce)
All-Bran with Extra Fiber	14	50
Raisin Bran	4	86
Spoon-Size Shredded Wheat	3	90
Nutri-Grain Wheat	3	90
Grape-Nuts	2	110
Wheat Chex	2	100

beans: *arabica* and *robusta* beans. Robusta beans contain more than twice as much caffeine as arabica beans. Most commercial brands of coffee use a mix of predominantly robusta beans, with a small portion of arabica beans. Therefore, commercial coffees have caffeine measurements toward the high end of the ranges listed in the following chart. Most speciality coffee shops carry both arabica and robusta beans, and coffee made from speciality coffee beans would have caffeine measurements toward the low end of the ranges given in the chart. Remember: The color of the bean is no indication of its caffeine content. Some very darkly roasted arabica beans have a very low caffeine content.

Table 10.3 can help guide your selections, and remember: American coffee mugs usually hold 10 to 12 ounces of beverage.

✔ *Cut back on alcohol.* Many people gravitate toward alcohol in times of stress, because it helps them relax. Providing your physician has not restricted your consumption of alcohol, we strongly encourage moderation in this area—meaning one serving per day for women and no more than two servings per day for men. One serving is equivalent to 12 ounces of beer (one can), 4 ounces of wine (a small wine glass), or 1 to 1.5 ounces of hard liquor (one shot). We recommend that women consume less alcohol than men because recent research has shown that women metabolize alcohol differently than men, and have a lower tolerance to its effects as a result. Women are also usually smaller than men.

These minor changes in your diet can make a big difference in how your body responds to and copes with stress. They can also help reduce the amount of fuel added to the fire of the potentially dangerous physical side effects of stress. You'll probably feel better and have more usable energy, something we all need more of when we're dealing with stress! Once again, you don't have to follow all of the suggestions all at once. Gradually work the changes into your lifestyle, and they will soon become second nature to you.

The following helpful hints can ensure that you integrate your diet changes into your lifestyle:

■ *Carefully think through why you want to make changes in your diet and lifestyle.* Try to think consciously about them every day. Plan for the long term, and make sure you understand the pros and cons.

■ *Expect to slip up—no matter how sincere your desire to change.* Everyone does at some point, and it really doesn't do you any good to beat yourself up when you slip. Just resolve to return to your planned diet and lifestyle changes as soon as you can. Try to anticipate those situations where you will be tempted to slip, and avoid them if possible.

■ *If you are giving up goodies that you just love for the sake of a healthier diet, develop a list of coping mechanisms you can use when you feel the old urge for a bag of chips, a hot fudge sundae, or whatever turns you on.* And then practice those coping techniques when the urge hits.

Table 10.3. Stimulant Contents of Common Foods and Beverages

Item	Serving size	Caffeine (mg)
Coffee (caffeine)		
Coffee, drip	5 ounces	110–150
Coffee, perk	5 ounces	60–125
Coffee, instant	5 ounces	40–105
Coffee, decaffeinated, brewed	5 ounces	2–5
Coffee, decaffeinated instant	5 ounces	1–5
Tea (theophylline)		
Tea—major U.S. brand, 5-minute steep	5 ounces	40–100
Tea—major U.S. brand, 3-minute steep	5 ounces	20–50
Tea—imported brand, 5-minute steep	5 ounces	50–110
Tea, instant	5 ounces	25–50
Tea, iced	12 ounces	67–76
Cocoa (theobromine)		
Hot cocoa	5 ounces	2–10
Chocolate milk	8 ounces	2–7
Milk chocolate candy	1 ounce	1–15
Bittersweet chocolate candy	1 ounce	5–35
Chocolate-flavored syrup	1 ounce	4
Chocolate cake	1 average slice	20–30
Soft drinks (caffeine)		
Coca-Cola		45
Diet Coke	one 12 oz. can	45
Mountain Dew	one 12 oz. can	54
Mello Yello	one 12 oz. can	52
Tab	one 12 oz. can	46
Pepsi-Cola	one 12 oz. can	38
Diet Pepsi	one 12 oz. can	36
Pepsi Light	one 12 oz. can	36
Dr. Pepper	one 12 oz. can	40
Sugar-Free Dr. Pepper	one 12 oz. can	40
RC Cola	one 12 oz. can	36
Diet Rite	one 12 oz. can	36
Kick	one 12 oz. can	31
Mr. PIBB	one 12 oz. can	40
Sugar-Free Mr. PIBB	one 12 oz. can	59
Nonprescription drugs (caffeine)		
Anacin, Empirin, or Midol tablets	2 tablets	64
Excedrine tablets	2 tablets	130
NoDoz tablets	2 tablets	200
Vivarin tablets	2 tablets	400
Triaminicin tablets	1 dose	30
Dristan Decongestant and Dristan A-F decongestant tablets	1 dose	16
Aqua-Ban (diuretic) tablets	2 tablets	200
Dexatrim (weight control) tablets	1	200

Table 10.3. (*Continued*)

Item	Serving size	Caffeine (mg)
Prescription drugs (caffeine)		
Cafergot (for migraine headache)	1 dose	100
Fiorinal (for tension headache)	1 dose	40
Soma Compound (pain relief,		
muscle relaxant)	1 dose	32
Darvon Compound (pain relief)	1 dose	32

■ *Give yourself a break when making major diet and lifestyle changes.* Most of us become compulsive when we make a major change in our habits. We find that the 80-20 rule applies very well here—stick to your resolutions 80 percent of the time and, unless you are on a special restricted diet recommended by your physician, allow yourself your newly taboo foods 20 percent of the time in smaller servings. This way, you don't feel cheated or deprived of your favorites, you know you will eventually be able to enjoy a smaller portion, and it *feels* easier to stick to your resolutions most of the time.

■ *Develop a network of people who practice healthy behaviors, and who can serve as your role models and provide support.* For some of us, that might mean joining a group like Weight Watchers at Work; attending Heart Smart or vegetarian cooking classes at a culinary institute or hospital; starting a "dinner exchange" group where friends take turns fixing healthy gourmet dinners for each other once a month; encouraging your lunchtime buddies to try someplace other than the local greasy spoon for lunch; or exchanging microwave ideas with friends. We need all the support we can get when we make major diet and lifestyle changes, and good role models can't hurt, either!

A Commonsense Approach to Vitamins and Minerals

Nutrition is still a "new" science: Many vitamins and minerals have not been completely researched, and new minerals are always being found to be important to human health. Much is still unknown.

However, a great deal is known. A major fact is that a balanced, typical American diet will supply all the necessary vitamins and minerals you need. Your body is even capable of synthesizing some vitamins from other materials if your diet doesn't provide them adequately. It also takes a long time for vitamin or mineral deficiencies to show up—a day or a week won't cause a deficiency. Much of what you read and hear about vitamin supplements is pure hype; most people do not need them.

However, it has been discovered that the B vitamins and vitamin C are used up more rapidly when people are under stress. But researchers still aren't sure how rapidly, or when stress becomes severe enough to use these nutrients up. But—and this is an important but—if you eat a balanced diet, you will still probably get enough of these vitamins without needing supplements.

If you are concerned about a deficiency, check with your physician, who can run a variety of blood tests to see whether you are indeed deficient. Most Americans are not. Exceptions are pregnant women (who need vitamins and minerals for two), people with genetically linked diseases that keep them from using vitamins and minerals properly (for example, pernicious anemia), people on prolonged antibiotic therapy, women on birth control pills, people who smoke or drink heavily, or people who have been on fasts for a long period of time.

Do not medicate or treat yourself. In this area, a little knowledge can be a dangerous thing. *Remember, vitamins and minerals are drugs.* More is not necessarily better when it comes to vitamins and minerals. Some vitamins (especially vitamin A) are toxic in large quantities. Too much potassium can cause severe side effects. So go easy, especially on fat-soluble vitamins. These are stored in your body and can build up to dangerous levels.

If you aren't sure your diet is adequate in vitamins and minerals, you might feel more secure if you took a multivitamin, multimineral supplement. Compare the RDAs (recommended daily allowances) for each vitamin and mineral in Table 10.4 with the amounts listed on the vitamin bottle. As long as you are getting 100 percent of your RDA in the supplement, that's all you need! Any additional you might need you will pick up in your diet. Take only the amount of tablets specified on the bottle—unless your physician directs otherwise. If you take more than one, you are just flushing your money away.

Expensive is not necessarily better when it comes to vitamins and minerals. All vitamins and minerals are generic. Differences in prices usually indicate fancier packaging, more advertising, and so on.

Some companies may use fillers to hold the vitamins and minerals together into a pill, and some sort of coating to protect the vitamins and minerals from exposure to air, make them taste better, and allow them to slide down your throat more easily. Sometimes people are sensitive to something in the fillers or coatings and can develop various gastrointestinal upsets (that is, when you burp that awful vitamin taste or have stomach cramps). Unless you already know what fillers and coatings you are sensitive to, you may have to experiment with different brands to find the one most tolerable for you.

Never take a supplement on an empty stomach! Many vitamins and minerals need to be combined with fats and other food by-products in order to be absorbed by your body. If you don't have something in your stomach, the supplement won't be broken down completely and will pass right out of your system.

How do you choose a vitamin and mineral supplement? It's easy if you follow these simple steps:

✔ Go to a reputable drug, discount, or grocery store.

✔ Look for products from reputable companies that make multivitamin-multimineral supplements.

✔ Check the RDAs in Table 10.4 against the amounts of the various vitamins and minerals listed on the supplement package. Check to see that you are getting at least 100 percent of the RDA for each vitamin and mineral on this list.

✔ Most likely you'll find several different products that fulfill the requirements from step 3. Now check the price: Take the number of capsules or tablets in the bottle and divide that into the price listed on the bottle to get your cost per capsule or tablet:

$$\frac{\text{cost of bottle}}{\text{number of pills}} = \text{cost per pill}$$

✔ Buy the brand that costs least per pill. Try this brand for a while. If you notice gastrointestinal problems, switch to another. Your supplement doesn't have to contain all naturally occurring vitamins. Naturally occurring vitamins are more expensive because they are more difficult to process into pills and tablets.

Women should gear their intake toward the lower RDA number, men toward the higher number.

Table 10.4. Recommended Dietary Allowances of Vitamins

Nutrient	Adult RDA	Purpose	Sources(s)
Vitamin A	800–1000 micrograms	helps increase night vision; important in maintenance of skin and mucous membranes in respiratory system.	carrots, apricots, dark green leafy vegetables, milk, squash, cantaloupe, peaches, tomatoes, eggs, cheese, butter
Vitamin D	400 I.U.s	helps us make use of calcium and phosphorus, important for strong bones and teeth.	sunlight, milk, milk products
Vitamin E	8–10 milligrams	protects polyunsaturated fats in cell membranes throughout the body from damage and may be important in slowing aging process.	corn, olive, safflower, peanut, and walnut oils; peanuts; wheat germ; spinach; asparagus; sweet potatoes

Table 10.4 (*Continued*)

Nutrient	Adult RDA	Purpose	Sources(s)
Vitamin K	65–80 micrograms	helps maintain the normal clotting properties of blood.	leafy dark green vegetables, egg yolks, soybean oil
Vitamin C	60 milligrams, but when under severe stress, suggested RDA is 250–5000 milligrams	necessary for the formation of collagen, backbone connective tissues. Also helps heal burns and cuts and may help in combating infections.	cabbage, oranges, grapefruit, cantaloupe, strawberries, broccoli, bananas, tomatoes, spinach, mung bean sprouts, pineapple
Vitamin B1 (Thiamine)	1.1–1.5 milligrams, but suggested RDA for people under severe stress is 2–10 milligrams	helps bodies change carbohydrates and proteins into energy by assisting in production of glucose.	brewer's yeast, whole wheat flour, wheat germ, pinto beans, soybeans, spinach, barley, navy beans, asparagus
Vitamin B2 (Riboflavin)	1.3–1.7 milligrams, but suggested RDA for people under severe stress is 2–10 milligrams	helps in biochemical processes that release energy and create proteins from amino acids.	cottage cheese, milk, yogurt, cheese, broccoli, mushrooms, squash, brewer's yeast, spinach, wheat germ
Vitamin B5 (Niacin)	15–19 milligrams, but suggested RDA for people under severe stress is 50–5000 milligrams	used for energy transformations in every cell.	tofu, soybeans, cottage cheese, mung bean sprouts, oatmeal, peanuts, peanut butter, wheat bran, eggs, potatoes, avocados
Vitamin B6 (Pyridoxine)	1.6–2.0 milligrams	helps metabolize proteins, create hormones, produce red blood cells, and maintain proper functioning of nervous tissues.	rice bran, soybeans, spinach, bananas, dried beans and lentils, whole wheat flour, broccoli, wheat germ, avocados

Table 10.4 (Continued)

Nutrient	Adult RDA	Purpose	Sources(s)
Vitamin B12 (Cobalamin)	2 micrograms	essential for the functioning of all cells—involved in synthesis of DNA and RNA. Also maintains cells of nervous tissues.	cottage cheese, milk, eggs, cheese, yogurt, whey
Folacin	180–200 micrograms	essential in formation of DNA and RNA and helps break down amino acids into useful materials necessary for formation of new cells.	dried beans and lentils, asparagus, broccoli, lettuce, spinach, sweet potatoes, cantaloupe, oranges, brewer's yeast
Pantothenic Acid	4–7 milligrams, but suggested RDA for people under severe stress is 20–100 milligrams	helps our bodies metabolize food and create other vitamins.	broccoli, soybeans, rice polishings, lentils, brewer's yeast, fresh peas, brussels sprouts, oatmeal, milk, egg yolks, cantaloupe
Calcium	800 milligrams	necessary for the formation of bones and teeth and makes possible the transmission of nerve impulses. Plays role in blood coagulation. Women should get adequate amount of calcium throughout lifetimes to prevent development of osteoporosis—brittle and easily fractured bones—in later years.	milk, yogurt, cheese, dark green leafy vegetables, broccoli, tofu, soybeans, hard water, mineral water
Phosphorus	800 milligrams	involved in all energy-creating biochemical processes in body and aids absorbtion of calcium.	pinto beans, cottage cheese, milk, bran, wheat germ, yogurt, tofu, corn, broccoli

Table 10.4 (Continued)

Nutrient	Adult RDA	Purpose	Sources(s)
Magnesium	280–350 milligrams	helps activate enzymes that make energy usable to all parts of body. Also helps conduct nerve impulses, create proteins, and contract muscles.	dried beans and lentils, wheat germ, bran, whole wheat flour, peanut butter, leafy green vegetables, apples, cantaloupe, oranges, cheese, milk.
Iron	10–15 milligrams	crucial in carrying oxygen to body cells.	liver, prune juice, dried beans and lentils, spinach, peaches, molasses, raisins, tofu, tomato juice, wheat germ, bran
Zinc	12–15 milligrams	essential for growth and repair of body tissues and cells.	dried beans and lentils, whole wheat flour, soymeal, bran, wheat germ, milk, spinach, whole wheat cereals
Iodine	150 micrograms	essential for normal thyroid gland functioning.	iodized salt, seafood, vegetables grown in iodine-rich soil
Selenium	55–70 micrograms	interacts with vitamin E to prevent breakdown of fats and body chemicals.	chicken, seafood, whole-grain breads and cereals, egg yolks, mushrooms, onions, and garlic
Copper, Manganese, Cobalt, Molybdenum, Chromium, Nickel, Tin, Silicon, Fluorine, Vanadium	none yet established	believed to work in conjunction with each other, and all previously listed vitamins and minerals. A deficiency in one element won't cause problems, but may make other processes less efficient. Can be toxic in high levels.	

A Few Words on Sodium and Potassium

There is a great deal of controversy in the field of nutrition concerning these minerals. Both are important in maintaining the electrolyte levels in the blood and in maintaining fluid levels in our bodies. These are rarely listed in terms of RDAs because people get more than they need from naturally occurring sources in their daily diet.

The typical American diet is adequate in potassium, unless a person is on certain types of diuretics for high-blood-pressure reduction, or is a marathon exerciser (high levels of exercise can cause potassium loss). Fluid loss caused by the diuretics can speed the removal of potassium from the body, and supplements prescribed by a physician may be necessary. Since potassium has severe side effects at high levels, potassium therapy requires the careful control of a physician who relies on blood tests to monitor potassium levels in the body.

Physical Fitness

It is hard to rationalize the time spent maintaining your physical fitness level when you're busy and under stress, but experts have found that by increasing your fitness level, you can effectively increase your energy level and do all sorts of good things for your body and well-being, such as:

- Helping lower blood pressure
- Lower the heart rate for walking, sitting, standing, and doing other physical activities, so your heart doesn't have to work so hard
- Raise HDL, a beneficial type of cholesterol
- Increase your stamina and endurance
- Improve your mood and outlook on life
- Decrease appetite, burn off calories, and raise your metabolism level
- Reduce excessive stress hormones present in your body
- Greatly increase your sense of self-control and control over your life—something that is often missing when we are under a great deal of stress

With all that going for it, physical fitness can be one of the most important ways you can cope with the effects of stress. Should you decide to increase your activity level, keep the following things in mind:

✔ *Check with your physician before you begin* any *fitness program.* Think about the kind of exercise program you might like to try, and discuss it with your doctor. Your physician may have some good reasons why you should or should not proceed with a fitness program at this time, and can help you select the most appropriate aerobic activities for your present level of physical conditioning.

🖛 *Make sure that you aren't too busy (tired, overworked, and so on) to exercise in some form every day.* You may *feel* too tired right now, but you can be guaranteed an extra hour of usable energy for every 45 minutes of physical activity you engage in. Activity will also help increase the quality, as well as the quantity, of your life in the long run. Work toward 30 minutes of aerobic activity 3 times a week—but don't exceed 5 times a week. You body needs a few days off, just as your mind does!

🖛 *Fitness is not a crash program!* It took your body 15, 20, or 30 years to get into the shape it is in now, and it's not going to change overnight. When you start increasing your activity level gradually, it is easier, hurts less, and is more fun, so you're likely to stick with your program longer. Many people under stress have lost touch with their bodies and natural body rhythms; it is important for them to increase their activity level gradually so that they can become aware of their inherent rhythms, how their bodies feel when they are being used effectively, and learn to enjoy physical activity.

🖛 *Don't take your fitness program too seriously.* Exercise can be lots of fun, but many people, especially Type As, turn exercise into work. Forget about points, times, miles, clocks—listen to your body and go with the flow.

🖛 *If exercise bores you, find some way to distract yourself.* That can mean changing where you exercise, how you exercise, what equipment you use, and so forth. It can also help if you reward yourself periodically throughout your program. These goodies can help you keep on track, even during the blahs that hit about two months into a fitness program when you don't see results as fast as you'd like.

Or work out to music. Researchers have discovered that music can help tremendously while you work out. The beat of the music can help you pace yourself and the music can increase your sense of rhythm. It also gives you something to think about other than your aching muscles! That's why every aerobic dancing or exercise class has loud, throbbing music, with the songs selected to match the type and speed of exercise being done.

The Sports Music Company (Box 767364, Roswell, GA 30076) makes a full range of tapes for beginning, intermediate, and advanced aerobics, for speed-walking, race-walking, and running. They make variable-pace tapes which include music for a warm-up, aerobic activity, and cool-down periods, steady-pace tapes which run at the same speed from beginning to end. The music selections are nearly endless: short tapes, New Age, Zydeco—you name it.

🖛 *Set fair expectations for yourself and your progress toward you activity goals.* Too many people poop out too early in an activity program because they expect their bodies to reach Olympic-caliber performance too soon. Remember, *you need only to reach the level of fitness recommended by your physician, and which is required by your lifestyle and environment.*

🖛 *No one sport does it all.* No one activity (except maybe aerobic dancing) can provide you with cardiovascular fitness, increased respiratory efficiency, muscle tone, and flexibility. It's as important to combine and experiment with different kinds of physical activity as it is to combine the proteins, carbohydrates, vitamins, and minerals we need to survive.

✔ *Above all, train—don't strain!* Always warm up, and always cool down. If it hurts, your body is telling you that you are either doing it wrong, doing it too much, doing it too fast, doing it too soon, or you shouldn't be doing it at all. Some mild soreness is to be expected as you begin to use muscles you haven't used in a long time, but any other kind of pain that lasts longer than a day or two is a warning signal. Listen to your body: It knows what is best for you! When it hurts, stop! It can save you a lot of grief later.

Learn how to do your activity of choice properly and get the proper equipment. Too many people get hurt because they don't do that. Did you know that there is a right way and a wrong way to run? So go buy a book or take a class. If you are into aerobics, check out Jane Fonda's aerobics tapes. Rated very highly by experts in the field, her tapes (available as cassettes or VHS tapes) cover a wide range of exercises and fitness levels. She has even done one for those of us over 35, called *Jane Fonda's Prime Time Workout*, which is also an excellent workout for those of us who are not physically fit and are just getting started after being away from exercise for too long. These tapes are widely available from booksellers and video stores, or you can get them by contacting The Workout, Inc. P.O. Box 2957, Beverly Hills, CA 90213).

✔ *If you don't do anything else—walk.* Walking is cheap, easy, safe (for most people), and a very effective aerobic exercise. Walking 30 to 45 minutes per day at a moderate pace (3 to 3.5 miles per hour) is beneficial for most people. If you are overweight, or if obesity or diabetes runs in your family, *how long you walk* is more important than how fast. Aim for 45 minutes to 1 hour of continuous walking daily at a comfortable pace. If you want to improve your aerobic fitness or reduce stress, you might want gradually to increase your speed—up to about a 15-minute mile (4 miles per hour). If you have respiratory or heart problems, make sure you walk indoors in a climate-controlled, pollution-free environment (breathing in car exhaust fumes is *not* for you!). Malls are perfect places for this! If you have arthritis or sports injuries to your back or legs, avoid steep hills—aim for level ground. You put less strain on weight-bearing joints that way.

Jane Fonda has put together two excellent tapes for walkers, called *Jane Fonda's Fitness Walkout.* Using specially selected music, timed to the speed at which you should walk, these tapes comprise four levels of walking, from beginner to very advanced. Also included are diagrams of stretching exercises to use during the warm-up and cool-down periods, as well as information on taking your pulse to determine your appropriate walking speed.

The activities listed in Table 10.5 can all qualify as fitness activities if the activities are continuous and vigorous. Different fitness activities appeal to different kinds of people, so check out your personality type for a good match:

In order to achieve the maximum aerobic benefits from any activity you choose, you need to exercise at 60 to 75 percent of your maximum predicted heart rate (but remember, if you are a beginner, over 40, or sedentary, this is a goal you must work up to gradually—never exceed 70 percent of your maximum heart rate in the beginning, and never exceed 75 percent of your maximum heart rate without being evaluated by your physician).

Table 10.5. Fitness Activities Matched to Personality Types

Activity	Type A	Type B	Type S
Aerobic dancing or exercising	X (maybe)	X	
Archery			X
Badminton		X	
Baseball		X	
Basketball	X (maybe)	X	
Bowling		X	
Canoeing	X	X	
Carpentry		X	X
Cross-country skiing		X	X
Cycling	X		X
Cycling—stationary		X	X
Dancing—ballet		X	X
Dancing—ballroom		X	
Dancing—jazz		X	X
Dancing—square		X	
Downhill skiing	X		
Fencing			X
Football	X		
Gardening		X	X
Golf		X	X
Handball	X		
Hiking	X		X (maybe)
Horseback riding		X	X
House cleaning		X	X
Ice hockey	X		
Jogging		X	X
Judo	X		
Karate	X		
Racewalking	X		
Racquetball	X		
Rowing			X
Running	X		X
Running—marathon	X		
Sailing		X	X
Sailing—competitive	X		
Skating		X	X
Squash	X		
Stair-climbing or step-climbing	X	X (in a group class)	
Swimming		X	X
Tennis—doubles		X	X
Tennis—singles	X		
Volleyball	X	X	
Walking—alone			X
Walking—with a group or a friend		X	
Water-skiing		X	X
Weight training	X		
Yoga or stretching		X	X

To figure your maximum predicted heart rate, subtract your age from 220. If you are 38, your maximum heart rate is 182 (220 − 38). Your beginning target rate should be 60 percent of your maximum heart rate, provided you are healthy enough to reach it. If you are 38, your minimum training rate should be 109 (60 percent of 182).

So now you know what your ideal heart rate should be while you are exercising. How do you tell if you have reached or exceed it? You need to take your pulse, at least twice during your exercise period while you are getting started until you are familiar with your body and its rhythms. To take your pulse, hold one hand in front of you with your palm up (the hand you don't wear a watch on). Place three fingers from you other hand on the thumb side of your wrist of the hand you are holding palm up. Feel around until you find an artery with a pulse or beat. Using your watch or a clock as a timer, count the number of beats for 10 seconds, beginning with 0 for the first beat, and then multiply by 6. This gives you your heart's beats per minute—your heart rate.

A good way to test your current level of fitness and determine whether the training heart rate you have determined is appropriate for you is to try the following exercise. Walk as briskly as you can until you have reached a heart rate that is 60 percent of your maximum predicted heart rate as figured earlier. Stop and listen to your body—do you feel anything in your joints, muscles, breathing, or chest that indicate you are pushing too hard? If so, back off and check with your physician before you go any further with an exercise program.

If you don't have any problems and feel good, then continue at your minimum training rate for up to 10 minutes, or as long as you can without feeling fatigue or discomfort. Then cool down for a few minutes by doing your exercise activity more slowly.

It is absolutely vital that you build up your time and the vigor of your exercise *gradually*. Don't expect to maintain your minimum training rate even for 10 minutes if you have been very sedentary. It can take up to six weeks, or even longer, to work up to maintaining your minimum training rate for 30 minutes. Then stay at that level for at least a month before you gradually move up to 65 percent of your maximum heart rate, and so forth. Don't hurry—listen to your body, and give yourself a break!

An excellent rule of thumb is, if you can carry on a conversation while you are doing your chosen fitness activity, you are exercising properly for your current body condition.

Sleep

Somehow, businesspeople have gotten a warped view about sleep. Many of the popular magazines tout ways to cut back on the amount of sleep you get, so that you can have more time to accomplish all the work and tasks you have to do. It has become very macho to brag to colleagues that you *really* need only four hours of sleep a night. People talk about pulling all-nighters when on deadline, just as they used to do in college—except we're not 19 years old anymore. Working women seem to be the most sleep-deprived of all—mainly because they still have work to do around the house when they get home from work.

The need for seven to eight hours of sleep a night is *not* a sign of laziness or emotional weakness; it's a biological imperative for the typical adult. True, people with different lifestyles need differing amounts of sleep, but people under chronic or dangerous stress need even more sleep. That's because the body repairs itself while you are sleeping, and there is more damage to repair when you are under stress.

Researchers are finding that sleep deprivation has become an important health problem in the United States. While their experiments have not shown conclusively that lack of sleep causes physical illness, we do know that mental alertness and performance definitely suffer when we don't get adequate sleep. People who don't get enough sleep can't think straight, can't make appropriate judgements, and can't maintain their attention spans for very long—which can add up to traffic accidents and accidents on the job.

How can you tell if you are getting enough sleep? The best way is to ask yourself how many times you've said "I've got to get more sleep." Do you need an alarm clock to wake up? Do you habitually hit the snooze button after the alarm goes off? How many times do you hit it? Do you fall asleep within 5 minutes of going to bed? Adequately rested people typically fall asleep within 15 minutes of retiring, sleep-deprived folks nod off as soon as their heads hit the pillow. Can you take a nap whenever you want? Many people like to boast that they can catch 40 winks at will, but what it really means is that they are sleep-deprived.

To get a good feel for how much sleep you need, think about how much sleep you had several days into your last vacation. How much you sleep on the weekend isn't a good indication: You are probably already sleep deprived by Friday night, and most people sleep in on Saturday and Sunday to make up for that sleep loss. But after three or four days into your vacation, you will have caught up on lost sleep, and be into your natural rhythms, which include sleeping until you wake up naturally. *That's* the amount of sleep you should try to get on a regular basis during the week.

On days when you haven't gotten adequate sleep, you will probably notice that your normal midafternoon slump is worse than usual. If you are lucky, you can take a nap—but taking a brisk walk is even better. It will rev you up a bit. Or have a piece of fruit—the carbohydrates and sugars will give you a small spurt of energy. Drinking something with caffeine in it may *feel* as if it works, but you will probably notice yet another slump in a couple of hours, once the caffeine wears off.

You need to be good to yourself when you are under chronic or dangerous stress, and getting enough sleep is one way to do that. Don't try to short-change yourself on sleep—it doesn't work in the long run, and can cause more harm than good. We discuss sleep problems later in this book, but if you aren't having trouble sleeping, just having trouble getting *enough* sleep, do yourself a favor. Go to bed 60 to 90 minutes earlier each night for at least a week. Yes, we know that means you might not get some things done around the house, you might miss the late news, or one bit of paperwork won't get done. But see how good you feel.

11
A Compendium of Coping Techniques

Behavioral Rehearsal

Behavioral rehearsal is just that—rehearsing a series of thoughts and actions you can use to cope with stressful situations before they happen. Not only does this sharpen your awareness of what stress feels like for you in certain situations, but it helps train you to plan and make use of self-instruction, creative thinking, and alternative coping methods.

Many people find it helpful to practice new behaviors with a friend, but you can also do it by yourself. You reap the most benefits from behavioral rehearsal if you practice a new behavior several times before actually using it.

Rehearsals are simple tools, but they require that you carefully think through situations that are particularly stressful for you. Remember, we usually imagine situations that are much worse than anything likely to happen in reality. The following guidelines can help make behavioral rehearsals work for you.

✔ *Become aware of what thoughts and feelings occur to you in a particular stressful situation that bothers you.* Ask yourself, "what thoughts or feelings tell me stress is near?"

✔ *Sort through ideas and beliefs that can make you more upset and tense.* Ask yourself, "What thoughts do I have about this situation that make me even more upset?"

✔ *Think about what you can do to prepare for the stressful situation.* Ask yourself, "What can I do to change the situation?" (There's almost always something you can do to make the situation less stressful.)

✔ *Now imagine yourself successfully handling the stressful situation.* Picture what your thoughts and actions would be.

☞ *Focus on how you will feel once you've handled the stressful situation successfully.*
Ask yourself, "How will I feel? What have I learned about myself and stress?"

☞ *Think about what you could do to reward yourself after you have handled the
stressful situation.* It is very important to reward yourself when you have done
something that ordinarily would be very upsetting or stressful for you to do. Ask
yourself, "What can I do to give myself a pat on the back and make myself feel
good about what I've accomplished?"

Most people find that it is most effective to tackle one stressful situation at
a time when they are practicing behavioral rehearsal. Remember, nothing
succeeds like success!

Don't worry if you are unable to reduce your anxiety and tension level
right away. Remember that you have been experiencing these familiar
reactions for a long time, and they have almost become habits. As with all
habits, you may lapse back into your old reactions after you think you've
solved the problem. This is normal and is to be expected. Just decide to
practice behavioral rehearsal again the next time you know you will encounter the stressful situation. You might want to try some alternative coping
techniques listed in this book as well.

Try to avoid a sense of failure. You can do that by not setting unrealistic
goals for yourself. It is also important to reward yourself when you master a
previously stressful situation. As adults we're taught that we shouldn't need
rewards for things we should be doing anyway. Nuts to that! When you do
something as great as mastering a stressful situation without feeling your old
familiar stress reactions, you've done a big piece of work! And you deserve a
reward! Remember that rewards work best when they are something you
really want, not something you *think* you should want.

Biofeedback

Biofeedback is finding increasing application in stress management today.
Essentially, it is a process in which information about a person's biological
activity is collected, processed in some way, and relayed back to the individual so that the biological activity can ultimately be modified. Biofeedback
is a high-tech treatment, because sophisticated machinery and trained personnel are used; but the process itself is really quite simple and effective in
managing stress on two fronts:

- Helping facilitate a relaxation response and, in doing so, treating the stress
  response itself

- Helping alter target-organ activity, and treating the symptoms of excessive stress
  arousal

Three kinds of biofeedback have proven very useful in helping people
cope with the effects of stress.

1. Electromyographic (EMG) biofeedback uses an electromyograph—an instrument in which electrical impulses are picked up through special sensors (called electrodes), that are applied to the skin with a special conducting jelly. These electrical impulses are signals that our body is doing something, and the electromyograph amplifies these impulses and displays them in some way so that we can see or hear them. It may display the impulses as a pattern of lights, the movement of a needle on a meter, a sound that gets louder as the impulse gets stronger, or any combination of these. Once people learn what these signals mean, they can begin to modify the body activity the impulse measures—usually muscle tension.

EMG biofeedback has proven especially useful for muscle-contraction problems, such as that found in muscle-tension headaches and bruxism (the grinding or clenching of the teeth and jaws). What happens in these problems is that, under stress, muscle contraction can increase so slowly and imperceptibly that the person is not aware of the increased muscle tension until the muscles go into spasm. The key is learning when the muscles just begin to tense up, and then working consciously on relaxing them. EMG biofeedback provides a visual or auditory display of muscle activity, so that people can learn to identify when their muscles are the least bit tensed up. Then they can consciously relax those muscles *before* they go into spasm.

2. Temperature biofeedback is another type of biofeedback useful in managing stress. The underlying concept in this approach is that skin temperature is a function of the dilation and constriction of blood vessels— the more the blood vessels are dilated, the more blood can flow through them, and the warmer the skin becomes.

Temperature biofeedback uses a sensor called a termistor, a small temperature-sensing device usually taped to a person's finger. The sensor is connected to a device that processes the temperature readings into some sort of display—either lights, a sound, or the movement of a needle on a meter.

Temperature biofeedback is useful for those stress-induced problems that involve the circulatory system, such as migraine headaches, hypertension, or even asthma. It is also a useful tool for helping teach general relaxation, because skin temperature is a good indicator of how aroused the nervous system is.

3. Electrodermal (EDR) biofeedback is also useful in helping to manage stress. EDR biofeedback works on the same principles as EMG biofeedback, but instead of measuring the electrical impulses of the muscles, EDR biofeedback measures the electrical impulses given off by the skin in the galvanic skin response. The higher our galvanic skin response is, the more stressed out we are. EDR can help us identify when we are just beginning to get stressed-out, so we can learn to spot the signs easily.

The key to successful use of any kind of biofeedback is the relationship the person develops with the trained therapist who runs the equipment and provides feedback to the stress victim on what the information means. In addition, the stress victim must be motivated to want to get better and to practice between sessions what was learned. If you think biofeedback might be useful for you, talk it over with your physician, who can help you determine whether biofeedback is an appropriate treatment for you, and can refer you to qualified biofeedback practitioners.

Breathing Exercises

How often have you heard people say, "If you want to calm down, just take three deep breaths?" They were telling you the truth! By taking deep breaths, you relax the muscles in your chest and stomach and slightly increase the carbon dioxide level in your blood, which has a tranquilizing effect. The following exercises can work wonderfully, but, remember, the idea is not to force your breathing but rather to relax and enjoy the experience. If you begin to feel dizzy or hyperventilated, just stop for a minute and rest.

Exercise 1: Calming Breathing

Inhale deeply through your nose, trying to take the air all the way down to your stomach. We rarely use our lungs to their full capacity. Most people breathe only with the top part of their lungs when they take short breaths. So expand your stomach so that you can fill your lungs completely. Exhale slowly through your mouth, trying to empty your lungs completely. As you exhale, your stomach should contract (some people do just the reverse). Relax, and repeat as often as you feel comfortable until you begin to feel calm.

Exercise 2: Timed Breathing

Inhale slowly through your nose to the count of 3. Hold your breath to the count of 3, then exhale slowly to the count of 3. Repeat this pattern for several minutes. Experiment a little. Some people find that a count of 4 or 5 works better. It's fun to do this exercise while you are walking or running, timing your breathing to your steps. Keep this a smooth, flowing process and you'll probably find yourself walking more slowly and enjoying the view!

Exercise 3: Feeling Sleepy

Breathing can also help you feel sleepy when you have insomnia. Researchers find that when people sleep, carbon dioxide levels in the blood are higher than when they are awake. Increasing the carbon dioxide level in your blood slightly can help you feel drowsy. Follow these simple steps:

1. Settle into a comfortable position. If your pillow is high enough to keep your head tilted backward a little, it will help relax the muscles in your throat and mouth.

2. Gently close your eyes.

3. Breathe in deeply, filling your lungs and expanding your chest. Breathe out, drawing in your stomach to exhale as much as possible. Repeat 2 more times.

4. Next, hold your breath for as long as you comfortably can. This increases the carbon dioxide level in your blood. When you feel you want to breathe again, repeat the process outlined in step 3. It is important not to take any more than three deep breaths in any part of this exercise in order to keep the carbon dioxide level just right. You can repeat this process as often as it takes you to feel sleepy. Some people need to repeat the process only a few times; others may need longer.

Favorite Passions: Hobbies and Leisure Activities

Leisure-time activities can be a great help in coping with the effects of stress. That's why everybody should have *at minimum* two or three favorite passions. Chances are good that if you are a typical stress victim, you haven't thought about hobbies or spare time in years.

But leisure time is even more important when you're trying to cope with stress in your daily life. Hobbies or passions can help in several ways: They take your mind off things that are worrying you, allow you time to recharge your batteries, expand your horizons, increase your self-esteem, expose you to new ideas, and let you have fun with people you like. Everybody needs time away from work and worries—you are no exception! In case you haven't thought about fun since you collected baseball cards or doll clothes, here are a few suggestions:

✔ *Everyone is gifted with creativity in some way, so forget about rules, other people's ideas, or what is acceptable.* Baking bread, painting your living room, rearranging your workshop, and so on are all creative pursuits. Experiment around and find out what suits you best, then do it in a way that suits *you*.

✔ *It is important to make your leisure time different enough from your work that you really do get a mental and physical break.* For example, if you are with people all day, your hobby might be most beneficial if you can do it off somewhere alone. If you are relatively quiet and sedentary in your daily life, your passion might be more fun if it involved other people, lots of action, and noise. If you do thinking— head work—as a job, it might be fun to do something that doesn't involve thinking, such as going to the movies or knitting (easy patterns). Experiment, and remember that it is important to complement your activities at work with your activities at play.

✔ *Your interests and passions will change as your life changes.* If a hobby gets boring, check out why, and then look around for something else. Very few things stay with us forever, and hobbies are no exception. You may be lucky enough to have a grand passion—that you have done since you were a kid, absolutely love, and can't imagine not doing. Hobbies such as painting, music, needlework, and cabinetry—to name a few—have enough depth and breadth to give you room to explore and experiment with new techniques, tools, and materials over the years, as you move from being a hobbyist to a true craftsperson. The hobby's scope gives it room to grow and change as your needs grow and change.

✔ *It's okay to make mistakes.* If your passion of choice involves a certain level of skill, such as needlepoint, tennis, fly fishing, or cooking, it is okay to make mistakes while you are learning. Once again, passions are more fun if you know how to do them right and have the right equipment. So go buy a book or take a class. Besides, you might meet some interesting people!

Friends, Family, and Supporters

Who do you turn to when you are under stress? Your spouse? Significant other? Best friend? Family? Support helps tremendously when we're under chronic or dangerous stress, and, when we get it, our bodies seem to work better. That's because the energy we would normally use to generate all our own support can be used for dealing with the stressful event—our adaptive energy can be used in other ways.

Granted, our primary support needs to come from within ourselves. Most of the time we can meet our own needs for support adequately, or with little help from others. Usually we can handle our own unhappiness and create our own good feelings. But when we are under stress, the support and nurturing we get from friends, family, and neighbors helps reaffirm that we are worthy people (which we often don't feel when we're under stress), and reinforces our connection with the larger community of human beings.

If you have workaholic tendencies, you will be inclined to let personal relationships slide by the wayside: You are always busy, on the road, or working on projects on the weekend. You don't notice this at first, but gradually you quit calling friends because you don't have time to see or talk with them, and then they quit calling you because they know that you'll be too busy to visit or get together. Pretty soon, you're down to a couple of friends and your spouse, significant other, or family.

It really doesn't hit you until one or more of your friends get transferred to other cities, laid off, or quit the company to join another; or some crisis occurs in your life and you need some help, but you find that all your friends live in different cities now and there is literally no one to help you. You can find yourself all alone—and lonely—and that feels even worse when you are in a stressful situation.

Many of us expect our spouses or significant others to meet all our needs for nurturing, support, companionship, advice, and so forth. But that's a pretty tall order. What happens if he or she is in a crisis situation at the same time you are? Neither of you will have the energy available to meet the other's needs adequately, and you both will end up feeling you've let the other down—on top of being stressed out. This situation is guaranteed to lower your already low feelings of self-esteem and worth.

We all need friends, and, although different people need different kinds and amounts of friends, all humans crave companionship and connectedness. Friends can provide that, but friendships take work, planning, and effort. When you are already stretched to the limit timewise, spending time on building a friendship may seem like the last thing you should do—but, the richness and warmth friends bring to our lives are great stress reducers.

Developing relationships at work is important, too. We don't expect you to tell your innermost secrets to your colleague in the office next to you (in many cases doing so may not be wise), but building alliances and networks is a powerful way to reduce stress on the job. Work friendships can: tie you into the office grapevine and provide you with information you might not otherwise be privy to; foster the development of a "mutual aid society" of people to commiserate with (especially important during reorganizations, mergers, and reductions in force); act as a reality check when stressful situations develop on the job; increase your pool of ideas on how to handle a crisis or stressful situation; link you into wider networks of colleagues and friends outside your company (also especially important during reorganizations and reductions in force); and sometimes, if you're lucky, even develop into close friendships.

Work friendships also take time, effort, and planning, but they enhance our feelings of self-esteem and worth in ways that outside friendships cannot. What we do in our careers comprises a tremendously large part of our self-concepts. We *are* what we do. When we are under stress at work, support, encouragement, and advice from work friends carries more weight with us than that provided by outside friends, simply because our work friends have been there with us and know the stressful situation intimately.

Keeping tied in with your extended family is also important. One of the great American myths is that, once you "leave the nest" (or graduate college, or get married, or whatever signifies adulthood to you), you shouldn't be closely tied to your family—you should make it on your own. What a rotten myth! For most of us, our family is one of the very few places where we can experience unconditional positive regard, as therapists say, meaning that we are accepted and loved just for being who we are. Families provide us with links to the past and our history, as well as our future.

Our relationships with our parents, brothers, sisters, aunts, uncles, and cousins change over the years. Just because you always fought with your brothers and sisters as a kid doesn't mean you have to continue to fight with them as an adult. You begin to view your parents as adults, with the same sort of concerns and problems we have in our own families. True, your mom may try to feed you too much whenever you visit, but it's important to get beyond this one aspect of the relationship and begin to treat each other as adults. It can be done, and the rewards are great. We all change, and sometimes our relatives change into pretty great people, if we give them half a chance. Besides, once you hit your late thirties, much of parents' advice starts to make sense!

Even pets can add a great deal to your life. They are a source of unconditional devotion and acceptance. Research has shown that people's blood pressure drops when then pet, play with, or groom their pets. Even watching fish swim around in an aquarium is soothing. Other research shows that people who have pets live longer than people without pets. Pets, particularly dogs, can provide you with a reason to get some regular exercise. Yes, they can be a hassle sometimes, but people who have had pets cannot imagine their lives without them. So think about it—there are lots of pets at your local animal shelter who could benefit from a good home.

So, do you have all the emotional support you need? If you hesitated even an instant in answering that question, get your address book. Call the friend you've been meaning to talk with for the last several weeks, but never got around to calling; phone your folks; and make plans to go out to lunch with someone from work who is interesting or who has been going through a tough time. Don't wait for people to come to you, your professional facade may be sending signals that you're just too busy for friendship, even if you really are looking for friends. Remember, giving is getting, and nowhere is that truer than in friendships.

A Good Cry

In our culture, crying has been given a bum rap. We are taught that grownups don't cry—only children cry. And men are *never* supposed to cry. Recent research is beginning to show that *not* crying may not be such a good idea.

University of Minnesota research has shown that there are two important chemicals present in tears—leucine-enkephalin and prolactin. Researchers believe that leucine-enkephalin could be an endorphin, a hormone released by the brain as a natural pain reliever, and that tears may rid the body of other substances that accumulate while a person is under chronic or dangerous stress.

So *not* crying could be harmful to your health. But granted, most of us would *die* before we burst into tears at work or in front of friends or family members. So do it on the sly—the shower is a great place (if your eyes get red you can always say you got soap or shampoo in your eyes); alone at home (with the curtains drawn, if you are really nervous about it); with your therapist; or when you are alone in your car (please pull off the road if you try this).

Guilty Pleasures

Guilty pleasures are great! They are those dumb (and not so dumb) things you love to do but are embarrassed to tell anyone about. Everybody has at least one or two guilty pleasures. People like yourself came up with these:

- Eating ice cream right out of the carton
- Pigging out on Frango chocolates
- Shopping—for anything!
- Eating animal crackers
- Sleeping until noon and skipping your workout on Saturday
- Zoning out in front of a fire with a "spot of brandy"
- Playing "air guitar" to rock music from the seventies and eighties
- Taking long bubble baths, with low lights and soft jazz on in the background
- Doing crossword puzzles
- Shopping for lacy lingerie
- Sleeping in the sun
- Reading trashy romance novels
- Reading bestseller mystery novels
- Watching reruns of *Star Trek*, *Bonanaza*, or *The Brady Bunch*
- Renting B movie videos
- Searching antique shops and sales for antique toys
- Cooking and eating "comfort foods"

Nothing is wrong with guilty pleasures as long as you don't go overboard and spend all your time doing them. In fact, as rewards during periods of stress, they can often make life seem worth living. People under stress tend to dismiss guilty pleasures as wastes of time, when, in reality, they can be sanity savers.

In fact, they are so important that we believe people should indulge in at least three per day. Guilty pleasures can last anywhere from two minutes to a full day. To help you begin to build up to three guilty pleasures a day, fill out the following list with ideas of things you can indulge in—at work, at home, and on the road—for the lengths of time listed in Table 11.1.

Table 11.1. Personal List of Guilty Pleasures

2–5 Minutes	5–30 Minutes	30 Minutes– half a day	Half a day or more

When was the last time you indulged in a guilty pleasure?

Hugs

Virginia Satir, a family therapist and counselor, believed people need a minimum of 10 hugs a day in order to survive. If people want to grow and develop, they need up to 15 hugs a day. Children need even more.

People under stress need even more hugs per day in order to function effectively—maybe as many as 20! Hugs make you feel good because they show you someone else cares about you and likes you. They reinforce your self-esteem, they give you a breathing space and a break from stressful situations, and they allow for contact with other people. When you are under stress, you cannot get too much of a good thing! Hugs in our society have become connected with sex, but hugs don't have to be physical. Consideration, courtesy, kind words, or just a smile can qualify as a hug.

What should you do if you're not getting your full daily quota of hugs? Ask for them! Nothing is wrong with asking; if the askee says no, just ask someone else. But you probably won't be refused. Most people are happy to give out hugs. You can also make it a point to give hugs. In fact, the benefits you get giving two hugs equals the benefits you get receiving one hug!

Humor

Humor is crucial to mental health—yes, crucial. When was the last time you laughed? In *Anatomy of an Illness*, Norman Cousins documents the positive effect laughter had on reducing pain he suffered from a severe arthritis-like illness—for him it was even more effective than painkillers. Researchers exploring the uses of humor have found that making fun of life's problems and our reactions to them can help us tolerate those problems for longer periods of time. Humor can be a tension breaker, a mood lifter, a relationship mender, and a pain reliever.

We're not talking about teasing, though. Many people confuse teasing with joking or kidding, but underlying all teasing is an element of hostility intended to pierce the receiver at a vulnerable point. These people are not being funny, they are being mean. Usually such people tease others because they feel inferior or inadequate, and teasing is a way they can feel superior for a while. Although teasers may be pitiable for this reason, the recipient of the teasing suffers too. Teasing can leave scars that last a lifetime, especially for children.

Joking or kidding means gentle ribbing about reactions or behaviors that are overdramatized or overblown, but only once and for the purpose of alleviating tension or cooling down a hot situation. This kind of kidding is not based on sarcasm, but on a realistic outlook.

There are all kinds of humor: slapstick, puns, cartoons, limericks, burlesque, parody, satire. Experiment and find what works best for you. As your mood changes, so can the kind of humor you find enjoyable.

But once you've latched on to what makes you laugh, try and laugh at least twice a day—not just "tee-hees," but big "ho-hos," every day. Our experience is that most businesspeople haven't *really* laughed in ages. In these serious times you are expected to be serious at work, and that tends to carry over into your life away from work. Think of laughter as sanity insurance!

Journals and Diaries

Keeping journals and diaries probably dates back to when human beings learned how to communicate with symbols on rocks or tablets. Journals must have something going for them, or the idea wouldn't have lasted so long.

Many people think that writing thoughts and feelings in a journal or diary is useful in sorting out problem areas, values, and goals. When your mind is whirling with thoughts chasing themselves in a circle, putting things down on paper can help. Things that seem insurmountable floating around in your head often become manageable when drawn out on paper. Values become clearer as you write about things and people that are important to you. Your goals may begin to take shape as you explore your relationship with the world.

Some people write daily in journals, others make entries only when the spirit moves them. Some write poetry, others write only thoughts or phrases that are meaningful for them. Journals can be used to make notes about dreams, which can be extremely helpful if you have recurring dreams or nightmares and want to know what meaning they have for you. Some people write down worries, gripes, concerns, or snappy comebacks to insults, and find that by doing so, they can stop thinking about them and fall asleep. Some researchers and writers use their diaries or journals to write down insights or ideas so they won't be forgotten.

The point is that journals and diaries can be anything you want them to be—from a special confidant to a record of history for your grandchildren. You might be intimidated by the prospect of writing down your thoughts or feelings, but grammar, spelling, phrasing, and readability are not important. No one will ever read your journal or diary unless you choose to share it with them, and then, we guarantee you, they won't be grading you on punctuation or spelling!

Putting your thoughts and feelings into words also becomes easier with practice, which is especially helpful if you have trouble talking about your feelings. When you find it difficult to think about what to write, you might, for a start, try writing your autobiography as you remember it. Thinking back over your experiences, you will be able to get a clearer picture of who you are and how you got that way. You will also clarify your values and feelings in the process.

Massage

Massage is an ancient tension reliever. When muscles get all knotted up from stress, massaging them helps bring blood back into the sore muscles, breaking down biochemicals that cause cramping. Some people think that the best kind of massage is the kind someone else gives them, but sometimes no one is around to do that! If that's the case, you can do it yourself and reap similar benefits.

When you're under stress, you might notice that particular muscle groups become tight and sore again and again. Those sore areas are your weak spots—groups of muscles you tense up almost automatically when you are in a stressful situation. The following are some quick ways to ease the soreness in those spots yourself.

Face

Facial massages are great for relieving tension and sinus headaches, as well as for providing a healthy glow. Facial massages are best done lying down with your eyes closed. Put both hands gently over your face and start by gently massaging your forehead with your fingers in a slow, circular motion. Be very gentle—facial tissue is fragile. Slide your hands down a bit and gently repeat the circular motion over your eyelids and eye sockets. Place your fingertips at the corners of your mouth and, stroking gently in an upward motion, massage your cheeks all the way up to your temples.

If you have a sinus headache, you may notice pressure under your eyes, along your cheekbones, and above your eyes. Massaging your cheekbones and jaw area using a circular motion with your fingertips might help relieve some of this pressure. Feel gently in your eye socket near the corner of your eye close to your nose and see if you can find a tender spot. Apply gentle pressure there for a few seconds, and some of the pain may be relieved. It also helps to use firm, stroking movements downward from your forehead to your ears.

Feet

Your feet are probably the hardest-working part of your body—and the most often ignored. As a result, you can easily get sore feet! Here are some ways to relieve the pain:

Sit comfortably with your left leg crossed over your right leg. Grasping your left foot, use your knuckles to massage the sole of your foot. Press firmly, moving in small circles. Go slowly and apply moderate pressure. Tender spots may mean that area needs more attention.

Now move to the top of your foot. Using the tips of your thumb, cover the top of your foot from the toes to the ankle, massaging in a firm, gentle, circular motion.

You will notice long tendons that run along the tops of your feet from the base of the ankle to each toe. Press firmly with the top of your thumb in the valleys between these tendons and run your thumb down the tendon to the toe.

Massage the bottom edge of your heel with fingertips and thumb. You can apply firm pressure here. Repeat these processes for your other foot.

Head

Using the index and middle fingers of your hands, massage your scalp using deep pressure for about five seconds. Gradually work your way around your whole head. Move your hands behind your head and place your index and middle fingers of both hands in the slight indentation at the center of the top of your neck, just below the base of your skull. Apply moderate pressure here for a few seconds, moving your fingers in a circular motion.

Now move your hands away from each other along the base of your skull about an inch or two and pause there to apply moderate pressure in a circular motion. Once again, move your fingers an inch or two more to the point where the base of your skull is adjacent to your ears. Pause for a few seconds and apply pressure here as well.

Neck

There is a large muscle that runs along each side of your neck from the base of your skull to your shoulders. Place the fingers of each hand on these muscles and knead them thoroughly for a few seconds. Move your fingers slowly down the muscle to your shoulders, kneading as you go.

Shoulders

Most people have a tender spot slightly to the rear of each shoulder, about halfway between the base of the neck and the edge of the shoulder. Find this spot by pressing gently along your shoulder and then applying moderate pressure on the tender spot for a few seconds. Repeat a few times on both shoulders.

Gently grasp the big muscle that runs along the top of your shoulder (the trapezius muscle) and gently knead all along the top of your shoulders. You may feel some bumps or knots—those are the parts of the muscle that are tensed up. Continue kneading until you feel the lumps or knots ease away and any pain subsides.

Upper Back

Yes, you can massage your own back! It will take some stretching, but it is really worth the effort. Reach your left hand over your right shoulder as far down the right side of your spine as your arm can comfortably reach. Using your index, middle, and third fingers, apply pressure up your spine. Repeat this using your right hand over your left shoulder.

Meditation

Meditation is really very simple—all it involves is a conscious clearing of your mind, silencing all the thoughts and conversations we constantly carry on with ourselves. These conversations can be a source of stress as we worry about a problem, scold ourselves, or think about upcoming events. You can give yourself breathing room by becoming aware of these conversations and learning to silence them.

Most researchers find that at least 20 minutes is necessary to reap the full benefits of meditation. When you are learning how to meditate, it can be helpful to set aside two 20-minute periods each day to familiarize yourself with how your body reacts to relaxation. The following guidelines explain the meditation process in a nutshell:

1. Find a quiet place where you can be by yourself and avoid interruptions.

2. Set a timer or alarm clock for 20 minutes, so that you don't have to worry about keeping track of time.

3. Loosen any clothing that is tight or uncomfortable.

4. Sit in a comfortable position or lie down on the floor, a couch, or a bed, placing a pillow or cushion under your head.

5. Close your eyes and try to concentrate on something that is pleasing to you. You will probably find that your brain is capable of focusing on a relaxing thought and still carrying on a conversation about something else, or you may find that your brain is focusing on your breathing or how your arm feels. Don't worry, just gently push that thought out of your mind, telling yourself that you will deal with it later. Return to your relaxing thought. If a relaxing thought doesn't seem to be working, try repeating a special word (something or someone you like), or even just a syllable, such as *om*. You can say it softly aloud if that helps—and it might when you are just getting started with meditation. As you become more practiced in meditation, you will find that mind wandering disappears.

6. Gradually you will feel relaxed, calm, and refreshed. When the alarm or timer sounds, open your eyes and slowly bring yourself back into your surroundings. Don't jump up right away and plunge back into your work! Stretch a little, yawn if you feel like it, and give yourself a pat on the back for taking such good care of yourself! Don't worry if you don't notice tremendous results right away. Relaxation will come the more you practice meditation.

Be patient with meditating. Most new users find that it takes a week or two before they begin to experience deep relaxation and rejuvenation. So stick with it, even if it doesn't seem to be doing you much good right away.

Many people report that their powers of concentration are greatly enhanced when they meditate. Other people find that meditation sessions allow them to think creatively about problems they are facing—their mind wanderings actually turn up solutions to their problems. So all mind wanderings aren't bad; they're harmful only if they make you uptight and tense when you want to relax!

Progressive Muscle Relaxation

Progressive muscle relaxation is a systematic way to relax all the major muscle groups in your body. It also helps to make you aware of what muscle groups you habitually "carry tense": Most people in chronic or dangerous stress situations have a muscle group that gets tensed up repeatedly. You may carry your shoulders up around your ears, or have the muscles around your diaphragm in your upper stomach always tensed. After awhile, that tensed-up muscle group begins to feel normal, and you may be unaware that the muscle is tensed. Going through progressive muscle relaxation for the first time is often a revelation for some people—they find tense muscles they didn't even know they had!

The basic principle of progressive muscle relaxation is that a muscle automatically relaxes after it has been forcefully contracted. The idea is to start contracting muscles forcefully from the top of your head down to your toes, and by the time you are done, all of your muscles will be completely relaxed.

It's easy to do. Wear loose clothing and sit in a comfortable chair or lie on a mat, your bed, or a firm couch. Don't hold your breath during the muscle contraction phase, and don't contract any muscle group that's weak or been injured.

Start with your forehead. Frown hard, and hold that frown for 5 seconds. Then let the frown go, and and let the muscles relax. Next move to your face, grimace hard, let go of the grimace, and let the muscles relax. Repeat the 5-second contracting and relaxing process with the following muscle groups in the order in which they are written: jaw, neck, shoulders, upper arms, lower arms, hands, back, chest, abdomen, buttocks, upper thigh, lower leg, and feet.

It takes some practice, but many people become so relaxed that they fall asleep by the time they reach their toes! If you have trouble remembering which muscle groups to contract when, try *Jane Fonda's Stretch and Stress Reduction Program* cassette (also available in VHS), on which she runs through progressive muscle relaxation step by step—with soft music in the background. The progressive muscle relaxation segment lasts approximately 15 minutes, and includes some breathing exercises.

Ultimate Relaxation (The Sports Music Company) is another excellent tape for practicing progressive muscle relaxation. The specially produced New Age-type music is combined with the sounds of a gentle, rolling surf—with a few birdcalls added in. It is truly a relaxing, soothing experience.

Rewards

In our society we are taught that rewards are okay for kids, but adults aren't supposed to need rewards. Rewards are important whatever your age—and they should be tangible, with a size or value equivalent to the magnitude of your accomplishment. Further, rewards *should not* be useful things, for example, a new calculator if you are in accounting or a new word processing software package if you do a lot of writing on your job (unless those are things you really want, but keep putting off getting for yourself).

Rewards should be things you ordinarily wouldn't get yourself or someone else wouldn't get for you. For example, an information technology planning manager in a large multinational corporation had always wanted a pair of diamond stud earrings. She had hinted again and again when asked about birthday and Christmas present ideas—all to no avail. The "puritan" in her said that diamond earrings were a frivolous waste of money, so she kept putting off buying them for herself. Then along came an information resources plan with a division that was nothing but problems from the word go. She worked miracles to get the planning process going, but it was very stressful for her. At times she thought the plan would never be completed. She decided that if she lived through this planning process, she had earned her stripes in corporate America—earned her diamond earrings. They became her personal goal—shopping for them kept her sane when the plan was bogged down in task-force bickering. The plan was completed, and approved by senior management, and she got her earrings. Were those earrings really a waste of money? Now she wears them every day to remind herself that she can do anything she sets her mind to!

Rewards can be very beneficial when you are working hard to change a behavior or a habit, such as cutting back on smoking, losing weight, starting a fitness program, or practicing assertiveness—especially when you are working on changing your life to cope more effectively with stress. All these things require work, an output of energy, and, usually, giving up old, comfortable ways of behaving. You deserve to be rewarded for a major decision and behavior change like that!

Think about things you could use as rewards for yourself: Come up with a list of about 10 rewards that you would enjoy. Then plan to give them to yourself at intervals during your change period: every few weeks, every fewer packs of cigarettes, and so forth. Most people experience a slump four to six weeks into any major change of lifestyle or behavior. Most people can maintain their initial enthusiasm for about three or four weeks. After that, things begin to get boring. If you haven't seen any major changes by six weeks, you'll probably give up. A couple of good rewards can provide you the impetus you need to keep going through that slump and beyond to the magic eighth or tenth week, when results usually begin to show up.

Rewards can even be effective on a smaller scale when you do something you ordinarily dread doing, such as confronting a coworker about something that angers you, telling your spouse when you have a need that's not being met, making a speech or giving a presentation, or working through all the papers on your desk. A long, hot shower, time spent reading a magazine or novel, a cup of tea or a glass of wine, or a phone call to a friend can be effective ways of giving yourself a pat on the back.

Rituals

Rituals is a term Alexandra Stoddard, in her book *Living a Beautiful Life*, uses to describe patterns that people create in everyday living that uplift the way we do ordinary things, so that a simple task rises to the level of something special, ceremonial, ritualistic. Rituals can make you feel better about yourself, your life, and your job, and make you feel more peaceful. We spend so much time and effort rushing around and saving up for tomorrow that we don't experience the individual days of our lives fully. But today is all we have, and, when we are under stress, we need constantly to remind ourselves of that, because our tendency is either to live in the past or the future.

What are some rituals that can make our job tasks more pleasant? Try on some of these ideas gathered from businesspeople like yourself:

- On Monday morning, when you know you will be in the office most of the week, buy flowers to put on your desk. The information technology manager who suggested this ritual now actually misses the flowers when they're not on her desk. She might get a single rose one week, a bunch of daisies another, tulips another time, and so forth. She doesn't spend much, the flowers brighten her office, and they add an incentive to drag herself into the office on Monday morning.

- After you shower in the morning, crawl back into bed with your breakfast, the morning paper, and the news on the radio or TV. The senior manager who does this religiously finds that it is a great way to ease into the day and makes dealing with reality more palatable. She *does* get *out* of bed after she finishes breakfast, though—no fair falling back asleep!

- Bring *good* coffee to work from home—either to make in the coffee maker or just carried in a thermos. You don't have to drink the stuff your employer provides just because it's free. The project manager who suggested this ritual says he can't believe how much better staff meetings seem when there's decent coffee to help you through.

- Use your favorite pen (or color of ink) to draft your memos, sign your name, doodle, and jot notes. The veterinarian who provided this ritual *loves* pens, but was always afraid to use her favorite fountain pens for fear she might lose them. But she hasn't lost one since she made it a ritual.

- Bring pictures of your family, friends, or pets to put on your credenza or desk. Yes, *everybody* does this, but look at it this way: they remind you that there is more to life than just work!

- Hunt out a place to get *really good* bagels or muffins for your daily snack, instead of junk food from the vending machine (it's always stale, anyway). The technical manager who suggested this ritual says a good bagel satisfies his urge to snack in a way Twinkies never could—so he's consuming fewer calories to boot!

- Order brightly colored file folders instead of boring manilla folders.

- Make a standing date to meet a special friend or colleague for lunch or coffee. This is important—see the section of this chapter, "Friends, Family, and Supporters."

- Take those who report to you directly to breakfast or lunch on a regular basis—and don't talk about work. It boosts morale, fosters goodwill and teamwork, and lets people get to know each other as people. The senior manager who does this says it's important to keep things casual (but away from the office), and to be willing to really *listen* to your people, and concentrate on making them feel comfortable.

- If your employer allows it, personalize your work space so that it works for you. That can be as simple as getting matching in boxes, out boxes, and pencil cups—or as artistic as using your favorite color for file folders, pencils, pens, and desk accessories.

- Get a really nice Daytimer, Filofax, or agenda—it might cost more, but you'll use it longer, won't lose it, and maybe even come to enjoy looking at it! You might also find yourself getting organized!

- Hang your kids' artwork up in your office. It will make your son or daughter feel great, and will remind you that life should be a balance of work and play.

- Daydream for a bit after lunch—it will promote creativity. The programmer who suggested this finds he gets some of his best ideas during this time.

- In nice weather, walk to appointments—don't automatically hail a cab. When you are out, notice the details of the buildings, the color of the sky, how the light looks. Or take a walk at lunch. The manager who does this every day (except when the Chicago weather prohibits it) says it makes all the difference in how he faces the afternoon. He says it helps him clear his head, reduce stress, and start fresh for an intense afternoon.

- Buy a nice mug in a color or pattern you like to use instead of Styrofoam cups. If you're a water drinker, invest in a small pitcher and matching glass—it will save you trips to the water cooler and remind you to drink eight glasses daily.

Get it? The idea is to transform daily tasks into meaningful activities by paying attention to the small details that go into those tasks. By doing that, we can enrich our daily lives, enhance our feelings of self-worth, and generally make work a little more fun!

Self-Talks

When was the last time you talked to yourself? If you are normal, it was probably within the last five minutes, and you probably weren't even aware that you were doing it! In this context, talking to yourself refers to those continuous thoughts and conversations we carry on inside our heads all the time.

Psychologists call these mental tapes self-talks. Some self-talks can be very positive, such as when you go over all the things you have to do over the course of the day and prioritize your agenda; when you come up with a new way to solve a difficult situation; or when you tell yourself how great you really are. Some self-talks are essentially background noise, such as when you think about what you want to eat for lunch, wonder if your flight will leave on time, remind yourself to pick up the dry cleaning after work, and so forth. But some self-talks can be harmful, such as ones in which you run yourself down, or ones where you foster a negative attitude and create stress without even knowing it.

What are some common negative self-talks? Read through the following list and check off how many you recognize saying to yourself in some form in the past week:

- "I'll never be able to compete for the new job that was just posted. They'll never think I'm competent enough."

- "I'll never make it to that meeting in time—traffic is terrible. I should have left earlier."

- "I never do anything right."

- "She couldn't possibly be interested in me because I'm too fat, too thin, too short, too tall—too whatever."

- "I can't tell my boss what I really think about this situation—he will just get angry, and I'll lose my job."

- "If I get laid off, it will be the end of the world. I don't know how I can possibly cope without a steady income."

- "It really irritates me how my coworker takes advantage of me when we are on deadlines. I know I should say something, but what if he complains to our boss?"

- "I don't know what's wrong with me. I should be able to complete this project on time. But what will happen if I don't?"

Sound familiar? You bet they do. Most of the time such messages impose unrealistically high expectations on us and those around us. They lead us to believe that we have no control over our lives, our feelings, or how we act. So we get all worked up, we focus on the worst that could possibly happen, and ultimately we start exhibiting stress-related problems.

But you can change your self-talks, even habitual ones. The hard part is realizing that you are carrying them on in your head all the time. When you are under a great deal of stress, make your goal doing the best you can under the circumstances—"good" is good enough. You don't have to be perfect. Expecting yourself to be perfect is unreasonable, because perfection is an unattainable goal—no matter what your parents told you when you were a kid!

Once you become aware of your self-talks, you can apply the test of logic to them. You may find that much of what you tell yourself is illogical. Ask yourself:

- Does this thought make any sense?

- What evidence do I have to support it?

- How do I know it's true? Who said so? What do they know about it anyway?

- Who says I should or shouldn't do something?

- Who says life has to be this way?

- Am I overgeneralizing or catastrophizing about this?

- What's the worst that could happen here?

It also helps to realize that many of our habitual self-talks are irrational. Psychologist Hermann Witte, in his book *Becoming Thick-Skinned,* lists 10 habitual, irrational self talks that are common, but contribute tremendously to feelings of stress. Read through this list, and think about how many of them you tell yourself:

✔ *"Things upset me."* In truth, you upset yourself. How you perceive an event or situation, and what you tell yourself about it determines how upset you get. Because you make yourself upset, you can also control how upset you get by changing your perceptions and self-talk.

✔ *"I don't control the nature, intensity, and duration of my emotional responses."* You can control the intensity of your reaction by rationally reviewing the situation and your perception of it. Even if an event happens suddenly and overwhelms you, you can lessen the duration of the stress by taking time to think through what happened and why. But don't totally cut off your emotional responses—experiencing them is very important, particularly in response to a major life event, such as losing a job, the death of a family member, and so forth. You can't begin to heal until you have experienced the pain. But you don't have to get permanently stuck in stress and pain because, while perhaps you can't control *getting* upset, you can control *how* upset you get and *how long* you stay upset.

✔ *"I inherited my emotional and stress responses."* You *learned* from your family how to respond to certain events, and because a certain response is learned, it can also be *unlearned.*

✔ *"I can't change the way I react."* Believe it or not, you have changed how you respond to certain situations over the years, and you will continue to change your reactions. But you will have more control over that change process if you look at your self-talks realistically.

✔ *"Things should and must go as I want them to."* Says who? As one manager so graphically put it to a colleague during a particularly frustrating team meeting, "Who died and made you God?" Believing this one is the mark of a perfectionist and sets you up for very unrealistic expectations of those around you—which is guaranteed to cause you great stress. You don't need any more *shoulds* in your life, nor do those around you. People who believe this self-talk also tend to expect much more from themselves than they do from other people. They push themselves harder, longer, and rate themselves on higher criteria. The first rule of life is to remember that you can't always control the way things go. If they turn out the way you want them to, great! But if they don't turn out as you might like, you can deal with it.

✔ *"I can't believe it. I don't understand it."* Telling ourselves that a situation has no rhyme or reason to it only serves to help us stay stuck in stress. A situation may not be completely understandable, but few situations are *completely* nonunderstandable. Carefully thinking through a situation and realistically analyzing it can help you see ways to cope. Now we don't mean *overanalyzing* the situation without getting information from others involved—when you do this, you only make yourself more stressed out because you tend to rely on your negative self-talk tapes for answers. So talk to others involved; find out what they are really thinking and feeling—as opposed to imagining what they are thinking and feeling. At first, asking might be hard, but it will save you much grief later on.

✔ *"It's horrible. I can't stand it."* This thought involves exaggeration, and as long as you continue to exaggerate, you'll stay stuck in the stressful situation and won't be able to move on to solve it. Think through what you are really feeling. Are you embarrassed? sad? uncomfortable? furious? Putting a label on your feelings defuses your reaction without preventing you from experiencing it. Remember, *you can always make things seem worse than they really are.*

✔ *"My shortcomings make me a bad person, a loser, a failure."* No, they just make you human. You'll never be perfect, nor will anyone else. If you are really dissatisfied with one of your shortcomings, work on changing that. But realize that you can still be loved, respected, and liked, even if you have a few shortcomings.

✔ *"Others think as little of me as I do of myself."* This is rarely true, but if you dwell on it long enough, you can turn it into a self-fulfilling prophecy. People almost always take us at our own value, so if we don't value ourselves, neither will they. Others accept you as you present yourself to them, and you can control how you present yourself.

✔ *"This is hopeless. Things will never get better."* Hopelessness makes stressful situations a thousand times worse. Things not only can, but probably will, get better. The simple passage of time does make a difference. During that passage of time, you can learn to cope more effectively with stressful situations.

So think hard about your self-talks. Are they increasing your stress? If they are, think about deliberately changing them. If you don't feel you can do that on your own, work with a clergyperson, counselor, therapist, social worker, psychologist, or psychiatrist. Get yourself the help you need to make the changes. You won't regret it.

Affirmations

Another kind of self-talk is an affirmation. According to Susan Jeffers in her book *Feel the Fear and Do It Anyway*, an affirmation is a *positive statement that something is already happening.* When we want to make changes in our lives, one of the greatest powers we can tap is our subconscious or preconscious mind. This part of our brain believes everything we tell it, which is why the negative self-talks mentioned previously are so powerful and why substituting positive self-talks works so well. It just so happens that our subconscious or preconscious brain will begin to believe that we are actually *living* new behaviors if we tell it those changes are *already happening.* It sounds crazy, but it really works that way!

The idea behind affirmations is to develop ones for yourself that talk about the changes you want to make in your life, and to talk about them as happening right now. Affirmations should always be stated in the present, for example:

Not: I will start to exercise regularly to make my body strong.

Right: I am exercising regularly to make my body strong.

Also, affirmations should always be stated in the positive, such as:

Not: I look better than I have in the past.

Right: I look great!

The more often you repeat your affirmations, the more your subconscious or preconscious mind will begin to believe them and to act as if they were true, giving you more personal power and strength to carry out the changes you desire. Most people find that they need to say them at least three or four times a day at first—in the morning when you get up, at lunch, in the evening when you get home from work, and before you go to sleep. Keep this up for at least a month, and you will see remarkable results. Keep it up for two months, and you will find your life changing almost effortlessly!

After a couple of months, you can go on a maintenance schedule of twice a day. Think of it as exercise for your brain—just as you need to keep exercising once you get into good physical shape. To keep up your level of fitness, you need to continue to say your affirmations to keep your positive attitude in shape.

Only you can determine what affirmations are appropriate for you—only you know the changes you want to achieve. And it is likely that the affirmations that are most beneficial for you will change as you achieve the life changes you want. To get you started, here are some sample affirmations to try on for a fit:

- I am achieving a balanced life.
- I am finding the perfect job for me.
- I am achieving what I want in life, easily and effortlessly.
- I am filling my life with peace and joy.
- I am creating a healthy body through diet and exercise.
- I am creating a more relaxing atmosphere at home and work.
- My world is filled with love and abundance.

It's easy! When you come up with five or ten affirmations that have meaning for you, put them around your home and office where you can see them frequently to remind yourself to pay attention to them. Some people write them on index cards, and keep a set in their appointment book and by the bedside. You can put them on the inside of the bathroom cabinet, so you see them when you shave or put on your makeup in the morning. Stick them on Post-It Notes and put them on mirrors, on refrigerator doors, anywhere where you will see them frequently. Tape them on your computer monitor or inside the front door so you see them every time you leave the house. If you've never tried them before, affirmations may sound silly, but they really are very powerful positive attitude motivators.

Therapy, Self-Help and Support Groups, and 12-Step Programs

Human beings need to feel connected to other human beings. The lack of connection can cause great stress, because that connectedness helps smooth over the rough spots in our lives. If we don't feel comfortable talking over those rough spots with friends and family members, whom can we turn to?

What Therapy Is

If you are under a great deal of stress, and you have tried a number of the coping techniques listed in this chapter but they don't seem to be working, you might want to think about whether or not some form of therapy could be useful to you. Therapy provides a safe place to work through the problems we face, try on new kinds of behaviors, and make decisions about what we want to do in our lives. Nothing is shameful or weak about deciding to explore therapy as an option—in fact, it is a sign of strength and self-protection. For stress-related illnesses, therapy is often much more effective than medication and has no side effects!

Therapy can take many forms. It can be short- or long-term and the sessions can be private or in a group environment. Many therapists and clinics have sliding scales for payment, and most health insurance provided by employers today covers at least some portion of the cost for therapeutic intervention, providing you have been referred by your physician.

When Should You Consider Therapy?

If you can answer yes to any one of these questions, therapy may be useful for you:

✔ "Am I spending alot of time dwelling on the past and neglecting the present?

✔ Have these kinds of stressful situations cropped up before in my life?

✔ Do I put myself down?

✔ Do I dislike myself?

✔ Do I have trouble letting go of my problems?

✔ Has my behavior changed suddenly?

One-on-One Therapy

If you would feel more comfortable in private sessions, one-on-one with a therapist, you need to shop around for a therapist the way you would for a good physician. Ask friends and family members if they can recommend someone. Your physician can be an excellent source of referrals, as can your company's employee assistance program. In fact, many employee assistance programs offer short-term private counseling through therapists paid for by your company. All such counseling is strictly private, and your employer is never told of the content of your sessions with the therapist.

You should also ask questions of therapists, just as you do of physicians. Some good questions to ask include:

✔ How long have they been in practice?

✔ Have they treated problems similar or identical to yours in the past?

✔ What is the usual course and duration of treatment?

✔ What kinds of results can you expect if you stick with the treatment plan?

Support and Self-Help Groups

Some people are more comfortable talking about their problems in a group setting with other people who share the same problems. This is the usual structure for support and self-help groups. Such groups help us realize we are not alone in our stressful experiences, and provide a safe place to air concerns and feelings. They are usually led by a therapist or counselor who manages the flow of the sessions and encourages participation by all the members. In some cases, the therapist may counsel each member individually as well.

Some people consider cults and "quick fix" groups, such as Scientology and EST, to be support groups. We do not—in fact, these groups can be harmful to your mental health and can increase your stress load.

What should you look for in a support group? Remember, a group is only as good as its leader and participants, so the same type of group can feel very different depending on who leads it and who attends the sessions. Overall, a good group should offer the following:

- *Structure.* Each person should have a set amount of time to share feelings with the group, and no one person should dominate.

- *Fairness.* Regardless of what they say or how they view things, all members of the group should be treated equally.

- *Goals, guidelines, and objectives.* You should have a clear description of the goals of the group, and the objectives they are trying to reach. During the sessions, the group should focus on those goals, and not get sidetracked into other areas. The rules or guidelines for behaving in the group should be clearly articulated to all participants.

- *Strong leadership.* The therapist or counselor leading the group should make sure that the guidelines for behavior are followed and that goals are met.

Because the success of groups is so dependent on how actively members participate in them, understand that you have to live up to your end of the bargain. Being a good group member involves:

- *Having a focus.* Be clear about what you want to achieve before you join a group.

- *Clarifying what you need.* Only you can make sure that you get what you need from the group—group members can't read your mind. If you are not getting the support you need, ask the group for it (yes, it's scary, but it is critical for your growth). If that doesn't work, ask the therapist for assistance. And if that doesn't work, ask for a referral to another group.

- *Treating other members fairly.* Observe the guidelines and don't hog all the time. Remember, you get only what you put into a group.

12-Step Programs

The most famous self-help group based on 12 steps is Alcoholics Anonymous. Today there are a wide variety of twelve-step programs that help people deal with everything from anorexia, bulimia, and overeating to drug abuse, being the adult children of alcoholics, and going through a divorce. Many of them have a spiritual aspect, encouraging members to rely on God (although "God" can be anything from a higher being to the group itself).

Benefits of Twelve-Step Programs.   We believe that twelve-step programs are best for helping people "come out of the closet," so to speak, with their problem—publicly admitting that they have a problem, learning that others have the same or similar problem, and learning that there is no shame in getting help to resolve that problem. Such groups are wonderful for people who are truly addicted to drugs or alcohol, because they offer the opportunity to build a new social support group which may be critical in kicking the habit.

Concerns About Twelve-Step Programs.   But we are less certain of the benefits of long-term involvement in twelve-step programs for people with other kinds of problems. Many twelve-step programs *focus* on the problem, as opposed to *solving* the problem, and for some people, that can become their whole identity—"I am a bulimic," for example. We want you to get past having your problem as the primary way you see yourself, so that you can grow to a healthier kind of life.

In addition, some twelve-step programs can give people a false sense of security by externalizing their problems—sort of "it's not my fault, I'm not responsible for my problem. It was caused by society, my family, or someone else." True, you may not be responsible for the creation of the problem, but we believe that you *are* responsible for making a decision either to continue to live in the problem or to get on with your life. And we want the therapy experience to help you get on with your life.

Summing Up Therapy

The bottom line is that therapy can be a valuable experience for two kinds of people:

1. People who are going through a period of acute stress caused by a specific problem in either their home or work life. Therapy can provide the breathing space to evaluate thoughts and feelings, decide what needs to be done to resolve the problem, make a plan, and then work on resolving the problem.

2. People who seem to experience stress caused by the same kind of problem repeatedly throughout their lives. In this case, therapy can help in identifying the situation as a problem, coming to grips with it, learning why it is causing stress, and providing a safe place to try out new behaviors and feelings to resolve that problem and eliminate the stress. In either case, stress sufferers come out winners, because they can resolve the problems causing the stress and move on in their lives. Isn't that worth the investment of time and effort?

Visualization

Visualization is a fancy term for learning how to use your imagination to help you relax. It can be helpful if your mind keeps working overtime, bringing up worries and problems you'd rather not think about. Visualization can also help you block out unwanted thoughts when you would rather concentrate on a task. Settle back into a comfortable position, relax any muscles that feel tense, and try one of the following exercises.

Exercise 1: Thought-Stopping

If a thought or problem keeps popping into your head, try saying no out loud each time you think of it. Practice this self-command repeatedly over a 5- or 10-minute period while remaining in a comfortable position. When the thoughts seem to be occurring less frequently, switch over to a silent no when the thought occurs. Eventually you won't even have to do that.

Exercise 2: Pleasant Scene

Imagine a pleasant scene, such as a sky with big white, fluffy clouds; a tropical paradise; your favorite vacation place; a place or situation that connotes comfort and safety for you; waves on an ocean; a fresh green forest. Focus on this scene to block out unpleasant thoughts. Picture yourself in the scene: what you would be doing, what you would be feeling, and so on. When you find that you have succeeded in blocking out unwanted thoughts, gradually let this scene fade away, focusing on the relaxed feeling it has left behind.

Let a black or gray nothingness appear before your closed eyes, on the "movie screen" inside your head. Gradually let patches of blue drift into the gray area on the "movie screen." As patches of blue come into your field of vision, hold on to the feeling that lets the blue appear.

Visualization Helpers. Some people have trouble picturing scenes, grayness, or fluffy clouds when they first try visualizing. This sort of mind stretching takes practice! If you have trouble visualizing pictures, you might want to consider using audio cues.

Audio cues involve using sounds to trigger your imagination and to help block out thoughts or worries. Some people enjoy listening to their favorite music while letting their minds wander and relax. Other people prefer to use white noise (any steady, low noise) from a white noise generator, fan, air conditioner, furnace, humidifier, and so forth to block out or mask outside noises. That's why some people can easily fall asleep listening to the whirring of a fan in the summer.

A considerable amount of research is being done in the area of psychoacoustics—the use of sounds to create a positive, relaxing atmosphere that can have an impact on feelings and emotions. The Sports Music Company's tape *Ultimate Relaxation,* discussed earlier in this chapter, may be helpful. The Nature Company's Environmental Sound Recordings™ (on compact disc and cassette) are helpful when practicing visualization. Naturally occurring sounds are recorded and then altered or amplified just enough to make the sounds seem incredibly real. Such tapes are like having a safe, effective tranquilizer as close as a CD player or stereo. The five recordings in the series include:

Distant Thunder	the sounds of a summer storm in the city, complete with distant thunder, the patter of rain on the patio outdoors, and distant traffic sounds.
Mountain Stream	the sounds of a babbling mountain stream in a forest filled with birdsong.
Gentle Ocean	an hour at the shore, with the sounds of breaking surf on the beach, lapping of waves, and distant gulls and evening shorebirds.
Equator	the sounds of African forests, Amazonian ponds, and gently rolling surf, plus a magical synthesized score.
Nature	one side has the dawn-to-dusk sounds of the wild. The other side has the same sounds combined with a synthesized musical score.

Exercise 3: A 30-Minute Vacation

A useful way to practice visualization is to take a "quick vacation" using the Nature Company recordings, your favorite music, or simply by picturing a place you particularly like. Turn on the recording of your choice, set a timer for 20 to 30 minutes, settle into a comfortable position, and close your eyes. Focus at first on the sounds you hear from the recording or picture your ideal vacation spot. Increase the vividness of your visualization by focusing on the answers to the following questions:

- Open your eyes in your "vacation spot" and look around. What colors do you see? What shapes can you see?

- Is it dark or light? Can you see shadows?

- What is the temperature of your "vacation spot"? Is it warm or cold? Can you feel the warmth or coolness against your skin?

- Can you feel the wind or a breeze against your skin?

- What sounds can you hear in your "vacation spot"? Where are they coming from?

- What does the ground feel like under your feet?

- What textures can you feel against your skin?

- Can you detect any fragrances in your "vacation spot"? Can you determine what they are?

- Are you with someone in your "vacation spot"? Who is it?

- What are you doing? Can you feel your body moving?

- What are your feelings in this happy "vacation spot"?

- Concentrate on what being completely relaxed feels like for you. Can you feel tension anywhere in your body? If you do, consciously relax those tense muscles. This good, relaxed feeling is one you want to bring with you when you leave your "vacation spot."

- When the recording ends or the timer rings, gradually bring yourself back into the room, gently increasing your awareness of your surroundings. When you're ready, open your eyes and look around, still keeping that happy, relaxed feeling with you. Stretch if you feel like it, or yawn, and enjoy feeling more relaxed than you may have been in a long time!

This sort of vivid visualization gets easier the more you practice it, so don't worry if you couldn't picture everything about your "vacation spot" the first time. As you relax more and more, you may notice your breathing slowing down, muscle tension slipping away, and pulse rate slowing. This is all for the good. They are signs your body is benefiting from relaxation.

Visualizing can help you, not only physiologically, but psychologically. Focusing your attention on the minute details of your "vacation spot" helps block out concerns that might be stressful and disturbing, giving you a breathing space and a chance to regroup your energies. For this reason visualization is helpful if you are having difficulty sleeping because you can't "turn off" your thoughts. As you become more skilled at visualization, you may not even hear the end of the record or tape—you'll already be asleep!

Visualization is also helpful for your body, even for time periods of less than 20 minutes. If you are feeling pressured, take a trip to the Caribbean for a few minutes! Give your mind a break! Businesspeople have told us that their favorite times to practice visualization are while on an airplane (bring your Walkman and a Nature Company tape to drown out the sounds of crying kids and bad movies), while commuting to and from work, when sitting in boring meetings, any time they're put on hold while on the phone, and when they can't sleep. Experiment and see when you could benefit from a free vacation!

Weekends and Vacations

How did you spend last weekend? If you are like many businesspeople today, you probably spent a full day running around doing errands you didn't have time to do during the week, doing laundry, cleaning, getting groceries, and maybe cooking ahead to store up meals for the coming week. Then you probably spent part of the second day doing homework you brought home from the office.

Did you do anything really *fun?* Did you spend some quality time together alone with your spouse or significant other? With your kids? Chances are pretty good you didn't, because our weekends have become an extension of work—not good for our mental *or* physical health.

We tend to get into ruts, doing the same things in the same way at the same times on the weekends. Just as nature abhors a vacuum, human beings abhor unstructured time.

Everyone needs a break—even *God* rested on the seventh day! But how can we break out of our ruts? How can we really relax? The ideas below are good places to start:

✔ *Choose at least* two *relaxing activities each weekend.* They should be completely different from what you do at work. If you work with a lot of people, a little solitude might help you unwind. If your job is fairly sedentary, try some sort of physical activity. If your work requires a great deal of head work and thinking, do something mindless that you don't have to think to do, such as needlework, cooking, working in a garden, remodeling a house. If your job is very competitive, sports in which you keep score are *not* what you should be looking for! If you are single, make it a point to get out with a group of friends or family members to get the sense of nurturing that couples get from each other.

✔ *Get away for awhile.* For many of us, if we can see the work around the house, the papers in our briefcase (which we dutifully carried home Friday evening), or the computer on our home desks, we can't stop thinking about working. The key is to have a change of scenery where you can't see your work. Take a drive in the country, go to the mall to window shop, check into a hotel for the night, visit a bed and breakfast inn, even go to a museum. *Anything* to get away for awhile.

✔ *Do something on the spur of the moment.* Yes, we know that your Daytimer or Filofax has your every waking moment scheduled. But just winging it does wonders in reducing your stress levels. A movie catches your eye in the newspaper, you drive by a new restaurant, your kids beg to go to the zoo—what you choose doesn't matter.

✔ *If you can't wing it, schedule it.* You can't get out of this so easily! Many overachievers can't tolerate spontaneity, so in order to do anything fun at all and pull ourselves away from working, we have to schedule it. Buy season tickets for sports events; the opera, the symphony, or the theater. Set up a weekly "date" with your kids, spouse, or significant other. With money and planning committed to an activity, you're more likely to do it.

✔ *Don't let chores take up a full day.* Set a time limit and do the most urgent jobs first. When you reach the time limit, quit! No one is going to look for the dust bunnies under your bed! Many working people also try to portion out the chores during the week, doing the washing one evening, the ironing on the night their favorite TV show is on (ironing seems to go faster with the TV on), getting groceries another evening, etc. That way, you can get your weekends almost completely free! Setting up such a system involves a mind set switch, though, and means you can't flake out on the couch when you walk in the door after work in the evening (at least until you get the evening's chore done!). Try breaking out of your rut and seeing what alternative chore schedule you can come up with.

Since we tend to treat vacations the same way we treat our weekends, all the ideas previously mentioned for unwinding on the weekend apply for vacations as well. There is a growing tendency for businesspeople to take several 2- or 3-day vacations instead of one or two longer vacations each year. This makes sense because often it is easier to get 3 days away than 10 days. So no more excuses about not taking all the vacation time allotted to you. You don't see CEO's short-changing themselves on vacation time, do you?

Worrying

Yes, worrying can help you cope with stress, if you worry *properly*. Worrying involves the mental production of a swirling cloud of thoughts focused on the fear of *what might happen* if we did or didn't do something.

Perhaps you are saying, "Hey, I've been worrying since I was a kid. You mean to tell me there is a right and a wrong way to worry?" Yes! Most of us worry ineffectively. We worry all the time, and we worry about everything. *Proper* worrying involves worrying about the right things and spending only a reasonable amount of time doing it.

Psychologist Thomas Borkovec believes you need to acknowledge that you have something worthwhile to worry about, but limit the time you spend worrying about it. His five step process to limit worrying works like this:

1. *Learn to identify your personal "worry symptoms."* They might be an upset stomach, repeatedly tensed muscles, sweaty palms, the inability to concentrate, or butterflies in your stomach. You need to be able to identify *when* you are wor-

rying. For a lot of us, worrying comes so naturally that we aren't fully conscious of the fact that we are doing it.

2. *Determine exactly what it is that you are worried about.* This might take some thinking. Your initial response might well be: *"Everything!"* But do your best to narrow it down to what is bothering you the most. Sometimes writing a list of the worries as they come into your head helps—pretty soon you will see a pattern forming and will be able to identify your "core" worry.

3. *Once you have identified your core worry, set aside a period of half an hour every day for the sole purpose of worrying.* Yes, a full half hour, every day. It sounds like a lot of time, but believe us, you are probably spending *much* more time than that worrying now!

4. *Use your half hour of worrying as a problem-solving session.* Think about possible solutions, explore potential remedies, and very important—think through a worst-case and a best-case scenario for your core worry. Worst-case scenarios rarely come true, but it helps to figure out exactly what your worst case is. You may be surprised to find that your worst case is fully survivable!

5. *Don't worry at other times of the day.* This is hard to do at first. But if you find yourself worrying about your core worry at times other than your half hour of worrying, deliberately push the worry out of your mind by reminding yourself that you will attend to it at the prescribed time, get involved in a task or conversation that will keep your mind occupied, or use visualization to think about something else.

Worrying properly means worrying effectively. We guarantee that you will come up with some good ideas for solving your core worry. If all else fails, do what one veterinarian does. When she has something she is worrying about, and really doesn't have time to worry properly (or simply doesn't have the energy), she explains the situation to her mother (who is a champion worrier), and asks her Mom to worry for her. Mom usually comes up with several possible solutions to the situation, and can easily envision a worst-case scenario!

12

How Stress-Related Illnesses Can Worsen

Stress-Related Problems and Disorders

As discussed in earlier chapters, when you have been under high levels of stress continuously for long periods of time, the hormones your body produces in response to that stress can cause physical damage. Research is continually verifying that more and more medical problems are related to stress, and we wanted to provide you with the most up-to-date information possible on those problems. In Chaps. 12–14, we look at the symptoms of such illnesses, what you can do to speed your recovery, when to see your physician, and what to expect when you do. These chapters may be particularly valuable if you have been diagnosed with a specific stress-related problem—you will find background information and hints on coping. If you have some symptoms that are worrying you, you may find a clue as to what is going on with your body, and alert you to when to see your physician.

Most young and middle-aged people don't develop serious medical illnesses; they develop problems that can turn into chronic conditions. First we discuss stress-related problems that can make chronic conditions worse, including insomnia, fatigue, and depression. Then we cover stress-related illnesses, including discussions on the following topics:

- *Head and neck complaints*
- *Chest complaints*
- *Abdominal complaints*
- *Musculoskeletal complaints*
- *Special topics*

Finding your own "Dr. Right" and building a solid working relationship are absolutely vital if you are suffering from stress-related problems. You will need lots of information and support to cope with, and recover from, a stress-related illness—and that takes a special kind of physician. You may need to shop around for a new physician if your current health care provider cannot provide the level and kind of care you need. Treat the process like you would hiring a consultant to work on a project at work—you want your physician to serve as a consultant for your healing process—and to oversee any other health care practitioners who need to be involved. Come up with a list of questions that are important to you (the rest of this chapter may give you some ideas), and then interview several physicians. It is perfectly acceptable to do this today—just let the physician know when you schedule the appointment. Then choose the physician with whom you feel the most comfortable working. It's really that simple! That's how you can become an educated consumer of medical services!

It's Not "All in Your Head"

Stress-related problems and disorders are often called psychosomatic (from the words *psyche*, meaning mind, and *soma*, meaning body). Many people think that means the problem is "all in your head" and will go away if you "just relax and stop worrying about it." This myth is a result of psychoanalytic theory that was developed before researchers discovered that stress could actually cause physical tissue damage and trigger many health problems.

The old psychoanalytic theory of psychosomatic illness went like this: A person experiences a stressful situation that is hard to resolve. As the situation becomes more overwhelming, the person begins to fear there is no way out, and at that point makes an unconscious choice to become ill as a way of coping with an intolerable situation.

As a result of this old theory, psychosomatic illnesses began to acquire a very negative connotation. You were somehow weak or lacking in will power if you developed a psychosomatic illness. And physicians began to label problems they couldn't adequately diagnose as psychosomatic.

A New Approach

It is time for a new definition of psychosomatic illness. We have worked with people suffering from a variety of psychosomatic illnesses, and often it wasn't all in their heads. Sometimes it was in their stomachs or muscles!

The old psychoanalytic theory of psychosomatic illnesses may be true for some people, but most of the time it is not. Research has documented that many kinds of psychosomatic illnesses are the result of prolonged impact of General Adaptation Syndrome on the human body.

Because of the complex hormonal changes and depletion of energy reserves, General Adaptation Syndrome (GAS) can cause actual tissue damage over a prolonged period of time. GAS can increase the amount of acid secreted in the stomach, leading to gastritis and ulcers; disrupt normal contractions in the intestinal tract, causing diarrhea; constrict blood vessels, leading to headaches and high blood pressure; and so on.

Consequently, these illnesses are not unconsciously chosen. They are the result of wear and tear on the body caused by GAS. What does this mean? Too often people classify such problems as mind-induced and go no further. But people suffering from them need to make sure that their problems are not physically based.

Checking It Out

If you are experiencing any physical symptoms that seem to be related to stress, it is a good idea to visit your physician and get those symptoms checked out. The most important and most difficult step is to be open to the idea that stress is indeed causing your symptoms. We hope you have a physician you feel comfortable with and trust. Your physician will probably take a careful history of your symptoms and give you a thorough examination. Laboratory tests and X-rays may be used, but not everyone needs them. If no evidence of serious organic illness is found (and fortunately, it usually isn't in stress-related complaints), changes in your diet, daily activities, or possibly medication may be used to help bring your problem under control. Don't be disappointed if your physician can't find anything physically wrong with you. *Stress causes many problems, but often leaves no footprints.*

When You Cross the Line into Illness

Three categories of complaints—sleeping problems, fatigue, and depression—can definitely be aggravated by stress. Although these complaints are not truly physical *illnesses*, they can make any stress-related illness, as described later in these chapters, seem much worse. Each complaint can be treated by your physician; so, if you suffer from them, we strongly recommend that you discuss them with your physician.

Sleeping Problems

Are You Getting Enough Sleep? As we said earlier, the need for seven to eight hours of sleep a night is *not* a sign of laziness or emotional weakness—

it's a biological imperative for the typical adult. People under chronic or dangerous stress need even more sleep. When you are under stress and have lots of things to do, you may tend to cut back on sleep to give yourself a few more hours during the day in which to get a few extra tasks completed. Although most people don't recognize it, not getting enough sleep is a significant stress-related problem.

In the past week, have you said to yourself "I've got to get more sleep"? Do you need an alarm clock to wake up? Do you habitually hit the snooze button after the alarm goes off? Do you fall asleep within five minutes of going to bed? If you answered yes to any of these questions, you aren't getting enough sleep!

To get a good feel for how much sleep you need, think about how many hours of sleep you needed when you were several days into your last vacation. How much you sleep on weekends isn't a good indication of how much you normally need because—you are probably already sleep-deprived by Friday night, and most people sleep in on Saturday and Sunday to make up for that sleep loss. But three or four days into your vacation, you will probably have caught up on lost sleep, and be into your natural rhythm, which means you sleep until you naturally wake up. *That's* the amount of sleep you should try to get on a regular basis during the week—especially when you are under a great deal of stress—as your body needs much sleep time to repair the damage caused by stress hormones.

Insomnia

Almost everyone has sleep difficulties at some point in a lifetime. Insomnia is the medical term that covers a variety of sleep disturbances. Some people have trouble falling asleep, others may awaken several times during the night, and still others may awaken early in the morning and be unable to fall back to sleep. Insomnia of a chronic kind has afflicted many famous, creative people, including Edgar Allen Poe, Robert Redford, and others. You're in good company while you toss and turn!

The most important thing to remember is that no one ever died from insomnia. You may be tired and feel awful—and make everyone around you miserable with your irritability—but your body suffers no real harm. It derives *almost* as much benefit from lying relaxed in bed as it does from actually sleeping. When your body and mind are tired, you will sleep.

The problem lies in how we *feel* about not sleeping. Rarely do people with insomnia get no sleep at all. Insomniacs may only remember only the times when they were awake (everyone awakens several times during the night, we just don't remember being awake); their sleep may be unusually light; or they may simply not feel rested when they get up. They then conclude that they haven't slept a wink.

Causes of Insomnia

Insomnia can be caused by a wide range of troublemakers: depression, which can cause a particularly nasty kind of insomnia; caffeine; too much alcohol; a too-full stomach; too much smoking (nicotine acts as a stimulant); worrying; a stuffy nose; a scratchy throat; a room that is too warm or too dry; or strenuous physical activity right before going to bed. All these troublemakers act to put your body into high gear and are adequate to keep almost anyone awake and staring at the ceiling.

Our own body rhythms can be the culprit as well. Like the rest of the natural world, human beings run on internal "clocks" that regulate the formation of hormones, determine when we feel hungry, and make us feel sleepy. If you keep track of your energy levels over the course of a few days, you'll probably discover that you have several sleepy periods during the course of the day. This is your prime time for sleep, and if you don't allow yourself to sleep during your prime time, it may be several hours before your energy cycle comes back around to a drowsy period—making it very difficult for you to fall asleep until then.

Vacations are great times to observe your natural energy cycles. Do what comes naturally. Eat when you are hungry and go to sleep when you are tired. After a couple of days you'll probably notice you eat and go to sleep about the same times every day. These are your prime times for eating and sleeping.

Treatments for Insomnia

✔ *Stick to a regular sleep schedule.* Our bodies seem to thrive on regular schedules, and they adopt habits quickly. Sleeping is no exception. Figure out the number of hours of sleep you need and then backtrack that many hours from the time you need to get up. Start following a schedule of going to bed at the time you determined (even if you aren't sleepy at first) and getting up at the desired time (even if you have to drag yourself out of bed the first few days). Within two weeks your body will adjust to the new schedule. The key is to stick to the schedule, even on weekends. Physicians have found that this sort of scheduling can cure even severe sleep problems.

✔ *Get some type of physical exercise during the day.* Physical exercise, not only reduces stress, but also tires out your body—particularly important when your regular job requires mostly sitting and using your head. When your body is tired, you will sleep. But don't exercise right before bedtime. The initial effect of exercise is to wake you up.

✔ *Avoid caffeine and chocolate beginning six hours before you plan to go to bed, and alcohol at least two hours prior to sleeping.* Caffeine, the theobromine in chocolate, and alcohol, all stimulants, are guaranteed to keep you awake.

✔ *Develop a bedtime ritual to serve as a cue for your body to begin to prepare for sleep.* Understand that you can't work right up until bedtime and expect to fall asleep the moment your head hits the pillow. Your body and mind need time to wind down. The process can take up to two hours, depending on the level of stress you are under and the type of work you were doing. Bedtime rituals help provide that chance to wind down and, over time, can be associated in your mind with sleeping. A ritual can be as simple as reading a book in bed until you feel sleepy, listening to music, taking a bath or shower, or working on a hobby—anything that is not strenuous physically or mentally.

✔ *Choose the right bedtime snack.* Some people find that a bedtime snack makes them feel drowsy, especially if it consists of milk (or milk products) or poultry. The tryptophan in milk products acts as a mild tranquilizer. Poultry also contains this chemical that makes people drowsy. So have a chicken sandwich!

✔ *Make sure your bedroom isn't too warm or too dry.* Eighty degrees feels the same to your body whether it is caused by summer breezes or too many blankets. A room that is too dry can dehydrate your throat and nose, which can keep you awake. The cure is a humidifier (or bowls of water standing around the bedroom) to add moisture to the air.

✔ *If you find that all these sleep-inducing tricks fail, get out of bed.* Medical thought is still somewhat divided on this issue, but the majority of research seems to indicate that if you have been lying in bed for an hour and can't either fall asleep or return to sleep, you should get up, go to the couch in the living room or the chair in the kitchen, and do something until you feel drowsy again. The theory is that if you stay in bed tossing and turning for hours, your mind may begin to associate sleep with stressful situations.

Another school thinks that, as long as you are resting comfortably, even though you are awake, you can stay in bed as long as you pursue *unstimulating* thoughts. Watch out for "racing"—where one worry or concern follows another at a faster and faster pace, or for becoming so distraught about not being able to sleep that you just make it worse for yourself. If either of these occurs, give yourself a break and get up out of bed for awhile until you feel drowsy again.

When to See Your Physician about Insomnia

Nearly everyone suffers occasional transitory insomnia—a period of a few bad nights now and then. But if the suggestions listed previously haven't helped; your insomnia lasts more than a week, or is seriously disrupting your lifestyle or causing other problems, a visit to your physician is in order.

Your physician may recommend some lifestyle changes, medications, or refer you to a special sleep clinic—where physicians specialize in treating chronic sleep problems. If your insomnia is linked to depression, your physician may refer you to a psychiatrist, psychologist, or therapist to help you resolve the underlying problem causing the depression. But expect some experimentation—no single treatment works equally well for all sufferers, and you may have to experiment a bit to come up with the right combination of lifestyle changes and, possibly, medications that work best for you.

What Doesn't Work for Insomnia

Over-the-counter sleeping aids are not an effective cure for insomnia. They usually contain antihistamines (normally used to alleviate symptoms of allergies) or scopolamine (for the symptoms of motion sickness). These medications make some people drowsy as a side effect; others are not affected at all.

Prescription sleeping medications differ from over-the-counter sleeping aids. Most have a sedative or tranquilizing effect and can help people to relax. But our bodies build up a tolerance to these medications very rapidly. Within two weeks it may be necessary to increase the dosage needed to achieve drowsiness. Sleeping pills can also become psychologically addictive. People believe they cannot sleep without pills and start taking them at bedtime whether they need them or not.

Prescription sleeping medications can be harmful for another reason. When we sleep, we cycle through several stages of sleep. The first stage is a light sleep, from which we can awaken very easily. The others are much deeper. It is during these deeper stages that we dream and that our bodies repair and replace cells and tissues to get them ready for another day. The chemicals found in prescription sleeping medications prevent us from reaching those deeper levels of sleep. That's why you can feel groggy in the morning if you took a sleeping pill the night before. Dreams are crucial to mental health; they allow you to sort through and process all the information picked up during the day. You especially need time for repairing and building cells and tissues if your body is coping with the biochemical results of GAS. So for most people, sleeping pills do more harm than good.

This is not to say that prescription sleeping medications are completely worthless. For some people, under the careful supervision of a physician and for a short period of time, sleeping pills can help provide a sort of rest or "oblivion" that may be sorely needed. Examples might be people adjusting to the death of a family member, people suffering pain, or people needing to sleep in a place not conducive to sleep (such as most hospitals). But sleeping medications should not be used indiscriminately.

Fatigue

Have you ever felt tired when you got out of bed in the morning or had days when it was all you could do to put one foot in front of the other? Have you ever fallen asleep while watching the evening news? Chances are you were experiencing fatigue—a very common stress-related problem. Physicians have found that there are three kinds of fatigue—physiological, pathological, and psychological.

Normal Physiological Fatigue

Physiological fatigue is a symptom of a host of physical disorders, ranging from diabetes and infections to heart disease. Some medications have fatigue as a side effect—tranquilizers and sleeping pills can build up in your body, making you feel tired far longer than might be expected. A deficiency in certain vitamins and minerals can cause fatigue. Sleeping-pattern changes can cause fatigue, as all new mothers and fathers are fully aware.

But the most common cause of physiological fatigue is overwork that tires out the muscles in your body. It results from trying to do too much in too little time. The cure for this kind of physiological fatigue is simple—more sleep. If getting more sleep for a few days doesn't help get your physician to rule out any other possible physiological causes of fatigue.

Pathological Fatigue

Pathological fatigue is rare. One kind is narcolepsy: an overwhelming and irresistible need for sleep. People suffering from narcolepsy have, during the course of a day, many "nap attacks" in which they simply fall asleep wherever they are and whatever they are doing.

Another serious problem that causes fatigue is sleep apnea. This disorder causes the sleeper, who is usually a heavy snorer, to stop breathing for up to 90 seconds. The person then struggles to start breathing again, and wakes up in the process. People suffering from sleep apnea usually fall asleep again immediately, but because their sleep has been disturbed, they often feel very tired the next day, for they are unable to spend enough time in the deep levels of sleep, where rest really occurs.

Finally, deep depression can cause tiredness. People suffering from a deep depression usually feel apathetic about life in general and sad about certain parts of their lives. Fatigue goes along with the apathy and sadness. Depression of this kind usually requires a combination of medical and psychological treatment.

Psychological Fatigue

Psychological fatigue is the most common type. Stress, anxiety, frustration, anger, and boredom are all culprits. Boredom in particular can be extremely fatiguing. Research has found that a half-hour of boredom can burn up as much energy as a full day's work.

To deal with psychological fatigue effectively, its causes have to be confronted and resolved. Confronting the life situations that cause you pain is not easy, but in this case you have to expend energy to get some. You might find it helpful to talk over your concerns with friends or family members. Their help and support might encourage you to change your life situation. Check out what needs you have that aren't being met, and be good to yourself by meeting some of them. You may find that the things you have to deal with can be faced more easily and may even become enjoyable.

If talking things over with friends and trying to meet some of your needs doesn't work, professional help might be in order. Sometimes we can't handle life crises on our own, and it is okay to seek professionals who make it their business to help. A social worker or counselor just might be able to help you get a new perspective on things so that they don't seem so overwhelming.

Chronic Fatigue Syndrome

Chronic fatigue syndrome (CFS), which appears to be a disorder of the immune system, has been getting a great deal of coverage in the media. Many people who suffer from depression, physiological or psychological fatigue, or a number of medical problems that have fatigue as a symptom mistakenly believe they have CFS. The Centers for Disease Control have established a list of symptoms that characterize true CFS, including: chronic fatigue that continues *for at least six months*; chills and/or fever; a sore throat; painful swollen lymph glands; unexplained muscle weakness; muscle discomfort; difficulty sleeping; inability to concentrate; headaches; and the absence of a thyroid condition (because the symptoms of a malfunctioning thyroid are very similar to CFS, thyroid problems must be ruled out first). And true CFS suffers must have had at *least eight of these ten symptoms for six months or longer.*

True CFS is very rare and it is not caused by stress, even though its sufferers may have lived very stressful lives prior to developing CFS. CFS sufferers are usually female, well-educated, and younger adults between the ages of 20 and 40. Physicians must rule out a wide variety of illnesses, including diabetes mellitus, mononucleosis, hepatitis, severe anemia, and others—all of which cause fatigue—before a diagnosis of CFS can be reached. The testing required to accomplish this can be lengthy and expensive.

Currently no cure for CFS is known, but a balanced diet, adequate rest, and moderate but not overly vigorous exercise are recommended. Time may be the only true cure because in some cases the symptoms of CFS resist treatment but then seem to go away on their own. Many quack cures have been offered for CFS, just as for other incurable illnesses. These quack cures don't work, nor do vitamin or herbal treatments. Doctor hopping—shopping around for a new physician in search of a cure—doesn't work either, because there are no quick cures.

Treatments for Fatigue

✔ *Make sure you are eating an adequate diet with plenty of healthy foods.* Many people who are dieting or under stress and unable to eat consume too few calories to provide adequate energy. Go for complex carbohydrates, such as grains, breads, fruits, and vegetables—they provide consistent energy levels for long periods of time. Avoid sugary foods, which may provide an initial rush of energy, but cause your blood sugar level to drop off quickly after that, making you feel more tired than before.

✔ *Get some kind of physical exercise every day, even if it's only taking a brisk walk.* You have to expend energy to get energy, and exercise can provide an energy boost that will last all day.

✔ *Don't skip meals.* If you skip breakfast, you hit a slump by 11 a.m. If you skip lunch, you'll be tired by mid- to late afternoon. Five small meals each day are much better than three large meals for keeping your energy levels up.

✔ *Get enough sleep.* Be sure to get extra rest on the weekend. But don't use sleep as an escape from depression.

✔ *Cut out late afternoon and late evening coffee or caffeine.* Caffeine can remain in your body for up to six hours and keep you wide-eyed at night.

✔ *Talk to a friend, family member, your physician, or a therapist if you think a personal problem is contributing to your fatigue.* Getting the problem out and talking about it is energy-enhancing, and getting support can reduce your feelings of depression.

When to See Your Physician about Fatigue

If you have felt fatigued for over a week, have tried getting more sleep and that doesn't work, or if fatigue is cramping your lifestyle—it's time to see your physician.

Your physician will ask you about major changes you may be going through; what you have done to alleviate your fatigue; the prescribed and over-the-counter medications you are taking to determine whether any of these may be causing your tiredness; your diet and exercise habits; and perhaps order special tests. Lifestyle changes, dietary adjustments, changes in medications, counseling, or new medications may be recommended. No single treatment works equally well for all people, so expect some experimentation until you and your physician find the best treatment combination for you.

What Doesn't Work for Fatigue

Many people think that, if they are suffering from fatigue, they should get a lot of rest, so they sleep a lot and don't expend much energy. But physicians have found that sometimes the old adage "you have to expend energy to get energy" is true. If you force yourself to get some sort of physical exercise—even just going for a walk—over time you will have more energy to expend and be less fatigued.

Another so-called cure for fatigue is caffeine, mainly for its pick-me-up effects. Fatigued people often drink lots of coffee under the false assumption that it will help alleviate the fatigue. Caffeine does not alleviate fatigue: It may provide a very short-term energy boost, but it doesn't solve the underlying problem. A cup of coffee when you feel tired won't hurt you, unless your physician has advised otherwise, but don't go overboard—you'll just feel jittery on top of feeling fatigued.

Fatigue has no quick cures. Curing fatigue requires the willingness to look for underlying psychological causes, such as depression or boredom, and a careful elimination of potential health-related problems. All that takes time, and fatigue sufferers sometimes get impatient. They expect to feel better instantly, and, when they don't, they start "doctor hopping," hoping for a cure, but never spending long enough with any one physician to uncover the causes of their fatigue. Doctor hopping only ends up prolonging the suffering so if you have already found your Dr. Right, do yourself a favor and stick with him or her until you see some results.

Depression

Many people under stress experience depression, ranging from a case of the blues or the blahs that lasts a day or so and is accompanied by feelings of sadness, listlessness, or weeping, to a full-scale illness that lasts for months, leaving the victim feeling listless, wrung out, and numb to the joys of life.

Depression usually results from an experience of loss: the loss of a role or position in life, of a valued relationship, of a skill or ability, of self-esteem, or public "face," or of a treasured possession. Even the imagined loss of any of these can bring about depression. Loss can also be cumulative: One loss, or even two, might not bother you, but when the third or fourth one comes along, you feel like you've been hit by a ton of bricks.

Most major life changes also involve feelings of depression, which occur just after the big change of some sort is made. This sort of depression is caused by the loss of our old ways of behaving and will subside as you become more comfortable with new roles.

The Blahs

Everybody gets the blahs from time to time. You know you have the blahs when you really don't want to drag yourself out of bed to go to work, you can't think of anything that appeals to you to eat, and thoughts about sex with your significant other don't get you going like they usually do.

The blahs usually happen when you are overworked, overtired, and generally stressed out. You have too much to do, not enough time to do it, and it seems that no one appreciates all that you are doing. Negative self-talk, discussed in Chap. 11, kicks in and you start giving yourself a hard time for feeling blah, and so on—compounding the gray cloud you feel caught under.

How do you cope? Sort through the blah feeling, and try to pinpoint where it is coming from. Does it have to do with a relationship? Is a specific situation at work causing it? Or is it something at home? Usually you get the blahs when you feel you aren't in control of a situation, and the cure is to get that control back. If you can figure out what is causing your blahs, you can think about ways to counteract the situation. Once you give yourself options, you regain control over the situation. If you ignore what is giving you the blahs and continue to think negatively, you set up a frame of mind that can sap your energy all day—and that's the last thing you need.

Suppose you uncover a situation that you can't make an immediate change to resolve, what then? What works best is making yourself do some activity that energizes or nurtures you—it quickly ups your energy level. Energizing activities include some sort of exercise; talking with a friend; thinking through all the things that are going well in your life; or just changing your routines for the day. Nurturing activities include indulging in guilty pleasures—a glass of fine wine, a cup of great coffee, a hot fudge sundae; or simply setting aside time in the day to do something you have wanted to do for awhile, but haven't had time to do.

The key is not to let the blahs overtake you and drag you down into the blues. So be nice to yourself—you'd do the same for one of your friends, wouldn't you?

The Blues

The blues are different from the blahs: You still feel listless, but you have an underlying feeling of sadness as well. The blues may last a day or two. They can be triggered by hormonal changes (for both men and women), but usually the blues hit after you have felt the stress of a of minor loss, or when you are *afraid* you might have some sort of loss. Most often, the blues have to do with stressful interpersonal relationships, either at home or at work, that aren't working out the way you had hoped. Some comment or off-hand remark made by the other person triggers your insecurities and sets off a round of negative self-talk. Soon you are feeling pretty rotten about yourself, about the relationship, about *everything* else.

The best way to cope with the blues is to understand that the thoughts that trigger the insecurities and negative self-talk are usually totally unrealistic. The initial situation may or may not have been negative, but because the person or situation is important to us, we "awfulize" it and read more into it than was probably intended. We pick up this skill at an early age and get good at it. But "awfulizing" is not an inherent force of nature, but something we do in our heads. We can change those self-talks to limit "awfulizing."

You have to think through the situation logically. Think through what you are telling yourself in your head. How realistic is it? What's the worst that could happen? Could you survive that? Are these emotions about something you feel you *must have* to survive? Chances are you don't absolutely, positively have to have whatever "it" is; you just *prefer* it. That's a big difference, and can make a big difference in blowing the blues away.

Confronting the person and asking directly what was meant by the comment or conversation—letting the other person know that the remark hurt your feelings may also be a useful approach. Doing this can be very scary, but it may be essential to help shut off the negative self-talk. You will probably find that the other person has no idea your feelings were hurt, and never meant to imply what you divined from the conversation. You may even be pleasantly surprised! If you find out the intent *was* negative you may be happy to have that information early on so you can evaluate whether you really want someone as a friend or lover who would intentionally hurt your feelings.

The idea here is to prevent the blues from growing unchecked by reality to the point where they drag you down into depression. You do have some control over whether or not that happens.

Grief-Related (Exogenous) Depression

Grieving over a loss of any kind is normal and healthy; it is not beneficial to cut short the grieving process. Unfinished "grief work" tends to crop up later in life, usually when you find yourself under stress again, and it compounds the new crisis.

Normal grieving is time limited, usually lasting four to six weeks in its acute phase. Some people may still experience sadness and a sense of loss for up to a year following the death of a family member or close friend. It takes us about that long to say goodbye and restructure our lives. Don't be concerned if you feel depressed after suffering a loss. The depression is actually helping you prepare for a new future.

Psychological Depression

Perhaps the most common form of depression is psychological depression. The depressing event, circumstance, or situation can usually be easily identified by the sufferer. But it is not really the event that does the depressing; rather, it is how we feel about ourselves as a result of it. Usually the event makes us feel impotent in some way, and we chastise and condemn ourselves for not being able to handle it in the manner (usually unrealistic) that we think is best. Pretty soon we have convinced ourselves that we are worthless to boot.

Stressful situations seem to trigger this sort of nonsensical thinking. We all carry around unrealistic expectations of how we should act and handle our lives, and, when we are under stress, we seem to put even more shoulds and oughts into our lives. And when we can't live up to them (and no one ever can), we see it as proof of how awful we really are.

So how do you break this cycle? It's hard to do it on your own, because chronic stress depletes the energy and initiative you need to get on with things. Most people benefit from counseling or therapy. Counseling can help you identify the inaccurate and illogical assumptions you are operating under, and learn how to change your self-talks. It also forces you to do things you enjoyed in the past, instead of just moping around the office or house. Hobbies, sports, guilty pleasures, and other coping techniques can distract you from your illogical self-talks while you work to correct what you think about yourself.

Biological Depressions

Biological depressions have several causes. Depression can be a side effect of some medications, such as antihistamines and beta blockers. In this case, the depression usually lifts after the medication is discontinued. Some medical problems can have depression as a side effect. For example, in hypothyroidism and premenstrual syndrome, people can feel depressed. Mononucleosis and chronic Epstein-Barr Syndrome, both of which produce fatigue, can also aggravate depression.

Chronic (Endogenous) Depression

Some people suffer from depression that lasts longer than a couple of months after a loss, and these people usually benefit from professional counseling. Counseling can help you come to terms with your loss and take your life in hand again.

Recent research has found that people suffering from long-term depression that seems unrelated to a loss may be suffering from a biochemical imbalance of some kind. Various neurochemicals present in abnormal concentrations in the brain can create feelings of depression. People with this kind of chronic depression often respond favorably to medications that counteract these neurochemicals or regulate their levels in the brain.

The newest research has found that neurohormones produced by our bodies during physical exercise can also counteract the hormones causing depression. Running seems to be particularly useful in this case, not only because endorphins (for example, "happy" hormones) are produced, but because it is easy to record your progress as you begin to run, and that increases your self-confidence.

Treatments for Depression

✔ *Eat a healthy, balanced diet.* When you are depressed, it is important to maintain even blood sugar levels, so that fluctuations in blood sugar levels don't add to your fatigue or depression. High carbohydrate intake often intensifies mood swings. People who are depressed often don't have much appetite, and it is important to get enough nutrients so that your body can repair the damage caused by General Adaptation Syndrome (GAS). So try to find healthy foods that appeal to you and make sure you don't skimp on meals.

✔ *Get some form of exercise every day.* The "happy" hormones mentioned earlier benefit everyone suffering from depression. So try walking, running, or some other form of aerobic exercise *that appeals to you.* Exercising also helps you feel that you can get control over at least some part of your life, and, for many people, not feeling in control contributes to depression.

✔ *Talk with friends, coworkers, and family members.* A shoulder to cry on, someone to bounce ideas off, or just someone to listen goes a long way in helping you feel less depressed. It's also important to know that others care about you—which is often forgotten when you are depressed.

✔ *Spend time with your hobbies and guilty pleasures.* When you're depressed, you eliminate from your life things that make you feel good. It takes an effort to do them, and, when you're depressed, you just don't feel you can make the effort. But force yourself to spend time in these leisure pursuits. They take your mind off what's bothering or worrying you, and they are a way to nurture yourself.

✔ *Monitor your self-talks.* Since self-talks can play a big role in maintaining and increasing depression, you must control it. Refer to the section "self-talks" in Chap. 11. It may be necessary to read that section daily for awhile!

When to See Your Physician about Depression

If you are feeling depressed, take a little time to think about losses you might have experienced in the recent past. Accept the grief process as an important part of mental health and be good to yourself. If you're not sure what caused your depression, if you seem to be stuck in the grief process, or if the suggestions listed previously haven't helped, make an appointment with your physician or a mental health professional to talk about it. Life is too short to be lived under gray skies or down in the dumps.

The American Psychiatric Association recommends that you see your physician if you experience four or more of the following symptoms consistently for more than two weeks:

- A noticeable change in appetite, accompanied by a significant loss or gain in weight
- A noticeable change in sleeping patterns, sleeping too much or too little
- Loss of interest in activities you once enjoyed
- Fatigue and loss of memory
- Feelings of worthlessness
- An inability to concentrate or think
- Recurring thoughts of death or suicide
- Overwhelming feelings of sadness and grief, accompanied by awakening two or more hours earlier than usual in the morning, feeling more depressed, and moving significantly more slowly
- Physical symptoms such as headaches or stomach aches

Your physician will: ask you about both prescription and over-the-counter medications you may be taking to see whether any of them could be causing your depression; talk with you about any major life changes or losses you may have experienced recently; evaluate your diet and physical fitness habits; and perhaps order some special tests.

Changes in medications or new medications may be recommended for an underlying medical condition; antidepressant medications may be prescribed if your depression is severe; diet and fitness changes may be advised; and referral may be made to a counselor or therapist. If your depression appears to be caused by an underlying medical condition such as diabetes or hypothyroidism, your physician may refer you to a specialist in that area.

Somewhat controversial at this time is the use of antidepressant medications. Antidepressants act to regulate an imbalance of neurotransmitters, such as serotonin and norepinephrine, inside the brain. These medications can help lift a severe depression and can be invaluable for someone suffering from chronic depression. For people with milder forms of depression, the side effects of antidepressants can be a major drawback: They range from low blood pressure to low libido, dry mouth, and constipation, depending on the drug prescribed. Some physicians believe these drugs should be used only for major depressions, with psychotherapy being the treatment of choice for milder depressions. Other physicians feel comfortable using antidepressants to short-circuit milder depressions, like depression-induced insomnia—to help the sufferer feel better at work and at home.

Discuss the use of any medication fully with your physician so that you understand the pros and cons of its use. Your physician may refer you to a psychopharmacologist—a psychiatrist whose subspecialty is tailoring drug therapy to specialized patient needs. But understand that antidepressants are often not a cure. In the best case, they act as a leveler, suppressing depression and improving a person's mood to enhance the response to psychotherapy or until the depression runs its course.

Understand that depression doesn't go away instantly, and you may have to work with your physician or therapist for awhile to see results. But everyone can be helped, given the rapid advances being made today in combating depression. So don't give up, hang in there!

What Doesn't Work for Depression

Once again, as with many stress-related illnesses, there are no quick fixes for depression. It takes time to sort out the underlying causes and to try different treatments.

People often turn to alcohol when they are depressed, thinking that the "buzz" will make them feel better or forget what is bothering them. Alcohol may do just that, but for the short term only. Over the long term, alcohol doesn't remove the underlying problems. Becoming dependent on alcohol can become another serious problem you have to confront. Others find that drinking alcohol when they are depressed just makes them more depressed. You don't need that. Your best advice is to avoid alcohol when feeling depressed—*period.*

One other concern is with the overuse of tranquilizers. Tranquilizers are often prescribed for people who are depressed, especially if they are also anxious. Tranquilizers may be useful to get someone through a short, difficult period. But our bodies rapidly develop a physical tolerance to tranquilizers: It takes more and more to have any effect. We can rapidly become psychologically dependent on tranquilizers, coming to believe that we can't get through the day without them—so we keep taking them, rather than try to manage without them. Either way, drug dependence becomes a big problem on top of depression. Withdrawal from tranquilizers is a lengthy, unpleasant experience. So do yourself a big favor, don't get hooked. Strictly limit the use of tranquilizers to precisely what your physician prescribed. Don't take them on your own.

13
A Compendium of Common Stress-Related Illnesses

Allergies and Upper Respiratory Infections

Allergies

Allergies are an inappropriate or exaggerated reaction of the immune system to an offending agent. That agent can be a chemical that comes in contact with the skin, causing a rash; a tiny airborne particle of dust, pollen, or animal dander that causes sneezing or makes sinuses or lungs clog up; or a food that causes gastrointestinal problems such as vomiting and diarrhea. As such, allergies are not *caused* by stress, but stress can definitely make allergy attacks occur more frequently, feel more severe, and last longer. This is particularly true for conditions such as asthma, hives, and allergic rhinitis (hay fever).

If you suffer from allergies, it is helpful to track your allergic episodes to determine whether your particular allergies are worse when you are under stress. If they are, it is important to share this information with your physician, so that your treatment plan can be modified to accommodate the effects of stress.

Upper Respiratory Infections and Flu

Over two hundred different viruses can cause upper respiratory infections (colds and flu), and they are around all year long. They all cause inflammation of the mucous membranes of the nose and throat, resulting in a stuffy, runny nose; sore throat; headache; general malaise; and sometimes a fever. Upper respiratory infections are not caused by stress, but because the General Adaptation Syndrome (GAS) commandeers a great deal of the energy you have available at any one time and may impact your immunity, your body may not have the energy it needs to fight off viruses that cause colds and flu. In addition, your general physical condition can become more run-down when you are under a great deal of stress, and fatigue can make colds and flu seem worse.

Most colds and flu clear up in 10 to 12 days—whether you take over-the-counter cold medications or not—and usually do not require a physician's care unless you run a fever or if the infection spreads. In some cases the infection can spread to the lungs (bronchitis), sinuses (sinusitis), larynx (laryngitis), or ear(s) (otitis media). When under great stress, or under significant stress for a long period, a cold can balloon into one of these conditions.

Treatments for Upper Respiratory Infections

There is no real way to prevent getting a cold or the flu, because if you are exposed to a virus for which you have no immunity, you will most likely "catch" it. The following ideas might help reduce your exposure, or make the cold or flu less uncomfortable:

- ✔ *Wash your hands thoroughly if people around you have colds or the flu, and try not to touch your eyes or nose.* This helps reduce the number of viruses that enter your body.

- ✔ *Eat right.* Malnutrition is a powerful immunosuppressant, whereas eating a healthy, balanced diet increases your resistance and prevents viruses from getting a foothold.

- ✔ *Get some form of moderate exercise at least three to four times a week.* Research shows that people who exercise moderately for about an hour three or four times a week increase their resistance to cold viruses. The exact reason is unclear, but the theory is that regular exercise increases your overall level of health, and reduces the impact of the general adaptation syndrome (GAS) on your body.

- ✔ *Keep your nose, sinus, and throat membranes moist by raising household humidity with a humidifier.* Moist membranes are less likely to be breeding grounds for bacterial infections. It is especially important to keep humidity high during the winter, when indoor heat rapidly takes humidity out of the air.

- ✔ *If you smoke, quit, and if you don't smoke, don't start.* Cigarette and cigar smoke can inflame nasal and sinus membranes, making them much more susceptible to bacterial infections. If possible, try to arrange for a smoke-free work space and a nonsmoking hotel room when you travel.

✔ *If you do catch a cold or the flu, drink lots of fluids, get plenty of rest, and take an over-the-counter pain reliever.* That's about all you can do. Fluids, especially weak tea or warm chicken soup (there is truth to the old wives' tale), can help soothe a sore, scratchy throat, and help keep mucus membranes moist. Rest is important, not only because you feel lousy anyway, but because your body needs all of its available energy to fight the cold. An over-the-counter pain reliever, such as aspirin, acetaminophen or ibuprofen, can help relieve headaches, aching muscles, and mild fevers.

✔ *If you have a cold, do yourself and everybody else a favor—stay home!* You are most contagious during the first several days, which is usually when you feel the worst anyway, and this is when you should stay home. You aren't proving anything to anyone about how dedicated an employee you are by dragging yourself into work and coughing or sneezing all over everyone—you're only spreading your cold.

What Doesn't Work for Upper Respiratory Infections

You have to be patient when you have a cold or the flu. The old adage is true: "Colds last two weeks if you take over-the-counter medications, and fourteen days if you don't take anything." It is also very common for them to recur, especially if your resistance is down because of stress.

But because colds and flu are caused by viruses, most home remedies don't work. For the most part antibiotics don't work either, because antibiotics are designed to treat *bacterial* infections, not viral infections. At this time there are no medications that eradicate cold *viruses*.

Vitamin C has gotten lots of press lately as a cold preventative, especially when taken in massive doses. No hard research has proven that massive doses of vitamin C will help you keep colds or the flu at bay. *Some* research suggests that taking vitamin C when you already have a cold can help keep the symptoms from becoming severe. But you don't need to take vitamin C tablets to achieve that—simply drinking more orange or grapefruit juice will achieve the same result, and you will be increasing your fluid intake as well.

Over-the-counter decongestant nasal sprays may temporarily relieve a stuffy nose for a day or two, but if used for longer can cause more harm than good. After using a decongestant nasal spray for about three days, you are likely to experience the "rebound effect"—when you stop using the nasal spray, you get even more congested, and you need more of the spray to get relief. If you start using the spray again, a vicious cycle develops, and you can become addicted to your nasal spray. This is not healthy, so your best bet is to stay away from such products altogether. If you are so stuffed up that you are miserable, limit your use to only two days.

Most over-the-counter combination cold products (Nyquil, Dristan, Contac, and others) have up to seven different medications in them, some of which may be unnecessary or may produce uncomfortable side effects. Therefore, we believe that combination cold products are best avoided completely. You are far better off using single-ingredient medications for a specific symptom that you may have. Nearly everyone develops a different combination of symptoms with each bout of a head cold or flu. Table 13.1 can help you determine which single-ingredient over-the-counter medications might relieve your specific symptom(s).

Chest Pain

One of the most frightening stress-related medical problems is chest pain, because we often fear that chest pain is a sign of a heart attack. In some instances, chest pain *can* be, and stress can play a role in causing it, especially if the sufferer is a man over 40 or a woman over 50 with a history of high cholesterol levels or heart problems. If the sufferer is younger and has low cholesterol levels, chances are very good that the chest pain is caused by something else.

Noncardiac chest pain can be caused by a number of non-stress-related problems, including injury (torn or pulled muscles), indigestion, bronchitis, pneumonia, or other viruses. But for a significant percentage of sufferers, stress can specifically impact noncardiac chest pain.

A very frequent cause of stress-related chest pain is gastroesophageal reflux (GER). GER (discussed in detail later in this chapter) is a condition in which stress causes the sphincter between the esophagus and stomach to relax, allowing stomach contents to back up into the esophagus. This can cause extreme pain of a burning type extending from just behind the breastbone to the upper stomach area. It might feel like a heart attack, but the pain does not feel "crushing," or radiate into the left arm, as it does in heart attack pain. It also gets worse when you lie down or bend over.

Another esophagus-related problem is esophageal spasm, in which the muscles of the esophagus that push food down into the stomach when you swallow go into spasm. While research has indicated the possibility of some underlying dysfunction in these muscles, we do know that stress can aggravate this condition. The pain it causes can be very severe, and gets worse when you swallow.

Severe or long-term stress can cause muscles in the chest wall to tense up over time, and ultimately go into spasm. This pain is sort of like getting a "charley horse" in your chest: it can be excruciating, come on suddenly, and mimic a heart attack. Like a "charley horse," it can occur during sleep, with the sufferer awakening due to the pain. All in all, the experience can be terrifying.

Table 13.1. Comparison of Selected Single-Ingredient Cold Remedies

Problem	Problem solver	Medication	OTC product	Side effect(s)
Congestion	Topical decongestant	Phenylephrine	Dristan, Sinex, Neo-Synephrine	Possible rebound effect if used for more than three days
		Oxymetazoline	Afrin, Duration	Possible rebound effect if used for more than three days
	Oral decongestant	Pseudoephedrine	Sudafed	May raise blood pressure; can cause dry mouth and throat
Sore throat	Medicated sprays and lozenges	Phenol compounds	Chloraseptic products	
		Benzocaine Hexylresorcinol Menthol	Spec-T Lozenges Sucrets N'Ice Lozenges	
Headache, fever, muscle aches	Pain reliever	Aspirin	Bayer, Bufferin	May irritate the stomach
		Acetaminophen Ibuprofen	Tylenol, Datril Advil, Motrin	May irritate the stomach
Coughs	Cough suppressant	Dextromethorphan	Benylin DM, Pertussin, Hold	Should not be used if you have chronic bronchitis or emphysema
		Codeine	Cheracol, Naldecon CX, Novahistine DH	Should not be used if you have chronic bronchitis or emphysema
	Expectorant	Diphenhydramine Guaifensin	Benylin Robitussin, Noritussin	May cause drowsiness

SOURCE: *Consumer Reports*, January 1989.

Treatments for Chest Pain

The best way to deal with cardiac chest pain is to prevent it from happening. You do that by lowering your risk factors for heart disease. If your cholesterol level is high, follow a low-fat diet to reduce it. Set up a regular aerobic exercise program to increase cardiovascular fitness. And practice the coping techniques outlined in Chap. 11 to reduce your overall stress levels.

A number of self-care treatments can be used to reduce the likelihood of developing severe noncardiac chest pain. Check out the section on gastroesophageal reflux later in this chapter for specific tips if that problem is causing your chest pain. If the cause is chest muscle spasm, the following home treatments can help when you first feel a twinge coming on:

✔ *Try over-the-counter painkillers such as aspirin, acetaminophen or ibuprofen.*

✔ *Use heat, either in the form of hot compresses, a heating pad, or a hot shower.* Heat helps muscles relax, and can be very effective in unkinking a spasm.

✔ *If you chronically tense your chest muscles when you are experiencing stress, progressive muscle relaxation and biofeedback can be helpful.* Both relaxation techniques can help you learn to identify when your muscles are beginning to tense up. When you sense them tightening, you can consciously relax that muscle group, short-circuiting the spasm creating process. Progressive muscle relaxation techniques are outlined in Chap. 11, and your physician can recommend a qualified biofeedback practitioner.

When to See Your Physician about Chest Pain

If the pain is sharp, lasts only for seconds, or has lasted for several days, it probably isn't a heart attack. If it feels more like a heaviness in your chest and lasts minutes to hours, it might be a heart attack.

But you should *never* disregard chest pain. Always check it out, especially if you are over 40 and develop it for the first time—whether or not you feel sick otherwise. The pain could be a heart attack, which is always a medical emergency. Call your physician and, if necessary, get an ambulance or a friend or family member to drive you to the emergency room. This is not the time to take chances.

If you have had chest pain before, you need to decide whether or not it requires a trip to the emergency room, a call to your physician, or simple home treatment. The following questions can help you decide:

■ *Is the pain crushing and/or does it radiate from the center of the chest to the jaw, neck, or arms?* If yes, and it has persisted despite 15 minutes of rest, a heart attack is possible, and you need to get to a hospital immediately. If the pain came on during exertion and you have had previous attacks, it could be angina pectoris, and you should call your physician without delay.

■ *Are you short of breath?* If yes, and you have recently had an operation, injury, or illness that kept you in bed, you may have developed a blood clot in the lung. You need to get to a hospital immediately. If you have a cough or a temperature over 100° F, you should call your physician immediately. You may have developed bronchitis or pneumonia. If you don't have a cough or temperature, you still need to call your physician without delay, as you may have a collapsed lung.

- *Does the pain get worse when you lie down, swallow, or bend over?* If yes, gastroesophageal reflux (GER) or esophageal spasm may be causing your pain. Try the self-care tips outlined later in this chapter for GER and consult your physician if they are not effective.

- *Do you have a burning pain in the lower chest and/or the upper abdomen?* If yes, and it came on after eating or eating too quickly or too much, indigestion may be causing your pain. Try over-the-counter antacids and consult your physician if it happens regularly.

- *Is the pain on one side of your chest only?* If yes, and you recently had a chest injury, a severe cough, or the area of the pain is tender to the touch, you probably have a pulled muscle or other injury. Consult your physician if the home treatments for sore muscles covered later in this chapter are not effective.

If you are unable to make a diagnosis from these questions, consult your physician without delay.

The kind of treatment your physician will recommend for your chest pain will depend on its underlying cause. A chest X-ray is often performed to examine the heart or lungs, and your physician may order other diagnostic tests. Medications may be prescribed, such as muscle relaxants for chest muscle spasms and medications that reduce the acid produced by the stomach for GER. But in most cases, lifestyle changes are recommended as well.

Dysfunctional Eating

Eating Too Much

Many people overeat when under stress. Since our culture seems to be obsessed with thinness, overeating as a response to stress piles on pounds and compounds the stress.

Eating a lot is not inherently bad. It is important to assess your eating patterns to see what overeating is telling you about your needs, values, and life situation. Ask yourself:

- Is there a risk to your health caused by overeating? Is your overweight problem severe? Do you have high blood pressure or diabetes, for example?

- Is there a pattern to your overeating? Check out the times, places, situations, and your feelings when you overeat. Are you really hungry at those times and places?

Can this information tell you about the ways to control parts of your life that are stressful for you?

■ Do you have favorite stress foods that you consistently binge on? What kinds of foods are they? Do you prepare them yourself or are they "fast foods"? Are they "comfort foods" from your childhood—foods you associate with nurturing and being comforted? Are they "lucky" or "magic" foods, like chicken soup? What do they tell you about your needs? Chewy foods may signify that you have a problem you need to chew on for a while. Crunchy foods might indicate that you'd like to bite somebody's head off! Mushy foods may mean you'd like to be taken care of for a while.

■ Do you otherwise eat a nutritionally adequate diet? If your overall diet is balanced, occasional binges are okay. If you can't get goodies from other people when you need them, you can behave responsibly by preparing them for yourself.

■ Could something else more healthy be an effective substitute if you consistently binge on junk foods? You can get clues to this from the texture, manner of preparation, and taste of your binge foods. Experiment and see what works for you.

The goal here is moderation. If overeating is not causing you any serious health problems and is serving as an effective crutch, use the crutch! Teddy bears are crutches, too, but nearly everyone outgrows them when their life situation changes. The same holds true for overeating.

If you have become bothered by weight gain caused by overeating while you are under stress, sort through your feelings about your weight and what that means for you. Beginning a diet when you are experiencing stress in other areas of your life is not always wise. Most diets begun during stressful periods don't succeed, simply because food serves as a good relaxer. Before you start dieting, ask yourself:

■ Why do I feel upset about my eating patterns and weight? What is it about my situation that is upsetting me?

■ What values do I have about my weight and overeating?

■ What are my reasons for wanting to start a diet?

■ Are these reasons realistic? (For example, losing 15 pounds most likely will not change your life dramatically, pick up your sex life, or make you witty and interesting.)

■ What functions are my eating patterns serving for me? What substitutes can I find for these functions?

If you feel that your weight is an important stress area for you, by all means cut back on your eating and start on a sensible, safe diet and exercise program. Be good to yourself while you are dieting. Remember, you are already under stress. Try not to create more.

Not Eating Enough—Lack of Appetite

Many people lose their desire to eat when they are under stress. They feel too nervous, or food just doesn't seem to taste good or to have much taste at all. As with overeating, this problem is usually transitory. As long as appetite loss is not causing you any serious health problems, hasn't lasted for more than a couple of weeks, or hasn't caused you to lose weight, don't worry about it. When things straighten out, your normal eating patterns will probably return without your even realizing it.

If you don't have much appetite, the meals you *do* eat must be well-balanced and healthy. You need to maintain good nutrition when you are under stress, so that your body has all the nutrients it needs to repair the damage caused by GAS. Keeping your blood sugar levels even throughout the day is important also, to prevent your becoming fatigued or depressed.

Try to find healthy foods that appeal to you, and avoid junk food if you can. Junk foods provide only empty calories, even though they may taste good. Eating four or five small meals or large snacks during the day can be better than eating three normal meals, particularly if an upset stomach accompanies your lack of appetite.

People who lose their appetites when they are under stress usually find that one or two foods still appeal to them: their "comfort foods." By all means, enjoy these as much as you want if they are at least somewhat healthy, or in moderation if your "comfort food" is a junk food. Use the crutch to nurture yourself when you are under stress.

Not Eating Enough—Anorexia Nervosa.

Anorexia nervosa is a serious dysfunctional eating problem, in which the sufferer refuses to eat and loses a great deal of weight. It can cause major physiological and psychological problems, including heart or kidney failure, irreversible hypoglycemia, and pulmonary tuberculosis—and, ultimately, starvation and death. Menstruation can cease in female anorexics, and osteoporosis—that is, loss of bone mass—can also occur. Both men and women can be affected, but the disorder is more common in women. Anorexics have a distorted body image and see themselves as fat, even when they are at a normal weight or very thin. Because our culture places a high value on being slim, many people can become obsessed about their weight to the detriment of their health—even without having all the symptoms of anorexia nervosa. Much debate is going on about the causes of anorexia nervosa, but stress seems to aggravate this condition and can cause relapses in people who previously had managed to overcome it.

Anorexia nervosa usually requires hospital treatment in a closely controlled refeeding program, combined with family therapy or individual psychotherapy. Even after anorexics return to normal weight, they may need to continue with psychotherapy for months or years.

Eating Too Much and Purging—Bulimia

Bulimia is a dysfunctional eating pattern characterized by severe overeating, usually followed by self-induced vomiting or extensive use of laxatives. As in anorexia, the sufferer may be of normal weight, but become obsessed about weight to the extent of vomiting or using laxatives sometimes after overeating (or even eating a normal meal), without having all the symptoms of bulimia. But damage to the person's health still results.

Sometimes, but not always, bulimia is a variant of anorexia nervosa. After years of eating very little, an anorexic may crave food and begin to binge. However, the fear of gaining weight remains, and the sufferer begins vomiting or using laxatives. Research has shown that stress can precipitate a binge and can trigger relapses months or years after treatment.

Treatment is very similar to that for anorexia nervosa. Hospitalization for several weeks may be required to carefully monitor eating, and psychotherapy is almost always required. Bulimia can cause serious health problems, including fatigue, muscle cramping, and seizures resulting from electrolyte imbalances following depletion of calcium, potassium, magnesium, and sodium; dental problems, because gastric acids contained in vomit can erode the enamel from teeth and cause gums to recede; esophageal ulcers and damage to the stomach, again caused by gastric acid; inability of the intestinal system to function without the use of laxatives if the bulimic made heavy use of laxatives; heart rhythm abnormalities; rashes, broken blood vessels, and swelling around the ankles, eyes, and feet; and, in rare cases, binging can result in pancreatic disease or fatal rupture of the stomach.

When to See Your Physician about Dysfunctional Eating

The rule of thumb is that you should discuss dysfunctional eating problems of any kind with your physician as soon as they begin to impact your lifestyle significantly, cause you worry, or create stress for you.

Your physician should openly discuss your concerns with you, asking you about the kinds and amounts of foods you eat, your physical fitness habits, and the kinds of stress you are currently experiencing. Specialized medical tests may be ordered to rule out any underlying medical problem, and a cardiac stress test may be done if you are over 40 or very inactive, to make sure it is safe for you to start a physical fitness program.

If overeating is your problem, your physician may recommend a reduced-calorie diet tailored to meet your special needs, help you set up an appropriate exercise program, and/or refer you to a registered dietician who can help in developing a balanced reduced-calorie diet or suggest you join a group such as Weight Watchers. If you need a specialized fitness program, you may be referred to a sports medicine specialist.

If your physician diagnoses you as suffering from anorexia or bulimia, hospitalization may be required until normal weight is achieved. Psychotherapy will also be recommended and, in some cases, antidepressant drugs may be prescribed.

Headaches

If you are a typical American, there is a high probability you had a headache within the past week. Everybody gets headaches once in awhile, and some people get headaches the way other people get nervous stomachs. Such people are chronic headache victims. A smaller number of people are faced with sometimes incapacitating migraine headaches.

There are as many causes of headaches as there are people. Therefore you need to learn as much as you can about your own headaches in order to figure out how to treat them effectively. You might want to keep a log of your headaches for a few weeks, noting where you are and what you're doing when they come on, how long they last, what seems to make them better or worse, and what you were thinking or feeling at the time. Then look for patterns. Do your headaches occur in similar situations, at similar times, and so on?

Simple Headaches

Simple headaches can be caused by any one of the following: sore throat; eye strain; fever; anemia; muscle spasm; holding your head at an odd angle for a long period of time; hunger; fatigue; squinting; allergies to foods and airborne particles; sodium nitrite (found in bacon, hot dogs, luncheon meats, and so forth); too much sun; monosodium glutamate (MSG), often used in Chinese, prepared, and frozen foods as a flavor enhancer; chocolate; caffeine; and cigarette smoke. Headaches caused by these culprits are easily cured once you change your habits, get some sleep, take care of the original health problem, or discontinue eating the offending food.

Tension Headaches

Most people suffering from headaches have tension headaches, which are caused by muscle contractions. These muscle contractions can be triggered by stress or a specific problem. You can distinguish this type of headache easily for yourself. They usually affect both sides of your head, may be felt across your forehead or down your neck, and happen again and again. You may even wake up in the morning with a tension headache in spite of a full night's sleep! Once you are able to pinpoint what triggers them you can take steps to remedy the situation. If you can do that, you will usually find that your headaches will go away without professional help.

Depression-Induced Headaches

Some people who have chronic headaches may have a "masked" or hidden depression, which shows up as headaches. People with depression headaches usually notice that their headaches are worse early in the morning and again late in the afternoon. Often there are other symptoms as well: You may awaken early in the morning and be unable to go back to sleep; backaches or chest pains may be a problem; you may suddenly cry for no apparent reason; or your behavior may change—if you love to eat you may lose your appetite; if you are usually neat, you may let your appearance go. Depression headaches are best treated by a physician and mental health professional together. A counselor or therapist can help you uncover and resolve the situation causing your depression, while a physician might recommend the use of an antidepressant drug for a short period of time to break the headache cycle.

Sinus Headaches (Sinusitis)

When you are run-down due to stress, a common cold or flu can spread to other parts of your respiratory system. If it spreads to your sinuses, the spaces in your skull between the facial bones, you can develop *sinusitis*—an inflammation of the mucous linings of the sinuses. Sinusitis is one of the most common chronic illnesses in the country. Many people think that sinusitis is just a head cold that seems to hang on for a long time, and don't realize they have the illness.

Your sinuses serve a valuable function: They secrete antibody-containing mucus, which protects the respiratory passages from irritants in the air. Once your sinuses are inflamed for any reason, they are much more susceptible to bacterial infection. When a bacterial infection sets in, the sinuses get even more inflamed, which makes them even more vulnerable. Dry air, airplane travel, "office pollution," and urban living often exacerbate this process. Over time, chronic sinusitis can leave those sinus membranes cracked, scarred, and swollen—prime sites for more bacterial infections.

How can you tell if your headache is truly a sinus headache? Most headaches are caused by muscle contractions due to tension. But if your symptoms include pressure or pain around your cheekbones, forehead, or behind your eyes, you may have a sinus headache. Your voice may be raspy; your eyes may be puffy; your ears can feel stuffed up; or you may develop bad breath—bacteria and pus in the nose and sinuses can give off a bad odor.

If you develop any of these symptoms, or if a cold just seems to last too long, it's time to visit your physician. If a bacterial infection is present, antibiotics are in order. Use of decongestants is often recommended, because they help drain the nose and sinuses. Several new prescription inhalers have been very useful in treating sinusitis; they help heal sinus membranes after the bacteria have been eliminated.

Some people develop chronic sinusitis, particularly if they have a number of allergies to airborne substances (such as dust, pollens, animal dander, or molds). Airplane travel can exacerbate this condition, especially if the sufferer is a frequent flyer. The changes in air pressure on ascent and descent can push bacteria-containing mucus into the ear area or into other parts of the sinuses, spreading the infection. So just when you start to get over an infection, it gets spread again. Climate can play a role here, particularly if pollen and mold levels are high and are combined with high humidity. High humidity can cause you to get stuffed up, and make chronic sinusitis worse. Lastly, "indoor air pollution"—frequently found in offices today, where the exchange of stale air for fresh air doesn't happen frequently enough—can help keep chronic sinusitis hanging on, as bacteria, viruses, cigarette smoke, pollutants, and other irritants continue to remain in the air long enough for you to breathe them in, where they can either cause inflammation of your sinuses, or spread infection.

Migraine Headaches

Many people suffer from migraines, and the majority are women. Stress doesn't *cause* migraine headaches, but it can increase their frequency, duration, and intensity. Migraine headaches tend to affect only one side of your head at a time; can cause nausea, vomiting, and loss of appetite; may be preceded by an "aura" (flashing lights across your field of vision, numbness in arms or legs, a taste in your mouth, or a noticeable odor); and seem to run in families.

Physicians used to believe that people who got migraines were perfectionists who worked hard to maintain their high internal standards of behavior. But recent research has found that migraines affect people across the entire spectrum of personality types.

Research has confirmed that careful control of diet can help control migraines. Aged cheese, fermented wines or liquors, chocolate, nuts, monosodium glutamate, and nitrites are all known to be capable of triggering migraine attacks. Changes in the level of sugar in your bloodstream can also trigger migraines. Eating balanced meals three times a day keeps blood sugar levels fairly stable, and is a useful preventive measure.

Changes in the weather, altitude, sleeping habits, and relaxation patterns can also trigger migraine headaches. Some sufferers notice that they get severe headaches on the weekend. This may be caused by changes in the eating, sleeping, and relaxation patterns followed during the work week.

The key here is to keep your body on a regular schedule, even during the weekends.

A serious problem can arise when women who get migraines take birth control pills. The hormones in birth control pills have been found to increase the frequency, severity, and duration of migraine headaches. If you are presently taking birth control pills and are experiencing headaches that resemble migraines, it might be a good idea to check with your physician. Switching to an alternative method of birth control has relieved considerable suffering for many women who experience migraines.

Physicians have a variety of medications available to help eliminate severe migraine problems. No single combination works for every sufferer, so your physician may have to experiment to find the correct medications and dosage for you. Biofeedback has also proven helpful for migraine prevention.

Treatments for Headaches

If you have a headache, the following tips might help make it more bearable, if not get rid of it entirely:

- *When you first become aware of your headache, check to see if muscles in your jaw, forehead, neck, or shoulders are tense.* Consciously relaxing or massaging these muscles may relieve your headache. Make sure your neck, head, and face muscles do *not* remain in the same position for long periods of time: This is especially important at work when you are working on a typewriter or computer, or are doing a lot of reading. Keeping muscles in a fixed position can cause them to tighten or "freeze," which can trigger or aggravate tension headaches. Take a five-minute break at least every two hours and do a little stretching.

- *Use heat, cold, or steam to ease the pain of a headache.* Usually cold applied at the first sign of a headache will help numb sensitive nerve endings, shrink blood vessels that have begun to swell, and diminish muscle spasms. Put some ice cubes in a plastic bag and wrap the bag in a damp towel or use a cold, damp washcloth or a frozen gel pack, which is available at most drug and discount stores, and put this cold compress directly on the area that hurts. It can also be soothing to put the cold compress on the back of your neck, the top of your head, and the base of your skull—all places where sensitive nerve endings converge.

  Some people find that heat works best for them when a headache is well under way. Heat and steam (standing over a sink of hot water with a towel over your head to trap the steam or taking a hot shower) are particularly effective in relaxing tense muscles and in easing sinus congestion. Heating pads placed on the back of your neck or on sore shoulders can also relax tense muscles. Experiment to see which approach works best for you.

- *Watch out for eyestrain.* Squinting at a computer screen, reading in dim light, wearing glasses or contact lenses that aren't right for you, or *not* wearing ones that are—all contribute to eyestrain, which occurs when the muscles around your eyes contract in an effort to help you see better. These tight muscles can trigger headaches and cause muscles in the face and scalp to contract as well, intensifying pain. If you are using a computer terminal or reading, take a five-minute break every hour, and look off into the distance to relax the muscles around your eyes. You might also want to try massaging the muscles around your eyes, or simply taking off your glasses or contacts and resting your eyes for a bit.

✔ *Try an over-the-counter pain reliever, but choose carefully and use wisely.* A wide variety of pain relievers are available over the counter. The buffering agents added to some pain relievers have proven very effective, but plain aspirin taken with a glass of milk or lots of water appears to work just as well and costs much less.

If you are allergic to aspirin or find it irritates your stomach, you might want to consider trying an acetaminophen-based pain reliever. However, unlike aspirin, acetaminophen is not effective in reducing inflammation (such as that found in arthritis, joint injuries, and so on). If you need an anti-inflammatory medication and cannot tolerate aspirin, your physician can prescribe a variety of such medicines.

Aspirin is aspirin, whether it comes in a fancy package or a plain bottle. Higher prices don't necessarily mean higher quality; they usually mean more advertising and fancier packaging. Check prices and purchase the brand that costs less per tablet. Aspirin decomposes rapidly when exposed to air. If your aspirin smells like vinegar, throw it out! It has begun to decompose and is no longer effective. Unless you get many headaches, buy smaller quantities so that the tablets don't lose strength before you use them up.

✔ *Consider using biofeedback: It has proven very useful in managing headaches, especially migraines.* Migraines are often triggered by changes in the flow of blood in the vessels of the brain. Biofeedback can help sufferers learn how to raise the temperature of their hands or relax scalp muscles. Cold hands are a symptom of migraine, and warming them can help abort a migraine attack by evoking the relaxation response. If you suffer from migraines, you might want to discuss this option with your physician, who can refer you to a biofeedback therapist if such treatment is appropriate.

✔ *Massage relaxes muscles, releases tension, and improves circulation—all keys to reducing headache pain.* You might want to try the massage techniques for the head, face, neck, and shoulders provided in Chap. 11.

When to See Your Physician about Headaches

If these suggestions don't help; over-the-counter pain relievers, such as aspirin (Bayer, Bufferin), ibuprofen (Advil, Motrin), or acetaminophen (Tylenol, Panadol) don't relieve your headache pain or if you are getting recurrent headaches, a visit to your physician is in order. You should also see your physician immediately if your headache: is much more severe than normal; is accompanied by any odd or unfamiliar symptoms; follows a blow to the head; is localized in a specific area such as your eye, ear, or nose; recurs in the same spot every time. A change in the pattern of your headaches is also an indication that you should see your doctor.

Your physician will ask about your headache patterns; check your eyes, ears, nose, throat, and sinuses for signs of infection; and perhaps suggest some lab tests. A neurologic exam is often enough to allay your fears of a brain tumor. Your physician may recommend lifestyle changes, diet modifications, and possibly medications. Expect that you and your doctor may have to experiment a bit to find the right combination of medications. You may be referred to one of approximately 800 headache centers across the country, where physicians specialize in treating chronic headache problems. Take heart though, with medications available today, virtually all headache sufferers can be helped tremendously.

What Doesn't Work for Headaches

More pain reliever does not necessarily mean better pain relief. Don't take more aspirin or nonaspirin pain reliever than is recommended. Aspirin does not eliminate pain; it only raises your tolerance for pain, and it can only raise your tolerance level a given, usually very limited, amount anyway. If the recommended dose of a pain reliever doesn't seem to work for you, see your physician. The pain may be indicating an underlying problem or you may need a prescription pain reliever.

Many pain relievers have caffeine added to them, on the theory that the caffeine would "speed relief through your bloodstream." Recent research has found that caffeine doesn't work that way and that it may not be effective at all in hastening pain relief. If you feel that the addition of caffeine does make your headaches go away faster, you might want to consider taking regular aspirin with tea, coffee, or cola drinks. This is cheaper than paying for higher-priced pain relievers with caffeine.

Hypertension (High Blood Pressure)

Hypertension is one of the top five chronic health disorders suffered by American adults, and the overwhelming majority have *essential* hypertension—the cause of the hypertension is not known. About half of the people with essential hypertension have what is considered to be borderline hypertension, meaning their blood pressure readings are in the resting range of 90 to 95 diastolic (the bottom reading) and 140 to 159 systolic (the upper reading). Stress does not *cause* hypertension, but it can make it worse—particularly if you are frustrated or angry. A good example of that is the fact that most people's blood pressure reading is a little higher when they have it taken at their physician's office, usually because they are nervous about being there! Type A people (are *you* Type A?) seem to be predisposed to hypertension.

Uncontrolled high blood pressure can be a real killer. The extra work for your heart and the increased pressure in your blood vessels can cause permanent damage. Hypertension doubles your risk for heart attack and stroke. If you also smoke or have high cholesterol, your risk of heart attack is significantly higher. If you are overweight on top of that, the risk doubles again. Hypertension is nothing to fool around with, but, because in its early stages it usually has very few symptoms, people may not treat it seriously enough.

Treatments for Hypertension

Although the primary treatment for hypertension is medication, there are several things you can do to help control it:

✔ *If you smoke, quit, and if you don't smoke, don't start.*

✔ *Cut back on salt in your diet.* True, your body needs some sodium, but you get all you need from the naturally occurring sodium found in the foods you eat (and we don't mean potato chips). Stop putting additional salt on foods, switch to unsalted margarine, and don't eat foods that contain a lot of salt (most junk foods and almost all prepared or frozen foods). New evidence suggests that chronic high salt intake may predispose people to *developing* hypertension.

✔ *Cut back on alcohol consumption.* If you are a heavy drinker, it is important for you to limit your intake of alcohol drastically. Excessive use of alcohol has been found to raise blood pressure.

✔ *If you are overweight, lose the weight.* Cutting back on the calories can have a positive effect on lowering your blood pressure.

✔ *Increase your level of activity and physical exercise.* Regular aerobic exercise for 50 minutes three or four times a week can work wonders in helping control high blood pressure. Even walking can help.

✔ *Practice progressive muscle relaxation, meditation, and/or biofeedback.* Stress doesn't cause hypertension, but it can make it worse. So any coping techniques that work for you in helping reduce the amount of stress you experience, will be beneficial in controlling high blood pressure. Progressive relaxation, meditation, visualization, breathing exercises, and biofeedback have all proven helpful for people suffering from hypertension.

When to See Your Physician about Hypertension

You should have your blood pressure checked whenever you visit your physician because, for the most part, hypertension has no obvious symptoms. You can check it yourself if you see a blood pressure reading machine at a mall or health fair. If your blood pressure is 140 over 90 or higher, repeat the reading on at least two more occasions. If your readings are consistently at 140 over 90 or above, see your physician.

Your physician will take your blood pressure several times—standing up, sitting down, and even lying down—and may order some special tests to rule out any physical cause for your hypertension. The aforementioned lifestyle changes are almost always recommended. Medications are usually prescribed to lower blood pressure; you and your physician may have to experiment a bit to find the combination of medications that works most effectively for you. A wide variety of medications are available that can dramatically reduce high blood pressure. It is very important that you take your medications exactly as prescribed, *every day*, so make sure you understand your treatment regimen before you leave your physician's office.

Many of the medications prescribed for hypertension can cause side effects, including fatigue, impotence, or a cough. But controlling hypertension doesn't mean you have to feel bad—in most cases, other medications can be tried that may not cause the annoying side effects for you. If you experience any side effects, discuss them with your physician as soon as you notice them.

Your physician will likely recommend lifestyle changes—especially that you find ways to cope with the stress you are experiencing, whether it is caused by problems on the job or at home. In addition to the coping techniques outlined here, you and your physician may want to discuss whether the kinds of stress you are experiencing could be helped with counseling or psychotherapy. Controlling stress can help control blood pressure.

What Doesn't Work for Hypertension

If you don't follow your physician's treatment plan, you will not be able to control your blood pressure effectively: It's that simple. It is mandatory that you watch your diet to lose weight and decrease your intake of salt. Once your physician starts you on medication, understand that you will be on it for life: Essential hypertension is a chronic illness for which there is no known cure at this time. To be effective, medications must be taken in the manner prescribed by your physician—you can't just take them when you don't feel right and skip them when you feel good.

Jaw Problems

Bruxism—Gnashing Your Teeth

Do you have a problem from the office or at home that you have been "chewing on?" Do you just grit your teeth and do it? Does your bedmate complain that the sound of you grinding your teeth is annoying at night? Do you wake up in the morning with your jaws aching? Are your teeth sore or are your gums bleeding when you wake up in the morning? Do you experience facial, neck, or ear pain on awakening?

If you answered yes to any of these questions, you may suffer from bruxism, a technical name for gnashing, grinding, gritting, clenching, clamping, clicking, or tapping of the teeth.

Stress plays a big role in bruxism, and acute bruxism can occur in anyone as a response to a stressful situation—as part of the widespread muscle contraction that can happen during the General Adaptation Syndrome. Clenching your teeth has been found to be a potent stress-release mechanism. Acute bruxism rarely causes any major problems, and usually resolves itself when the stressful situation ends.

Sometimes chronic bruxism can develop when people are under stress for long periods. There are three kinds of chronic bruxism. *Clenching* the teeth (which more often happens during the day when you find yourself in a stressful situation) generates severe biting pressure and can damage the bones of the jaw. *Clicking* involves intermittent pressure on the jaw, and does little damage (but the sound can be aggravating). *Grinding* (which most often occurs during sleep), not only causes severe biting pressure, but can abrade tooth surfaces, wearing away enamel. Chronic bruxism can also lead to temporomandibular joint syndrome.

Temporomandibular Joint Syndrome (TMJ)

The temporomandibular joint is located at the head of the jawbone (mandible) where it fits into the underside of the temporal bone of the skull. You can feel this joint move when you move your lower jaw. Temporomandibular joint syndrome (TMJ) causes pain that affects the head, jaw, and face when the joint and the muscles and ligaments around it don't work properly. The most common cause for that is a spasm of the chewing muscles— triggered by chronic bruxism.

The common symptoms of TMJ include: headaches, especially around the temples; dull, aching facial pain; tenderness of the jaw muscles; clicking or popping sounds when the mouth is opened wide; the sensation of a "locking" jaw or jaws getting stuck in one position; and difficulty in opening the mouth. Although TMJ is not life-threatening, it can be extremely painful and a real nuisance.

Treatments for Bruxism and Temporomandibular Joint Syndrome

The best way to treat bruxism and TMJ is to reduce the stress you are experiencing, because bruxism is directly correlated to stress. You might want to try the following ideas:

✔ *Experiment with progressive muscle relaxation, meditation, and biofeedback.* These coping techniques, discussed in Chap. 11, are helpful for people suffering from bruxism or TMJ.

✔ *Reduce your overall levels of stress by actively practicing whatever coping techniques work best for you.*

✔ *Hot, moist compresses can help ease sore muscles.* Applying a hot washcloth to sore jaw, neck, or facial muscles can help ease pain and muscle spasm, as can taking a hot shower. Even resting with the side of your face on a heating pad set at low can help.

✔ *Switch to soft, nonchewy foods for a little while.* The idea is to temporarily lessen the work the jaw muscles have to do. Caramels, apples, and thick steaks are definitely out!

✔ *Try a gentle massage of the affected muscles.* All muscle spasms respond to gentle massage to "get the kinks out."

When to See Your Physician or Dentist about Jaw Problems

If the home treatments listed in the foregoing don't help, or if you are experiencing a particularly painful TMJ spasm, make an appointment with your physician. Your physician may prescribe muscle-relaxant medications; recommend special bite or jaw exercises; or, if your problem is very severe, refer you to a dentist.

A dentist may fit you with a bite splint, a device that fits over the teeth at night to prevent clenching or grinding. You may also need to have your bite corrected with selective grinding or the use of braces or other orthodontic devices. In some cases, if much damage has been done, jaw surgery may be required.

What Doesn't Work for Jaw Problems

Expensive orthodontia and surgery may alleviate the symptoms of TMJ and bruxism for a while, but if you don't work on the stress that is causing you to have these problems, TMJ may recur. Chiropractors and osteopathic physicians are not qualified to treat TMJ.

Lower Gastrointestinal Tract Problems

Irritable Bowel Syndrome (Irritable Colon Syndrome, Spastic Colon)

Irritable bowel syndrome (IBS) is a broad term that refers to a variety of types of altered bowel functions *that are not caused by a specific disease.* IBS is not caused by stress, but stress definitely makes it worse, and can increase the frequency, duration, and intensity of attacks. Symptoms can subside and even disappear for periods of time, but IBS usually recurs throughout life. Although not life-threatening, it can cause great distress. IBS is more common in women than men, and onset usually occurs between the late 20s to 40 years of age.

Irritable Bowel Syndrome Symptoms. IBS can make you feel genuinely miserable and manifests itself through a bewildering array of symptoms: intermittent cramplike abdominal pain or discomfort (which never awakens you at night), excess gas or belching, abdominal distention (swelling), sensations of fullness, lack of appetite, nausea, transient relief of pain by bowel movement or passing gas, mucus in the feces, sense of incomplete evacuation of the bowels, heartburn, back pain, weakness, faintness, agitation, tendency to tire easily, palpitations, and altered bowel habits—usually either constipation or diarrhea (which does not usually awaken you during the night), although some people alternate between constipation and diarrhea. The pain sufferers feel is highly variable in terms of severity, location, and duration: Some people feel discomfort after meals; some feel pain in the lower left side of the abdomen; some experience pain under the left rib cage; and some, in the stomach area.

The exact cause of IBS is not known. Research suggests that the basic abnormality is a disturbance of involuntary muscle movement in the large intestine—which may be inherited. Stress exacerbates this underlying dysfunction, and initial onset of the condition and subsequent recurrences are linked to high stress.

Physicians divide IBS into two main types: *spastic colon* (the most common), which produces constipation, *painless diarrhea*, in which stools are semiloose but not watery, often come on urgently, and are associated with cramping.

Treatment for Irritable Bowel Syndrome. If you have IBS, you can do a number of things:

✔ *Track your IBS episodes on a calendar, along with your periods of stress.* If you are female, also track your menstrual periods as well. Female IBS sufferers may find that their IBS gets worse just after ovulation, when progesterone is secreted by the body. Research has found that some people have delayed reaction, that is, they don't experience IBS symptoms at the moment they are experiencing great stress, but have a delayed reaction from one to three weeks after the stress has subsided. Just knowing that your body responds in this manner can help you plan for IBS episodes.

✔ *Experiment with your diet to determine which food(s) trigger your IBS episodes, and avoid them.* Start keeping a diary of when you experience IBS, noting what you ate prior to the episode and what stresses you might have been feeling. You may see a pattern develop—for example, foods with garlic in them, or that are spicy, cold, or gas-producing may initiate IBS symptoms. Once you know which foods are particularly bothersome, make it a point to eliminate them from your diet. Fatty or fried foods particularly aggravate IBS. Experiment with eliminating dairy products from your diet to see whether your symptoms decrease. A fairly large percentage of IBS sufferers are *lactose intolerant*. They cannot digest the sugars found in dairy products. When this happens, cramping and excessive gas result. Coffee combined with IBS can cause diarrhea.

Foods that produce gas, and so should be evaluated to see whether they bother you, include apples, bananas, beans, broccoli, cabbage, carbonated beverages, cauliflower, corn, cucumbers, meringues, milk, oats, onions, and turnips.

✔ *Make sure to eat your meals on a regular schedule every day.* Human bodies thrive on regularity. Particularly in the case of IBS, physicians find that skipping a meal, then eating a heavier one later, can result in cramping and diarrhea. When you do eat, chew thoroughly and slowly.

✔ *Reduce your fat intake.* Research has proven that cholekinin, which is produced by the body in response to fat intake, slows down the muscle movements of the colon. Cut back on foods that are fried or high in fat. Good choices are turkey, chicken, and fish that are baked, grilled, or poached. Complex carbohydrates, including most fruits and vegetables (and also provide fiber), as well as pasta, rice, and breads are also good choices. Although this recommendation is particularly important for IBS sufferers, it makes good sense for everyone.

✔ *Gradually increase the amount of fiber in your diet by eating a wide variety of high fiber foods.* This is important whether you suffer from constipation or diarrhea. Fiber tends to normalize transit time through the large intestine. Additional bulk drops the pressure in the abdomen and decreases uncomfortable sensations. High-fiber foods include almonds, apricots, beans, blackberries, bran, brussels sprouts, corn, coconut, dates, figs, kiwi, lentils, parsley, peaches, pears, pineapple, pistachio nuts, popcorn, prunes, raspberries, strawberries, walnuts, and whole-grain products.

✔ *Use high-fiber psyllium hydrophilic mucilloid (Metamucil, Konsyl, Hydrocil) on a regular basis.* This adds bulk to the stools and makes them softer and easier to pass. Start gradually increasing your intake, according to package directions. It works best if you work up gradually to the maximum dosage over a period of two to three weeks. Otherwise you may experience cramping and excess gas. If you have diarrhea, try taking it 30 to 40 minutes prior to meals. For constipation, try taking it at bedtime.

✔ *Respond promptly to urges to have a bowel movement.* It may be more difficult to have one later. Realize however, that a daily bowel movement is not necessary for good health.

✔ *Get your body in the habit of having a bowel movement at the same time each day.* You can do this by allowing yourself enough time to relax after eating an *unhurried* breakfast or dinner, because food in the stomach triggers the gastrocolonic reflex (movement of the intestines), which is necessary to produce a bowel movement. You can also time the taking of psyllium hydrophilic mucilloid, for example, after breakfast or after dinner, and, over the period of about two weeks, your body will normalize with a bowel movement around those times.

✔ *Drink plenty of fluids—at least six glasses per day.* Fluid is important for keeping stools soft, and even more important if you are taking psyllium hydrophilic mucilloid.

✔ *Get regular, mild aerobic exercise.* Yes, it works for IBS, too. Regular exercise can stimulate bowel movements. It also reduces the effects of stress, which can dramatically aggravate IBS.

✔ *Practice the coping techniques in Chap. 11 to reduce stress.* Biofeedback, meditation, and progressive muscle relaxation are particularly effective for IBS. Any other coping technique that works for you, and which you enjoy, can be used as well.

✔ *Avoid smoking and excessive use of alcohol.* These "bad guys" can increase IBS symptoms.

When to See Your Physician about Irritable Bowel Syndrome.   If self-treatments don't help, the change in your bowel habits was sudden, or you are experiencing more frequent recurrences of IBS, a visit to your physician is in order.

To diagnose IBS, your physician needs a careful history of your symptoms, their severity, and what you have tried in an effort to cope with the discomforts of IBS. If you have mild symptoms, no lab tests may be necessary. But if your symptoms are severe, or if there has been a sudden change in your bowel habits, lab tests may be required to rule out other diseases. A blood test may be done to check for anemia, which sometimes indicates internal bleeding. Stool cultures to check for parasites or bacteria are often indicated when diarrhea is the problem. Sometimes a sigmoidoscopy and/or a barium enema is done. Sigmoidoscopy is a procedure in which the physician uses a special instrument to view the lower colon directly. A barium enema provides a diagnostic X-ray of the intestine.

Your physician may prescribe special drugs to lessen your symptoms, but realize that, while they lessen symptoms, they don't cure the problem. The most important components of treatment are diet and lifestyle changes.

What Doesn't Work for Irritable Bowel Syndrome.   Over-the-counter laxatives may seem helpful when you are having acute constipation, but when used for more than a day or two, they can seriously disrupt an already upset bowel system. They also cause nutrient losses and attendant deficiencies, and can result in dependency—a potentially serious problem. Enemas and "colonics" don't work either, and can seriously disrupt your lower gastrointestinal system.

The same holds true for Kaopectate, Pepto-Bismol, and other over-the-counter antidiarrhea medications. Other IBS sufferers try antacids, but these have not been proven beneficial in long-term use, and can increase both constipation and diarrhea.

Nor do fad diets work, especially those that focus on either the elimination or increased intake of one particular type of food. Your best bet is sticking with a high-fiber diet, moderate exercise, and psyllium hydrophilic mucilloid. There are no magic cures for irritable bowel syndrome.

Ulcerative Colitis

The symptoms of this serious bowel problem often mimic IBS. If you have frequent blood in your stools or weight loss, your colitis may be of this serious type. Stress, particularly that surrounding major life changes, can also aggravate ulcerative colitis, the chronic inflammation (swelling) and ulceration (forming of sores) of the lining of the colon and rectum.

If you are under a great deal of stress and suffer from ulcerative colitis, it is important to let your physician know about the stress you are under. Making use of the coping techniques in Chap. 11 may help reduce your stress and lessen the severity and frequency of your ulcerative colitis episodes.

Menstrual Irregularities

Women experiencing high levels of stress often report irregularities in their menstrual periods because women's reproductive systems are very sensitive to the hormones produced as a response to stress. An individual's response to stress is idiosyncratic: Your body may not behave like your sister's or friends' bodies when you are under stress. Periods can come earlier or later than normal; the flow may be heavier or lighter; cramping may be more painful; spotting or light bleeding between periods may occur; or, in severe stress-overload situations, women may find that their periods stop entirely. Business traveling can also throw off a woman's monthly cycle.

When to See Your Physician about Menstrual Irregularities

Usually these minor irregularities are not a cause for concern and correct themselves when the stressful situation ends. But all women should track their menstrual cycles on a calendar and note any irregularities. If your period comes more than a week earlier or later through two monthly cycles, see your physician. The same holds true if there is a mild or moderate change in the flow through two monthly cycles or you experience spotting or light bleeding.

If you miss a period entirely, or if it is more than three weeks late and you are sexually active, see your physician soon to check out the possibility of pregnancy.

It is important to contact your physician immediately if you are sexually active and your menstrual flow suddenly gets abnormally heavy to the point where you fill up a tampon or pad within two or three hours, or if you pass large clots. These can be signs of a miscarriage, and your physician may want to see you immediately.

As we said before, menstrual irregularities most often correct themselves when stress levels are reduced. But those same irregularities can be valuable early warning signs for more serious reproductive problems, and they should not be ignored. In this case, it is better to err on the side of caution.

Musculoskeletal Complaints

Sore Muscles

Muscle Spasms. A muscle spasm is a muscle that has become abnormally rigid, or has knotted up. Although not serious, spasms can be very painful. They can occur anywhere in the body and can be caused by strain or injury: Nearly everyone is familiar with this kind of pain after exercising hard over the weekend, doing a great deal of gardening or lifting, or just moving wrong. In this case, muscles that haven't been used in awhile suddenly get called into play, and end up getting strained. This sort of muscle spasm often occurs approximately 48 hours after exercise or a wrong movement.

But people who are under a great deal of stress can experience a slightly different kind of muscle spasm. It is not uncommon to "carry your stress" habitually in a certain muscle group: Some people "carry their shoulders up around their ears," tighten their abdominal muscles, clench their teeth, tense the muscles in the upper stomach area, or contract muscles in their legs. Most of us can sense when our muscles are beginning to tense up, but some people are so used to carrying a particular muscle group tightened up that the tensed muscles begin to feel *normal*. When muscles are tensed up for a period of time, they can go into a painful spasm.

Fibromyositis. People who are experiencing a great deal of life stress sometimes develop *fibromyositis*, which is chronic, diffuse pain and stiffness in the muscles around the joints and sometimes in the back. The role that stress plays in this condition is not completely clear and its cause is not known at this time, but sufferers report nearly continual radiating, burning, or tingling pain in the lower back, neck, and shoulders, chest, buttocks, or knees. Fatigue and frequent awakenings from sleep at night are often reported as well. Fibromyositis is most common in middle-aged and elderly people.

People with fibromyositis report no restrictions in movement of the affected muscle group, but trigger zones (specific places on the muscle group that can be pressed to recreate the pain) may be felt in the affected muscles, and these spots are tender to the touch. Attacks can be worse in cold, damp weather or when stress on the job or at home gets more severe.

Treatments for Sore Muscles. Nearly everyone is vulnerable to muscle spasms; you can try a number of self-care treatments either to prevent or to reduce the duration of a spasm, including:

✔ *If possible, avoid the event that triggered the muscle spasm, and give the affected muscle group a rest.* If you developed the muscle spasm playing touch football or sitting hunched over in your chair at a stressful staff meeting, it just makes sense to moderate your activities to prevent a recurrence of the spasm. You might not be able to avoid staff meetings, but you can watch to be sure that you maintain proper posture for their duration!

✔ *Try over-the-counter painkillers such as aspirin, acetaminophen or ibuprofen.* Aspirin and ibuprofen also reduce inflammation, which can be important if your muscle spasm is the result of strain.

✔ *Apply heat, either in the form of hot compresses, a heating pad, or a hot shower.* Heat helps muscles relax, and can be very effective in unkinking a spasm.

✔ *Try a gentle massage.* Again, the idea is to help the muscle relax. You might want to try some of the self-massage techniques outlined in Chap. 11. If your tensed-up muscles are in a place you can't reach, consider a professional massage. Just remember, go easy on the sore muscle—excessive pressure can further irritate a muscle in spasm.

✔ *If you chronically carry a certain muscle group "tight" when you are experiencing stress, progressive muscle relaxation and biofeedback help.* Both techniques can help you learn to identify when your muscles are beginning to tense up. Then you can consciously relax that muscle group, short-circuiting the spasm-creating process. Progressive muscle relaxation techniques are outlined in Chap. 11, and your physician can recommend a qualified biofeedback practitioner.

✔ *Begin a physical fitness program that includes exercises geared toward increasing muscle tone and overall flexibility.* If muscles are used regularly, they become stronger and more resistant to strain. Stretching exercises can help you achieve flexibility, which is just as important as muscle strength.

When to See Your Physician about Sore Muscles. Most muscle spasms respond well to the self-care guidelines listed previously. But if, after a week of home treatment and resting the muscle group, you feel no improvement, or if you feel a tingling or weakness in the affected body part, it's time to see your physician. He or she will want to make sure that you haven't torn or seriously injured the muscle and may prescribe a muscle relaxant medication and physical therapy. Muscle relaxant medications are prescribed only for severe spasms, and physical therapy can help, first to unkink, and then to tone and strengthen the sore muscle group. Fibromyositis responds well to bedtime antidepressants, which normalize sleep patterns and allow muscles to relax.

What Doesn't Work for Sore Muscles.   It is not wise to continue pushing, exercising, or using a muscle group that has gone into spasm. Doing so only serves to irritate an already knotted-up muscle, and may prolong the duration and intensity of the spasm.

Backaches—Upper and Lower

Various surveys have shown that between 60 to 90 percent of the population will experience back pain at some point in their lives. Most back pain sufferers are between 30 and 50, and frequently have their first severe episode of back pain in their thirties. This is partly because the spine starts to age when people hit their thirties; partly because people in their thirties are very active on the job, at home, and in leisure activities; and partly because during our thirties we may go through a number of major life changes, including promotion, marriage, divorce, loss of a job, relocation, or taking that vacation we've always dreamed about. These major life changes all cause significant stress.

Within the medical community there is some argument as to whether stress by itself can be the sole cause for backache. But few disagree that stress can greatly aggravate back pain.

Upper Backaches.   Physicians consider the upper back to be that part of the back from the neck to about two-thirds of the way down to the waist. Upper back pain is most frequently the result of muscular spasm, strain, or tearing. It can be caused by sports (trying to do too much on the weekends when our bodies are out of shape); improper ergonomic design in the workplace (see the section of this chapter that discusses work-related injuries); lugging heavy carry-on luggage through airports while racing for a connecting flight; or trying to put the entire contents of our desks into a briefcase to take home in the evening or on the weekends.

Less frequently, the muscle spasms can be caused primarily by stress. As discussed previously, some people habitually carry their stress in certain muscle groups. Whenever muscles are kept tensed for long periods of time, they can become fatigued and go into spasm. Even more rarely, upper back pain can be caused by fibromyositis.

Lower Backaches.   Lower backaches, which are probably more common than upper backaches, are more complex. They can be the result of muscular spasm, strain, or tearing; arthritis; fibromyositis; a skeletal deformity or injury; or a nerve injury or problem. Sufferers often have a family history of back pain or arthritis.

The most frequent type of low back pain, and one of the largest single causes of missed work days, is "nonspecific back pain." Nonspecific back pain is not completely understood at this time, but physicians believe it is due to a mechanical disorder that affects one or more parts of the back, such as a ligament strain, a muscle tear, damage to a spinal facet joint, or even a prolapsed disk. Stress can greatly aggravate nonspecific back pain, and severe stress can precipitate the onset of the initial episode of back pain.

Treatments for Backaches. Many self-care treatments can be used to help control back pain. The first rule is: "If it hurts, don't do it!" The last thing you want to do is reinjure or strain an already sore or stiff set of muscles in your back. So be good to yourself; take it easy when attempting *any* of these self-care treatments, and don't push your back beyond what it is able to handle comfortably!

✔ First, refer to the section just covered on treatments for sore muscles. All those treatments work for back pain as well. Also consider these other options.

✔ *Remember, ice is nice if used right.* Ice can help relieve pain at its onset, but only at the onset. Cold can help contract blood vessels so that blood cannot rush in to inflame the area. It can also help numb tender nerve endings. Try putting an ice pack or cold pack (preferably wrapped in a small towel to prevent your skin from getting too cold) on the affected part of your back for 20 or 30 minutes. Then keep the cold pack off for two to three hours. If the pain still persists, repeat this procedure—but only once or twice more.

✔ *Rest your back, preferably in a firm bed.* Sometimes rest is all that a muscle needs to help it start healing. If your bed is old or soft, try slipping a bed board (fiberboard or other stiff board approximately three-fourths of an inch thick) between the mattress and box spring for extra support. Waterbeds provide the proper amount of support only if filled adequately. Some other back pain sufferers swear by them—especially if they are heated.

✔ *Lay on the bed the right way.* Yes, there is a correct way to lie on your bed! When you are suffering from back pain, it is important to reduce the pressure on your back and gently stretch the muscles out. The best way to do that is to lie on your side, with your arms out in front of you, your hips and knees slightly bent, and your knees angled up toward your chin. Another alternative is to lie flat on your back with knees and hips bent so that your knees are straight up in the air. You may find other positions that are even more comfortable for them, so experiment (gently!) to see what works best for you.

✔ *Follow the commonsense rules for lifting, sitting, and standing.* Always use a foot rest (alternate putting your right and left foot on it) when you will be standing up working at a table or other waist-high platform. When you lift a heavy object, bend at the knees and hips and lift straight up, rather than bending over at the waist with your knees straight. Hold heavy objects (or babies) close to your body, not at arm's distance. Never bend over (at a table, desk, sink, etc.) without bending your knees. Don't slump in your chair or on the couch to watch TV (or to sit through a boring staff meeting). Don't push a heavy object in front of you with your arms straight, push backward with your arms behind you instead—this dramatically reduces the stress placed on your back.

✔ *If you are overweight, lose the weight.* Carrying excess weight, especially in the stomach and abdominal area, puts tremendous pressure on the back, as any woman who has been pregnant knows. Many people report a marked reduction in back pain once they've brought their weight down to appropriate ranges for their height and build.

✔ *Begin a physical fitness program that includes exercises geared toward increasing muscle tone of the abdominal area and overall flexibility.* The abdominal muscles support the back, so it makes sense that strong abdominal muscles can help prevent back injury and ameliorate back pain. Stretching exercises can help you achieve flexibility in your back muscles, which is just as important as muscle strength.

✔ *If you spend a great deal of time at your desk, invest in a chair that supports your back properly.* Simply changing desk chairs can markedly reduce back pain, especially if you are at your desk for large blocks of time. What constitutes the "best" chair varies from individual to individual, but there are certain characteristics to look for. It should have adequate, *adjustable* (both for height and amount of tilt) support for the small of your back. Arm rests are crucial, because they help take some of the pressure off the lower back. The seat itself should be wide and large enough to support your seat and thighs comfortably. Its height should be adjustable so that your feet can comfortably touch the floor.

✔ *If stress seems to make your back pain worse, or if you were under severe stress right before your back pain started, work on combating those stressors.* Practicing some of the stress reduction measures outlined in Chap. 11 can help you lower your overall stress levels, help you rest better, and generally improve your outlook on life.

When to See Your Physician about Backaches.   For the most part, back pain does not indicate a life-threatening condition. Self-care treatments are usually the recommended course of action, particularly if the pain came on gradually or occurred as the result of overenthusiastic pursuit of a sport or household chore. If you are still in pain after a week of rest using heat and over-the-counter pain relievers, visit your physician.

In some instances back pain can indicate a more severe medical problem. You should call your physician if: there was a sudden onset of pain with no known precipitating event (such as turning the wrong way, swinging too vigorously with your golf club or tennis racquet, or lifting something heavy); when it is associated with weakness in the leg or problems with bladder control; when lower back pain radiates down into your buttocks or leg (this sort of pain is usually quite severe and can indicate sciatica, which is caused by pressure on a nerve); or when upper back pain radiates into an arm (which can also indicate a nerve problem).

Your physician will need to determine exactly what is causing your back pain, because the course of treatment depends on that cause. X-rays and other special tests may be ordered, especially if conservative treatment hasn't worked. Medications typically prescribed include anti-inflammatory or muscle relaxant drugs. Special exercises or braces and corsets may be recommended to help support your sore back, and your physician may refer you to a physical therapist for massage, acupressure, or other special treatments. Lifestyle changes are often indicated. Spinal injections or surgery are usually reserved for very severe cases, and then only after all other avenues tried have proven unsuccessful.

What Doesn't Work for Backaches. Unfortunately, as with almost every other stress-related medical problem, there are no instant cures for back problems, and experimentation is necessary to uncover the combination of treatments that most effectively controls your back pain. Patience is required, as experimentation takes time.

Chiropractors and physical therapists are useful in the treatment of backaches. However, if you find you are going for treatments every week for longer than two months, you may be having your wallet, not your spine, manipulated.

The biggest mistake back pain sufferers make is doctor hopping—hoping for an instant cure to relieve their pain. Approximately 50 percent of all patients with low back pain improve after one week of bed rest, and the rest usually improve within two more weeks. However, your back pain problems will *not* be resolved in one or two visits to your physician. You have to invest the time to develop a good working relationship with your physician, seriously implement the treatments recommended, and give them a chance to work.

Repetitive Stress Injuries

The proliferation of desktop computers and computer terminals has changed the way most of us who labor in offices work. We spend more of our time sitting at a desk, staring at computer screens, and typing information into those computers. And most of our work spaces are not set up to accommodate properly either the equipment or our bodies as we use that equipment.

The result is potentially the biggest workplace health problem corporations will have to face in the decades to come—repetitive stress injuries. Human beings are simply not designed to do repetitive motions over and over again (translated into thousands of keystrokes a day), and when we do that (even a fraction of it), the result is damage to muscles and nerves in the fingers, hands, wrists, arms, neck, head, and back. How much and how severe this damage is depends on how well or how poorly our workspaces are designed. Recent research indicates that repetitive stress injuries suffered by office workers are also affected by work pacing, work stress, environmental conditions, and personal traits.

Repetitive stress injuries have long been common in meat-cutting factories, or in other jobs where people on the line did repetitive motions for long periods of time. Usually such injuries were associated with heavy lifting or hard physical labor. According to U.S. government statistics, over half of the workplace injuries in 1989 were repetitive stress injuries—up from 18 percent in 1981. With more people than ever using computers, that number is guaranteed to rise.

Repetitive stress injuries take many forms, depending on the kind of repetitive motions a person makes, how the work space is set up, and what inherent bodily weaknesses. One injury that has been getting a lot of press is carpal tunnel syndrome—a severe injury of the tendons and nerves of the wrist and hand—which can require surgery and may be disabling. But all types of repetitive stress injuries are painful, debilitating to some degree, and reduce worker' productivity.

The kinds of problems computer users have reported include:

- Shooting pains in the arms
- Acute pain or stiffness in the arms, legs, neck, shoulders, and/or back
- Acute wrist or finger pain
- Numbness or tingling of the fingers, hands, arms, or shoulders
- Chronic pain in the neck, shoulders, or back

If you are experiencing any of these symptoms, Table 13.2 may give you an idea on how to alter your work space:

Table 13.2. Repetitive Stress Injuries and How to Avoid Them

Symptom	What to Check
Backache	Chair height and design, including foot support and backrest; inadequate back support; incorrect height for keyboard and monitor; location of monitor and work materials; bifocals/trifocals worn; time spent on task
Neck and shoulder pain	Seat height and inadequate back support; chair design; work material arrangement; monitor screen contrast; environmental stressors; glasses worn
Arm, hand, wrist pain	Arm rest adjustment; work materials arrangement; height adjustment and poor wrist postures; highly repetitive keying and time spent on task
Leg Pain	Seat height; foot support; leg clearance; time spent on task

The important fact to remember about repetitive stress injuries is that, when you or your staff feel pain, the damage is already done, and it may be too late to repair it. Prevention is key.

Treatments for Repetitive Stress Injuries

✔ *Select work-station chairs and desks that are flexible and can be adjusted to meet users' special needs.* Chairs should be adjustable, at least for height. Desks should have special height-adjustable modules for keyboards and monitors.

✔ *Use a foot stool or box if you feet don't touch the floor when you sit in your desk chair.* Leaving your feet dangling reduces the circulation to your legs and can cause pain.

✔ *Put your desk up on blocks.* If your desk is too low for you to comfortably use your computer, try putting pieces of two-by-four blocks under each leg to raise it.

✔ *Support your back.* If your chair lacks a lumbar support, a small pillow or rolled up towel, placed behind your back will help keep your posture correct, and relieve strain on your lower back.

✔ *Put a phone book or a thick computer manual under your keyboard to raise it to a comfortable level.* Conversely, if your desktop is too high to use your keyboard comfortably, put a pillow in your lap and place the keyboard on top of it or put your keyboard on a board placed over the desk drawer.

✔ *Don't use your mouse on top of your desk for prolonged periods of time.* This causes a great deal of stress on your neck, arm, and shoulder. Try putting the mouse and mousepad on a board placed over a side desk drawer to lower it to a more comfortable level.

✔ *Avoid flexing your wrists.* Your hands should be level with your forearms when you type on your keyboard. If it is hard to hold this posture, use a covered board or brick as a wrist rest.

✔ *Take work breaks.* Even just for a few minutes, stretch, roll your neck, or stretch your hands by squeezing a tennis ball. Stand up, move around, and focus your eyes on something in the distance.

✔ *Keep your monitor approximately at arm's length (24 inches) from your face.* This provides the proper viewing distance and can reduce both eyestrain and muscle strain in your neck.

When to See Your Physician about Repetitive Stress Injuries. If these suggestions don't help, or if you feel pain regularly, see your physician. When you have pain, damage has been done; unless the work environment and work habits are altered and corrective steps taken, the damage will only get worse.

Many primary care physicians aren't familiar with workplace injuries, and you may need to provide the clues. Your physician will ask you to describe the kind of computer or typing work you do; have you do range-of-motion exercises to determine the extent to which your ability to move the affected body part has been hampered; and may recommend X-rays or other specialized medical tests. Work-space or work-habit changes, physical therapy, special exercises, medications, specialized braces, or (as a last resort) surgery may be recommended.

Skin Problems

Seborrheic Dermatitis

Dermatitis refers to an inflammation of the skin. Allergies can cause dermatitis, but usually physicians aren't sure what causes skin to become inflamed. It is clear, however, that stress can aggravate an existing skin inflammation, and can trigger an outbreak of seborrheic dermatitis—a red, scaly, itchy rash that develops on the face, especially under the eyebrows, on the bridge of the nose, and around the mouth, scalp, chest, and back.

Although uncomfortable and aggravating, seborrheic dermatitis is not life-threatening. Topical corticosteroids, such as hydrocortisone, and/or antifungals can be helpful in bringing the problem under control. If you develop seborrheic dermatitis, handle your skin gently: Use gentle, mild soaps and cleansers; avoid washcloths, facial sponges, and scrub brushes; and try not to scratch (which only makes the dermatitis worse and increases the risk of infection).

Neurodermatitis or Eczema

Eczema is a type of dermatitis characterized by itching, scaling, or blisters that weep a clear or straw-colored fluid. Eczema can be caused by an allergy, but in some cases occurs for no known reason.

Atopic eczema is a chronic, superficial inflammation that often occurs in people who have a family history of allergies. This rash is very itchy, and the red pimples can leak a clear fluid when scratched. Leaking pimples can join to form large weeping areas if the sufferer scratches the affected area a great deal, and the risk of infection is increased.

Mild cases of atopic eczema can be helped by applying emollients, such as petroleum jelly, to keep the skin moist. In severe cases, physicians may prescribe corticosteroid ointments to control the inflammation. Antibiotics may be used to control infection, and antihistamines may be prescribed to reduce itching.

Nummular eczema appears as circular, itchy, scaling patches on the skin. Again, corticosteroid ointments can be used to reduce inflammation. However, nummular eczema is often very persistent, and may be resistant to treatment.

Perhaps the most annoying type of eczema is *hand eczema*, which as you would imagine from its name, appears on the hands and forearms. Itchy blisters, up to approximately 1 inch across, can form on the hands and arms, and the hands may be covered with cracks and scales. The blisters weep a clear or straw-colored fluid when scratched.

Hand eczema can sometimes be caused by exposure to detergents, household cleansers, and dishwashing liquids. But, more often than not, it is triggered by stress. Allergies can also trigger hand eczema, and outbreaks can be worse in the spring and summer. Occasionally, a fungal infection on the feet can trigger eczema of the hands. Treating the feet actually clears up the hands!

Your physician will likely recommend wearing rubber gloves over white cotton gloves during a hand eczema outbreak when you come in contact with detergents or cleansers. Your hands should be patted dry every time you wash them, and a mild, unscented hand cream should be applied several times a day. For moderate cases your physician may prescribe a corticosteroid ointment to curb inflammation and/or antibiotics to control infection. For severe cases, oral corticosteroids may be required for a limited period. These require careful monitoring by a physician.

When to See Your Physician about Dermatitis or Eczema

Since most skin problems are more aggravating than life-threatening, many people put off seeing their physician. As a result, problems can settle in and be much harder to eradicate. A good rule of thumb is: If you have tried the over-the-counter treatments suggested in this section for a month, and the problem hasn't subsided, it's time to schedule a visit with your physician. Make an appointment if your skin problem suddenly gets worse, or when it really begins to cause stress for you.

Your physician may need to examine you to rule out any underlying medical problem; ask you about prescription and over-the-counter medications you may be taking to see whether any of them could be aggravating your skin problem; talk with you about the kinds and amounts of stress you are experiencing; evaluate your diet and physical fitness habits; ask you about the cleansing and makeup products you use, and how you apply them; and may order some special tests.

Based on this information, your doctor may prescribe new medications; change medications your are currently taking; recommend different cleansing products and methods; or refer you to a dermatologist for specialized care. Realize that no single treatment works equally well for everyone, and some experimentation may be required before you and your physician or dermatologist hit on the combination of treatments that works best for you. Skin problems take time to heal and require lots of patience on your part, but if you stick with your treatment program, you will see results!

What Doesn't Work for Dermatitis and Eczema

Physicians have found that over-the-counter medications such as hydrocortisone creams and anti-itch medications, don't usually work well for severe dermatitis. That's because they usually aren't sold over the counter in a strength potent enough to do much good. They also don't help clear up any underlying infections.

Expensive does not necessarily mean better when it comes to prescription treatments. A hand eczema treatment that works very well for some sufferers is simply soaking the hands four times a day in a basin of warm water mixed with several tablespoons of vinegar! So trust your physician or dermatologist: The prescribed treatment may seem unique, but such treatments often work.

Adult Acne

Have you been furtively checking out Clearasil and other acne remedies at your local drug or discount store—while at the same time you check out the merits of moisturizers? If so, you're not alone: Dermatologists' offices reflect that trend. Many are treating more adults than teenagers for acne.

Unfortunately for many of us, acne comes back to haunt us when we least expect (or want) it—in our twenties, thirties, and even forties. The official line was that acne disappeared when you left your teens, but that story didn't account for the stressful lives most of us are living today. Both men and women are vulnerable, although women seem more prone to it than men (perhaps because of the use of cosmetics and hair care products that can aggravate the condition).

Luckily, most adults suffer from low-grade acne composed of blackheads (a darkened oil duct opening), whiteheads (a firm white bump), or pimple (a small elevation of the skin filled with pus), not the cystic kind many teenagers get. But fast-trackers (and normal adults) fear that even *that* could bump them off the road to success. People tend to feel that a breakout projects, not just a lack of competence, but a general untogetherness. Sufferers feel that people will look at them with their breakouts and feel that they couldn't possibly manage an important position, presentation, case, etc. So how a person feels about having acne can become a major stressor.

What causes adult acne? Dermatologists have concluded that it is a hereditary disease—if your parents had acne, you'll probably have it, too. It is triggered by hormonal changes, and stress hormones can kick off the process. Stress can cause an increased secretion of androgens—hormones that control oil production. This fact is reflected in where adult acne shows up: mostly on the chin, jawline, back, or neck—areas where the most hormonally sensitive hair follicles are located. Many things can aggravate a breakout, including: heat and humidity (because they rev up oil production); overzealous cleansing; certain hair products, especially mousses and gels; some medications, such as bromides, iodides, aspirin, ibuprofen, corticosteroids taken orally, lithium, Dilantin, phenobarbital, and birth control pills containing progesterone; pollution, by contributing to the clogging of pores; foods and vitamin supplements high in iodides and fluorides, such as shellfish, seaweed, asparagus, spinach, and iodized salt. Pressure, such as from holding a phone against your chin or sitting with your chin in your hand, and irritation, for example, where your workout clothes rub against your skin when you are perspiring from exercise can also trigger breakouts in sensitive individuals. But there is some good news: Chocolate *does not* cause acne, so if chocolate is one of your guilty pleasures, you can continue to indulge!

Treatments for Adult Acne

✔ *Shampoo regularly.* When your hair comes in contact with your face or neck, its oils add to the surface oils already there, and contribute to clogging the surface of your pores. Wash daily in the summer, and at least every other day during winter.

✔ *Try a different method of washing your face.* Try a mild glycerine soap, a mild cleansing gel, or an antibacterial soap (if it doesn't irritate your skin) twice a day followed by a mild nonalcohol astringent.

✔ *Stay away from washcloths, facial sponges, and scrub brushes, as these may further irritate inflamed skin.* Use clean hands and fingers only.

✔ *Avoid oil-based makeup and oily moisturizers.* Stick with oil-free or water-based preparations—you don't want to put more oil on top of a problem already caused by too much oil.

✔ *Become a label reader.* Be sure that the suntan products, moisturizers, shaving preparations, and cosmetics you purchase are noncomedogenic (won't clog pores). Many on the market today won't contribute to causing acne.

✔ *Avoid squeezing pimples.* Your mother told you this when you were a teen, but it's still true. You can cause permanent scarring and increase the risk of infection.

✔ *Test your sensitivity to any new skin preparation before use.* Rub a small amount onto the inside of your wrist, and take care not to wash it off for 24 hours. Any reaction or sensitivity will show up in about a day.

✔ *Try an over-the-counter acne preparation specifically designed for adult skin.* These usually contain benzoyl peroxide (try the 2.5 percent and 5 percent doses. You can go as high as 10 percent over the counter, but such products tend to irritate adult skin), sulphur, salicylic acid, or resorcinol. All of these medications loosen and increase the shedding of skin cells and sebum (the oils your skin produces). Start first using the preparation every other day for two or three weeks. After that, you develop a tolerance, and you can increase applications to twice a day or use the medication only at night. But never treat acne with an over-the-counter product more than twice a day. If you notice excessive redness or dryness, stop using the preparation for a day or two, and then use it half as often as you did before. If you still have problems, you may need to switch to a preparation containing one of the other medications listed in the foregoing.

When to See Your Physician About Adult Acne.   Because adult acne is more aggravating than life-threatening, many people put off going to see their physician. As a result, problems can settle in and be much harder to eradicate. If you have tried the over-the-counter treatments suggested in this section for a month, and the problem hasn't subsided, schedule a visit with your physician. Make the appointment if your skin problem suddenly gets worse, or when it really begins to cause you stress.

Be prepared to discuss the history of your skin problem—what prescription and over-the-counter medications you are taking (to see if they could be aggravating your skin problem); the kinds and amounts of stress you are experiencing in your life; your diet and physical fitness habits; and the cleansing and makeup products you use and how you apply them.

Depending on the type and severity of your acne, your physician may prescribe Retin-A; topical antibiotics such as erythromycin and clindamycin; oral antibiotics such as tetracycline, erythromycin, or Minocin; or prescription-strength benzoyl peroxide, an antibacterial agent. None of these treatments work overnight; antibiotics and benzoyl peroxide can take four to six weeks before improvement is visible. Retin-A may need to be used for as long as six months before significant changes are visible. Remember, the acne you see today took several months to form, so don't expect instant results.

For very serious cases of acne, your physician may refer you to a dermatologist, who may prescribe the use of the drug Accutane if your acne is very severe or cystic. Accutane requires close medical supervision because it can have serious side effects such as elevated cholesterol levels and birth defects.

But although it can be controlled, there really is no cure for acne. Most dermatologists say that acne eventually burns itself out if you bring your stressors under control—which may be the best advice of all!

Sores On or In the Mouth

Cold Sores.   Cold sores are those nasty, tingling, painful blisters that occur around the mouth—often in clusters—especially when we are under a great deal of stress. They are caused by the herpes simplex 1 virus. Most people have been infected by the herpes simplex virus as children, and, once we've been infected, the virus never goes away. It lays dormant for awhile, but the blisters seem to crop up again just when we need it least—like the day before we're scheduled to give a presentation to a very important potential customer or to the board of directors. The problem can also flare up when we're exposed to hot sunshine or cold winds; when we have a cold or are generally run-down due to stress overload; or, for women, around the time of their period.

If you suffer from frequent cold sores, you know the symptoms well. First there is a tingling in the area of the mouth where the blister will appear. Next comes a tiny blister, which either grows larger or is joined in a cluster by other blisters. Within a day or two, the blisters itch like crazy, are very sore, and look red and irritated. Within another day or so, they burst and a crust forms over them, which can be very painful if cracked open. The cold sores usually disappear within a week, but if they last longer, they can leave scars behind.

At the first tingle, start applying a medicated lip ointment, such as Blistex, using a cotton swab to apply it. Continue regular application until the blister(s) crust over. Then, a dense moisturizer such as Vaseline, may help keep the crust pliable and prevent it from breaking open. If it the crust does break open and bleed, try applying the lip ointment first under the Vaseline. Always blot cold sores with a tissue, don't rub with fingers, to prevent spreading the active virus to other parts of your body.

If your cold sores are particularly troublesome, large, or aren't healing properly, see your physician. You want to avoid infection and possible scarring. Your physician may prescribe idoxuridine paint (which "burns off" the top layer of the cold sore and starts the healing process) or the antiviral drug acyclovir to soothe the area. No effective preventive treatment has been found for cold sores, but some people find lip salves like Chapstick or Blistex, applied prior to exposure to sun and wind, can help.

Canker Sores. A canker sore is a small, painful ulcer or sore that develops on the inside of the cheek or lip or underneath the tongue. It usually lasts one to two weeks and then heals by itself. These sores are typically caused by stress overload, overvigorous brushing of the teeth, or allergies. Approximately 20 percent of people suffer from canker sores at any given time; the problem is most common between the ages of 10 and 40. Women get them more often than men, and are more likely to develop them just before their menstrual period.

Canker sores usually heal by themselves and are not a cause for worry, even though they are a painful nuisance and make eating difficult. If the canker sore is in a particularly awkward place, use of over the counter painkillers or waterproof brush-on ointments can help.

If it is large, abnormally painful, or located so that eating or brushing your teeth becomes next to impossible, see your physician. A corticosteroid ointment or an antibiotic mouthwash may be prescribed to speed healing. In severe cases, a special waxy waterproof covering with an anesthetic (which usually lasts a couple of days—long enough to jump-start the healing process) can be placed directly on the canker sore to seal it off, numb the pain, and prevent food and beverages from further irritating it.

Upper Gastrointestinal Tract Problems

Nervous Indigestion

Nervous indigestion covers a variety of symptoms, including heartburn, abdominal pain, nausea, and excessive gas. It is a *very* common side effect of stress. Most people experience it at some point and some people experience it frequently, the way others get tension headaches. It can be exacerbated by eating too much, too quickly, or by eating very rich, acidic, spicy, or fatty foods. Excessive intake of caffeine can also make it worse.

Nervous indigestion is rarely serious, although it can be extremely aggravating. Some people find that over-the-counter antacids ease their discomfort, and that the liquid form works more effectively than tablets. But avoiding foods and situations that seem to trigger your symptoms and finding time to eat three or four meals a day at regular times, *without rushing*, work even better than antacids.

If you have persistent nervous indigestion, if it recurs frequently, if the pain lasts longer than six hours or is accompanied by vomiting, vomiting blood, passing very dark stools, or feeling weak or faint, you may have developed a more serious upper gastrointestinal problem (gastritis, gastroesophageal reflux, or peptic ulcer) and a visit with your physician is in order.

Gastritis

Gastritis, an inflammation of the mucous membrane that lines the stomach, is usually not *caused* by stress, but stress makes it worse. Pain in the upper abdomen, which can be moderate to severe; nausea; loss of appetite; and vomiting are typical symptoms. Gastritis may occur as a sudden attack, or it can be chronic, developing over a long period.

Gastritis is usually a benign condition, but you should see your physician if the attack occurs suddenly, if you are vomiting blood, or if your stools are abnormally dark. The greatest concern is internal bleeding of the stomach, and problems resulting from the blood loss, such as anemia. Acute gastritis may cause erosions in the stomach lining, which bleed easily. In its chronic form, blood may ooze continually. A short course of ulcer-treating medications may be prescribed, which should provide rapid relief within days. Recurrences of gastritis are common, especially when aggravated by stress and lifestyle.

Heartburn and Gastroesophageal Reflux

At some time during their lives, most people experience heartburn, which is a burning sensation behind the breastbone. The burning sensation may extend all the way up into the throat. This is a *very* common side effect of stress, and the discomfort can usually be handled with the short-term use of an over-the-counter antacid. If heartburn occurs on a regular basis, it is a symptom of gastroesophageal reflux (GER).

To understand GER, you have to understand how the upper gastrointestinal system works. When you swallow your food, it passes through your throat into a tube, the esophagus, which carries it to the stomach. At the base of the esophagus, where it joins the stomach, is a ringlike muscle called the lower esophageal sphincter. This muscle opens to permit food to enter the stomach, and then closes to prevent stomach contents from backing up into the esophagus and throat. When you are under great stress this muscle may not work properly—it may be weakened or improperly regulated. Cigarettes, caffeine, alcohol, and stomach acid all relax the sphincter and may directly "burn" the esophagus. Typical sufferers work 12-hour days; eat large business dinners, complete with two drinks and three cups of coffee; go straight to bed; and awaken two or three hours later feeling as though their chests have been split open.

The walls of the esophagus do not have any protection from stomach acids, and the reflux causes pain, which is experienced as heartburn. Over time, repeated exposure to stomach acids can cause painful erosions or ulcers to develop on the esophagus. Particularly bad episodes of reflux can cause great pain, and sufferers may think they are having a heart attack.

Symptoms of Gastroesophageal Reflux. GER has many symptoms, including: the *effortless* return of stomach contents up into the throat, the sensation of slow or blocked passage of food from the mouth to the stomach, heartburn, the production of more saliva than is normal, the sensation of having a lump in the throat (which usually goes away when swallowing), hoarseness, belching or burping excessively, nausea, feeling full soon after beginning a meal, and bloating or abdominal distention.

Most GER sufferers experience a combination of several of these symptoms; one alone is usually not enough to indicate GER clearly. The combinations are idiosyncratic, that is, they differ for each individual.

Treatment for Gastroesophageal Reflux. The symptoms of GER can be controlled in many ways, including the following:

✔ *Experiment with your diet to determine which food(s) trigger GER episodes and avoid them.* You may see a pattern develop—for example, foods with garlic in them may set your GER off, or spicy or peppery foods may trigger GER. Once you know what foods are particularly bothersome for you, eliminate them from your diet—even if they are your favorites!

One school of thought is that a high-protein, low-fat diet may be particularly beneficial in helping control GER. High-protein foods appear to increase the pressure of the lower esophageal sphincter, helping prevent stomach contents from refluxing into the esophagus.

✔ *Avoid fatty or fried foods.* A diet high in fats (the typical American diet) aggravates GER. Red meat, pork, salmon, some shellfish, and ham are all high in fat. You do better with turkey, chicken, and fish. Forego preparations that add fat, such as frying, and skip rich sauces and added margarine or butter. Peanut butter, other nut butters, chocolate, rich ice creams, most desserts, and all cooking oils are high in fats, which can trigger a GER episode. This modified diet may take some getting used to, but it is far healthier overall than our typical diets. You may also lose weight in the process!

✔ *Eat several small meals throughout the day, rather than three large ones.* Eat them on a regular schedule. Remember to eat *slowly* and to chew well.

✔ *Don't eat anything for at least 3 hours before going to bed.* Three hours is enough time for your meal to have moved from your stomach down into your small intestines, so there is less chance that you will have anything in your stomach to reflux into the esophagus.

✔ *Steer clear of coffee (regular or decaffeinated), tea, colas, chocolate, and alcohol.* The caffeine in coffee, tea, and colas can aggravate GER, as can the theobromine in chocolate. Alcohol also makes GER worse. The acids present in coffee and tea can aggravate an already inflamed esophagus.

✔ *Avoid foods that can irritate an already sore esophagus.* This includes acidic foods, such as tomatoes and tomato juice, citrus fruits and their juices, apples and apple juice, and whole milk and cream, which can stimulate acid production in the stomach. You may find that you can tolerate fruit nectars, such as peach, pear, apricot, guava, and mango, much more easily than orange or grapefruit juices. Also avoid carbonated beverages because the acid which makes the bubbles can be very irritating to GER.

✔ *Quit smoking. And if you don't smoke, don't start.*

✔ *Take liquid over-the-counter antacids one hour before meals and at bedtime.* The goal here is to neutralize any acid present in the stomach contents to prevent its reflux into the esophagus. Taking antacids *before* meals seems more effective than taking them *after* meals.

✔ *Elevate the head of your bed 4 to 6 inches.* Lying flat increases the chance that stomach acids can reflux into the esophagus. By raising the head of your bed 4 to 6 inches, you can use gravity to keep the stomach contents where they should be. You can put the head of your bed up on wood blocks, or use a Bedge (a long wedge-shaped foam support for the entire upper body, which is 9 inches high at the top from BEDGE, Inc., 400 S. Farrell Dr., Suite 8-102, Palm Springs, CA 92262), or try a Bed Rest/Wedge (available from the Comfortably Yours catalog, 2575 E. 43rd St., P.O. Box 102216, Chattanooga, TN 37422-7216).

✔ *Avoid clothes that are tight around the waist, bending at the waist, and other pressure on the abdomen.* The resulting pressure can force stomach acids back up.

✔ *If you are overweight, lose the excess weight.* Additional weight can put pressure on the abdomen, forcing stomach acids into the esophagus.

When to See Your Physician about Gastroesophageal Reflux. If the self-care treatments haven't worked, or you find that you are having GER episodes more frequently, visit your physician.

Perhaps the most important tools at your physician's disposal for diagnosing GER are a thorough history of your symptoms, including what you have done to relieve your discomfort, and your family's health history. When you visit your physician, you might want to take with you a list of your symptoms, and the self-care treatments you have tried.

If your symptoms are severe, your doctor may order an upper gastrointestinal barium X-ray series to rule out the possibility of a peptic ulcer. Only the most severe or refractory cases require the care of a gastroenterologist (a physician who specializes in problems of the gastrointestinal system).

Medications are usually required to help reduce GER and keep it under control and to heal erosions of the esophagus. In very severe cases of GER, or cases that don't respond well to drug treatment, surgery may be performed. But surgery is always a last resort, and is recommended only after other treatments have proven unsuccessful over an extended period.

Some people develop chronic GER (particularly those with a family history of GER) after a first onset during a highly stressful period. Chronic GER usually requires some kind of maintenance drug therapy, and the same drugs used for treatment are usually used for long-term therapy. In this particular case, the medications don't cure the problem, they only keep it under control; eventually, addressing the lifestyle causes of GER become essential!

Peptic Ulcers

Peptic ulcers are sores or ulcers of the lining of either the stomach or the first part of the small intestine just below the stomach called the duodenum. One in ten Americans will suffer a peptic ulcer at some time, either because the stomach secretes too much acid or pepsin (a digestive juice), or because the lining of the stomach or duodenum is weak and cannot tolerate normal amounts of pepsin and acid. Stress does not *cause* peptic ulcers, but it can make an existing ulcer worse.

If you have a peptic ulcer, it is important to let your physician know when you are experiencing increased levels of stress in your life. It may be necessary to alter your medication or treatment plan to accommodate the effects of stress on your body. Practice the stress coping techniques outlined in Chap. 11 to help bring your stress level under control.

What Doesn't Work for Upper Gastrointestinal Problems

Certain things definitely don't alleviate upper gastrointestinal problems. Some years ago, common wisdom held that milk or cream was good for heartburn or an ulcer, because it coated the stomach. It was not uncommon for ulcer patients to be given diets that specified drinking lots of milk. But research has since determined that dairy products (especially milk and cream) actually cause the stomach to produce more acid, increasing the risk of irritation.

Antacid tablets made predominantly of calcium carbonate, such as Tums or Rolaids, are not terribly effective in reducing heartburn or stomach pain. Sufferers report that liquid antacids made from aluminum or magnesium hydroxide are more effective.

Some people think that over-the-counter painkillers can reduce heartburn or stomach pain because after all, they work on other kinds of pain. But such products are not effective in reducing upper gastrointestinal pain, and aspirin and ibuprofen can actually irritate the lining of the stomach, causing even more pain.

14
Special Topics in Stress-Related Illness

Panic Attacks

Panic attacks affect between 10 and 15 million people in the United States. They usually occur after prolonged stress. What is a panic attack? Imagine revving up your car while it is in park—it's ready to speed off, but there is no need for it to do so. The engine is racing, but it can't move. Panic attack suffers feel the same way. Some people feel that they are losing their minds and even disassociate a bit.

Pretty strange stuff and, after awhile, sufferers begin to avoid situations that they think could trigger an attack. When that happens, a full blown phobia develops. Experts disagree on whether the cause is primarily psychological or biological—but all agree that brain chemistry is affected.

Neurotransmitters sense danger and the general adaptation syndrome kicks into full gear, helping your body prepare to fight or flee. Your heart rate goes up, and blood is directed away from the skin, hands, and feet to help the large muscles in the arms and legs get ready for action—leaving hands and fingers tingling or cold and clammy.

Breathing increases, to supply more oxygen to the large muscles, which can cause hyperventilation and a pounding heart, shortness of breath, a choking or smothering feeling, and even lightheadedness and dizziness. Those symptoms represent a normal physiological reaction to perceived danger: Your body is trying to protect you, even though the danger isn't readily apparent. In fact, panic attacks often occur when you are most relaxed and your guard against stress is down.

Researchers have shown that certain kinds of stress appear to trigger panic attacks. Those stressors usually involve separation from others (panic attacks often occur while driving alone; you are in an enclosed space away from loved ones), and moving to a new area. Again, suffers are usually removed from important people in their life. There may be a genetic predisposition to release GAS hormones and steroids in the presence of those special stressors, but the link is not clear. For reasons that are not yet understood, panic attacks are more common in patients with mitral valve prolapse syndrome.

When to See Your Physician about Panic Attacks

Having a single panic attack does not mean you have panic disorder. Experts don't consider such attacks a disorder until you have at least four over a one-month period. Because panic attacks are so scary, even one or two will send most people to their physician. This is perfectly OK; when the episodes bother you, see your physician.

If no underlying medical problems are uncovered, your physician may prescribe medications that block the symptoms caused by an overstimulated nervous system, including anxiolytic agents of the benzodiazepine family, monoamine oxidase inhibitors, or tricylic antidepressants. All of these drugs have significant side effects, and their use has to be closely monitored by your physician. The drug treatment cycle usually lasts for about six months.

Your physician may recommend either individual or group counseling to help uncover the underlying problem situation, or may refer you to a therapist, psychologist, or a special clinic that specializes in panic episodes. Many people benefit from desensitization drills, where they repeatedly, and in a gradual and controlled manner, confront the object or situation that provokes the fear response. Researchers have also found that practicing relaxation techniques such as breathing exercises, visualization, and progressive relaxation (covered in Chap. 11) helps prevent panic attacks from reccurring once under control. The vast majority of panic attack sufferers are able to control the episodes with medication and therapy—often within a few months—and go on to lead normal lives.

What Doesn't Work for Panic Attacks

Continually avoiding the situations that you think might have triggered the panic attacks does not work. Because many people feel that the panic attacks happen out of the blue, they begin to restrict their activities, and eventually are afraid to go anywhere. They may refuse to drive or to travel. But most of the time, the situations sufferers try to avoid are not the cause, and they restrict their lives needlessly. Fear feeds on fear. The more fearful you become, the harder it is to resolve the problems triggering the panic episodes. So do yourself a favor, work with your physician. It won't be easy and there are no quick cures, but panic attacks can be controlled and you can resume a normal life.

Hyperventilation

Most of the time we are unaware of our breathing patterns. Our brains manage that task for us. But when under stress, many people become aware of their breathing process and notice that their breathing patterns change. For example, you may notice that your breathing is shallower (you don't completely fill your lungs) and/or faster. Some people notice that they may sigh more frequently than normal, take frequent deep breaths, or even hold their breath a bit between inhalations. These are common side effects of stress, and usually are no cause for concern.

But some people, especially those suffering from great stress, asthma, or other lung or heart problems, start to hyperventilate due to stress. *Hyperventilation* is abnormally deep or rapid breathing, and can be accompanied by feelings of anxiety. Normally, the chemicals in our blood are carefully balanced, but hyperventilation can throw off the balance and cause an abnormal loss of carbon dioxide in the blood, increasing blood alkalinity. This causes numbness or tingling in the hands or feet, faintness, painful spasms of hand or foot muscles, and the sense of being unable to take a full breath. This can be frightening and, if added to feelings of anxiety already present, can cause the sufferer to experience a feeling of impending doom.

Some people develop chronic hyperventilation problems when under stress in the way that other people consistently get headaches, stomach-aches, or diarrhea. The reason for this is not completely understood, but these people may have an underlying predisposition to respiratory problems.

Treatments for Hyperventilation

Although frightening, hyperventilation is usually not life-threatening. You can do several things to cope with hyperventilation, including:

✔ *Breathe into a paper bag.* By breathing in the same air you exhaled, which contains carbon dioxide, you can gradually increase the amount of carbon dioxide in your blood and keep it from becoming too alkaline, which helps prevent tingling in hands and feet and feelings of faintness and anxiety.

✔ *Practice the breathing exercises outlined in Chap. 11.* These exercises make you more aware of your breathing patterns and slow down breathing. They can also help you reduce stress and prevent hyperventilation.

✔ *Practice the progressive muscle relaxation exercises outlined in Chap. 11.* Many people who experience breathing problems carry their stress in the muscles surrounding the chest, diaphragm, or upper stomach areas. They gradually tense those without realizing it, making it more difficult for the lungs to work properly. Breathing can become shallower. Knowing when these muscles begin to tense up, rather than waiting until they go into spasm, can make a difference in heading off a hyperventilation episode.

✔ *Get adequate aerobic exercise.* Aerobic exercise can help increase lung capacity and lower the resting breathing rate. Exercise also reduces stress and relaxes chest wall muscles, which can help prevent hyperventilation. Look through the list of exercise activities in Chap. 10, and choose one that appeals to you.

✔ *If you smoke, quit. If you don't smoke, don't start.* Smoking irritates the lungs and reduces lung capacity, both of which can increase the possibility of hyperventilation.

✔ *Track your hyperventilation episodes and examine your lifestyle.* If you frequently experience hyperventilation, start logging the episodes, noting what was going on in your life just before the episode, what kinds of stress you were experiencing, what emotions you felt, what symptoms you developed, how long the episode lasted, and how you resolved it. Eventually you will begin to see a pattern developing—usually similar situations trigger attacks. Once you know what your triggers are, you can modify your lifestyle to eliminate them or practice coping techniques to help you deal with those stressors. Specifically, biofeedback, imagery, and behavioral rehearsal can all be helpful, as can any other techniques that help you lower your overall stress levels.

When to See Your Physician about Hyperventilation

If you frequently experience hyperventilation episodes or if they begin to be more severe, a visit to your physician is in order. Sometimes hyperventilation signifies more serious lung or cardiac problems, and your physician will want to eliminate these as possible causes.

If you suffer from allergies or have had allergies for a long time you may have developed asthma. Asthma is a serious, chronic condition that requires ongoing medical management. Your physician may want to make sure this is not causing your hyperventilation episodes.

What Doesn't Work for Hyperventilation

Many people think that, because anxiety or stress can cause hyperventilation, tranquilizers can cure it. Although in very severe cases tranquilizers may be used briefly to reduce extreme anxiety, overall, tranquilizers are not effective against hyperventilation.

Mitral Valve Prolapse Syndrome

Mitral valve prolapse syndrome (MVP) is caused by a slight deformity of the mitral valve, which is located on the left side of the heart. This deformity lets one part of the valve billow somewhat back into the upper chamber of the heart during the contraction of the heart to pump blood. It is probably the most common cardiac variation seen by physicians, and affects approximately 6 percent of the population.

Although MVP has been found in both men and women, it is most common in young to middle-aged women, and causes a characteristic heart murmur which can be heard through a stethoscope. Most of the time it causes no problems, but a common symptom is disturbance of heart rhythms, which feels like palpitations or skipped beats. While the exact cause of MVP is not known, evidence suggests that it may be inherited.

MVP is usually not life-threatening, but it can cause additional frightening symptoms. Approximately 14 percent of MVP patients have moderate symptoms, and only about 1 percent have severe symptoms. Sufferers of the severe type of MVP may experience more bothersome symptoms, including profound fatigue, chest pain, anxiety, depression, panic attacks (which can occur in the middle of the night, awakening the sufferer), shortness of breath, inability to think clearly, and dizzy spells. It is believed that this deformity of the heart valve is often associated with a slight variation in the function or balance of the autonomic nervous system—which develops in an unborn baby at the same time as the heart valve. This slight imbalance, called dysautonomia, causes many of the more severe symptoms listed.

Recent research indicates that nutritional changes and severe emotional stress (such as death of a loved one, divorce, or a new job) or severe physical stress (such as an accident, surgery, or severe illness) can precipitate dysautonomia-related symptoms in MVP patients who previously had no severe symptoms.

Treatments for Mitral Valve Prolapse Syndrome

If you suffer from MVP, there are a number of things you can do to help reduce the amount and severity of your symptoms:

- ✔ *Get regular, mild aerobic exercise.* Plan on three times a week, for at least 30 minutes per session. You will strengthen your cardiovascular system and gradually provide yourself with more energy so you don't feel so fatigued. The endorphins created during physical exercise can help relieve depression and anxiety. Exercise also helps counteract the hormones created by stress and fosters relaxation. Any kind of exercise is fine, even walking.

- ✔ *Practice coping techniques outlined in Chap. 11 to reduce your levels of stress.* Biofeedback, progressive relaxation, meditation, behavioral rehearsal, and imagery have proven particularly beneficial for MVP sufferers. Any coping technique you enjoy can be used to help reduce your overall stress levels.

- ✔ *Avoid smoking and excessive use of alcohol.* These "bad guys" can increase MVP symptoms by stimulating the nervous system.

- ✔ *If you are experiencing dysautonomia-related symptoms, eliminate caffeine from your diet.* Caffeine is a stimulant, and your body is already hypersensitive to stimulation. Avoid the caffeine-containing foods, beverages, and medicines listed in Chap. 11.

- ✔ *If you are experiencing dysautonomia-related symptoms, eliminate sugar from your diet.* Eating sugary foods, pure sugar, honey, or fructose causes rapid swings in blood sugar levels, which play havoc on the autonomic nervous system. Although they give you a burst of energy that may be tempting when you are tired, when the sugar level in your blood drops, you will feel more fatigued than ever. Focus on complex carbohydrates and the complex sugars found in fruits and vegetables. These are broken down in your body over a longer period of time, giving you a more stable and uniform outpouring of fuel.

✔ *Drink 8 to 10 glasses of fluids per day.* Not only is this important for general health, but some MVP sufferers experience symptoms because of a decrease in circulating blood volume and low blood pressure, which causes them to tire easily. Getting enough fluids helps counteract this tendency. Try water, decaffeinated beverages, sugar-free soda, and fruit juices.

When to See Your Physician about Mitral Valve Prolapse Syndrome

If the self-care treatments previously outlined don't adequately reduce your symptoms, if you suddenly develop symptoms, or if symptoms get more severe, it's time to visit your physician. Severe MVP symptoms, such as panic attacks, depression, anxiety, and mental confusion often require long-term medication.

Much research has been done in the area of medical management for MVP, and your physician has a number of medications available that can help dramatically reduce these bothersome symptoms. The exact combination of medications needs to be customized for each patient, so expect a certain amount of experimentation until you and your physician arrive at a combination that works for you. Don't give up hope, help is available!

What Doesn't Work for Mitral Valve Prolapse Syndrome

There are no easy answers or shortcuts for controlling MVP symptoms. Medication alone won't eliminate symptoms; lifestyle changes are mandatory. No drugs work overnight, and lifestyle and dietary changes require time to take effect. Such changes are not easy to accomplish and we are often tempted to give up too early when we don't see immediate results. Patience is required, and faith that you will eventually achieve the results you seek.

Doctor shopping doesn't work either. True, many MVP sufferers have been to many physicians before receiving the diagnosis of MVP, and they may have lost faith in the physicians' ability to provide them any relief. But with the new medical treatment programs formulated through research, if you have a good working relationship with your physician and are willing to make the necessary lifestyle changes, you will eventually see a reduction in your symptoms.

You need to communicate effectively with your physician, describing precisely how different treatment regimens affect you, particularly if you experience unpleasant side effects from a medication. Your physician can tell you if the side effects will gradually go away, or whether the medication needs to be changed.

Adjusting the dosage of your medications in response to changes in your day-to-day symptoms doesn't work. In fact, it can be dangerous. Some people take more medications on days when they feel badly and less on days they feel better. *Always take the medications exactly as directed.* To be effective, most medications should be present in your body at stable levels; taking more than the recommended dose could cause serious side effects.

Finally, never mix medications prescribed by more than one physician. Some MVP patients may have several specialists working on their case, and each may prescribe certain medications. Your primary care physician, who coordinates for your care, needs to know of what those medications are, to make sure that none of them conflict or counteract each other. So keep your doctor informed!

Substance Abuse

Smoking

Smoking is not good for human bodies, *period*. There is no way around it—even a little bit can have long-range effects on your health. Many people start smoking (or start smoking more) when they are experiencing stress, but this is one crutch that's really self-destructive. You probably know about most of the negative effects of smoking, but perhaps you don't know that cigarette smoke stimulates the body's production of stress hormones. Smoking may *feel* relaxing, but it may actually make the general adaptation syndrome (GAS) worse!

If you smoke now, think seriously about quitting. Nicotine is addictive and you will experience stress when you try to quit. But there is never a "good time" to quit—only a "right time"—and that time is as soon as possible. Many programs have been proven to help people quit, for example, SmokEnders. You physician can refer you to a group in your area, and can prescribe new medications such as Nicorette, which can help reduce your craving for nicotine while you work on modifying your behaviors in a smoke-reduction support group.

Alcohol Use and Abuse

Many people gravitate toward alcohol during times of stress, because it seems to help them relax. If your physician has not restricted your consumption of alcohol, we strongly encourage moderation in this area—one serving per day for women and no more than two servings per day for men. One serving is equivalent to 12 ounces of beer (one can); 4 ounces of wine (a small wine glass); or 1 to 1.5 ounces of hard liquor (one shot). We recommend that women consume less alcohol than men because recent research has shown that women metabolize alcohol differently than do men, and have a lower tolerance to its effects as a result. Women are also usually smaller than men.

Although alcohol can have adverse effects, drinking doesn't seem to do harm if done in moderation, and may have a small cardiovascular benefit. If you are concerned about drinking too much, ask yourself:

- Is there a risk to your health or lifestyle from the drinking pattern you've established?

- Is there a pattern to your overconsumption of alcohol?

- Can you use a less harmful substitute for alcohol?

- What needs does alcohol fill for you? Can you find other ways to meet these needs?

There are several schools of thought on the right and wrong ways to go about reducing your alcohol intake. If you have a serious drinking problem, the most successful way to quit is to get professional help, either from a peer-group program such as Alcoholics Anonymous or from professional mental health practitioners. If you have been drinking heavily for a long time, your body needs special care while you quit drinking, and you'll find the support and encouragement you receive in an organized program to be helpful. Discuss this with your physician, who can offer a referral to an appropriate treatment program.

If you're a social drinker and are concerned about drinking more and enjoying it less, try the following suggestions.

✔ *Try alternatives to hard liquor.* "Coolers" or "spritzers" (soda plus wine, liqueurs, or liquor) can give you a tall drink that lasts longer when you sip it. People find that a single cooler can adequately take the place of two or three normal drinks.

✔ *Try the new nonalcoholic drinks.* Nonalcoholic mixed drinks are no longer limited to the wretched Shirley Temple. Many establishments produce an array of exotic drinks without a drop of alcohol. You might also want to try some of the new nonalcoholic beers. Some taste just like the real thing.

✔ *Become terribly chic and order bottled mineral water.* Most restaurants offer a selection of bottled mineral waters, including the ubiquitous Perrier, and it is currently "in" to order mineral water with a slice of lemon or lime.

✔ *Rely on the tried and true nonalcoholic beverages.* What's wrong with asking for a lemon-lime soft drink, cola, ginger ale, or fruit juice? It is becoming more acceptable to ask for something nonalcoholic, especially when you have to drive home.

Drug Use and Abuse

Tranquilizers.   Tranquilizers are the most overprescribed category of drugs in the world. Several years ago researchers estimated that 140 million new prescriptions (not refills) were written each year for tranquilizers. Women are far more likely to get prescriptions for tranquilizers than men.

Tranquilizers are usually ineffective in reducing stress because they do nothing to solve the problems that caused it in the first place. They just numb your brain and reduce the anxiety that might serve as an impetus to begin working on the problems and resolving the stresses.

Tolerance to tranquilizers increases rapidly: In a short time it takes more of the drug to get the same effect. Some tranquilizers are physically addictive, but all are psychologically addictive; and withdrawal is a long, unpleasant, difficult process.

This is not to say that tranquilizers are completely worthless. In certain situations, such as death of a loved one, coping with the immediate effects of a disaster or a disease, or in the treatment of stress-induced high blood pressure and other chronic diseases, tranquilizers do have a *limited* role to play. But only for a short period of time under a physician's careful supervision. Remember, tranquilizers are drugs that can be deadly if abused.

Sleeping Pills. Sleeping pills probably rank second as the most abused prescription drug in the United States. The problem with prescription sleeping medications is that they don't really help you sleep, they only provide oblivion for a short time. Tolerance of prescription sleeping medications increases rapidly. Some physicians contend that after two weeks of continuous use, sleeping pills in any amount are no longer effective in inducing sleep. Their only value is as a placebo. If chronic use of sleeping medication is required, one has to consider underlying depression as a strong possibility.

Sleep-inducing drugs are psychologically addictive as well, and withdrawal is lengthy and agonizing. Because they can interact with other medications, prescription sleeping medications can precipitate adverse reactions and cause death.

Again, this is not to say that sleep-inducing medications are never useful. They may be helpful in times of crisis or to break a stubborn cycle of insomnia. But they should be used only for a limited period under the strict supervision of a physician—with careful regulation of any additional medications or alcohol.

Amphetamines. Amphetamines, or uppers, are also widely abused. Many people have gotten prescriptions for amphetamines to help them lose weight or cope with fatigue. Unfortunately, they help with neither in the long run. These drugs can be physically, as well as psychologically, addictive and withdrawal is lengthy and painful. Dependence on uppers often fosters dependence on sleeping pills as well, in an effort to come down. This leads to a vicious cycle of uppers to wake up and sleeping pills to sleep. Withdrawal from this double-drug dependence is even more difficult and unpleasant. So avoid these drugs if they are offered to you for weight loss!

There is a place for amphetamines in psychiatric medicine, albeit a *very* small one. They can be useful in breaking the cycle of chronic fatigue or depression complicated by severe fatigue. But amphetamines should be used only for a short period of time under the strict guidance of a psychiatrist or physician.

Antidepressants.   Antidepressant medications are less abused in our society, only because they are somewhat harder to obtain. Antidepressants should not be used as an occasional "pick-me-up." They are a serious medication for serious conditions. Nor will they cure the blues.

Antidepressants can be useful for certain psychiatric conditions such as psychotic depressions (severe depressions lasting for months with deep apathy and fatigue), manic-depressive illnesses (in which people swing from tremendous emotional highs to devastating emotional lows in a cyclical pattern), and sleep disorders. But they don't take effect immediately: It may be several weeks before improvement is noticed. Those medications require careful regulation by a physician or psychiatrist for maximum effectiveness.

Mind-Altering Drugs.   These drugs were very popular in the 1960s and early 1970s, but their use appears to be on the decrease. This category includes marijuana, LSD, STP, Quaaludes, heroin, cocaine, morphine, and so on. The major problem with these drugs is that for the most part, they are extremely addictive physically, as well as psychologically. Tolerance of them increases very rapidly, and they interact with other drugs to cause potentially lethal reactions. Withdrawal is very painful and lengthy.

These drugs are also almost impossible to get legally without a prescription, which means that they usually must be purchased on the street. The quality of street drugs varies enormously, and a buyer can never be certain of the dosage or purity of the purchase. As a result, street drugs are frequently deadly.

People react differently to mind-altering drugs, and even individual reactions vary from use to use.

Morphine does plays a role in pain reduction. It has been found helpful for people suffering great pain, particularly pain caused by diseases such as cancer. Codeine is used to lessen pain from surgery or other medical conditions, but these drugs are never completely safe, even under the supervision of a physician. They are best used for short periods under carefully controlled conditions.

Marijuana is an object of controversy. Initially researchers thought it was relatively safe, but more recent research has begun to uncover potential long-term risks. It is also psychologically addictive, and its use can be a difficult habit to break. Purchased on the street, its strength and purity cannot be assured, and it is illegal in most places to grow your own. Marijuana doesn't reduce stress, since it acts in the same way as tranquilizers, numbing the brain, not solving the problems that caused the feelings of stress in the first place.

Marijuana has only two uses for which its effectiveness has been documented: (1) the treatment of various eye diseases related to increasing pressure of the fluid inside the eye, and (2) reducing the nausea that is a common side effect of chemotherapy treatments for cancer. In many states even medical use of marijuana is illegal.

Cocaine has become fashionable in several high-stress occupations. It was once considered to be relatively harmless. Sigmund Freud was one of many who promoted its use. Recent research has proven, however, that even one casual dose can cause a stroke, cardiac arrhythmia, heart attack, or death. A single dose can kill. It is also psychologically addictive and can react with other drugs to cause potentially lethal combinations. In addition, when sniffed through the nose ("snorted"), cocaine destroys membranes and tissues in the nose. Complicated reconstructive surgery may be necessary to rebuild damaged nasal passages.

In conclusion, it seems that drugs of any kind have the potential for doing far more harm than any good they might do in dealing with stress-related problems and disorders—particularly when their use is not prescribed and carefully monitored by a physician. They are not to be taken lightly. The drugs mentioned earlier do not relieve stress, so why use them? There is a whole smorgasbord of techniques and tricks that are safer and far more effective in helping us cope with stress.

When to See Your Physician about Substance Abuse

Your physician needs to know about any use of nonprescription or illicit drugs. Physicians are trained not to be judgmental, so you don't have to fear getting a sermon. Your physician's goals are: helping you reduce your dependency on alcohol or drugs, reducing the stress that is causing it, making sure that any prescribed medications will not cause you harm.

You can expect your physician to ask you about major changes you may be going through and stresses you are experiencing; ask you to describe what you have done to control your drinking or use of drugs; perform a physical examination to determine whether your substance abuse has caused medical complications; go over both prescribed and over-the-counter medications you are taking to determine whether any of these may be addictive or harmful in conjunction with your use of alcohol or drugs; discuss your diet and exercise habits; and perhaps order special tests.

Your doctor may recommend lifestyle changes, dietary adjustments, changes in medications, counseling, or new medications, and/or refer you to a special substance abuse program, such as Alcoholics Anonymous. If your addiction is severe, in-patient treatment in a hospital-based substance abuse treatment program may be recommended. These programs usually offer counseling in conjunction with supervised reductions in dosages of the drugs you take. Sometimes, less harmful drugs may be given, as well as treatment for withdrawal symptoms. No single treatment works equally well for all people, so expect some experimentation until the best treatment is found.

Stress and Sex

How Stress Impacts Desire and Performance

Prevailing permissive and open attitudes about sex and sexuality have certainly changed our thinking about sex, and have also added anxiety and stress.

With the increased knowledge of sex and sexual activities came an assumption (or in some cases, an expectation) that now everyone should be a superb sexual performer. Now we worry not only about how our partner is responding, but also about whether or not we are performing or responding correctly. Partners worry about the length, intensity, type, and timing of orgasms, and many people are beginning to wonder if something is wrong if they don't achieve them. Add to this scenario increasing pressures from work, problems managing home and family tasks while working, and guilt for just about everything else. The result is an explosive situation.

Stress reduces our ability to become aroused sexually. Because we have only a limited amount of energy available at any one time, having much of that energy drained away with worry or anxiety reduces the amount left for other things, including sex. Since time began (partly for survival reasons), one of the first areas to suffer from "energy cutbacks" has been sexual responsiveness. If you can't become aroused, you can't respond.

Our society also places great value on being in control of our feelings. This is a paradox. We're expected to be repressed in all areas of our emotional lives except in sexual relationships. Once we learn how to control our feelings, we become afraid to let loose, even during sex. Another problem is that bottled-up emotions usually have to come out somewhere, and when they do, they very often affect sexual arousal, response, and performance.

This whole idea of sexual performance can be disastrous. Almost everyone experiences some kind of stress-related sexual problem at some point in a lifetime. This normal stress reaction can be compounded if you begin to worry about your problem of arousal or responsiveness. A vicious cycle can begin.

How can these stress-related sexual problems be solved? Actually, most solve themselves once you eliminate the idea of performance. The idea of "pleasuring" is much more conducive to arousal and response. Pleasuring involves understanding that sex does not ultimately need to result in intercourse and mutual orgasm in order to be enjoyable and fun. If you believe that sex must always result in intercourse and orgasm, you're missing out on a lot. Sex also includes hugging, kissing, stroking, caressing, massaging, talking, and so on. These activities can be enjoyable ends in themselves.

More truthful, realistic information can also be helpful. Unfortunately, most of the information available in the media is based on fantasy, with little relation to what goes on in most people's lives. It is a wonderful fantasy that people are always thinking about sex, always ready, always perform superbly. But that's only fantasy. People also worry about bills, responsibilities, and obligations; agonize over presentations, speeches, reports, business deals, and budgets; worry about being laid off or getting fired—and sometimes cannot respond sexually because of these concerns. That is normal, that is real life

It is also true that men and women respond differently and require different things in order to become aroused, mainly as a result of socialization. It could be helpful for partners to learn more about these differences. The "Good Reads" section at the end of the book lists some books you might want to explore.

It is also helpful for partners to discuss together how important sex is for them and how they want to arrange their lives to spend time together. Most people become aroused more easily and are more responsive sexually when their relationship with their sexual partner involves more than just sex—when they share similar interests, spend time together apart from sexual activity, and are understanding of each other's needs and preferences.

Common Sexual Problems

Although stress most typically impacts *desire* for sex, it sometimes can make other sexual difficulties worse. Most people experience the following difficulties at some point during their lifetime.

Painful Intercourse.   Both men and women can experience painful intercourse. The pain may be superficial, occurring around the external genitals, or it may be experienced deep within the pelvis. Usually there is an underlying medical condition that causes the symptoms, such as a sexually transmitted disease; a reaction to spermicides in barrier-type birth control methods; anatomical abnormalities; prostatitis in men; insufficient vaginal lubrication, especially after menopause; pelvic disorders for women; cystitis; or other infection. But stress, especially that caused by problems at home or unresolved conflicts in the relationship, can make the pain worse. Sometimes, stress is the only cause, and, in that case, special counseling may be needed to resolve the problems causing the stress.

Premature Ejaculation.   One of the most common sexual difficulties experienced by men is premature ejaculation, which happens when ejaculation occurs before or very soon after penetration. Most adult men occasionally experience premature ejaculation during their lifetimes, often because of overstimulation or stress caused by concerns about sexual performance.

Techniques such as sensate focusing (covered later in this section) and the "squeeze technique" for delaying ejaculation can help significantly. The squeeze technique is very simple—either partner squeezes the penis when the man is about to ejaculate, pressing just beneath the glans (head of the penis), using the thumb and two fingers. This helps lessen the ejaculation reflex, and can be repeated several times during a sexual encounter. It helps the man begin to learn to control the ejaculation reflex.

Erectile Dysfunction (Impotence).   Impotence, the inability to achieve or maintain an erection, is another very common sexual difficulty experienced by men, and most men will be affected by it at some time in their lives. Stress can cause temporary impotence, as can fatigue and depression. In a small percentage of cases, impotence can be caused by a physical disorder, such as diabetes mellitus or a hormonal imbalance; a neurological disorder, such as spinal cord damage; a circulation problem; or chronic alcohol abuse. Many drugs, such as antihypertensives, antidepressants, diuretics, and antipsychotics, can cause impotence as a side effect.

If you experience difficulty achieving or maintaining an erection more frequently than "once in a while" and if the episodes don't seem to occur when you are under a great deal of stress, check it out with your physician. Your doctor may order a variety of tests to eliminate the possibility of any physical disorder. Medications may be altered or stopped to aid in diagnosis as well. Once the cause is identified, the underlying problem can be treated, and normal sexual function can be restored.

Orgasmic Dysfunction.   The most common sexual problem experienced by women is the inability to achieve an orgasm, and 30 to 50 percent of women experience it at some time in their lives. Stress is a major cause, especially if the stress is caused by anxiety about sexual performance, problems at home, or unresolved conflicts in the couple's relationship. In some cases, the inability to reach orgasm can be a side effect of certain medications or pain during intercourse. Sometimes, however, it is as simple as not enough foreplay to get beyond the excitement phase—most women need an average of 13 minutes of stimulation, compared to only about 3 minutes for men.

If you have difficulty reaching orgasm more often than "once in awhile," or if the episodes occur even when you are not under stress, discuss it with your physician. Once the cause is identified, the underlying problem can be treated, and normal sexual function restored.

Anxiety about Catching Sexually Transmitted Diseases. Sexually transmitted diseases (STDs) have always been around. It used to be that we only had to worry about pubic lice, syphilis, and gonorrhea—which could be treated successfully with antibiotics. Then came chlamydial infections and trichomoniasis (also treatable by antibiotics); genital warts, which may predispose women to cervical cancer; and genital herpes, which turned out to be a problem people had to live with for the rest of their lives and could be only controlled, not eradicated, by medication. Most recently we discovered acquired immune deficiency syndrome (AIDS), which is usually fatal and for which at present there is no known cure.

Sex is now a high-risk activity, and any high-risk activity is scary. Scary situations cause stress, particularly when you know that you can catch something that could be fatal. This stress can impact both desire and performance.

How can you cope with this kind of stress? First, get to know your partner well and ask questions about herpes, previous partners, and any other concern you may have. If your partner refuses to answer the questions, you probably don't want to have a relationship with that kind of person. Second, have sex later in a relationship rather than earlier—not only because sex is usually better if you know and trust each other as friends, but because some sexually transmitted diseases take time to develop symptoms.

If you are in a committed, monogamous relationship, both of you can visit your physician and get tested for STDs. If you both come out negative, and have not slept with other partners within several months prior to the test—great! As long as you remain monogamous, you shouldn't have to worry about getting STDs.

If you are *not* in a monogamous relationship, your best offense is a good defense—in this case the use of condoms and spermicides in addition to your regular form of birth control. Condoms and spermicides help prevent the spread of the AIDS virus, as well as syphilis, venereal warts, and gonorrhea. If you have many partners, you may also want to talk with your physician about getting tested for a variety of STDs. In this case, it is far worse *not* to know if you have acquired an STD than to know definitely that you *have*. If you don't know you have an STD, not only could you could pass it on to someone you care about, but delaying treatment only compounds the problem.

Anxiety about "Biological Clock" and Fertility Issues. When couples delay pregnancy because of schooling or the demands of high-pressure careers, anxiety increases over loudly ticking "biological clocks." For a woman to wait until her thirties used to be considered late for having babies, but recent research has proven that healthy women can safely have babies even into their early forties. Maybe we should give ourselves a break and set the alarm back just a little bit!

Stress can also impact fertility, for both men and women. In women, severe stress can affect ovulation, making menstrual periods irregular, or even causing them to stop. Men under stress may find that their sperm counts go down or that their sperm are less active, both important factors for conception. Once stress is reduced for both partners, ovulation and sperm counts and motility return to normal, usually within a short period of time.

Even if everything is in working order, a couple has to be able to spend time together making love in order to conceive! And spending lots of hours on the job or having to travel much of the time hinders that! If having a baby is high on your list of priorities, you may need to take a hard look at your career demands, and adjust your respective schedules and agendas to accommodate that goal. Medical science has yet to find a way to facilitate conception for a couple who find themselves in different time zones.

If you have been trying to conceive, and haven't been successful after 9 to 12 months, visit your physician. (Notice that we said *months*, not weeks.) Ninety percent of women conceive within a year of unprotected intercourse. Although some couples are lucky enough to conceive the first time, most are not—especially if one or both partners are under a lot of stress, or if the woman has been using birth control pills for several years. Mother Nature works at her own pace, and often can't be rushed. Your physician may order special tests to rule out physical problems, and talk with you to determine whether intercourse is taking place at the right time for conception. You may be referred to a specialist for additional testing and treatment.

If physical problems are discovered, take heart. Great strides have been made in helping couples conceive, and most problems can be corrected. Today, over half the couples seeking help from specialists achieve a pregnancy—far more than ever before.

Treatments for Sexual Problems

Eliminating the notion of performance from sexual encounters greatly reduces the potential for stress overload. *Sensate focusing*, often used in sexual therapy, is one of the best ways to do this. Sensate focusing involves becoming aware of all the body's erogenous areas—in fact, the entire body is capable of being an erogenous zone. Try the following steps to build your awareness of how your body responds and becomes aroused. Remember, this does not necessarily have to lead to intercourse to be pleasurable and fulfilling.

1. Start by taking a long, warm bath or shower. (Together with your partner if you enjoy that; if not, that's okay.)

2. Turn down the lights, lock the doors, put on some soft music, open a bottle of wine if you enjoy that. Give yourself and your partner time to unwind, relax, and turn off the worries of the day. If you have children, it might be helpful to wait

until they're asleep. Or ask a friend or babysitter to care for them while you and your partner go to a hotel, motel, or a friend's cabin or cottage. The goal is to prevent interruptions, or the worry about potential interruptions. Even putting a latch on the inside of your bedroom door and unplugging the phone can help.

3. When you and your partner are relaxed and feeling good, climb into bed, first taking off robes, nightgowns, pajamas, and so on. Flip a coin or draw straws to see who gets a chance to be pleasured first.

4. Once the first pleasuree has been chosen, go over the ground rules. No direct stimulation of the breasts, nipples, or genitals at first, just explore other parts of the body. The pleasuree is to give the pleasurer feedback on what feels good, what would feel better, and what doesn't feel so good. Remember, you can't read each other's minds, so it is important to ask for what you want. The pleasuree is to return the pleasure by pleasuring the partner in turn.

5. Now comes the best part! The pleasurer begins caressing, stroking, touching, and exploring the pleasuree's body—everywhere. That includes the pleasuree's neck, shoulders, back, tummy, legs, thighs, arms, lips, ears, eyelids, face, scalp, toes, fingers, and so on. Some people like to use lotions or creams to make the caressing and massaging smoother. Others find such lotions (even flavored ones are available) messy and might want to try baby powder or dusting powder instead. Such powders can also act as lubricants and reduce friction. The pleasurer doesn't have to rely just on fingers and hands to caress and touch. Experiment with your tongue, lips, toes, legs, eyelashes, and so forth. Tiny kisses on the inner thigh or eyelash "tickles" on the face can feel fantastic!

6. The pleasuree should keep the pleasurer aware of what feels good and what doesn't feel good. If you want your pleasurer to touch you somewhere else or do something differently, just say so!

7. If the pleasuree wants to have breasts, nipples, or genitals stroked or caressed, that's fine, but only *after* other areas of the body have been explored. Try to refrain from actual intercourse, at least at first. As you become more aware of the various ways to pleasure each other, you may want to explore alternative ways to caress, touch, or massage each other's breasts, nipples, and genitals.

8. Believe it or not, the pleasuree will reach a point of being satisfied and content. Then it's the pleasuree's turn to please the pleasurer, making sure to follow the same guidelines previously listed. You will probably find that it is just as much fun to give pleasure as it is to receive it!

9. Some people may have difficulty accepting pleasure from their partner. In this case it is helpful for them to do the pleasuring first, allowing them to become more comfortable with receiving pleasure by first experiencing what it is like to give pleasure.

10. If you or your partner have difficulty "getting into" sensate focusing at first, don't worry. We're not taught much about how our bodies and emotions react to this sort of activity, and the new feelings might seem weird at first. That's normal, just go slowly and go only as far as you feel comfortable. As you become more comfortable with caressing and being caressed, you will discover that you have erogenous zones where you never even knew they existed.

Very few people need sex therapy. If couples give themselves some time away from performing and focus on pleasuring while they sort out other stressful parts of their lives, most sexual response and arousal problems take care of themselves. If this doesn't work, there may be a relationship problem the couple needs to confront and work out. In this case, assistance from a mental health professional is very helpful. Only people with very severe sexual problems need the assistance of a sex therapist, and that help is most useful after assistance from mental health professionals has been found to be insufficient.

Stress and Normal Midlife Changes

Midlife Crisis

Many people, when they hit their late thirties or early forties, go through a period of intense examination of their lives—looking at both work and personal components. Opportunities for career advancement often dwindle; salary increases and options to increase the scope of responsibility become less available (and the new staffers just out of college seem like such "kids"). People who work for big corporations think about chucking it all and striking out on their own; those who have their own businesses wonder whether it might be safer to be part of a large group or corporation. Married people start noticing how their partner has changed and wonder how the partner sees them; single people start worrying about forever missing out on the joys and contentment of a committed relationship; parents see their children growing up and needing them less; people who don't have children worry that it will soon be too late to have any. In addition to these worries, we wonder whether our incomes will be able to keep up with our increasing outgo as we try to provide adequate income while raising children; we have to adhere to diets more strictly, exercise longer, and work harder to stay fit (*everything* seems to be settling in several inches lower than before). Our parents are aging, and we're starting to worry about their care; and we start thinking about really adult things like retirement planning, 401k plans, investment portfolios, and real estate—in short, we're coming face to face with mortality and realizing that our time is not infinite.

This period of self examination is extremely stressful, because it causes us to question our basic goals and values—the core of our personalities. And this stress can cause mood swings, untypical behavior (such as buying trendy clothes our kids would wear, trying different hairstyles (both men and women do this), and experimenting with lifestyles different from what we have been accustomed to. Some people find this kind of self examination so stressful that they get involved with self-destructive behaviors (such as substance abuse, sexual promiscuity, and breaking up marriages and relationships) as a way to ameliorate the stress.

True, it is a painful process, but people have gone through it from the dawn of time—it's just that nobody really talked about it. For most people, this self-examination period lasts about a year. The vast majority of sufferers end up staying in the jobs and relationships they already have (and go back to looking like they always did), but make minor modifications in their lives to make them more enriching and rewarding. Even today, men often decide to focus flat out on grabbing the brass ring (or promotion) at work, and rededicate themselves to doing extra work to achieve that goal. Working women often decide that all the career demands aren't worth the sacrifice, and choose to cut back a bit at work so that they can devote more time to family and personal relationships.

Most people are able to get through this midlife crisis with the support of friends and family, and by practicing coping techniques as outlined in Chap.11. If the stress is severe, you may find yourself beginning to develop the symptoms of one or more of the medical problems discussed in Chap. 13. In that case, follow the self-treatment guidelines outlined for the problem and, by all means, visit your physician if those self-care techniques are not sufficient.

If you feel that you are getting stuck in your self-examination, working with a counselor or therapist can be very valuable, as can joining a support group. Your physician can refer you to a therapist, counselor, or support group, or you can call your local mental health center, a clergyperson, or even your company's employee assistance program for referrals. Get the help you need to get you back on the new or altered path you want to follow: You owe it to yourself, your spouse or significant other, and your family.

Menopause

Menopause, the cessation of menstruation, is also a normal midlife event, typically occurring when a woman is between the ages of 45 and 50, and taking place over a two- to five-year period of time. Changes linked with menopause often begin several years before menopause, and can occur for several years afterwards. Menstrual periods become irregular as the amount of estrogen produced by the ovaries decreases, causing ovulation to become irregular and then cease. Menstrual flow becomes lighter, vaginal dryness may develop, and hot flashes or sudden sweating may occur.

Many women can get the estrogen they need from other sources in their bodies, but those who do not may experience some menopausal discomfort. As a result of these hormonal changes, they may experience mood swings; nervousness; irritability; fatigue; insomnia; mild depression; pounding heartbeat; or aching joints, limbs, or back.

Many women are placed on estrogen replacement therapy for these complaints. Some women improve; some do not. If your symptoms do not improve, examine the role of stress in causing these symptoms, because such symptoms are classic signs of stress overload as well as of menopause. So if you are around your middle forties, get these symptoms checked out by your physician. They may not all be caused by stress, and it is important to know that for sure.

Pregnancy is still possible while you are going through these changes, and what you use for contraception may need to change. Becoming pregnant at this stage of your life can be a major stressor! Your physician can advise you on your contraception options.

The Effect of Stress on Chronic Diseases

Stress overload can negatively impact many chronic diseases, including diabetes mellitus, rheumatoid arthritis, hypertension, and asthma. This happens in several ways:

1. The actual stress hormones can alter the course of these chronic diseases and destabilize the delicate balance we strive for when we try to keep these conditions under control.

2. When we are under a great deal of stress, we often don't follow (or forget to follow) our medical regimens properly, causing further destabilization.

3. Third, stress victims typically don't eat balanced meals, exercise appropriately, or get enough sleep, which can negatively impact the destabilization process.

4. If people have had episodes when their illness was particularly bad, they may worry about when the next bad time will occur, causing additional stress.

This all adds up to a potentially dangerous situation, one in which chronic diseases can become worse or flare up with acute episodes that, in some cases, could be life-threatening. So let your physician know when you are experiencing significant stress; he or she may choose to alter your medical regimen to accommodate the negative effects of stress on your chronic disease. It may also be helpful to track when you *do* get flare-ups of your chronic disease, and see if you were under stress at the time. Sometimes just knowing when to expect a flare-up goes a long way in reducing the fear (and stress) of worrying about when it will occur.

Adhere strictly to your medical regimen, even though the tendency is not to do so. Leave yourself notes around the house to take your medicine or follow your special diet or exercise plan; get a weekly or daily pill dispenser to hold your medications; ask friends or family to remind you and provide support. Use any crutch you can think of to help you remember!

Chronic disease sufferers under stress can benefit greatly from the coping techniques in earlier chapters. Think about expanding the variety of coping techniques you use daily and the frequency with which you use them, or try new ones that appeal to you. Such coping techniques not only lower your stress levels, but help counteract the hormones produced by your body when you are under stress, which can help short-circuit the destabilization process.

Faux and Spurious Illnesses

Hypoglycemia

Hypoglycemia is a condition in which sufferers have abnormally low levels of glucose (or sugar) in the blood. In its true form, its symptoms include sweating, weakness, hunger, dizziness, trembling, headache, palpitations, confusion, and sometimes double vision—all caused because the cells in the body are not getting enough energy. Almost always this occurs two to four hours after eating and is called reactive hypoglycemia. All of us may experience this complex of symptoms on occasion, especially after a period of high sugar, caffeine, or alcohol intake. These "hypoglycemic" symptoms may occur even when our blood glucose levels are normal!

Many people incorrectly think that they are suffering from hypoglycemia if they are frequently fatigued. But medical research has not linked fatigue to hypoglycemia. Most cases of hypoglycemia occur in people who are insulin-treated diabetics. The myth that reactive hypoglycemia predicts the future likelihood of diabetes is just that, a myth. It is far more probable that the fatigue experienced by self-diagnosed hypoglycemia sufferers is caused by either stress or depression. But only your physician can tell for sure, so get it checked out.

Systemic Yeast Infections

Systemic yeast infection is a "disease" that is currently in vogue. Many popular books and articles claim that the consumption of yeast in foods such as breads, baked goods, or beer can cause fatigue, depression, insomnia, and other vague, low-grade "ills" that make you feel run-down. The thesis is that, if you eliminate yeast and yeast products from your diet, you can clear your body of yeast and reduce these unpleasant symptoms.

No medical evidence supports the existence of systemic yeast infections. However, as with hypoglycemia, symptoms experienced by self-diagnosed sufferers are caused by stress or depression. Eliminating yeast from your diet will not make stress or depression go away—only working with your physician and using coping techniques will do that.

Premenstrual Syndrome (PMS)

The most frequent emotional symptoms of Premenstrual Syndrome (PMS) are: irritability, tension, depression, insomnia, headaches, and fatigue. Some women have trouble controlling their tempers. Physical symptoms can include breast tenderness, fluid retention, headache, backache, and abdominal pain. As many as 30 percent of women experience some of these problems each month, but only about 5 percent have one or more severe symptoms. PMS can occur at any time during adulthood, and can get worse as we age. The popular media have focused mainly on the emotional symptoms, and would have you believe that women can suffer from PMS all month long.

But that is not the case. PMS is most likely influenced by hormonal changes that occur throughout the menstrual cycle, but it only kicks in during the last 7 to 10 days prior to menses. Medical research has found that high-carbohydrate or high-salt diets may intensify the mood swings. At other times, the symptoms attributed to PMS usually have stress or depression as the underlying cause.

If you think you suffer from PMS *all the time*, do yourself a favor, make an appointment with your physician, who can help you determine if PMS is the real problem or if the cause is stress or depression. Once identified appropriately, the real problem can be dealt with and you can get on with your life. If your physician does find that PMS is a problem for you, changes in your diet or even antidepressant medication can be useful. Regular exercise can help reduce stress. Progesterone, once touted as a cure, has proven ineffective in managing PMS, and may even make you feel worse.

What is Really Going On Here? The Patient's (or Physician's) Need for a Diagnosis

When it comes to these *faux* or spurious illnesses, which do not have a sound medical basis, we have to ask why people persist in believing that they suffer from them. In many cases, the reason is simple: Patients need a label for their problems to get them off the hook for not dealing effectively with them, or, because of the "invisible footprints" conundrum, they need a label that will legitimize their suffering.

Some physicians continue to diagnose these faux illnesses for several reasons. In some cases, they simply do not understand completely the impact stress and depression can have on symptomatology. In rare cases, physicians tire of having patients claim to have symptoms that are difficult to diagnose, or they discount the patient's (typically a female patient's) perception of the symptoms. Either way, it is easier to pronounce a diagnosis of hypoglycemia or PMS than to deal with the uncertainties. Luckily, this state of affairs is changing rapidly.

The bottom line is that stress as a major cause of symptoms is not always well-accepted in our society today: we like to have clear-cut causes for our problems. Because stress leaves "invisible footprints," its role as a cause of physical problems is not clear-cut. Through more research and education, this national perception may change, and stress in and of itself will have the legitimacy accorded other real illnesses.

15
Anger, Communication, Gentle Assertiveness, and Conflict Resolution

This chapter deals with four typically high-stress areas in most people's lives—anger, communication, considerate or gentle assertiveness, and conflict resolution. Anger—how we express it and cope with it—often poses problems for effective communication, so it is discussed first. Understanding how effective communication works is essential to appreciating considerate assertiveness techniques, so communication is covered second, and assertiveness is discussed third. Effective conflict resolution relies on a thorough understanding of all these issues, so it is presented last.

Anger and How It Works

When do you get annoyed? What happens when you lose your temper? How do you feel? Most of the time anger happens to us so quickly that we don't have a clear picture of how it progresses. We've also been taught as children that anger is bad. When we get irritated, we also get upset about the fact that we are exasperated! However, a definite pattern of escalation leads to the expression of anger, and if we know how that works, we can learn how to break the process.

Causes of Anger

In the initial phase of the anger cycle, a person is confronted with a situation that poses a personal threat in some way, or that frustrates attempts to get needs met. Six possible kinds of situations can trigger these feelings:

- *Loss of self-esteem.* This kind of loss is most keenly felt internally. We have a sense of having failed somehow or of having let ourselves down.

- *Loss of face.* This loss is felt publicly. Our friends and family may have learned about a failure or inadequacy of ours, or the image of ourselves we present to society has been tarnished in some way.

- *Threat of physical violence or harm.* Our self-preservation instinct comes in here.

- *Loss of valued possession(s), skills, or abilities.* When something we value is taken away from us, we can feel threatened because of the problems involved in replacing it, the pain of readjusting our lives if it cannot be replaced, or simply because we have an emotional investment in the object, skill, or ability.

- *Loss of a valued role.* We define ourselves to society and to ourselves in terms of the various roles we play. Since most of our identity is based on these "performances," losing one is painful. If the role we lose is important to our lives and society, we can feel worthless and "faceless."

- *Loss of a valued relationship.* Relationships with others are very important to most people, and losing a valued connection—especially if you don't think you can find an alternative way to meet the needs it fulfilled—can be very painful and threatening.

The Power Analysis

In the few seconds that it takes your brain to register the potential loss or threat in the situation in front of you, you also conduct a power analysis, which includes an evaluation of the type and severity of the threat or loss and an analysis of the resources you have available to deal with this situation. If the analysis is positive, meaning that you can handle it or you can survive on your resources, you will not get angry, and the cycle ends here.

If, however, your power analysis comes up negative—that is either the situation is menacing or you do not have adequate resources to deal with it—angry feelings will be triggered.

Individual Reactions to Angry Feelings

What happens when angry feelings are triggered? Individual reactions depend on both the outcome of the power analysis and the person's personality, but some common reactions include:

- *Inability to talk or express angry feelings.* When some people get really upset, they simply cannot talk. No words come out, no matter how hard they try. When such people are moderately to really furious, they *can* talk, but the words come out very softly, slowly, and clearly. Family and friends may know that when these folks sound this way, they are furious, but people who don't know them well don't believe they are really upset, and that can cause problems.

- *Withdrawal.* This reaction involves giving someone you're annoyed with the silent treatment, or withdrawing physically or mentally from the situation itself.

- *Avoidance or distraction.* Some people go to great lengths to avoid situations that could lead to angry feelings or try to turn attention elsewhere to distract themselves and others.

- *Blowing up.* Some people yell, scream, shout, kick, hurt, fight, stomp their feet, or even kill when they get upset.

- *Practicing passive-aggressive behaviors.* People who use passive-aggressive behaviors look, at least on the outside, as if they are going along with the situation and are not angry. But beneath the surface they are planning and executing all sorts of sneak attacks to get back at the others involved in the situation. The sneak attacks are usually little things that irritate the others the most.

- *Internalizing the anger.* People who internalize anger literally swallow it. They turn their frustration inward and develop headaches, high blood pressure, ulcers, and other gastrointestinal problems. Because this approach to dealing with anger can have such negative effects on health, it is important to channel anger properly.

- *Developing depression.* Many therapists believe that most common depression is caused by anger that is turned inward. If for some reason you believe that you cannot confront your anger and its source, you may choose to ignore it. But the anger doesn't go away, it becomes depression—a kind of depression that is very hard to shake until its causes are uncovered and resolved. This depression is a terrible energy drainer as well, and can lead to fatigue, insomnia, and numerous other health problems.

- *Panic.* Many people literally panic when they get upset. They are so frightened of their own anger that they get scared and confused.

- *Projecting anger onto others.* People who project their feelings onto others deny their own anger and attribute it to others involved in the situation. By doing that, they can be somewhat righteous when they finally blow up.

- *Placating or pacifying the other person involved to prevent the loss or threat that triggered the angry feelings.*

- *Confrontation.* People who are angry discuss their angry feelings with others involved in the situation and ask for a response.

- *Negotiation with others involved in the situation to resolve it.*

The most effective reactions to anger are confrontation and negotiation. Only these two reactions have the potential to resolve the situation that triggered it. This is not to say that any of the other reactions are bad (except blowing up, when it endangers you and others), *they are just less effective.* Most of the time these patterns were learned in order to survive while we were growing up. Sometimes they may be very wise things to do, but most of the time they are ineffective because they do not resolve the initial problem.

Once we have reacted to our angry feelings, our minds and bodies also respond to the reaction itself. As mentioned before, some people are afraid of anger, and their fear can escalate and intensify the threat or loss posed by the situation.

Our bodies respond physically to anger as well, and these feelings can be very scary if you are not familiar with them. There are as many different physical reactions as there are people and triggering situations, but some common reactions include dry mouth, pounding heart, dizziness, feeling faint, shaking, cold hands, red face, stuttering over words, not being able to talk, headache, stomach ache, fatigue, not being able to think clearly, not being able to move (freezing up), crying, or feeling a tremendous need to release pent-up energy in some way. These physical reactions, and our intellectual response to them, can also escalate and intensify our feelings.

After we have responded to our physical and emotional reactions to our anger, they combine to create a reaction of some sort to the other people and the situation. This response is perceived by the person(s) involved as a new situation and they then go through the same steps in the anger cycle. The process can go on and on, and the situation can escalate almost indefinitely.

Breaking the Anger Cycle

Once you know how the cycle works, you can see that there are several opportunities for breaking or altering it. One very important opportunity involves the perception of the threat or unmet need. We usually zip right through this part without stopping to get a clear picture of what is really going on, but putting everything on hold for a few seconds can be extremely helpful. Ask yourself whether this threat or frustration is realistically based and whether it is really *your* responsibility to begin with. Anger based on someone else's threat or frustration is very contagious. Make sure the problem is really yours!

Once a clear picture of the situation is established, you have a better chance of making an accurate power analysis. Think through what resources you have on hand for coping, and you may find that you *do* have adequate resources to meet your needs and can defuse the anger cycle right here. Determine what sorts of capabilities you could add to increase your power base for responding to the initial situation.

Studying your individual anger reactions and your responses to them can be very helpful. The more you know about yourself and your body, the less likely you are to be taken by surprise by how you behave and feel. Being aware and in control can help you prevent escalation of the cycle. Finally, learn how best to structure your overall response to the initial situation so that the problem can be resolved.

Structuring Your Responses to Anger

Ideally you would become so personally secure and confident of yourself and your abilities that nothing would threaten you at all! Because that scenario is not realistic, here are ideas on how to structure your responses to increase their effectiveness for resolving situations.

Acknowledging your anger and telling the other person(s) how you feel can be very useful. The best way to do this is to use "I" statements. "I" statements help you express your feelings and clarify what is happening. They are less threatening than statements that blame others, and they are more likely to be listened to and considered. For example, if you are upset because your spouse or child was late for dinner, it would be more effective to say, "I really get annoyed when you are late for dinner and don't call. I get worried and scared that something happened to you. I also get panicky because I know the rest of the family is on a tight schedule and I worry that holding up dinner might make them late." Chances are the other person will be less threatened by this approach than he or she would if you started screaming.

Calibrating your response to the needs of the situation is also important. It is senseless to use an atom bomb when a frown will do. You waste your overall energy and greatly risk escalating the situation. Conversely, pitching a fit can be extremely effective in the appropriate situation. Anger is not an all or nothing emotion. The feelings span a whole continuum from slightly irritated to furious. Learning to categorize various levels accurately can help you to clarify your resources for dealing with the situation.

Analyzing the threat can be useful. At many times, doing so shows you that the situation was caused by a difference in values, goals, upbringing, or ways of behaving; or clarifies that the situation was provoked unintentionally or unknowingly. Analysis helps reduce the personal threat or loss facing you and may end the anger cycle right there.

You can defuse the intensity of your feelings and clarify your perceptions of the situation by talking to others. Talking gives you feedback about how you are perceived, as well as validation of your feelings. You may also get much-needed support and encouragement.

Forgiving the other person means letting go of your anger and welcoming resolution, while paving the way for more effective handling of similar situations in the future. "Let's forgive and forget" is very to easy to say, but hard to do. Holding grudges never really hurts anyone but ourselves; people get back whatever they give out. People who have hurt others *always* wind up getting put down somewhere else along the line, and in ways more devastating and damaging than anything they could have managed.

People who are comfortable and secure in themselves have no need to go around trampling on other people's feelings. Those whose purposely hurt others feel inadequate and inferior in some way, and that inadequacy will trip them up somewhere else along the line.

If forgiving and forgetting simply is not possible for you, you might want to train yourself to turn off emotional investment in a person or a relationship. That person simply no longer exists for you. Turning off means training yourself to stop mulling over old hurts and slights, to stop plotting revenge, and to get on with your life. It takes a while, but it can be done!

Coping with Someone Else's Anger

Coping with someone else's anger can fall under one of two categories: (1) dealing with someone's fury about a situation in which you played no part, or (2) facing another's wrath that you helped to trigger. The first category usually produces anger by contagion—you're left all hot and bothered by a situation you can do nothing about. The second category can lead to escalation of the other's feelings and can add to your own. Some techniques can be used to defuse both types of situation, however, and the following ideas may be helpful.

- *Affirm the other person's anger.* Say that you are aware of the anger and are willing to talk about it. Not doing so will usually increase the intensity of the upset. Saying something like "Yes, I hear you. I'm not sure what I did to make you angry, but I want to know about it" can be enormously stress reducing.

- *Talk about how the anger makes you feel.* This may be hard if you feel the other person has power over you, but expressing your tenseness and its impact on your perception of the situation can pave the way to negotiation and compromise.

- *Find out what is really going on.* Clarify with the other person what triggered the anger—what needs or wants were not met. Are those realistic? Is the situation your responsibility? What are the options as seen by the other person? Getting at hidden agendas—the unexpressed needs, wants and expectations that we all carry around—is crucial. When all the cards are on the table, resolution is much more likely.

Working it out involves coming to grips with the cause of the problem and assessing the reality of the options available. If a behavior is the cause of the anger, new ways of behaving can be discussed and agreed on. Talking about how similar situations will be handled in the future is also a good idea. Apologize if you are at fault, and if you can't apologize for the situation, at least say you're sorry for getting the other person upset.

If, after negotiation and compromise, you still don't get anywhere, discuss bringing in a neutral third party to act as mediator. Labor unions and management do it all the time. Good mediators could be superiors and supervisors at work, clergypersons, mental health professionals, more experienced family members, or lawyers. It's best to consider these people only as a last resort. Try to resolve the situation on your own first.

A Final Word on Anger

Anger does not go away if we ignore it, deny it exists, or fail to resolve it. It goes underground and makes sneak attacks on your health (in the form of physical and emotional symptoms) and other relationships (through unrealistic expectations, unmet needs, and garbled thinking and communication). Buried anger can also surface the next time another crisis comes along, intensifying the effect of that crisis on you. Harnessing anger by confronting it and resolving it can unleash a powerful source of energy for you (even in the "Oh, yeah? Well, I'll sure show you!" form). Some of humanity's greatest achievements have been attained and some of the greatest risks taken in the name of showing others that they were wrong. Making use of anger this way can increase your personal sense of power, promote your continued growth, and facilitate improved communication with people around you.

How Communication Works

Communication is something everyone does and everyone thinks they do well, yet very few people do it effectively. It is the glue that binds the human species together. As the late Virginia Satir, a renowned family therapist, was fond of saying,

> Communication is the largest single factor determining what kinds of relationships a person makes with others and what happens to him or her in the world. It determines how we survive, how we develop intimacy, how productive we are, how we make sense, and how we connect with our own divinity.

Communication is learned. We come into this world with the raw materials needed to communicate—brains, mouths, faces, bodies, etc. But how we use those tools, in conjunction with our self-concepts, and our experiences with communicating, are learned as we grow up in our families: Most of it is learned and solidified before we are 5 years old!

The communication skills that worked for us at age 5, within our families, may not continue to serve us well as we get older and our life situations change. But because all communication is learned, we can change our styles and skills if we want to. And knowing that simple fact is very powerful. We can become effective communicators at any time in our lives.

Effective communication requires an understanding of how the process works. First, we convey information, not only with our words and actions but also with our tone of voice, phrasing, and the types of words we use: our expressions and tiny movements of our limbs or muscles; our energy level; the type and style of clothing and personal grooming; and with touch, taste, and smell. *In short, you cannot* not *communicate.* Everything you do or say, or don't do or say, conveys volumes.

Communication takes two: One person to send the signals and another to receive them. We bring several things to our encounters, including our bodies and brains, our values, our expectations of what is going to happen in this particular encounter, our ability to share, and our remembered past experiences with similar situations.

These elements of communication affect, not only how we say what we say, but how we interpret other people's attempts to reach us. They combine to create a series of screens through which we obtain information about the situation and on which we base our perceptions. Each of these screens has different size "holes," which allow only certain bits of information to get through. The result is that we can never know or understand completely the true reality of any message or situation because our understanding of the situation is based on the much smaller amount of information that makes it through the holes in our screens. Because everyone has different filters, *no one ever views any situation or communication attempt in exactly the same way,* even if the people involved are from the same family or have known each other for a long time.

Based on incomplete information and our evaluation of it, we respond in some way. The other people then evaluate this new communication through their filters, and the cycle continues. Knowing this, we are absolutely amazed that people can communicate effectively as often as they do! The communication process has an inherent tendency to become confused, but there are ways to compensate for that tendency and to make our communication more understandable.

Analyzing Communication Breakdowns

Having experienced and observed many communication breakdowns, we've found it can be useful to ask the following questions to help pinpoint what happened and to figure out how to resolve the situation:

- *What is similar about this situation and others I have experienced?* What was going on with me and the other(s) involved at times when communication broke down? Did the same problem trigger the breakdown this time around?

- *When have I observed similar feelings?* What was going on in that situation? How did I react?

- *Does this person remind me of someone else?* Many times aspects of a person's personality remind us of someone else without our being aware of it. We can easily transfer our feelings and expectations of that other person onto the new person. Most of the time this is beneficial, and we transfer warm, friendly feelings. But sometimes we carry over negative feelings that are totally unrealistic in the new situation.

- *Has anyone else acted like this toward me or treated me this way before?* Who was that person? What was happening at that time? Are any parts of this new situation similar to that old one? How did I respond?

✔ *What am I getting out of this situation or from feeling this way?* Remember, we rarely continue doing something unless we are getting *something* from our efforts.

✔ *What part did I play in the communication breakdown?* How am I continuing to contribute to it? This is the hardest question to ask ourselves, because we never like to admit we could have done something wrong! But we need to assess accurately whether we are indeed responsible!

The answers you came up with for these six questions can give you ideas about where to go and what to do to resolve your communication breakdown. They can also teach you a great deal about yourself and how you communicate.

Preventing Communication Breakdowns

Yes, you can prevent communication breakdowns, or at least greatly reduce the likelihood of their happening. The following tips will help you increase your ability both to send and to receive effective communications. Trying all of them at once would be too stressful, try incorporating one or two techniques into your communication style and see what happens.

■ *Remember that your actions speak louder than your words.* When confronted with words and actions that don't match each other, most people instinctively (and correctly) put more emphasis on the meaning conveyed by actions. Only trained actors can alter their actions enough to be truly convincing; most of us act out our feelings accurately because most of the things we do are outside our awareness.

■ *Intentions don't count, effects do.* You may have had the best intentions in the world, but if a communication breakdown occurred, use that as your guide. It is telling you that your meaning is not being communicated to those around you. To put it another way, the *other person's perception* of the situation needs to become *your reality.*

■ *Be positive whenever you can.* People don't like to hear bad things about themselves all the time. Who wants to hear nothing but gripes and complaints? On the other hand, people can recognize a phony compliment five miles away. You can usually find something positive to say, but, if not, don't say anything at all.

■ *It is impossible to read minds.* We don't care how long you have known someone, it is absolutely impossible for you to know what that person is thinking because people are constantly changing, growing, and evolving. Test all your assumptions verbally and recognize that any situation can be seen from as many sides as there are people involved. When you don't know what is going on with someone, just ask. If you phrase your question in the following terms, you can foster sharing of information and feelings: "I'm curious, what did you mean when you said...?" "Help me understand what that means for you..." "What was it exactly about the situation that made you upset?" "What does that look like for you?" "I'm not sure I understand what that means to you. Can you explain it to me again?" "I think I heard you say that..." "Did I understand you correctly? I took what you said to mean..."

■ *Be clear and specific in your communications.* You know that you can't read others' minds, neither can other people read yours. They can't hear what you are saying in your head, so say it out loud! But remember, *if the people around you are preoccupied, they may hear only half of what you say!* Timing can be everything in communication, so choose an appropriate time to bring up the discussion. In the car on the way to work may not be the best time for a major discussion!

■ *Accept all feelings and try to understand them.* People are entitled to any and all feelings they may have. This fact is very important. Your responsibility is to understand them and accept them as real for that particular person, at that time, and in that situation. *No* feelings are ever crazy, stupid, or wrong. However, society does not have to accept or tolerate all *actions*, particularly those that could cause harm to others. When people know they can have all sorts of feelings, that they are okay, and that they can talk about those feelings, the need for acting out the feelings decreases dramatically.

■ *Treat your family and coworkers with the same kindness you show your friends.* We tend to be nice to everyone but the people who are around us most of the time! It is high time to return to good manners and politeness! Those little conventions were established to keep people and communication running smoothly, and, as such, they are great stress reducers!

■ *Try not to nag, yell, whine, or preach.* Think for a moment what you do when a friend goes off on a tirade of complaining. What did you do when your parents nagged you as a child? Chances are good you tuned out both your friends and your parents. People soon begin to tune out naggers, preachers, and whiners as soon as they open their mouths. So if you have something important to say and you say it in a whiney or preachy manner, no one will be listening anyway. Asking questions works better.

■ *Learn to listen.* Force yourself to pay attention beyond a few words and work to knock holes in your screens so that more information can come through. Researchers have found that most people attend only to the first few words or phrases of a sentence or communication attempt; then they focus on creating their response to what they think they have heard. To break away from this habit, try the following:

1. Give the speaker your full attention—don't let your mind wander!

2. Put aside any preconceived ideas about what the speaker is going to say.

3. Interpret what is going on descriptively (by looking at the speaker's facial expressions and body language and listening to word choice, etc.) rather than judgmentally (putting your own interpretations on what was said).

4. Be alert for any confusion on your, or the speaker's, part—and ask for clarification.

5. Make it clear that the speaker has been heard.

■ *Avoid unfair communication and fighting techniques.* There is a way to fight fair. Several books listed in the "Good Reads" section at the end of this book can help you learn these new techniques. Essentially, the techniques are based on fair play, common sense, and courtesy. You've got all those skills, so use them!

Dealing with Mixed Messages

Sometimes it seems that no matter how hard we try to communicate effectively, we give and receive mixed messages—messages in which the words don't match the "metamessage" (or the big-picture message) communicated by facial expressions, body language, tone of voice, eye movements, and so on. In nearly all of these cases, the person speaking is completely unaware of sending conflicting signals.

Why does this happen? Virginia Satir, in her book *The New Peoplemaking*, said she believes that double messages occur when the communicator holds one or more of the following views:

- I have low self-esteem and believe I am bad because I feel that way.
- I am afraid I might hurt the other person's feelings.
- I worry about retaliation from the other person.
- I fear that our relationship will be harmed and I could be abandoned.
- I do not want to impose on the other person.
- I am unconscious of anything but myself and do not attach any significance to the other person or the interaction itself.

What can you do if you are confronted by mixed messages? You could just listen to the words and go with the information you get from them. You could tune into the nonverbal signals, thinking that only the very best actors and actresses are able to control their actions effectively enough to hide their true feelings. You could just ignore the whole message, believing it is too much bother to try to figure out what is really going on. Alternatively, you could try to assimilate both messages, and end up getting very confused and spending hours ruminating on what the person *really* meant. Finally, you could choose to comment on the double message, and give the communicator the opportunity to clarify it for you.

Most of the time, people rely on the information they pick up from nonverbal signals they receive during a mixed message. In the majority of situations, this is a safe bet; but there are always times when the nonverbal signals are not accurate, which is why checking out mixed signals is so important—especially if they happen frequently in a specific type of situation. Asking for clarification in a nonthreatening way not only helps *you* get a better picture, but it may also help the *communicator* become aware of sending the double messages.

A Final Word on Communication

Effective communication is not difficult or tricky; it involves respecting those you are talking with, understanding your own biases and shortcomings, and making an effort to express yourself in ways that are understandable to those around you. Following the ideas outlined in this chapter can increase your effectiveness as a communicator and interpreter. By achieving that, you can greatly reduce the potential for stress and stress overload.

How Gentle Assertiveness Works

Assertiveness is not aggression. Aggression involves demanding your own way no matter what and stepping on whomever's toes it takes to get your needs met. Gentle assertiveness involves standing up for your rights while fully respecting the rights of others, and negotiating and compromising to get the most needs met for everyone—making sure every encounter is a win-win situation for all participants. Nonassertiveness means denying your own needs and wishes to satisfy someone else's. Your unmet needs have the potential to become major stressors.

People are *nonassertive* for many reasons. They may not believe (or know) that they have rights and they are special, unique, and important; they may have come to believe that awful things will happen or other people will be hurt if they ask for what they want; or they prefer playing games to communicating fairly or interacting honestly with others.

People are *aggressive* for many reasons, too. They may feel inferior or inadequate in some way; they may believe that being aggressive is the only way to get their needs met; they don't have the skills necessary to be assertive; they are transferring feelings about prior situations onto new situations; or, more rarely, they simply like to bully others.

Assertiveness, on the other hand, is really an extension of effective communication. It means standing up for your rights, while respecting the rights of others. When you do that, you can usually fulfill your needs and maintain good interpersonal relationships.

Your Personal Bill of Rights

The first step toward becoming more assertive involves learning what rights you have as a human being. Yes, *you do have rights,* and they include:

- *Judging your own behavior, thoughts, and emotions without assistance from anyone else, and accepting any and all consequences and responsibilities for them.*

- *Choosing not to give anyone reasons or excuses to explain or justify your behavior.*

- *Deciding for yourself alone whether you have the responsibility to solve someone else's problem and whether you wish to do so.*

- *Changing your mind whenever you want to without owing anyone an explanation.*

- *Making mistakes and accepting the consequences and responsibilities for them.*

- *Saying "I don't know" and accepting the fact that it is impossible for anyone to know everything.*

- *Creating your own self-esteem without relying on the goodwill and regard of others.*

- *Making your own decisions, based on your needs, values, goals, priorities, resources, and situation.*

- *Asking what other people's needs and wants are, and then deciding whether you want to fulfill them.*

- *Deciding you don't care about a situation or problem, without owing anyone an explanation or apology.*

Putting Your Rights to Work

The rights you have as a human being carry over into all aspects of your life. If you are like most people, though, you may be more assertive in certain areas of your life than in others. Our upbringing and past experiences with assertiveness influence our degree of comfort practicing it in various situations, so it is important to know exactly how we feel.

Take a few minutes and think through your past experiences with, and feelings about, assertiveness. Then draw up an "assertiveness hierarchy" on paper, with lines numbered from 1 through 10. On line 10 list a situation in which you feel very comfortable exercising your rights. On line 9 list a situation in which you feel slightly less comfortable, on up to number 1—the situation in which you feel least comfortable being assertive. Is there a pattern in your responses? Can you identify specific feelings or fears as you go higher up on your hierarchy? Are those fears realistic? Do any of your rights as a human being ameliorate those concerns? What can you do to make yourself more comfortable in these situations? Are you confusing gentle assertiveness with aggression?

Gentle assertiveness is a skill, just like many other things we do in our daily lives. The more you practice skills, the easier they become, until you no longer have to think consciously about doing them. Being gently assertive is very much the same. It feels weird and scary at first, but the more you practice it, the easier it gets.

The purpose of an assertiveness hierarchy is to give you some sort of framework to use in practicing those skills. The idea is to start with situation 10, apply your rights, and practice until you feel very comfortable being gently assertive in that situation. Once you acheive that you can move up to situation 9, repeating the same process. Eventually you can work yourself all the way up the chart and feel comfortable in your number 1 situation.

Why work this way instead of tackling the worst first? Because effectiveness in being gently assertive rests on a cumulative experience. Each little success adds another brick to the foundation, allowing you to feel more secure and comfortable. Jumping feet first into your personally scariest situation can produce severe stress, and when you are already suffering from stress overload, you certainly don't need to give yourself any more!

Gentle Assertiveness Tricks and Tips

As with all skills, there are some tips, tricks, and techniques that can make assertiveness easier and more effective. Go slowly, clarifying your own values, goals, priorities, thoughts, and feelings. Consider your timing when you ask to get your needs met. Reward yourself every time you take a new step. Be as honest and as open with others as you can be. *And practice whenever you get the chance.*

Assertive people exhibit certain nonverbal behaviors that convey to others that they are to be taken seriously. Those behaviors include:

- Standing straight and tall
- Looking directly at people with whom they are communicating
- Maintaining eye contact while talking
- Speaking in a clear, steady, strong voice
- Speaking without hesitation and with assurance and confidence (you can even write out a speech beforehand and practice if you want!)

Acting assertively is as important as what you actually say, because the tendency of people is to trust nonverbal messages more than verbal messages, as discussed earlier. Yes it's scary and, yes, you have to do it before the fear goes away, but if you want to *be* assertive, you have to *look* assertive. You can develop an assertive demeanor through lots of practice in front of your bathroom mirror or with a close friend.

After you've done all that, you might want to try experimenting with the following techniques:

- *Use Describe, Express, Specify, and Choose (DESC).* This assertion technique outlined by Bower and Bower can be used to organize what you want to say. To use it:

  1. *Describe:* Paint a verbal picture of what situation or behavior is bothering you. "When you..." "When..."

  2. *Express:* Explain the feelings that the situation or behavior triggers in you. "I feel..." "I think..."

3. *Specify:* Identify several specific ways you would like the situation or behavior to change. "I would like..." "I would prefer..." It would make me happy if..."

4. *Choose:* Select the consequences you have decided to apply to the situation or behavior if the other person does not alter them. "If you do..., I will do..." "If you don't do..., I will..."

■ *Try being a broken record.* One of the most important aspects of being assertive is being persistent in stating what you want, even when other people try to distract you. Don't get angry, irritated, or start screaming. Don't give reasons or explanations. Just keep saying what you want over and over, like a broken record.

■ *Try a workable compromise.* If your self-esteem or public "face" is not at stake, you might consider offering a workable compromise as a way out of the situation. Compromises are often accepted by others involved because they offer a way out without losing face.

■ *Try fogging when you don't want to fight.* "Fogging" involves appearing to agree with statements intended to provoke an argument. You can *agree in principle* with statements people use to criticize you. For example, if your partner says you are a lazy slob, you could reply, "Yes, I can see how some people might think I'm a lazy slob." Or you can agree with any possible truth in a statement. You could say, "I can see how you might think I'm lazy. Some days all I want to do is sleep." Or you can agree with *any truth contained in the statement.* You might say, "That's one thing about me for sure—I like to take the lazy way out." All these responses defuse the situation and render the criticizer speechless!

■ *Try negative assertion.* Many times criticism is based on different values, goals, or priorities. We don't stop to think that such things won't be altered or changed no matter what we say or do, and we start screaming anyway. Negative assertion involves accepting the fact that you made an error while avoiding an argument. For example, if someone accuses you of not doing something you promised you would do, you could say "Yes, I didn't do it. And I didn't do it because I was uncomfortable doing what you asked me to do. I have the right to change my mind, and that is exactly what I did."

When someone is being unduly hostile, your best bet is to admit you made a mistake, but to exaggerate it a bit so that the hostility comes across as being out of line. For example, if you forgot to pick up the dry cleaning and your mate is being hostile, you could say, "Oh my god! You mean I forgot to pick up the dry cleaning? What a stupid idiot I am! I'll run down and get it right now!" If the person is giving you valid criticism, even though they are being hostile, you best defense is to say, "Yeah, you're right, I blew it. Sorry."

■ *Use negative inquiry.* Negative inquiry is a nondefensive response that prompts criticizers to make further critical statements, but in the process to clarify their values and expectations. If your boss criticizes you unfairly, for example, you could say, "I don't understand. What is it about me that makes you say that?" After each response, request further clarification. Eventually the criticizer will realize the absurdity of the criticisms, and you will have avoided a fight.

■ *Provide free information and practice self-disclosure.* Gentle assertiveness involves, not only stating your opinions and needs, but being an active participant in the process and facilitating communications from others. One way to keep conversation going is to provide *free information*—revealing your feelings, your interests, and things about yourself in the course of a conversation. Following up on free information provided by others increases their participation in the conversation. *Self-disclosure* involves revealing information about yourself and your interests in response to direct questions.

A Final Word on Gentle Assertiveness

Gentle assertiveness is not all take and no give. It involves being an active listener, doing your part to keep communication flowing smoothly, and helping others to express themselves, as well as standing up for your rights, needs, and wants. Since stress symptoms can be produced by keeping strong feelings inside and not getting needs met, practicing gentle assertiveness in our daily lives may be one very good way to reduce stress overload. Try it. It really works!

Win-Win Conflict Resolution: Bringing It All Together

In the win-win school of conflict resolution everyone gets at least part of what they want out of a situation, anger and confrontations are minimized, everyone is able to express their position and needs assertively, and people walk away from the encounter respecting each other. True, our society tends to glorify and reward encounters in which someone wins and the others lose, but, in the long run, relationships are fostered more effectively when people come out of an encounter liking and respecting each other. Can this nirvana be achieved? Yes, it can with a little work, when you understand how anger, communication, and assertiveness work. All three are necessary to achieve a win-win situation.

In her book *Hidden Agendas*, Dr. Marlin Potash covers some important ground rules for achieving win-win situations. They are based on effective communication techniques discussed earlier in this chapter, but they bear repeating:

✔ *Think before you speak.* Although you have the right to express yourself, you have the responsibility to do it in a way that does not hurt others or push their anger buttons.

✔ *Say what you mean and mean what you say.* Conflicts are not the time or place to give only hints about what you want or to give mixed signals (words and body language that are incongruent), expecting others to read your mind. If you don't ask directly for something, chances are very good that you won't get it.

✔ *Listen, and listen actively to the other person.* The tendency is to shut down when confronted with a conflict, and to start preparing a defense as soon as the other person utters the first sentence. But force yourself to "stay in the moment" instead, and really listen. Then paraphrase the communication back, checking out whether your interpretation of what was said is correct. Only after you have restated the communication to the other person's satisfaction, are you ready to start expressing your feelings about what you heard. This is a very difficult skill to master, but it can be done, and it can save you a great deal of stress and heartache!

✔ *Never put words into the other person's mouth.* Never put your interpretation of the situation into another's mouth: It never gets you anywhere. For example, saying "You think I'm irresponsible," or "You're not really angry about this, you've just had a bad day" demeans both your communication partner and you.

✔ *Specify exactly what problem or situation is under discussion and stick to that only.* Don't bring in the "kitchen sink"—old hurts, slights, or other situations. Doing so only confuses the issue and distracts both of you from understanding what is really going on.

✔ *Forget who is at fault.* It takes at least two people to create a conflict: One person can't do it alone. Therefore, blaming, criticizing, justifying, and defending will not help you resolve your differences. Acknowledging your feelings about a specific behavior or problem and suggesting alternatives will help you achieve a win-win outcome.

✔ *Treat this conflict just as you would a conflict at work:* Identify what the best possible outcome could be (what would happen if you could get it "your way"); determine your nonnegotiables (the least you could get and still meet your most pressing needs); analyze any other options that could occur; and finally think through what you are willing to give or give up in order to get what you want. You can't get something for nothing, so the last part of that sentence is crucial. It is the core of a win-win philosophy of conflict resolution.

Summing Up

Although anger, communication, assertiveness, and conflict resolution can become major stressors, we all have the capability to relearn our ways of communicating. In doing so, these potential stressors can become powerful sources of energy and satisfaction instead. Our words of advice can be boiled down to the following:

✔ *Be as nice to others as you would like them to be to you.* (Your mom was right about this, too!)

✔ *Listen before you talk.*

✔ *Begin with agreement.* You'd be amazed at how much better you can communicate with people with whom you disagree if you start off your discussion with some area on which you both agree. Even if it requires really digging to uncover that common ground, do it! It's worth the effort.

✔ *Say "and," not "but."* We've found that the word *but* acts like an eraser inside people's heads: It erases the value of anything said before it in a sentence. If you say to people "Yes, your opinions have value, but..." they hear you saying inside their heads "...but I really don't give a fig what they are!" If you use *and* instead, the value of what you said stays in the message, and adds something to it. "Your opinions are valuable, and ..." says to the other person "your opinions do have weight and we will add them to what else we are considering here." It's so simple: Use fewer "buts" and more "ands."

✔ *Make lots of "I" statements; limit "you" statements; and forget about making "why" questions.* "I" clarifies for the other person what you think and feel, while "you" can make a person feel criticized. "I" reduces defensiveness, and fosters communication. "Why" questions automatically put other people on the defensive, because they feel they must justify their behavior or the situation. "Why" questions, as in "Why don't you spend more time with me?" are usually veiled criticisms, which get you nowhere.

Try it, you may find that effective communication, assertiveness, and conflict resolution can be a whole lot of fun!

16
Preparing for Changes: Values, Goals, Decision Making, and Taking Risks

When was the last time you thought about your values? Can't remember? You are not alone. In our society, many people's lives are a collection of habits—habits acquired when a situation arose that had to be resolved. Some people think about their values only when faced with a crisis—usually a crisis that requires immediate action.

Almost everyone has at least two sets of values: *personal values*—those values that apply just to them as a person, in their personal life, and provide guidance in how they want to act and interact in their intimate and social spheres; and *work* values—values that apply to their jobs and careers—which provides a similar grounding at work. Many people also have *family* values— values they hold jointly (we hope) with their mate and any children, which embody the way they want to live as a family.

These different sets of values must be both *consciously understood* and *congruent* with each other. If they are not, great stress can result, for several reasons:

1. Acting or living contrary to our values promotes guilt and, subsequently, stress. If we're not certain what our values are, we either tend to feel guilty about everything or, conversely, about nothing. Most people tend to fall into the first category to some degree, probably as a result of all those "shoulds" and "oughts" taught to us as children.

2. If our personal, work, and family values are incongruent, or at odds with each other, we may experience great stress when called on to make a decision in one

sphere of our lives where the values called into play conflict with a value held in another part of our lives. All in all, such a situation is not pleasant.

3. Because values may be formed as rules to deal with specific situations, we may still be operating by those values, even after the original situation that prompted the value has changed considerably.

Clearing Out the Garbage

Values that have lost their utility we call "garbage," and all of us carry plenty of garbage around with us all the time. Some common pieces of garbage are the following: "You should work at one company or job your entire life," "Your income should be double your age in thousands of dollars if you want to be considered successful," "You should have a vacation home by the time you are 40 or you are not successful," "If you haven't been promoted in three years, your career is off track and you should consider leaving your company," "Children should be seen and not heard," "A lady never raises her voice," and on and on. This kind of value may have been beneficial when it was first formed, but times and lifestyles have changed drastically—so much so, in fact, that for some people these values may no longer be useful. By keeping values past the "expiration date" of their usefulness, we increase our possible sources of stress by setting standards for ourselves that may be impossible to reach.

Much of the time we can alter these values and reassess their usefulness and, in the process, greatly reduce our levels of stress. All of us need to air out our values periodically and throw away the garbage. Doing so ensures that treasured values don't get lost in the shuffle.

The fancy name for this proces is values clarification, and it lies at the root of successful goal setting, wise decision making, and creative risk taking—three other potentially stressful areas of life. To set goals, make decisions, and take risks, you need to be clear about your values. Values clarification takes some time and thought, but it's really not hard to do. In fact, it can be fun! The following exercises are designed to tell you a great deal about yourself and your values. Grab a pencil or pen and paper, a cup of coffee (decaffeinated) or glass of wine (a small one), and spend some time airing out your values.

Evaluating Your Personal and Work Values

Start off with your personal and work values. We talk about family values later in this chapter.

What Does Your Life Line Look Like?

Every person's life line, that is, a graphic representation of a person's life path, is different. Each line has its own shape, ups and downs, beginnings and endings. Your life line can reveal a great deal about you: your values, goals, hopes, successes, and wise and not-so-wise decisions. This interesting exercise takes between 15 and 30 minutes, and is well worth the effort.

Get a large piece of paper (or tape two pieces of note paper together). You are literally going to draw a line that depicts the hills and valleys of your life. Use a pencil for this, because you will need to make revisions to it: Later events will trigger memories about earlier events, and vice versa. Start at one outer edge of the paper, at about the middle of the page's width with your birth. Your life line begins at your birth and then continues through where you think your life is going. Take a few minutes to think about important events in your life and mark them down on your life line. Mark the highs and lows of your life as well—with the highs as the peaks and the lows as the valleys. For each important event or series of events, list your age when it happened to you. Once you've done that, you're halfway home!

When you've finished sketching your life line, add the following symbols:

! where you took the greatest risk of your life

✗ where you encountered an obstacle that prevented you from getting or doing what you wanted to achieve

○ where a critical decision was made for you by someone else

+ where you made the best decision you've ever made

− where you made the worst decision you've ever made

? where you see an important decision coming up in the future

Consider your life line carefully now, complete with symbols. Can you see anything that surprises you? Do you see any patterns relating to risks and decisions? How have decisions affected the shape of your life? Did you actually make the decisions that altered your life?

Many people are surprised by two patterns that often show up in life lines. The first is a pattern that usually follows the worst decision they ever made. Most people notice a sharp dip in their life line immediately after their worst decision, but then their life line begins to climb back up, usually going higher than where it was before they made the "bad" decision. That should tell you that bad decisions often don't turn out to be so bad after all. They can offer tremendous learning experiences and can sometimes change the pattern of life for the better.

The second pattern is the sharp dip in their life lines most people notice after a decision that was made for them by someone else. That tells us that people very rarely make wise decisions for someone else. Only you know what your best interests are and how best to fulfill them—*so make your own decisions! No one will ever be able to make them as wisely for you as you can yourself.*

The Place Where You Live

One theory holds that we keep around us only those things that are meaningful or useful in some way. The things you've chosen for your house, apartment, room, or condominium can be revealing in that regard. Take a few minutes now to walk around the place where you live. What messages do the furnishings, knickknacks, clutter, messes, and so on send to you? What do they say about the person who lives there? Jot down your thoughts as they come to you—don't edit or censor them in anyway. Remember, you're not acting as an interior decorator here, you want to be an archaeologist of sorts.

What Do You Carry with You?

Values clarification experts have found that the things you carry with you all the time can also reveal your underlying values. Chances are you wouldn't carry something around with you unless it was important for some reason.

Take a few minutes to grab your briefcase, handbag, tote bag, backpack, or wallet. Pick out 5 or 10 things you carry with you all the time, things that would send you into a panic if you suddenly lost them. Make a note of your answers to these questions: What things did you choose? Why? What meanings do they have for you? What does that tell you about yourself? Again, remember to be an archaeologist, not an editor!

Things I Like to Do for Fun

Your values can also be revealed by looking at the things you enjoy doing. Using Table 16.1, make a list of 15 things you truly enjoy doing. (If you can think of more, terrific! But try to come up with at least 15.) When you've completed your list, add in the following symbols:

$ for every activity that costs more than 10 dollars to do (or 5 dollars if you are on a tight budget)

A next to things you enjoy doing alone

F next to things you enjoy doing with friends

T next to things that require thought or planning

S next to things that can be done only during a specific season

H next to things you can do at home

C next to things that require closeness or intimacy

M next to things you would like to spend more time doing

W next to those things your family, friends, or conscience say are a waste of time, money, or energy

Table 16.1

Things I like to do for fun	Symbols	Date

After you've added the symbols to your list, take a few minutes to think about when you last enjoyed each of the activities on your list. Can you remember back that far? Write down a date if you can remember one, or estimate how far back in terms of weeks or months (hopefully not years).

Now look at your completed list and jot down the answers to these questions: Can you see any patterns? Do you have more things you like to do alone or that you like to do with friends? How many things cost money? Can you do very many of the things at home? Do the things you like to do require thought or planning beforehand? How many things do you want to spend more time doing? Do any of the items on your list that have an M beside them also have a W next to them?

What the Symbols Tell You. *If you had more than five Fs or Cs:* You enjoy the company and friendship of other people and place a high value on maintaining and building those friendships.

If you had more than five $s: You value the pleasures money can buy, even if you don't value money itself. It may be important for you to have a stable level of income in order to feel comfortable and secure.

If you had more than five Ts: Since many of the activities you enjoy doing require planning, it may be useful to begin planning ahead so you can do more of them. If you are very busy and have trouble clearing your calendar, you might want to consider developing interests that don't require planning, ones you could enjoy when you suddenly found yourself with some free time.

If you had more than four Ss: You may need to develop other interests that aren't dependent on a specific season, or consider relocating to a climate that will let you enjoy these activities for longer periods of time.

If you had more than five Hs: If your responsibilities keep you away from home much of the time, you are depriving yourself of a great source of pleasure and stress reduction. You may need to rethink your work and social schedule, giving yourself permission to set aside blocks of time at home, so you can do the things you enjoy doing there.

If you had any *Ms:* Keep these activities in mind when you select coping techniques to help you reduce your stress levels. These activities may be excellent stress reducers for you. Plan to build at least some amount of time into your day so that you can enjoy these activities more often, and examine why you're not able to spend more time doing these activities now. Are other values or situations interfering in some way?

If you had any *Ws:* Ask yourself the following questions: Where did you get the idea these activities were time wasters? Whose voice can you hear telling you that? Why are they considered wastes of time, money, or effort? Do these reasons stand up in your current life situation? Why do you feel guilty doing them? What is causing your guilt?

If you haven't done more than five activities on your list within the past week, what does this pattern tell you? Either you're not allowing yourself time to do what you enjoy doing, or you may have listed those activities you say you enjoy doing, but really don't enjoy. Are they activities you feel you *should* enjoy doing? Unless you resolve this conflict in some way, chances are good you'll continue feeling stress in these areas.

Checking Out Your Personal and Work Values

Our actions are *always* the clearest indicators of what we value. If you invest time and effort in doing something, you are revealing your values. What you value has a great deal to do with what is stressful for you, because if things are not going as you would like in areas that you value highly, you will experience more stress than if the situation did not involve areas you value.

The chart in Table 16.2 is a values grid. Beside the numbers on this grid, list 16 things you have done in the past year. Just jot them down as you think of them: Anything goes—your hobbies, job-related activities, important events or experiences, trips, and so forth. If possible, try to keep an even split between things from your personal life and things relating to work.

Listed along the top of the grid are numbers corresponding to some common values. Under each number put a check in that column for each activity or experience you listed that involved the corresponding value in some way. For example, if you listed "took an art class" as one of your activities, you would put a check by that activity in column 8 for self-expression; maybe in column 7 for independence, and so on for all the values involved.

Values

1. Love

2. Money

3. Growth or achievement

4. Recognition or reward

5. Self-esteem

6. Security

7. Independence

8. Self-expression

9. Leadership

10. Variety or thrill

After you have thought through all 10 activities, total the check marks in each value column. You will be able to see the relative strengths of your personal and work values as you compare the number of times you have a check mark in each value column. Ask yourself the following questions: Are the values what you thought they would be? Any value that got *more than four check marks* should be considered very important to you, and any value that rated *more than eight check marks is critical for you.* Are your values for work and your personal life congruent? Are there any major areas of conflict?

Table 16.2

Activity or experience	1	2	3	4	5	6	7	8	9	10
_____	—	—	—	—	—	—	—	—	—	—
_____	—	—	—	—	—	—	—	—	—	—
_____	—	—	—	—	—	—	—	—	—	—
_____	—	—	—	—	—	—	—	—	—	—
_____	—	—	—	—	—	—	—	—	—	—
_____	—	—	—	—	—	—	—	—	—	—
_____	—	—	—	—	—	—	—	—	—	—
_____	—	—	—	—	—	—	—	—	—	—
_____	—	—	—	—	—	—	—	—	—	—
_____	—	—	—	—	—	—	—	—	—	—
_____	—	—	—	—	—	—	—	—	—	—
_____	—	—	—	—	—	—	—	—	—	—
_____	—	—	—	—	—	—	—	—	—	—
_____	—	—	—	—	—	—	—	—	—	—
Totals	—	—	—	—	—	—	—	—	—	—

What Is Important to Me?

Now it's time to prioritize a little. Look back over your responses to the previous exercises and make two lists of approximately six things that are important to you. One list should focus on your personal life, and the other list should be work-related. These lists could include activities, traits, skills, experiences—anything your responses showed were important to you.

After you have jotted down your lists, go back over the items in each list and try to rank them in terms of how important they are to you. Put a 1 by the item that is most important, a 2 by the second most important, and so on, until each item you listed has a number or priority. What are the three things you want most in your personal life? What values do they reflect? What three things do you want most out of your work life? What values do they reflect?

Are there any areas of conflict between what you want for your personal life and your work life? For example, let's say you had at the top of your list for work that you wanted to push really hard to get a promotion, but to do so would mean really putting in many extra hours until job evaluation time. At the top of your list for your personal life was spending more time with your spouse or significant other or family. It is highly unlikely that you will be able to achieve both of these things: You have uncovered a powerful stressor. You may need to do additional evaluation and thinking to determine which of the conflicting priorities is most important to you. This is the process of adjusting your priorities!

Now think about what you've done recently that has been related to those three most important work and personal values, activities, or behaviors that move you toward what you want out of life. Do your actions support what is important to you? How? If the majority of your actions and behaviors are not moving you toward what you want most out of your personal and work life, they can be a source of significant stress.

If you're not happy with the actions you've taken, can you think of situations that may be preventing you from getting where you want to be? Can you think of any ways of getting around those roadblocks? What would they be?

Setting Personal and Work Goals

Once we've sorted out our values, it is time to look at our goals. If we have identified what we truly want out of life (rather than what we think we should want, or what other people want for us) and when we have made our goals congruent with the essence of our being, we can reduce the stress we feel in our daily lives by removing potential sources of uncertainty and ambiguity.

Most of us are carrying around outmoded goals: goals that we outgrew long ago, goals that no longer fit us because our values are different, or goals that simply no longer work for us because our lives and careers have changed. These outmoded goals can be powerful stressors because, in the back of our minds, we keep trying to move toward them—when we cannot reach them, we become frustrated.

So we need, not only to periodically "air out our values," but also to reassess our goals frequently to see whether they are still a good fit. Ideally, our goals should be reassessed after every major life change or transition (for example, when we get married, after the birth of a child, after a major job change, when we approach middle age or retirement, and so on) or major acute stress episode. If you haven't had any major life changes or acute stress episodes lately, a good rule of thumb is to reassess your goals every three to five years, just to see whether they are still in sync with your life. The following exercises will help you set both long- and short-term goals for yourself.

Five-Year Wish List

Stop for a few minutes, close your eyes, and really think about where you'd like to be in your life five years from now, both in terms of your personal life and at work. If you could do or be anything in the world, what would your ideal life look like? Keep in mind your values and think in terms of job, home life, family, leisure-time activities, location, and so forth. What would you be doing? Where would you be living? How would you be living? Would you be sharing your life with someone special? Who would that be? What would your family be like? What would your social or community activities be? What would you do for fun?

Jot down your thoughts about these questions as they come to you—remember, no editing! You're an archaeologist (or maybe an explorer in this case), not an editor! Based on your answers, can you aggregate your thoughts into some sort of pattern? What five components of your ideal life are most important to you? Some people find it useful to write these components down, others find that keeping a written list just makes things more stressful. Do what is most comfortable for you, but if you don't write them down, make sure you visualize them clearly enough and in enough detail that you will be able to remember them.

One-Year Wish List

Now repeat the process and questions outlined in the foregoing for the five-year wish list, but think in terms of what your ideal life would be and look like a year from now. As you pull your thoughts together, think about this: Does where you want to be a year from now put you farther along the path to where you want to be in five years? If not, you may have uncovered a powerful source of stress for yourself. If your short-term goals are not in sync with your long-term goals, you cannot help but feel stressed-out.

Things I Do Well

Another aspect of setting goals is thinking carefully about what we do well and what we don't do well. It's logical that things we do well will be much less stressful for us than things we are not so good at doing.

Think for a few minutes about what you're good at. Don't look at this as blowing your own horn; view it as giving yourself credit for your many talents and skills! *Everyone* has lots of those! Make a note of all the abilities, talents, skills, and so forth you have that make you a unique individual. Be as specific as possible, and think about your personal and work lives.

Things I'd Rather Forget

Now it is time to evaluate the things you're not so good at doing, both in your personal and work lives. Everyone has areas of weakness or lack of skill, and it is important to know what these "nontalents" are. If you continually push yourself in areas where you do not have adequate knowledge or skill, you will experience great stress. But if you can acquire the needed skills or knowledge, you can lessen your stress levels.

When you've listed your "nontalents," take a look back at your one- and five-year wish lists. Are any of your "nontalents" acting as roadblocks on your path to your ideal life? What would it take to get around these roadblocks? Can you pin down specific skills or knowledge you need to acquire? How can you acquire what you need?

Reassessing Personal and Work Goals and Making Plans

Now comes the fun part: You get to pull all of this new self-knowledge together and determine new, better-tailored personal and work goals for yourself. You should be able to define your goal in 15 words or less. If it takes more than that, your goal may actually incorporate multiple goals, and you may end up confusing yourself.

Choose at least one personal and one work aspect from your five-year wish list and one personal and one work aspect from your one-year wish list and complete the following:

My new and improved *five-year personal goal*:

_____

_____

_____

Specific steps I need to take to get to my *new five-year personal goal*:

_____

_____

_____

_____

_____

My new and improved *one-year personal goal*:

_____

_____

_____

Specific steps I need to take to get to my new *one-year personal goal*:

_____

_____

_____

_____

_____

My new and improved *five-year work goal*:

_____

_____

_____

Specific steps I need to take to get to my new *five-year work goal*:

_____

_____

_____

_____

_____

My new and improved *one-year work goal*:

_____

_____

_____

Specific steps I need to take to get to my new *one-year work goal*:

Evaluating Family Values and Goals

Family goals are the goals you and your mate hold that guide your life together and help shape how you live as a family if you have children. Most couples, however, never conosciously discuss the values and goals that shape their relationship and their family life: They just assume that their mates operate under the same frame of reference that they themselves do. It's usually not until a major blow-up or crisis occurs that partners discover that they hold values and goals that are quite different from one another's.

The situation can cause a great deal of stress for several reasons:

1. We may read different meanings into behaviors based on our differing frames of reference.

2. Decisions we make on a daily basis without consulting our mate, using our personal frame of reference, may have unintended consequences according to the other partner's point of view.

3. Our family values and goals may be incongruent with our mate's family values and goals. And finally, many of them may be carryovers from our childhoods and reflect the way things were done in our families of origin. But those values and goals may no longer be relevant, given the changes in the couple's lives and careers.

The way to avoid this kind of stress is to discuss with our mates, consciously and clearly, our frames of reference and what we see as important family goals and values. Sounds simple, but for many people, doing so is very threatening and scary. It doesn't have to be, however, if you use the exercises provided in this section. The goal is for both of you to share thoughts and feelings, learn more about each other's perspectives, and be open to looking at family values in new ways. These exercises can be very powerful for you as a couple, and can help you develop greater closeness and intimacy. So make a pot of decaffeinated coffee, open a bottle of wine, relax, and have some fun!

The following exercises will help you and your mate clarify your expectations, perceptions, and desires regarding family values and goals. Each step will take between two and three hours of uninterrupted time to complete, and may even take longer, depending on how involved you get with the resulting discussions. It is probably most feasible to complete the steps on different days, as you both may be talked out after completing each step! Make a date with each other to complete the subsequent step within a few days, so that your discussions are still fresh in your minds.

Step 1: Clarifying Personal Values and Goals

Our recommendation is that both you and your mate complete the series of exercises from the preceding section, "Evaluating Your Personal and Work Values."

✔ Things I like to do for fun

✔ Checking out your work and personal values

✔ What is important to me?

✔ Five-year wish list

✔ One-year wish list

✔ Reassessing personal and work goals and making plans

After you both have completed these exercises, discuss the results with each other—openly, honestly, and without accusation. What you are striving for here is a more complete understanding of your mate's frame of reference, values, and goals. This experience can be very powerful for couples—you might not have shared so much with each other in a long time! As you have this discussion, make note of the areas where your and your mate's values and goals differ or are incongruent. This can be a way to uncover hidden potential stressors in your relationship.

Step 2: Clarifying Perceived Family Values and Goals

The process for exploring shared family values and goals is somewhat different. At this point, it is important to discuss with each other what each mate *perceives* to be the *current* family values and goals. To do this, we recommend that you both complete the following exercises independently.

Checking Out Family Values

Table 16.3 is a repeat of the values grid we used to evaluate personal and work values—but with a difference. This time each mate lists ten things you, as a couple or family, have done in the past year. Just jot them down as you think of them—again, anything goes.

Table 16.3

Activity or experience—Mate #1	1	2	3	4	5	6	7	8	9	10
Totals										

Activity or experience—Mate #2	1	2	3	4	5	6	7	8	9	10
Totals										

As before, numbers corresponding to some common values are listed along the top of the grid area. Under each number put a check in that column for each activity or experience you listed that involved the corresponding value in some way. For example, if you listed "took a vacation to Hawaii" as one of your activities, you would put a check by that activity in column 10 for "variety or thrill," maybe in column 1 for "love," and so on for all the values involved.

1. Love

2. Money

3. Growth or achievement

4. Recognition or reward

5. Self-esteem

6. Security

7. Independence

8. Self-expression

9. Leadership

10. Variety or thrill

After you both have thought through all ten activities, total the check marks in each value column. You will be able to see the relative stengths of your family values as you compare the number of times each of you have a check mark in each value column. Ask yourselves the following questions: Are the values what you thought they would be? Any value that got *more than four check marks should be considered very important* to your current frame of reference for your family, and any value that rated *more than eight check marks is critical* for your frame of reference for your family. Are the values you and your mate identified congruent? Are there any major areas of conflict?

This exercise always prompts interesting (and at times spirited) discussions between couples. It can be an eye-opening experience if you approach it from a learning perspective, and don't get bogged down in blaming or accusing each other. What you want to identify are values that may be in conflict with each other—so you know it up front, and can negotiate shared values a bit later on.

Five-Year Wish List for the Family.   This next exercise is a bit more complicated. Each partner needs to think about where he or she would like the family to be five years from now. Independently jot down the answers to the following questions: If you could have, do, or be anything or anywhere in the world, what would your ideal family life look like? What would the family be doing? Where would you be living? How would you be living? What would your social or community activities be? What would you do for fun?

Based on answers to these questions, each mate next tries to aggregate his or her thoughts into some sort of pattern. Using that pattern, each spouse lists which five components of the ideal family life are most important to him or her.

One-Year Wish List for the Family. Next, each partner needs to think about where he or she would like the family to be one year from now. Independently, jot down the answers to the following questions: If you could have, do, or be anything or anywhere in the world, what would your ideal family life look like? What would the family be doing? Where would you be living? How would you be living? What would your social or community activities be? What would you do for fun?

Again, based on answers to these questions, each mate next tries to aggregate his or her thoughts into some sort of pattern. Using that pattern, each spouse lists what five components of the ideal family life are most important to him or her.

Sharing Lists. Now comes the fun part! Exchange lists! Do the lists contain things you expected? How are they different? Are any of the top priorities incongruent or in conflict with other priorities? You can really learn a great deal about your partner through this exercise. Did you find out anything new, interesting, or surprising about your mate?

Step 3: Developing Shared Family Values and Goals

Once you have clarified personal and perceived family values and goals, it's time to develop a shared vision of where you want your family to be in life. This involves negotiating with each other over personal and perceived values and goals that are incongruent, celebrating existing shared values and goals, and coming up with a group of values you both are comfortable using to guide your life together.

Once that is done, we strongly recommend that you jointly come up with a five-year and one-year family goal, along with a plan outlining the steps you both need to take to achieve that goal. Look carefully to see that these new shared family goals are congruent with any personal or work goals each of you may have—you want to eliminate potential sources of stress and conflict. This process is not easy, and it may take some time to talk through all the feelings and issues that surround such an important topic for a couple, but the rewards are well worth it. Couples can move mountains if they are both pulling or pushing in the same direction!

Dealing with Fear

If you are not growing as a human being throughout your lifetime, you are stagnating. There are too many wonderful experiences available to you, just waiting out there, for you to sit back and say "this is as good as it gets, so I'm not going any further." Being stagnant is very stressful, because frustration and boredom lead to unhappiness. Growth can be stressful, too, especially in the beginning, because you are taking risks and making changes. But it is a good kind of stress, the kind that makes people stronger and happier.

Some people say it's just not their personality to take risks, and that they shouldn't behave counter to their personality. But no one has as a personality trait an inherent aversion to risk taking or to making changes. What these people are *really* saying is that they are *afraid* to take risks and make changes, and because of that fear they are stuck, stagnant, in their lives.

Taking risks, making changes, and making decisions do involve fear, and fear is something most of us try to avoid. Some people handle fear better than others, but everyone worries about it. In her book, *Feel the Fear and Do It Anyway*, Susan Jeffers says that we can be educated to understand how fear works, and hence become less afraid of fear.

She outlines three levels of fears that affect us when it comes to taking risks and making decisions.

1. First-level fears involve the surface story—things that happen to us, such as aging, becoming disabled, dying, illness, loss of financial security; and things that require action on our part, such as making decisions, changing careers, ending or beginning relationships, asserting oneself, and so on. New skills or knowledge can help us get over these fears and take the risk or make the decision.

2. Second-level fears involve our reactions to events *inside our heads*, such as rejection, success, being vulnerable, failure, loss of image, and so on. These fears mirror our self-image and self-esteem, and how we feel about our ability to handle our world. As our self-esteem and self knowledge increases, we may find that these fears aren't so scary after all.

3. Third-level fears are the big ones—the ones that hold us back from taking risks, from growing, from changing our lives, from expanding our worlds. The third level of fear is: *I can't handle it! At the bottom of all our fears is the simple fear that we can't handle whatever life may bring us.*

Think about that last sentence for a minute. If you can handle anything that comes your way, you have *nothing* to fear. What a powerful concept! It is powerful because it means that to diminish your fear of taking risk and making decisions, *all you need to do is to develop more trust in your ability to handle whatever comes your way.*

And how do you do that? You learn the *skills* that help you take calculated risks and make wise decisions. Skills are the secret to those two scary activities, risk taking and decision making. In the rest of this chapter we cover important skills as well as information that will help you feel more comfortable taking risks and making decisions.

But first we want to let you in on a few very important truths about fear that have been treated as secrets, and which Jeffers also covers in her book.

1. *Fear will never go away as long as we continue to grow and change.* Bet you don't want to believe this one, huh? But unfortunately it's true—fear will always be a part of your life when you make changes. It is a normal human reaction to the process of initiating change and trying new things for the first time. But most of us believe incorrectly that the fear should go away; and that, if we feel fear, we are doing something wrong or shouldn't be taking the risk or are making the wrong decision. So we start worrying and second-guessing ourselves, which makes everything that much worse. So think of it as a relief: You no longer have to work so hard at getting rid of fear!

2. *The only way to get rid of the fear of doing something is to go out and do it.* Bet you didn't want to hear that one, either! In many instances, *doing it* comes *before* the fear goes away. Think about that for a minute, and then think about scary things you've done in your life, for example, giving your first presentation to a large group of people, making your first sale, asking someone out for the first time, making love for the first time, having the first baby. What happened after you did each of those the first time? If you are like most people, the next time got easier, the third time was easier yet, and by now, while you may get a little nervous before you do it, *the fear is gone because you know you can handle it.*

3. *The only way to feel better about yourself is to go out and do something.* Once again, doing it comes before feeling better about yourself. You get a big bonus when you do something scary: After it's done, you get a big self-confidence boost. Think about that in your own life—remember how good you felt after the first time you drove a car, skied downhill, made a sale, or completed a cold call on a customer?

4. *Not only are we going to experience fear whenever we're on unfamiliar territory, but so is everyone else.* What this means is that all those people you have envied because they've made changes, taken risks, and made decisions were also afraid while they were going through it—just as you are. You're not different, or defective, or weird. You're just human. *But if others can do it, in spite of their fears, so can you.*

5. *Working through the fear is less frightening than living with the underlying fear that comes from a feeling of helplessness and the thought that we can't make it.* Reread that sentence and let the meaning sink in. No matter how safe we feel in our stagnant little pond, we live with the underlying fear that some day, some time, out of the blue, the day of reckoning will finally

come—the day that our worst "what if..." happens. Talk about a prime situation for stress overload! This is probably the worst! And the more helpless we feel, the greater are the fear and stress. So take heed, even a stagnant pond isn't a haven from stress!

But knowing these truths intellectually is not enough, you have to retrain yourself to think about fear in a new way. Jeffers recommends rereading these truths to yourself several times a day over several months, until they become part of you. And then you will find yourself starting to reverse your behaviors and moving *toward* your new goals, rather than staying stuck and stagnant and helpless.

Fear is not the problem; the problem is how we *perceive* the fear. We all hold the power within us to alter our perceptions. We can react differently to developments in our lives, we can get the skills we lack, and we can get the information we need to make calculated risks, wise decisions, and successful changes. The rest of this chapter helps you learn how to do just that.

Making Wise Decisions

Most people think of decisions in terms of good and bad, and right and wrong, with "right" or "good" decisions being those that turn out well, and "bad" or "wrong" decisions being those that don't turn out as expected. In reality there are no such creatures, decisions are of two kinds only: decisions that are arrived at using a definite process, and decisions that happen. Both types of decisions create paths through life that are strewn with opportunities. But one path, created by decisions arrived at using a definite process, may be less stressful overall.

Decisions that are arrived at using a definite process are wise decisions because deciders use a process that allows their values to come into play, carefully consider alternatives and options, and plan reassessment of the decision and its effects. Wise decisions don't always follow prevailing societal norms or expectations. They are right for the decider at the time they are made, given the information the decider has to work with at the time. *And that's all that matters!*

Ten Steps to Wise Decisions

The following outline can provide a framework for you to follow to make your own wise decision, and it can apply to any situation you need to make a decision about:

1. *Define exactly what the decision is that has to be made.* Is this a decision for you to make, or does the responsibility really belong to someone else? Do you really

have a decision to make? (Remember, you can't make a decision unless you have two or more options from which to choose. If you don't have at least two options, you need to learn to cope with the inevitable.) When does the decision have to be made? Whom does it involve? Why is it an important decision for you? What values does it involve for you?

2. *Write down all the alternatives you can imagine.* This sort of brainstorming can be extremely helpful. Jot down everything that comes into your head. Don't edit yourself—*everything* goes down on paper.

3. *Think about where you could get more information about possible alternatives.* If you were only able to come up with a few alternatives, it might be useful to think about possible sources for more information. The more information you have, the easier it is to create alternatives. Possible information sources might be friends, family members, community agencies, clergypersons, newspapers, books, magazines, and so on.

4. *Check them out!* Explore these additional sources and brainstorm again. List every new alternative as it comes into your head.

5. *Sort through your alternatives.* Once you have a completed list, you can begin to evaluate your alternatives systematically. Write down the values that would come into play for each alternative. Look to see which alternatives would let you involve the most values. Cross off the alternatives that don't fit into your personal value framework.

6. *Picture the outcomes.* For the alternatives that remain on your list, try to picture what possible outcomes could result from trying those alternatives. It helps to write these down, too.

7. *Sift for reality's sake.* Now go back over your possible outcomes and decide which ones are most likely to happen. Cross off those that most likely *won't* happen to you.

8. *What fits you?* Look over the remaining alternatives on your list along with their possible outcomes and determine which one(s) would be the most comfortable for you. This (or these) is (are) your "wise" decision(s). If you are very happy with an alternative, but not so happy with its probable outcome, this is a clue that the decision is not a wise one for you. You might dislike an alternative but be thrilled with its possible outcome: Be careful in this instance because chances are that this decision would not be wise for you, either. Most likely you will have to choose between the lesser of two evils. If you feel that you can live with both the alternative and the possible outcome, then you would be "wise" to follow it.

9. *Get to it!* Put your decision into action and, once you've made it, *stop worrying!* You have done your very best for the present. Remember, you can always change your mind! Very few decisions are ever carved in granite. You have the right to change your mind at a later date without owing anyone an explanation!

10. *Does it still work?* It is important to evaluate your decisions at specified times after you begin to get an idea of how the outcomes are shaping up. Think through whether the outcomes are what you expected, whether you are happy with them, and whether you want to leave the decision as it stands. If the decision

did not turn out as you planned, go through the previously outlined process again. Did you need more information? What values actually came into play? *Remember, there's no law·that says you can't change your mind.*

Common Decision-Making Mistakes

Looking Through Screens.   How we *perceive* a situation plays a big part in the kind and number of alternatives we are able to create in order to make a decision. Our information about any event or situation is filtered through a series of "screens." Each screen alters, distorts, or blocks out bits of information about the actual situation. How *much* each screen blocks out depends on: the strength and clarity of the values involved in the situation; the types of past experience we've had with similar situations; the kind and intensity of expectations we hold about the event; the culture and subculture that shaped our personalities and responses while we were children; and of hidden agenda personal gratifications or needs we want to get met in the situation.

All these serve to block out bits of the situation or event, so that *we never see the entire situation as it exists in reality!* There's nothing inherently wrong with this "screening" process, it is only human. But it can cause problems if the screens we place between ourselves and the situation block out helpful information or distort our perceptions of the event so much that what we *think* happened bears very little resemblance to what *actually* happened.

Compensating for Screens.   To compensate for this human weakness, we need to make every effort possible to increase our pool of resources, information, and alternatives when making decisions. The following suggestions might help you knock larger holes in your personal screens:

🖊 *Do not rely exclusively on "expert" information.* Remember, experts are human too, and they process *their* perceptions of events through the same types of screens you do. Seek out information from several sources to broaden your outlook.

🖊 *Be careful not to overestimate or underestimate the value of information you receive from others.* Our society has a tendency to *overestimate* advice or information given by physicians; parents; people of high rank, class, or status; the wealthy; the powerful; "experts" or "authorities"; people we respect; people who appear to "have it all together"—to name just a few. Ask yourself, "Do these people have a stake in my decision? Do they know only one side? What values might come into play for them?" In other words, *take everything with a grain of salt,* and, when in doubt, *get a second opinion.*

We have also been taught to *underestimate* information from the following sources: women; children; older people; people of lower rank, class, or status; the poor; people with limited formal education; people in certain professions such as the arts, blue-collar occupations, agriculture, social work, education, homemaking, and so forth—to name just a few. Our reaction is often, "What could *they* possibly know?" Many times they know quite a lot, and chances are they can add different "bits" of information to your total picture—because their screens are different. So when you start to discount a piece of advice, stop first and ask yourself *why* you are discounting it.

✔ *Listen to what you do* not *want to hear, as well as to what you expect or hope to hear.* Process everything that relates to your decision. When we're faced with a decision, it is amazing how selective our hearing can be! We are perfectly capable of tuning out anything we don't want to know or hear about, especially if we've settled on a risky alternative. But processing and considering the things you don't want to hear is important, because you just might be able to save yourself some grief that way.

✔ *Most importantly, listen to your feelings and gut reactions!* Your body doesn't lie! Have you ever made a decision and then gotten a stomach ache, headache, or even a feeling of apprehension? What outcome resulted from that decision? Was it negative or unhappy? If you've experienced something like that, you're not alone. Nearly everyone has had it happen at some time. Why did it happen? Our brains are remarkable creations. They are capable of picking up masses of information all the time through the screens we've erected. Because our conscious thought processes can't handle focusing on all that data at once, much of it gets filed away at a *preconscious* or *subconscious* level. For example, your conscious thought processes are involved with reading the words on the pages of this book and making sense of them for yourself. If you are concentrating deeply on this book, you may not be consciously aware of anything else. However, your brain is picking up and storing information on the temperature of the room, the amount of light available, traffic sounds from outside, whether or not you are getting hungry or sleepy, the texture of your clothes against your skin, how your chair seat feels, which muscles need to be moved, variations in air currents, and so on.

When you deal with people, your brain picks up and stores information on tone of voice, eye movements, choice of words, muscle tension, body position, and so on—without your being aware of it. Your brain stores away these bits of information as well. All this information stored at the preconscious level is sorted and organized, often while you're dreaming, and takes the shape of what we call intuition. Have you ever *known* something without understanding exactly how you knew it? That's your intuition at work. Intuitive thinking has been discredited by some people, but we think that's a real shame. In certain respects intuitive thinking may be more accurate than conscious thinking. Your conscious brain can be fooled, but your intuitive or preconscious brain cannot. So listen to those gut feelings—only very rarely are they off target!

Remember, *information is power.* Make sure you're getting full benefit from the power available to you. Anyone, and everyone, can make wise decisions, including you! And each subsequent decision gets easier. You may not have to use all the steps in this process for every decision you make, but for the major decisions—those that impact a number of values; affect other

people; involve large sums of money, your health, or well-being—the more
parts of the process you use, the wiser your decision will be!

Taking Smart Risks

The Myth of a Risk-Free Life

First, let us pass on a nugget of valuable information to you: *Life involves
uncertainty*. In today's world, people can't get away with setting up a life plan
for themselves when they are young and then sticking to that plan unwaver-
ingly for the rest of their lives. The world, business, lifestyles, and relationships are changing too rapidly for that to be feasible. You might be able
to get away with gambling less frequently if you are willing to give up some of
the goodies out there in the world, *but you cannot completely avoid taking a
chance*. Hence, all of us have to be able to take smart risks; and, therefore, all
of us have to learn how to manage this process so we don't jeopardize our
safety or mental health.

You need to understand that *all* decisions involve some level of danger,
because nothing is ever completely certain. Alternatives and options may be
more or less certain and, hence, more or less hazardous, but the outcome
from any decision can never be predicted with 100 percent accuracy. The
amount of risk any decision or alternative carries will vary from person to
person, depending on the person's resources, possible gains, possible losses,
and values involved. Only *you* can determine how much potential peril an
alternative or decision holds for you. This in turn determines in part the
desirability of that option for you.

Your Personal Risk-Tolerance Level

Everyone has a unique tolerance for risk. This intolerance level may vary for
different parts of our lives as well. For example, you may be willing to take
advantage of many new opportunities on the job, but feel very uncomfortable in situations that involve uncertainty with respect to your partner or
family. Tolerance for risk for any part of our lives is shaped by the following
seven components.

- *The resources at our disposal to use in coping with the situation and the alternatives
we create.*

- *Our socialization as children.* This includes the "shoulds" and "oughts" we were
taught as children concerning taking risks. Women have usually been taught *not* to
leap before they look, while men are taught to go for broke.

- *Our past experiences with similar situations.* If our past experiences with taking
risks were positive, we will be better able to tolerate higher levels of uncertainty in

new situations. If our past experiences were negative, we may not feel comfortable with new opportunities. That's okay, but it is important to know that up front, and to take it into account when considering new alternatives and options.

- *Our self-esteem.* If we feel good about ourselves and our abilities, we are more likely to trust our judgments of potential hazards in a situation, and be willing to tolerate higher levels of ambiguity in new situations.

- *Our support systems.* Support systems are important because they can help dilute the guesswork involved in a decision and any fear that results from taking a chance. Support systems are the friends and family members we can count on to help us through tough times while we wait to see how a decision turns out, or who can help us out if the decision doesn't turn out as we expected it would.

- *The number of people involved in making the decision.* The more people who share responsibility for making a decision, the less threatening that decision is for each person, because there is someone else to fall back on.

- *Responsibilities and obligations.* It stands to reason that the more responsibilities and obligations to others we have, the more careful we have to be in making decisions. You can't gamble and feel comfortable doing so when you know that other people are depending on you for their physical or psychological livelihood. People without families to support can be more daring than people with familial responsibilities.

Many people are uncomfortable taking risks. Doing so raises their stress levels, and they shy away from precarious situations. Most of the time this self-protective stance is realistic and sane, but sometimes our survival and growth may depend on making changes. In these cases such people lose out and end up being miserable.

Increasing Your Risk-Tolerance Levels

You can increase your tolerance of risk, however. The following suggestions can help:

- ✔ *Increase your resources.* Increase the skills, abilities, experiences, etc. that you have to fall back on.

- ✔ *Make a plan with a timetable.* A good plan and timetable give you direction and reinforce the belief that your plan is working. Your plan or timetable might be wrong, or may need to be changed once you see how things begin to turn out. But forcing yourself to go through the process of building a plan and a timetable can help you uncover hidden roadblocks and pitfalls, as well as give you an even clearer picture of what you are up against.

- ✔ *Get more practice taking risks.* The more you practice or use a behavior, the easier it becomes. It also gradually becomes less frightening. Think about the first time you ever drove a car. That was certainly scary and involved taking a chance! How did you feel? How do you feel now? You probably don't think that much about driving a car. You just do it. You can practice taking risks on a small scale every day and gradually increase your tolerance by doing things such as initiating contact with potential friends, doing more things on your own, asking to have your needs met, and so on. All these things can be a bit threatening, and when you learn that taking little steps can have positive rewards, big risks seem less overwhelming.

✔ *Strengthening your support system.* Talk about your feelings with friends, family members, and perhaps coworkers, letting them know what your needs for support are. Few people will turn down an honest request for support.

✔ *Involve other people in the decision-making process and talk about the peril involved.* In this way responsibility is shared, and the individual threat decreases. Understand fully the potential losses and gains, possible mistakes, and likely outcomes. Also understand your limits: Where you are willing to take a chance, and how much, and where won't you gamble, no matter what? That information is very important to have.

✔ *Clarify your obligations and responsibilities.* Many times we feel accountable for people and things that, in reality, are not our responsibility. Can you "weed out" any of your responsibilities?

✔ *Sort through your "shoulds" and "oughts."* Many of the "shoulds" and "oughts" we were taught as children were realistic *when we were children.* They may *not* be realistic for adults, living very different lives in very different times. Examine your personal "shoulds" and "oughts" concerning risk taking. Can you toss out any of them?

✔ *Increase your self-esteem.* Give yourself a pat on the back! Most of the time we focus only on our failures or negative points. Take some time to look at your successes and good points as well. Don't say you don't have any; you wouldn't have gotten this far in life if you didn't have at least a few!

Dos and Don'ts of Smart Risk-Taking

Okay, so you've decided to go for broke, and you've increased your resources. What then? In his book *Risking*, David Viscott shares some thoughts on the Dos and Don'ts of taking smart risks:

■ *Do have a goal.* This is so obvious, you'd think that people would just naturally think of it. But many people do not have a clear purpose, which is trouble from the start. How will you know when you have lost, or won?

■ *Do know the potential loss that could be involved.* If you rush into a decision without checking this out, you are not only naive, but stupid as well. If you don't fully understand what you could lose, loss will catch you by surprise and undermine your efforts. As Viscott says, "If you don't understand the loss, you don't understand the risk."

■ *Don't ignore the fear.* In the previous section we said that every change involves fear, and that you should feel the fear and do it anyway. This is true, but don't ignore fear that doesn't go away, or doesn't ebb after you have made your decision and lived with it for awhile. It may be a valuable signal to you that you are still in danger or that you are risking too much, given where you are in your life right now.

- *Don't count on being 100 percent successful.* No one is ever completely successful when they take a chance, because the ultimate outcome never completely matches the outcome we have pictured in our minds. If you expect the picture to match the reality, you will only be disappointed unnecessarily, and find yourself less willing to take a smart risk the next time.

- *Don't assume risk out of emotion.* This is important. Don't gamble out of fear, anger, hurt, guilt, or depression. Viscott says emotional chances should be taken only on emotional issues. In other words, don't act out your feelings, they only mess up your decision.

- *Do take time to correct mistakes.* Even when a plan is underway, mistakes can be fixed. Think of them as midcourse corrections, which can make a smart risk even smarter by compensating for errors you didn't know you had.

- *Don't give up too soon, but don't hang on forever.* As the song goes, "you have to know when to hold and know when to fold them." Taking risks is not easy; the process requires perseverance and patience—and faith that the outcome will happen as it was meant to be. We know this sounds rather "New Age-ish," but there is some truth to the statement. Sometimes the outcomes we least expect turn out to be the most wonderful of all.

  But, conversely, don't hang on past the point of pain. People just *know* when the cause is lost. You will too. At first blush, hanging on might seem to be better than letting go, but it never is. Let go and learn from the experience.

- *Don't take time out when you are executing your plan.* Many people make this big mistake. You might miss something important. As Viscott says, "when you are risking, you are risking, and that is all that is important. The secret of success in most risks is not letting up while there is something you can do to affect the outcome in a positive way or to limit losses."

Taking risks is not easy. It requires enormous courage, perseverance, and patience. But everyone has the power within to take smart risks, which can enlarge and enrich one's life. You can unleash that power, you can make the changes that are right for you, and you can handle the results!

17
Making and Living with Changes

Seeing the Effects of Change

This is the end of the book, but hopefully only the beginning of a happier and less stressful life for you! If you practiced, tried, and experimented with the ideas presented in this book and don't really feel any different yet, take heart. It takes awhile to incorporate major lifestyle modifications such as those we've suggested into your daily activities, and it may take some time before you notice any significant progress.

When It Gets Worse Before It Gets Better

Some people who have been under a great deal of stress without really being aware of it may actually find that things will get worse for a bit before they get better. That is only because they were not aware of the effect stress was having on them, and now that they understand what stress can do, they see it everywhere. If you create a package of coping techniques and work on the underlying causes, your symptoms and physical effects will eventually diminish. We wish we could say that any discomfort goes away completely, but that is impossible. Life will always involve some level of stress.

What to Expect When Making Changes

Whenever we encourage people to make major renovations in their lives, we want to make sure they know what to expect during that process. Some very common side effects occur, not all of them expected or pleasant, and you should be alerted to them in advance.

Reactions from Friends and Family

Here you are, all fired up and excited about the new adventure you have embarked on, which you (and we) believe will increase your health and happiness and decrease your stress levels. So why aren't the people closest to you as excited as you are, and supporting you in your efforts?

The people closest to you are used to interacting with you in a certain way, and having *you* react to *them* in predictable ways. You have rearranged this pattern, and you are evolving as a person. That is scary for people around you, and, inevitably, varying levels of upset result—not the least of which is the anger you may feel because, just as you are beginning to deal with the fears of moving forward, your cheering squad turns on you!

There are several reasons for this:

1. *Your family and friends may be afraid that if you continue to grow, you won't want or need them anymore.* They may even have a hidden interest in your previous stressed-out, weakened behavior. They may feel that they have a great deal to lose by the readjustments you are making. That can be a real fear for some people, and it may take awhile for them to come around to see that they also have much to gain.

In the meantime, they may try unconsciously to sabotage your efforts—by, for example, making you rich desserts when you are trying to cut back on fats and sweets; telling you that the exercise program you have embarked on won't be effective because it didn't work for someone else; or belittling your efforts at trying to modify your job or home situation. The best way to deal with this kind of situation is to let those close friends and family members know, in a diplomatic way, that you still love and need them, and that you hope they will come to be supportive to your efforts. Then just shut your ears to their negative comments and don't take the attempts at sabotage personally.

2. *Your close friends and family members may not know how best to support you right now, and may fall back on the ways they used to use to make you feel good*—like making you rich desserts! In this case, it is up to you to let them know clearly, *specifically* what they can do to help you execute your plan. This means you have to take some time to think through what you really need right now: Most of us know we need support when we rearrange our lives, but we expect those around us to be mind readers to determine how to provide it!

Most family members and friends are more than willing to help you, as long as you tell them *how*. If they are unable to provide the encouragement you have requested from them, for whatever reason, look elsewhere for that support.

3. *Your friends and family may be members of the "moan and groan" club.* Most of us are not aware that we are members of that club until we stop

moaning and groaning about work or our lives: It kind of becomes a habit, albeit a very negative one. Complaining may be working for your friends and family at this point in their lives. If that's the case, seek reinforcement elsewhere.

If you are lucky, your new motivation and commitment to change will rub off on your friends and family members. They may even join you on that journey. If that's so, terrific! Enjoy their backing, have fun, and go for it! But if not, read on.

Building a Support Network

Even if your family and friends turn out to be the best cheerleading squad a person could hope for, it is beneficial for you to begin to broaden your support system to include different kinds of people when you are living through a major remodeling of your life. At these times, you need people who will make you feel *wonderful* about yourself, and provide you with new information and insights to help keep you on the path you have chosen.

Where can you find new friends like this? Support groups are a great place to get lots of positive support for changes you are making. Your physician or clergyperson can probably provide you with referrals. There are self-help groups for people overcoming almost every kind of stress-related problem. A support group can even be a walking club, the people you work out with at the health club, or a hobby club. Wellness workshops, personal growth seminars, and evening classes are other good sources.

Friends who are a bit further along than you in transforming their lives can also be helpful. They can act as mentors and role models. Look and listen as you talk with people, and when someone says something that is intriguing to you, make a note of his or her name—and then *follow up*.

You must make the effort. You can't expect people to read your mind and decide to call you to initiate a friendship. Nothing is going to come to you, especially in the beginning. Most people are flattered that you think they manage stress well, and are more than willing to share helpful techniques and information with you. But you have to ask, you have to initiate, you have to take the risk! Isn't that a very small step compared with all the other advances you are already making?

What to Expect from Yourself

Wellness Bores.   You need to be aware of what we call the overcompensation syndrome. When people first begin to reshape their lives, they tend to go to extremes, adhering rigidly to their new patterns of behavior. That is normal and a necessary part of beginning to incorporate new behaviors into your life. But some people become very inflexible about the areas of their lives they are attempting to alter. Think of all of the people you know who quit smoking, and then, for the first several months afterwards, hassled everyone who smoked about their "nasty habit." See what we're getting at here?

If you find yourself getting a great deal of grief from friends and family, stop for a minute and take a hard look at your behavior. Are you overcompensating? You might be, and that's OK, because you probably aren't aware you are doing so. But if you find that you are going overboard, give your friends, family, and yourself a break by not taking yourself quite so seriously. Eventually your behaviors will moderate themselves, but if those behaviors are causing you aggravation, it may be best to consciously restrain them right away.

The *Real* Road to Growth

The path to successful modification of our lives is never easy or straightforward. We all expect that once we commit to the change and take the risk, we will be able to execute according to plan. It doesn't work that way. The road proceeds in fits and starts, with lots of zig zags. For every three steps forward you take, you will feel that you take one or two steps backward. You may also find that you slip back into your old behaviors from time to time.

It's frustrating, but that's the way human beings advance. We're not computers or machines, we can't be programmed to evolve precisely on schedule along a predetermined path. Humans are fallible. To be honest, if we don't see occasional setbacks or slip ups in behavior, we start to worry that the new activities the person has started, whatever they are, are not truly significant for him or her. Real changes are messy! So be kind to yourself, give yourself a break, and try to go with the flow!

The Pace of Change

Expect that change will be very slow, and sometimes it may feel like you aren't making any progress. There is no way to speed up the process. It won't all happen in a month, in two months—it may not even happen in a year! But it does happen, and everyone's pace and timing is different. So don't be discouraged if a friend or colleague seems to be making more headway than you are. If you are really worried, talk with a physician or mentor about it—someone who can help you see the big picture again, and show you that you are still on track.

When You Feel Overwhelmed

From time to time you may feel overwhelmed by the enormity of the reconstruction you have undertaken. If that happens, you may be attempting too much too soon. Remember, "inch by inch is a cinch, yard by yard is too hard." You have to walk before you can run. If your new behavior feels too difficult and you think of giving up, check to see whether you can break the change down into more manageable steps. Your likelihood of success will be greater!

When *Not* to Initiate Change

When Your Life Is in Turmoil

As much as we value lifestyle reform, we do believe that there are times when it is not a good idea. Change requires energy, *tremendous* amounts of energy, and sometimes when we have a great deal going on in our lives that we cannot control, we may not have the resources we need to readjust successfully. Attempting the change would simply result in frustration. As long as your physician believes that your health is not negatively impacted by not initiating and following through with the new behavior, it may be wiser to wait a bit until things calm down. You have lots of time, and you can choose exactly when you want to start transforming yourself—and that is OK.

When You Are Already Making Changes

If you have already begun major renovations in one area of your life, we think it is unwise to start altering other areas. This is partly because of the "energy thing," but also because making changes and taking risks requires that you be very focused and intent on executing your plan. By attempting too much, you scatter your focus and make it impossible to be fully conscious of what you are doing.

Unfortunately, many people decide to overhaul their entire lives, all at once, rather than make changes one at a time. Invariably, no readjustment succeeds, the person gets terribly frustrated, and turns off on the process.

As long as your physician believes there is no threat to your health, do yourself a favor. Change one aspect of your life at a time. You'll experience less stress, the process will be easier, and you will have a much greater chance of being successful.

The True Role of Stress in Life

We hope you will come to appreciate stress as a great growth producer, pushing you to try new things, take risks, and continue developing and evolving as a human being. Stress can be a very positive force in our lives, once we determine what our individual, unique optimal level of stress is—that level of stress that keeps us active, on our toes, and involved in life, but doesn't overwhelm us or tire us out. Harnessing the energy it produces will help you accomplish great things.

If you picked up this book even though you weren't experiencing very much stress or many of its symptoms, we hope you've learned how to prevent yourself from ever reaching serious overload levels. By taking care of your body, maintaining high levels of wellness, and expanding both your self-knowledge and your bag of tricks, you can create the optimum conditions for your continued growth and development as a human being.

If nothing else, we hope this book brought you a few chuckles and made you think about a new idea—at least once! If we've been able to accomplish that through this book, all the hours we've spent and the stress we've experienced writing it have been worth it!

Keep growing!

Good Reads

American Medical Association. *Encyclopedia of Medicine.* New York: Random House, 1989.

Andre, R. *Positive Solitude: A Practical Program for Mastering Loneliness and Achieving Self-Fulfillment.* New York: HarperCollins, 1991.

Babcock, D. E. and T. D. Keepers. *Raising Kids OK.* New York: Avon, 1976.

Bach, G. R. and R. M. Deutsch. *Pairing: How to Achieve Genuine Intimacy.* New York: Avon, 1970.

Bach, G. R. and R. M. Deutsch. *Stop! You're Driving Me Crazy.* New York: Putnam, 1979.

Baldridge, L. with S. Gelles-Cole. *Letitia Baldrige's Complete Guide to Executive Manners.* New York: Rawson Associates, 1985.

Bardwick, J.M. *The Plateauing Trap: How to Avoid It in Your Career and Your Life.* New York: AMACOM, 1986.

Bepko, C. and J. Krestan. *Too Good for Her Own Good: Breaking Free from the Burden of Female Responsibility.* New York: Harper & Row, 1990.

Berne, E. *Beyond Games and Scripts.* New York: Grove Press, 1976.

Blonder, T. J. *For Goodness' Sake: An Eating Well Guide to Creative Low-Fat Cooking.* Charlotte, VT: Camden House Publishing, Inc., 1990.

Brody, J. *Jane Brody's Nutrition Book; Jane Brody's Good Food Gourmet.* New York: Bantam Books.

Comfort, A. *Joy of Sex; More Joy of Sex.* New York: Simon & Schuster.

Cooper, K. H. *Aerobics for Women; The Aerobics Way; The New Aerobics.* New York: Bantam, 1979.

Davis, J. T. *Walking!* New York: Bantam, 1979.

Deal, T. E. and A. A. Kennedy. *Corporate Cultures: The Rites and Rituals of Corporate Life.* New York: Addison-Wesley Publishing Compapny, Inc., 1982.

Dubin, J. A. and M. R. Keveles. *Fired for Success.* New York: Warner Books, 1990.

Ellis, A. *How to Stubbornly Refuse to Make Yourself Miserable About Anything.* New York: Carol Publishing Group, 1988.

Fassell, D. *Working Ourselves to Death.* New York: Harper & Row, 1990.

Fixx, J. *The Complete Book of Running; Second Book of Running.* New York: Random House.

Fonda, J. *Women Coming of Age.* New York: Simon & Schuster, 1984.

Frederickson, L. *Confronting Mitral Valve Prolapse Syndrome.* San Marcos, CA: Avant Books, 1988.

Friel, J. and L. Friel. *An Adult Child's Guide to What's "Normal."* Deerfield Beach, FL: Health Communications, Inc., 1990.

Grundy, S. M., ed. *The American Heart Association Low-Fat Low-Cholesterol Cookbook*. New York: Times Books, 1989.

Jeffers, S. *Feel the Fear and Do It Anyway*. New York: Fawcett Columbine, 1987.

Kinder, M. *Going Nowhere Fast: Step Off Life's Treadmills and Find Peace of Mind*. New York: Prentice-Hall Press, 1990.

King, P. *Never Work for a Jerk!* New York: Dell Publishing, 1987.

Koltnow, E. and L. S. Dumas. *Congratulations! You've Just Been Fired*. New York: Fawcett Columbine, 1990.

Leinberger, P. and B. Tucker. *The New Individualists*. New York: HarperCollins, 1991.

Mayer, J. I. *If You Haven't Got the Time to Do it Right, When Will You Find the Time to Do It Over?* New York: Simon & Schuster, 1990.

McGee-Cooper, A. *You Don't Have to Go Home From Work Exhausted!* Dallas, TX: Bowen & Rogers, 1990.

Mirkin, G. *Mirkin Report: A Journal of Fitness, Nutrition, and Health* (monthly). Silver Spring, MD.

Peck, M. S. *The Road Less Traveled*. New York: Simon & Schuster, 1978.

Phillips, L. and W. Phillips with L. Rogers. *The Concise Guide to Executive Etiquette: Absolutely Everything You Need to Know About Business Protocol*. New York: Doubleday, 1990.

Saltzman, A. *Down-Shifting: Reinvesting Success on a Slower Track*. New York: HarperCollins Publishers, 1991.

Satir, V. *The New Peoplemaking*. Palo Alto, CA: Science and Behavior Books, 1988.

Selye, H. *The Stress of Life*, rev. ed. New York: McGraw-Hill, 1976.

Sills, J. *A Fine Romance: The Passage of Courtship from Meeting to Marriage*. New York: Ballantine Books, 1987.

Smith A. and W. Reid. *Role-sharing Marriage*. New York: Columbia Press, 1986.

Smith, M. J. *When I Say No, I Feel Guilty*. New York: Bantam, 1975.

Spear, R. *Low Fat and Loving It: How to Lower Your Fat Intake and Still Eat the Foods You Love*. New York: Warner Books, 1991.

Steiner, C. *Scripts People Live*. New York: Bantam, 1975.

Stoddard, A. *Living a Beautiful Life*. New York: Random House, 1986.

Tannen, D. *You Just Don't Understand: Women and Men in Conversation*. New York: Ballantine Books, 1990.

University of California School of Public Health. *University of California at Berkeley Wellness Letter: The Newsletter of Nutrition, Fitness, and Stress Management*. Berkeley, CA.

Viscott, D. *Risking*. New York: Pocket Books, 1977.

Winston, S. *Getting Organized: The Easy Way to Bring Order into Your Life*. New York: W.W. Norton & Co., Inc., 1978.

Winston, S. *The Organized Executive: New Ways to Manage Time, Paper, and People*. New York: Warner Books, 1983.

Woititz, J. G. *Marriage on the Rocks; Struggle for Intimacy; The Self-Sabotage Syndrome; Adult Children in the Workplace*. Deerfield, FL: Health Communications, Inc.

Wurman, R. S. *Information Anxiety*. New York: Doubleday, 1990; *The Passage of Courtship from Meeting to Marriage*. New York: Ballantine Books, 1987.

Index

Acquired immune deficiency syndrome
(AIDS), anxiety about catching, 281
Acute stress, 30
Adult acne:
causes of, 258-259
treatments for, 259-260
when to see your physician about, 260
Aerobics, 169-170
hyperventilation and, 269
mitral valve prolapse syndrome and,
271
Affirmations, 196-197
Alarm phase, general adaptation syndrome (GAS), 31
Alcohol, 160
abuse of, 273-274
depression and, 223
gastroesophageal reflux and, 263
hypertension and, 240
insomnia and, 211
jet lag and, 110
mitral valve prolapse syndrome and,
271
See also Substance abuse
Allergies, 224, 234
hand eczema and, 257
Amphetamines, abuse of, 275-276
Anatomy of an Illness (Cousins), 184-185
Anger:
causes of, 290-291
cycle of, breaking, 293
harnessing, 296
individual reactions to, 291-293
power analysis, 291
someone else's, coping with, 295
structuring responses to, 294-295
Anorexia nervosa, 232
Antidepressants, 222
abuse of, 276
Appetite, lack of, 232
Assertiveness, 301-305
personal bill of rights, 301-302
putting to work, 302-303

Assertiveness (*Cont.*):
tips/tricks, 303-305
Asthma, stress and, 286-287
Atopic eczema, 256
Audiotapes:
business information, 112
progressive muscle relaxation and, 190
visualization and, 202
Autonomous professionals, 45

Baby boomers:
downshifting by, 152-153
as employees, 56-57, 67-68
Baby busters, as employees, 56
Backaches:
doctor hopping and, 253
lower, 250-251
treatments for, 251-252
upper, 250
when to see your physician about, 252-
253
See also Massage
Becoming Thick-Skinned (Witte), 195
Beef, 157
Behavioral rehearsal, 175-176
mitral valve prolapse syndrome and,
271
Behavior styles, management, 58
Best-friend bosses, 64
Bet-the-Company Organizations, 25, 48-
49
Biofeedback:
headaches and, 238
mitral valve prolapse syndrome and,
271
therapist, relationship with, 177-178
types of, 176-177
"Biological clock," anxiety about, 281-282
Biological depression, 220
Bosses:
difficult bosses, identifying, 63-65
managing, 63-66
tactics for, 65-66

Breakfast, 158
  recommended cereals, 159
Breathing exercises, 178-179
  hyperventilation and, 269
Broken record technique, 304
Bruxism:
  definition of, 241-242
  treatments for, 242-243
Bulimia, 233
Bureaucratic Organizations, 25-26, 49
Burn out, 116-124
  causes/cures, 119-120
  definition of, 116
  dysfunctional family members and, 121-
    124
    myths about workplace/working rela-
      tionships, 122-124
    struggle for workplace success, 121
  reactions to, 118-119
  symptoms of, 117-118
Burn Out Checklist, 21-22
  scoring, 22
Business environment:
  changing, 45-46
  stress-management techniques and, 2
Business travel, 102-110
  jet lag, dealing with, 109-110
  preparing for, 103-106
  surviving, 106-109
Butter/margarine, 157

Caffeine, 159, 173
  fatigue and, 216, 217
  gastroesophageal reflux and, 263
  insomnia and, 211
  in pain relievers, 239
  See also Coffee
Calcium, 166
Canker sores, 261
Cautious behavior style (Type C), man-
    agement, 58
Chameleon bosses, 64
Changes:
  pace of, 339
  reactions from friends/family, 337-338
  seeing effects of, 336
  support network, building, 338-340
  when not to initiate, 340-341
Chest pain:
  causes of, 227
  treatments for, 229
  when to see your physician about, 229-
    230

Chocolate:
  gastroesophageal reflux and, 263
  insomnia and, 211
  migraine headaches and, 236
Cholesterol, 156
Chromium, 167
Chronic diseases, effect of stress on, 286-
  287
Chronic (endogenous) depression, 220-
  221
Chronic fatigue syndrome (CFS), 215
Chronic stress, 30-31, 34, 35, 173-174
Chronic Stress Pattern, 34, 35
Clenching teeth, 242
Clicking teeth, 242
Cobalt, 167
Cocaine, 276-277
Codeine, 276
Coffee, 159-160, 192
  fatigue and, 216, 217
  gastroesophageal reflux and, 263
  See also Caffeine
Cold sores, 260-261
Communication, 296-301
  breakdowns:
    analyzing, 297-298
    preventing, 298-300
  filters, 297
  as learned skill, 296
  mixed messages, dealing with, 300
Company Culture Checklist, 22-26, 47
  scoring, 25-26
Company cultures:
  Bet-the-Company Organizations, 25, 48-
    49
  bottom line on, 49-50
  Bureaucratic Organizations, 25-26, 49
  identifying, 46-49
  importance of, 46-47
  Tough-Guy Organizations, 25, 26, 46,
    47, 49
  Work Hard/Play Hard Organizations,
    25, 48
Compartmentalizing, 120
Competition, 51-54
  couples, 139
Complex carbohydrates, 157
  at breakfast, 158
Computerization, 113-115
Content plateaus, 70-73
  boredom/"blahs," dealing with, 71-73
Control, feelings of, perceptions of stress
  and, 40

Coping, determinants of, 32-33
Coping Behavior Checklist, 7-9
  scoring, 9
Coping techniques:
  behavioral rehearsal, 175-176
  biofeedback, 176-178
  breathing exercises, 178-179
  crying, 182-183
  family/friends/supporters, 180-182
  guilty pleasures, 183-184
  hobbies/leisure activities, 179-180
  hugs, 184
  humor, 184-185
  journals/diaries, 185-186
  massage, 186-188
  meditation, 188-189
  progressive muscle relaxation, 189-190
  rewards, 190-191
  rituals, 191-193
  self-talks, 193-197
  support and self-help groups, 199-200
  therapy, 198-201
  twelve-step programs, 200-201
  visualization, 201-204
  weekends/vacations, 204-205
  worrying, 205-206
Copper, 167
*Corporate Cultures: The Rite and Rituals of
  Corporate Life* (Deal/Kennedy), 47
Corporate professionals, 43-44
Couples:
  daily living, chores of, 137-138
  dual-career, definition of, 131
  money, 136-137
  relationships/friendships, 138-139
    competition, 139
    power conflicts, 138-139
    separate activities/friendships, 139
  work time vs. personal time, 131-136
    career changes, 132-133
    making transitions between work/
      home, 133-135
    managing two careers, 131-132
    time management, 135-136
  See also Working parents
Credit monger bosses, 64
Crying, as coping technique, 182-183

Daily living chores:
  couples, 137-138
  singles, 128-129
Dangerous Stress Pattern, 35-36, 173-174
Death, as stress reaction, 38

Decision making, 328-332
  mistakes, 330-332
  screens:
    compensating for, 330-332
    looking through, 330
  wise decisions, ten steps to, 328-330
Denial, as stress reaction, 37
Depression, 37, 217-22
  alcohol and, 223
  biological, 220
  the blahs, 217-218
  the blues, 218-219
  chronic (endogenous), 220-221
  exercise and, 221
  fatigue and, 214
  grief-related (exogenous), 218
  -induced headaches, 235
  insomnia and, 212
  mitral valve prolapse syndrome and,
    271
  psychological, 219-220
  tranquilizers and, 223
  treatments for, 221
  when to see your physician about, 221-
    223
Dermatitis, 256-261
  over-the-counter medications and, 258
  seborrheic, 256
  when to see your physician about, 257
  See also Adult acne; Eczema; Skin prob-
    lems
Diabetes mellitus, stress and, 286-287
Diaries, as coping technique, 185-186
Diet, 156-168
  alcohol, 160
  beef, 157
  breakfasts, 158
  butter/margarine, 157
  B vitamins, 156
  caffeine, 159, 173
  cholesterol, 156
  complex carbohydrates, 157
  depression and, 221
  eggs/egg yolks, 157
  fiber, 158
  fish, 157
  fruit, raw, 157, 158
  integrating changes into lifestyle, 160-
    162
  luncheon meats, 157
  migraine headaches and, 236
  mitral valve prolapse syndrome and,
    271

Diet (*Cont.*):
  organ meats, 157
  peanut butter, 157
  polyunsaturated oils, 157
  pork, 157
  poultry, 157
  processed foods, 156, 158
  salt, 156, 158
  stimulant contents of foods/beverages, 161-162
  sugar, 156, 158, 271
  theobromine, 159
  theophylline, 159
  vegetables, raw, 157, 158
  vitamins/minerals, 162-168
  whole milk products, 158
Difficult bosses, identifying, 63-65
Discrimination, 68-69
Diversion, as stress reaction, 37
Do-it-yourself stress assessment, *See* Stress assessment
Dominant behavior style (Type D), management, 58
Downshifting, 152-153
Downsizing/layoffs, overseeing, 60-61
Drug abuse, 37, 274-277
  amphetamines, 275-276
  antidepressants, 276
  mind-altering drugs, 276-277
  mood-altering drugs, 276
  sleeping pills, 274
  tranquilizers, 274-75
  See also Substance abuse
Dual-career couples, *See* Couples
Dysfunctional eating:
  anorexia nervosa, 232
  bulimia, 233
  lack of appetite, 232
  overeating, 230-231
  when to see your physician about, 233-234
Dysfunctional family members:
  burn out and, 121-124
    struggle for workplace success, 121-124
    workplace/working relationships myths, 122-124
  common myths of, 149-151
  struggle for intimacy, 148-149

Eczema:
  atopic, 256
  hand, 257

Eczema (*Cont.*):
  nummular, 256
  over-the-counter medications and, 258
  when to see your physician about, 257
Eggs/egg yolks, 157
Egomaniac bosses, 65
Electrodermal (EDR) biofeedback, 177
Electromyographic (EMG) biofeedback, 177
Electronic mail system, turning on prioritization features of, 114
Emotional exhaustion, burn out and, 117
Employees:
  age differences in, 56-57
  behavior styles, 58
  cultural differences in, 57-58
Energy level, as coping determinant, 33
Environment, as coping determinant, 32-33
Erectile dysfunction (impotence), 280
Exercise/physical fitness:
  aerobics, 169-170
  backache and, 252
  benefits to body/well-being, 168
  depression and, 221
  fatigue and, 216
  fitness activities, combining, 169
  hypertension and, 240
  insomnia and, 211
  irritable bowel syndrome (IBS) and, 246
  jet lag and, 110
  matched to personality types, 171
  maximum predicted heart rate, figuring, 171-172
  mitral valve prolapse syndrome and, 271
  sore muscles and, 249-250
  strain, avoiding, 170
  upper respiratory infections/flu and, 225
  walking, 170
  warnings about, 168-170
Exhaustion phase, general adaptation syndrome (GAS), 32
Exogenous depression, 218
Eyestrain, headaches and, 237-238

Face massage, 186-187
Family relationships, 180-182
Family values/goals:
  evaluating, 320-325
  five-year wish list, 324-325
  one-year wish list, 325

Family values/goals (*Cont.*):
  perceived, clarifying, 321-324
  personal values/goals, clarifying, 321
  shared, developing, 325
  sharing lists, 325
  values grid, 322-323
Fat:
  at breakfast, 158
  gastroesophageal reflux and, 263
  irritable bowel syndrome (IBS) and, 245
Fatigue, 213-217
  caffeine and, 217
  chronic fatigue syndrome (CFS), 215
  mitral valve prolapse syndrome and,
    271
  pathological, 214
  physiological, 214
  psychological, 214-215
  treatments for, 216
  when to see your physician about, 216
  See also Depression; Insomnia; Sleep
Faux and spurious illnesses, 287-289
  diagnosis, need for, 288-289
  hypoglycemia, 287
  premenstrual syndrome (PMS), 288
  systemic yeast infections, 287
Fear:
  dealing with, 326-328
  See also Panic attacks
Feel the Fear and Do It Anyway (Jeffers),
  196
Fertility issues, anxiety about, 281-282
Fiber, 158, 159
  irritable bowel syndrome (IBS) and, 245
Fibromyositis, 248-249
Fifty Plus-ers, as employees, 57
Fish, 157
Five-year wish list:
  for family, 324-325
  for reaching personal goals, 316
Flexible work schedules, 144
Flu, *See* Upper respiratory infections/flu
Fluid intake, mitral valve prolapse syn-
    drome and, 271
Fluorine, 167
Fogging, 304
Folacin, 166
Foot massage, 187
Freelancing, 144
Fruit:
  at breakfast, 158
  raw, 157, 158

Gastritis, 262
Gastroesophageal reflux (GER), 36, 227,
    262-265
  symptoms of, 263
  treatment for, 263-264
  when to see your physician about, 264-
    265
General adaptation syndrome (GAS), 209,
    273
  coping determinants, 32-33
  phases of, 31-32
  short-circuiting, 33
Generally incompetent bosses, 64
Gentle assertiveness, *See* Assertiveness
GER, *See* Gastroesophageal reflux (GER)
Glass ceiling, 68-69
Glucocorticoids, 31
"Going crazy," as stress reaction, 37
Grief-related (exogenous) depression, 218
Grinding, teeth, 242
Guilty pleasures:
  as coping technique, 183-184
  depression and, 221
  personal checklist of, 184

Hand eczema, 257
Hazardous Stress Pattern, 35, 36
Headaches:
  aspirin and, 238-239
  depression-induced, 235
  migraine, 236-237
  pain relievers and, 239
  simple, 234
  sinus (sinusitis), 235-236
  tension, 234-235
  treatments for, 237-238
  when to see your physician about, 238-
    239
Head massage, 187
Health level, as coping determinant, 32
Heartburn, 262-263
Heredity, as coping determinant, 32
Heroin, 276
Hidden Agenda (Potash), 305
High blood pressure, *See* Hypertension
Hobbies:
  as coping technique, 179-180
  depression and, 221
Home-based work, 144
Hugs, as coping technique, 184
Humor, as coping technique, 184-185
Hypertension:
  episodes, logging, 270

Hypertension (*Cont.*):
   medication and, 241
   stress and, 286-287
   treatments for, 240
   uncontrolled, 239-240
   when to see your physician about, 240
Hyperventilation:
   treatments for, 269-270
   when to see your physician about, 270
Hypoglycemia, stress and, 287

IBS, *See* Irritable bowel syndrome (IBS)
Illness, as stress reaction, 37-38
Imagery, mitral valve prolapse syndrome
      and, 271
Impotence, 280
Influencing behavior style (Type I), man-
      agement, 58
Information Anxiety (Wurman), 110
Information overload, 110-113
   coping with, 111-113
Insomnia:
   causes of, 211
   definition of, 210
   over-the-counter/prescription sleeping
      medications, 213
   treatments for, 211-212
   when to see your physician about, 212-
      213
   See also Fatigue; Sleep
Iodine, 167
Iron, 167
Irritable bowel syndrome (IBS):
   antidiarrhea medications and, 246
   definition of, 243-244
   fad diets and, 246-247
   laxatives and, 246
   symptoms of, 244
   treatment for, 244-246
   when to see your physician about, 246-
      247

Jane Fonda's Fitness Walkout, 170
Jane Fonda's Prime Time Walkout, 170
*Jane Fonda's Stretch and Stress Reduction
      Program*, 190
Jaw problems:
   bruxism, 241-242
   temporomandibular joint syndrome
      (TMJ), 242
   treatments for, 242-243
   when to see your physician about, 243
Jekyll-and-Hyde bosses, 64-65

Jet lag, dealing with, 109-110
Job hunting, 82-83
Jobs:
   redesigning, 119-120
   stages of, 116-117
Job sharing, 144
Job splitting, 144
Journals, as coping technique, 185-186

Karoshi, 38

Lack of appetite, 232
Lactose intolerance, 245
Layoffs:
   causes of, 73
   compared to being fired, 77
   feelings associated with, 77-78
   overseeing, 60-61
   surviving, 80, 85-87
      adjusting to larger workload, 87-88
      developing person plan B, 89
      employers and, 89-90
      using coping techniques, 88-89
   See also Reductions in force (RIFs); Ter-
      minations
Leisure activities, as coping techniques,
      179-180
Life Experience and Hassles Checklist, 15-
      18
Life Satisfaction Checklist, 12-15
Living a Beautiful Life (Stoddard), 191
Lower backaches, 250-251
Lower gastrointestinal tract problems:
   irritable bowel syndrome (IBS), 243-247
   ulcerative colitis, 36, 247
LSD, 276
Luncheon meats, 157

Magnesium, 167
Management:
   behavior styles of, 58
   bosses, managing, 63-66
   developing new mind set, 54-56
   downsizing/layoffs, overseeing, 60-61
   employees, 56-66
      age differences in, 56-57
      cultural differences in, 57-58
   in stress-intensive environments, 54-66
   terminations, 62
Manganese, 167
Marijuana, 276-277
Massage:
   face, 186-187

Massage (*Cont.*):
    feet, 187
    head, 187
    headaches and, 238
    neck, 188
    shoulders, 188
    sore muscles and, 249
    upper back, 188
Meditation, 188-189
    mitral valve prolapse syndrome and,
        271
Menopause, 285-286
Menstrual irregularities, 247-248
Mental exhaustion, burn out and, 117-118
Midlife crisis, 284-285
Migraine headaches, 236-237
Milk, 158
    insomnia and, 212
    upper gastrointestinal tract problems
        and, 265-266
Mind-altering drugs, abuse of, 276-277
Minerals, 162-168
    calcium, 166
    chromium, 167
    cobalt, 167
    copper, 167
    fluorine, 167
    folacin, 166
    iodine, 167
    iron, 167
    magnesium, 167
    manganese, 167
    molybdenum, 167
    nickel, 167
    pantothenic acid, 166
    phosphorous, 166
    potassium, 168
    selenium, 167
    silicon, 167
    sodium, 168
    supplements, choosing, 163-164
    tin, 167
    vanadium, 167
    zinc, 167
    See also Diet; Vitamins
Minorities:
    glass ceiling/discrimination, 68-69
    stress and, 59
Mitral valve prolapse syndrome (MVP),
        270-273
    doctor hopping and, 272
    medications:
        dosage adjustments to, 272-273

Mitral valve prolapse syndrome (MVP)
    medications (*Cont.*):
        mixing, 273
    treatments for, 271-272
    when to see your physician about, 272
Mixed messages, dealing with, 300
Molybdenum, 167
Money:
    couples, 136-137
    singles, 128
Mood-altering drugs, abuse of, 276
Morphine, 276-277
Mouth sores:
    canker sores, 261
    cold sores, 260-261
Muscle spasms, 248
Musculoskeletal complaints:
    backaches, 250-253
    repetitive stress injuries, 253-256
    sore muscles, 248-250
MVP, *See* Mitral valve prolapse syndrome
    (MVP)

Narcolepsy, 214
Nature Company, Environmental Sound
    Recordings, 202
Neck massage, 188
Negative assertion, 304
Negative inquiry, 3-4
Negative manipulators, 54
Nervous indigestion, 262
Neurodermatitis, See Eczema
New Peoplemaking, The (Satir), 300
Nickel, 167
Nummular eczema, 256
Nutrition, *See* Diet

One-on-one therapy, 198-199
One-year wish list:
    for family, 325
    for reaching personal goals, 316
On-line data sources, 112
Optimal Stress Pattern, 34
Organ meats, 157
Orgasmic dysfunction, 280
Overcompensating syndrome, 338-339
Overeating, 230-231
Overweight:
    backache and, 252
    gastroesophageal reflux and, 263

Panic attacks:
    definition of, 267

Panic attacks (*Cont.*):
  mitral valve prolapse syndrome and, 271
  stressors that trigger, 267-268
  when to see your physician about, 268
  See also Fear
Pantothenic acid, 166
Parents, *See* Working parents
Part-time work, 144
Pathological fatigue, 214
Peanut butter, 157
Peptic ulcers, 36, 265
Perceptions of stress:
  factors affecting, 38-40
  mechanism of, 40-42
Personal exhaustion point, 32
Personal goals:
  reassessing, 318-320
  setting, 316-320
    five-year wish list, 316
    one-year wish list, 316
    "things I do well" list, 317
    "things I'd rather forget" list, 318
Personality style, stress-management techniques and, 2-3
Personality Type Checklist, 26-29
  scoring, 28-29
Personal relationships, coping and, 180-182
Personal stress, causes of, 3
Personal values:
  clarifying, 321
  evaluating, 309-316
Pets, stress and, 182
Phosphorous, 166
Physical exhaustion, burn out and, 117
Physical fitness, *See* Exercise/physical fitness
Physiological fatigue, 214
Physiological side of stress, 30-33
  acute stress, 30
  chronic stress, 30-31
  reactions/general adaptation syndrome (GAS), 31-32, 38
  stress patterns, 34-36
  stress reactions, 36-38
Plateauing, 67-115
  business travel, 102-110
  computerization, 113-115
  content, 70-73
  information overload, 110-113
  promotions, 90-98
  reductions in force, surviving, 73-90

Plateauing (*Cont.*):
  relocations/transfers, 98-102
  structural, 67-70
Pleasant-scene exercise, 201-202
Politics, 51-54
  win-win politics, 53-54
Polyunsaturated oils, 157
Pork, 157
Positive Solitude (Andre), 126
Potassium, 168
Poultry, 157
  insomnia and, 212
Power, 51-54
Power analysis, 291
Power conflicts, couples, 138-139
Premature ejaculation, 280
Premenstrual syndrome (PMS), stress and, 288
Priorities, reassessing, 120
Processed foods, 156, 158
Professional type, determining, 43-45
Progressive muscle relaxation, 189-190
  hypertension and, 240
  hyperventilation and, 269
  mitral valve prolapse syndrome and, 271
Promotions, 90-98
  authority, handling, 92-93
  impostor phenomenon, 96-97
  leaving old job, 93-94
  managing, 90
  new position, adjusting to, 90-92
  old peers, managing, 94-96
  power and, 52-53
  transition, handling, 93
  turning down, 97-98
Protein, at breakfast, 158
Psychoacoustics, 202
Psychological depression, 219-220
Psychological fatigue, 214-215

Quaaludes, 276

Reductions in force, surviving, 73-90
Reductions in force (RIFs):
  developing "plan B," 74-77
  finances, managing, 81-82
  job hunting, 82-83
  personal life, 84-85
  severance package, negotiating, 78-80
  signs of, 74
  what to expect from, 77-78
  See also Layoffs

Relationships/friendships:
  couples, 138-139
  singles, 129-130
  working parents, 146-147
Relocations/transfers:
  children, impact on, 99-101
  disruption of, 98-99
  pros/cons, clarifying, 101-102
Repetitive stress injuries:
  avoiding, 254
  definition of, 253-255
  treatments for, 255
  when to see your physician about, 255-256
Resistance phase, general adaptation syndrome (GAS), 31-32
Resources, perceptions of stress and, 39
Retin-A, adult acne and, 260
Rewards, as coping technique, 190-191
Rheumatoid arthritis, stress and, 286-287
"Risk creators," 71-73
Risk taking, 332-335
  dos/don'ts of, 334-335
  personal risk-tolerance level, 332-333
    increasing, 333-334
  risk-free life, myth of, 332
Rituals:
  bedtime, 211-212
  as coping technique, 191-193

Salt, 156, 158, 168
  hypertension and, 240
Seborrheic dermatitis, 256
Selenium, 167
Self-disclosure, practicing, 304-305
Self-Sabotage Syndrome, The: Adult Children in the Workplace (Woititz), 122
Self-talks, 193-197
  affirmations, 196-197
  depression and, 218-221
  logic of, 194-196
  negative, 194
Semiautonomous professionals, 44-45
Severity of stressful situation, as coping determinant, 33
Sexual problems, 278-284
  "biological clock"/fertility issues, anxiety about, 281-282
  desire/performance, stress and, 278-279
  erectile dysfunction (impotence), 280
  orgasmic dysfunction, 280
  painful intercourse, 279
  premature ejaculation, 280

Sexual problems (*Cont.*):
  sexually transmitted diseases, anxiety about catching, 281
  treatments for, 282-284
Shoulder massage, 188
Silicon, 167
Singles:
  daily living, chores of, 128-129
  money, 128
  relationships/friendships, 129-130
  single life, 126
  solitude vs. loneliness, 126
  stress at home, 125
  work time vs. personal time, 126-128
  See also Working parents
Sinus headaches (sinusitis), 235-236
Skin problems:
  adult acne, 258-260
  eczema, 256-257
  mouth sores, 260-261
  seborrheic dermatitis, 256
  See also Adult acne; Dermatitis; Eczema
Slave-driver bosses, 63-64
Sleep, 172-174
  breathing exercise for, 178-179
  fatigue and, 216
  See also Fatigue; Insomnia
Sleep apnea, 214
Sleeping pills, abuse of, 274
Small is Beautiful (Schumacher), 153
Smoking, 273
  gastroesophageal reflux and, 263
  hypertension and, 240
  hyperventilation and, 269
  mitral valve prolapse syndrome and, 271
  upper respiratory infections/flu and, 225
  See also Substance abuse
Sodium, See Salt
Sore muscles:
  exercise and, 250
  fibromyositis, 248-249
  muscle spasms, 248
  treatments for, 249
  when to see your physician about, 249-250
  See also Progressive muscle relaxation
Steady behavior style (Type S), management, 58
Stimulant contents of foods/beverages, 161-162
STP, 276
Stress:
  perceptions of, 38-42 factors affecting,

Stress (*Cont.*):
  38-40
  physiological side of, 30-33
  role of, 341
Stress assessment:
  Burn Out Checklist, 21-22
  Company Culture Checklist, 22-26
  Coping Behavior Checklist, 7-9
  Life Experience and Hassles Checklist,
    15-18
  Life Satisfaction Checklist, 12-15
  Personality Type Checklist, 26-29
  Stress Symptom Checklist, 9-11
  Workplace Stress test, 18-21
Stressful Situation Checklist, 18-20
Stress-intensive environments:
  company cultures, 46-50
  competition, 51-54
  continually changing business environ-
    ment, 45-46
  managing people in, 54-66
  politics, 51-54
  power, 51-54
  price paid for success, 59-60
  professional types, 43-45
Stress-management techniques:
  diet, 156-168
  exercise, 168-172
  failure of, reasons for, 2-3
  sleep, 172-174
  warnings/cautions about, 5-6, 155-156
Stress patterns:
  chronic, 34, 35
  dangerous, 35-36
  hazardous, 35, 36
  optimal, 34
  typical, 34, 35
Stress reactions, 36-38
  styles, understanding, 120
Stress-related illness, 35-38, 60, 207-289
  alcohol, 273-274
  allergies, 224
  chest pain, 227-230
  chronic diseases, effect of stress on,
    286-287
  depression, 37, 217-222
  dysfunctional eating, 230-234
  fatigue, 213-217
  headaches, 234-239
  hypertension (high blood pressure),
    239-241
  hyperventilation, 269-270
  hypoglycemia, 287

Stress-related illness (*Cont.*):
  insomnia, 209-213
  jaw problems, 241-243
  lower gastrointestinal tract problems,
    243-247
  menopause, 285-286
  menstrual irregularities, 247-248
  midlife crisis, 284-285
  mitral valve prolapse syndrome (MVP),
    270-273
  musculoskeletal complaints, 248-256
  new approach to, 208-209
  panic attacks, 267-268
  premenstrual syndrome (PMS), 288
  sexual problems, 278-284
  skin problems, 256-261
  substance abuse, 273-278
  systemic yeast infections, 287
  upper gastrointestinal tract problems,
    262-266
  upper respiratory infections/flu, 224-
    227
Stress Symptom Checklist, 9-11
  scoring, 11
Structural plateaus, 67-70
  common reactions to, 70
  discrimination, 68-69
  glass ceiling, 68-69
Substance abuse, 273-278
  alcohol, 273-274
  drugs, 274-277
  smoking, 273
  when to see your physician about, 277-
    278
Sugar, 156, 158, 271
Superwoman myth, 143
Support and self-help groups, 120, 199-
  200
Systemic yeast infections, stress and, 287

Tea, 159
  gastroesophageal reflux and, 263
Telecommuting, 144
Telephone, forwarding calls, 114
Temperature biofeedback, 177
Temporomandibular joint syndrome
  (TMJ):
  definition of, 242
  treatments for, 242-243
Tension headaches, 234-235
Terminations:
  feelings associated with, 77-78
  managing, 62

Termination (*Cont.*):
  See also Layoffs; Reductions in force (RIFs)
Theobromine, 159, 211
Theophylline, 159
Therapy:
  one-on-one, 198-99
  support and self-help groups, 199-200
  twelve-step programs, 200-201
  when to consider, 198
Thought-stopping exercise, 201
Time management, couples, 135-136
Tin, 167
Tolerance, as stress reaction, 37
Tough-Guy Organizations, 25, 26, 46, 47, 49
Track record, perceptions of stress and, 39- 40
Tranquilizers:
  abuse of, 274-275
  depression and, 223
Transfers, *See* Relocations/transfers
Twelve-step programs, 200-201
Typical Stress Pattern, 34, 35
Tyrant bosses, 64

Ulcerative colitis, 36, 247
Ultimate Relaxation (Sports Music Company), 190, 202
Upper backaches, 250
Upper back massage, 188
Upper gastrointestinal tract problems:
  antacid tablets and, 266
  gastritis, 262
  gastroesophageal reflux, 262-265
  heartburn, 262-263
  milk/cream and, 265-266
  nervous indigestion, 262
  painkillers and, 266
  peptic ulcers, 265
Upper respiratory infections/flu, 224-227
  over-the-counter cold products and, 226-227
  single-ingredient cold remedies, comparison of, 228
  treatments for, 225-226
  Vitamin C and, 226

Vacations:
  coping techniques, 204-205
  singles, 127
Values:
  clearing out the garbage, 309

Values (*Cont.*):
  evaluating, 309-316
    items you carry with you, 311
    life line, 310-311
    residence, 311
    Things I Like to Do for Fun list, 311-313
    values grid, 314-316
  perceptions of stress and, 38-39
  reassessing, 120
  See also Family values/goals; Personal goals; Work goals
Vanadium, 167
Vegetables, raw, 157, 158
Videotapes:
  aerobics, 170
  of business information, 112
  muscle relaxation, 190
Visualization:
  definition of, 201
  exercises, 201-204
  mitral valve prolapse syndrome and, 271
  psychoacoustics, 202
Vitamins, 162-68
  A, 164
  B, 156, 162, 165-166
  C, 162, 165 and upper respiratory infections/flu, 226
  cobalamin (B12), 166
  D, 164
  E, 164
  K, 165
  niacin (B5), 165
  pyridoxine (B5), 165
  recommended dietary allowances, 164-167
  riboflavin (B2), 165
  supplements, choosing, 163-164
  thiamine (B1), 165
  See also Diet; Minerals
Voice mail system, turning on prioritization features of, 114

Walking, 170
Weekends:
  coping techniques, 204-205
  singles, 127
Whole milk products, 158
Win-win conflict resolution, 305-306
Win-win politics, 53-54
Withdrawal, as stress reaction, 37

Women:
  glass ceiling/discrimination, 68-69
  migraine headaches and, 237
  stress and, 59
Workable compromises, 304
Work environment, changing, 119-20
Work friendships, self-esteem and, 181
Work goals:
  reassessing, 120, 318-320
  setting, 316-320
    five-year wish list, 316
    one-year wish list, 316
    "things I do well" list, 317
    "things I'd rather forget" list, 318
Work Hard/Play Hard Organizations,
  25, 48
Working parents, 140-147

Working parents (Cont.)
  fathers as heroes, 143-144
  home life vs. work life, 140-142
  needs of, 145
  raising children, 145-146
  relationships/friendships, 146-147
  superwoman myth, 143
  workplace alternatives for, 144-145
  work time vs. personal time, 142-143
Work values:
  evaluating, 309-316
  setting goals, 316-320
Worrying, as coping technique, 205-206

Zinc, 167